COGNITIVE-BEHAVIORAL INTERVENTIONS FOR EMOTIONAL AND BEHAVIORAL DISORDERS

Cognitive-Behavioral Interventions for Emotional and Behavioral Disorders

School-Based Practice

Edited by

MATTHEW J. MAYER
RICHARD VAN ACKER
JOHN E. LOCHMAN
FRANK M. GRESHAM

THE GUILFORD PRESS
New York   London

Library of Congress Cataloging-in-Publication Data

Cognitive-behavioral interventions for emotional and behavioral disorders :
school-based practice / edited by Matthew J. Mayer.
    p. ; cm.
  Includes bibliographical references and index.
  ISBN 978-1-59385-976-3 (hardcover : alk. paper)
  1. Cognitive therapy for children. 2. School mental health services. 3. Emotional
problems of children—Treatment. 4. Behavior disorders in children—Treatment.
I. Mayer, Matthew J.
  [DNLM: 1. Mental Disorders—therapy. 2. Adolescent. 3. Child. 4. Cognitive
Therapy—methods. 5. Education, Special—methods. 6. School Health Services.
WS 350.2 C6765 2008]
  RJ505.C63C63 2009
  618.92′891425—dc22

                                                              2008026719

About the Editors

Matthew J. Mayer, PhD, is Assistant Professor of Educational Psychology in the Graduate School of Education at Rutgers, The State University of New Jersey. He is actively engaged in research on school violence and disruption, using structural equation modeling with national-level data sets to foster better understanding of processes associated with school violence and disorder. Dr. Mayer also focuses on developing new models of training for teachers and allied professionals, integrating professional preparation in cognitive-behavioral methods into graduate training programs. Dr. Mayer has a long professional history as a school-linked practitioner, a special educator, an educational case manager in foster care, and an educational support specialist working with high-risk youth. He serves as a manuscript reviewer and a member of the editorial boards for several major journals and is President of the Board of Directors of the Consortium to Prevent School Violence, a national organization engaged in research, dissemination, technical advisement, and advocacy work to prevent school violence.

Richard Van Acker, EdD, is Professor of Special Education at the University of Illinois at Chicago. His research involves efforts to prevent the development of serious antisocial behavior in children and youth, with a special focus on violence and aggression and the social interaction between teachers and their students. Dr. Van Acker was a key investigator in the Metropolitan Area Child Study (MACS) project, a major longitudinal study that involved providing social-cognitive interventions to students, combined with teacher training and consultation. Formerly President of the Council for Children with Behavioral Disorders, he has written over 100 publications and has participated on the editorial boards of several major research journals.

John E. Lochman, PhD, ABPP, is Professor of and Doddridge Saxon Chairholder in Clinical Psychology at the University of Alabama, where he also directs the Center for Prevention of Youth Behavior Problems (CPYBP). A major focus of the CPYBP is to investigate how evidence-based programs can be effectively disseminated into real-world settings. He has received the Blackmon–Moody Outstanding Professor and Burnum Distinguished Faculty Awards from the University of Alabama, and was awarded an honorary doctorate by the University of Utrecht in The Netherlands in 2004 for his prevention research. Dr. Lochman has written over 200 publications on risk factors, social cognition, and intervention and prevention research with aggressive children. He is Editor in Chief of the *Journal of Abnormal Child Psychology*; serves on the National Institutes of Health Study Section on Psychosocial Development, Risk, and Prevention; is a Fellow in the American Psychological Association and the Academy of Cognitive Therapy; is a member of the Board of Directors of the Society for Prevention Research; and is President-Elect of the American Board for Clinical Child and Adolescent Psychology.

Frank M. Gresham, PhD, is Professor of Psychology at Louisiana State University. His research and practice interests are in social skills assessment and interventions with children at risk for or with emotional and behavioral disorders; response-to-intervention practices; treatment integrity; and applied measurement practices. He is the coauthor of the *Social Skills Improvement System* and has written over 250 journal articles, books, and book chapters. Dr. Gresham holds Fellow status in three divisions of the American Psychological Association and is a member of the National Association of School Psychologists, the Association for Behavior Analysis, and the Council for Exceptional Children.

Contributors

Jaleel Abdul-Adil, PhD, Institute for Juvenile Research, University of Illinois at Chicago, Chicago, Illinois

Diana Antinoro, MA, Graduate School of Applied and Professional Psychology, Rutgers, The State University of New Jersey, Piscataway, New Jersey

Lauren A. Arbolino, PhD, College of Education, Lehigh University, Bethlehem, Pennsylvania

Genery D. Booster, MEd, College of Education, Lehigh University, Bethlehem, Pennsylvania

Brian C. Chu, PhD, Graduate School of Applied and Professional Psychology, Rutgers, The State University of New Jersey, Piscataway, New Jersey

Ann P. Daunic, PhD, College of Education, University of Florida, Gainesville, Florida

George J. DuPaul, PhD, College of Education, Lehigh University, Bethlehem, Pennsylvania

Melissa Fisher, MA, Department of Educational Psychology, College of Education, University of Texas at Austin, Austin, Texas

Michael M. Gerber, PhD, Center for Advanced Study of Individual Differences, University of California at Santa Barbara, Santa Barbara, California

Julia A. Graber, PhD, Department of Psychology, University of Florida, Gainesville, Florida

Frank M. Gresham, PhD, Department of Psychology, Louisiana State University, Baton Rouge, Louisiana

Nancy Guerra, EdD, Department of Psychology, University of California at Riverside, Riverside, California

Jenny Herren, MA, Department of Educational Psychology, College of Education, University of Texas at Austin, Austin, Texas

Laura Grofer Klinger, PhD, Department of Psychology, University of Alabama, Tuscaloosa, Alabama

John E. Lochman, PhD, ABPP, Department of Psychology, University of Alabama, Tuscaloosa, Alabama

John W. Maag, PhD, College of Education, University of Nebraska at Lincoln, Lincoln, Nebraska

Matthew J. Mayer, PhD, Department of Educational Psychology, Graduate School of Education, Rutgers, The State University of New Jersey, New Brunswick, New Jersey

Richard J. Morris, PhD, Department of Special Education, Rehabilitation, and School Psychology, College of Education, University of Arizona, Tucson, Arizona

W. M. Nelson III, PhD, Department of Psychology, Xavier University, Cincinnati, Ohio

Gretchen Schoenfield, BS, Department of Special Education, Rehabilitation, and School Psychology, College of Education, University of Arizona, Tucson, Arizona

Janet R. Schultz, PhD, Department of Psychology, Xavier University, Cincinnati, Ohio

Stephen W. Smith, PhD, College of Education, University of Florida, Gainesville, Gainesville, Florida

Emily Solari, PhD, University of Texas Health Science Center, Houston, Houston, Texas

Kevin D. Stark, PhD, Department of Educational Psychology, University of Texas, Austin, Austin, Texas

Susan M. Swearer, PhD, Department of Educational Psychology, University of Nebraska–Lincoln, Lincoln, Nebraska

Patrick H. Tolan, PhD, Department of Psychiatry, University of Illinois at Chicago, Chicago, Illinois

Michael D. Toland, MA, Center for Research on Children, Youth, Families and Schools, University of Nebraska–Lincoln, Lincoln, Nebraska

Richard Van Acker, EdD, College of Education, University of Illinois at Chicago, Chicago, Illinois

Adam S. Weissman, MS, Department of Psychology, Rutgers, The State University of New Jersey, Piscataway, New Jersey

Amie Williams, MA, Department of Psychology, University of Alabama, Tuscaloosa, Alabama

Preface

This book was developed as an outgrowth of The Guilford Press's *Handbook of Research in Emotional and Behavioral Disorders*. Credit for the idea to launch this project belongs to the late Dr. Robert B. Rutherford Jr. of Arizona State University, who proposed the creation of a text to discuss cognitive-behavioral interventions (CBIs) for youth with emotional or behavioral disorders (EBD), including content specific to special education. Dr. Rutherford was a leader in special education for more than 30 years, addressing issues pertaining to students with EBD, with particular attention to the needs of youth with disabilities involved with, or at risk for involvement with, the juvenile justice system. Dr. Rutherford played an instrumental role in the maturation of the field of EBD within special education, facilitating the well-known annual Teacher Educators for Children with Behavioral Disorders (TECBD) conference, which has been a cornerstone of the profession over the past 31 years. It is at this conference that researchers and faculty who train professionals in education and allied disciplines are able to meet and share ideas within a uniquely intimate and collaborative environment. The TECBD conference under the stewardship of Dr. Rutherford helped to advance the field in many ways, including fostering increased interdisciplinary work to address the needs of students with EBD. Thus it is fitting that this text is dedicated to the memory of Dr. Rutherford, who provided great leadership and inspiration to many in the field and in so many ways helped to change the lives of countless at-risk young people for the better.

Although there have been numerous texts addressing various CBIs and related interventions, there has been limited collaboration in this area among special education, school psychology, and clinical psychology. That began to change in 2005 with a special edition of the peer-reviewed research journal *Behavioral Disorders*, which addressed CBIs with the collaboration of many authors across these three disciplines. That trajectory continues with this text. Researchers and practitioners in multiple disciplines face similar challenges with service delivery to young people who experience a variety of social, emotional, and behavioral problems. Many of these professionals incorporate one another's disciplines to some degree, and tools that they use often share a common professional heritage. Yet at times, these disciplines have remained somewhat insular.

This text examines research and practice in CBIs across multiple areas of need. Related discussions of the research base are sometimes varied as a result of the population under consideration. When we consider categorical and dimensional models of mental health that may relate more or less to psychological and psychiatric perspectives, versus an educational framework, questions emerge as to exactly whom we are talking about when we refer to the clientele. Further muddying the waters are issues of research project-based and existing school-based, university-based, and community-based clinics and the groups they may serve. The terminology *emotional or behavioral disorders* is closely aligned with the research and service delivery professionals in special education, yet there is significant overlap in group membership for the young people receiving CBIs through any of the venues just mentioned, and those formally identified under the Individuals with Disabilities Education Act as emotionally disturbed. Any examination of CBIs for children and adolescents *necessarily* needs to address the multiple disciplines and venues where such service delivery exists, with particular attention to schools in general and in concert with the special education system. This text represents a significant advance in that direction, with increased attention to a combination of school-related and disability-related issues in the provision of CBIs. We hope that this text marks a milestone in a path of increasing interdisciplinary collaboration across special education, school psychology, and clinical psychology to help better address the mental health needs of young people.

Contents

PART I

FOUNDATIONS OF COGNITIVE-BEHAVIORAL INTERVENTIONS

CHAPTER 1

Historical Roots, Theoretical and Applied Developments, and Critical Issues in Cognitive-Behavior Modification

MATTHEW J. MAYER
RICHARD VAN ACKER

Cognitive-behavior modification (CBM) is not a singular approach, but rather a body of methods and strategies used to change behavior through the active engagement of clients in understanding and taking control of their thoughts, feelings, and behaviors. CBM has a rich history of research to practice from the 1970s through the present day. CBM evolved over several decades, drawing on theory and research in behavior modification, modeling, and related aspects of social learning theory, self-instruction, problem solving, and self-control. CBM looks beyond a purely behavioral training approach that manages overt behaviors and also addresses change in covert thoughts. CBM approaches were developed in part based on the idea that behavior is mediated through inner speech. This implies that language can be directed to change cognitions, and, as a result, behavior can be altered. In sum, cognitive-behavioral interventions (CBIs) represent an integrated approach, blending behavioral therapy with supports for cognitive change (Kend-all, 1993) while also addressing contextual and environmental issues. Activities such as discussion, client homework (e.g., cognitive and be-havioral activities), behavioral enactment, and performance-related ac-tivities (e.g., role play, rehearsal) are used to assist clients in altering their thoughts, feelings, and, subsequently, their behaviors. Research in multi-ple fields of study has established the efficacy of CBIs (Kazdin & Weisz, 1998; Kendall, 2006; Ollendick & King, 2004; D. B. Wilson, Gottfred-son, & Najaka, 2001).

Youth with emotional or behavioral disorders (EBD), some of whom are formally served by the special education system, as well as those at risk for serious mental health impairments can benefit from CBIs. Reports on long-term outcomes for students with EBD are trou-bling. Students with EBD have the highest dropout rate among students with disabilities—more than 50%. They face an elevated risk of arrest during and following their school enrollment (Wagner, 1995; Leone, Mayer, Malmgren, & Meisel, 2000). Difficulties continue into the young adult years, with ongoing problems with social relationships, trouble maintaining steady employment, and lower earnings than nondisabled and other disabled peers (Carson, Sitlington, & Frank, 1995; Green-baum et al., 1996; Malmgren, Edgar, & Neel, 1998; Wagner, 1995). These difficulties may in part be connected to deficiencies in anger con-trol, aggressive behaviors, limited social problem-solving skills, anxiety, and depression, all of which have been treated using CBIs (Kazdin & Weisz, 1998; Kendall, 2006; Ollendick & King, 1998; Weisz & Hawley, 2002).

This text explores current research related to CBIs for several mental health disorders displayed by children and youth. When con-sidering therapeutic interventions for students with EBD, the priority should not be the disability label per se, but rather the individual need being addressed. This point relates to the work done by special educa-tors with students with EBD and to the missions of researchers, teacher educators, and practitioners who work to improve the lives of these individuals. Prior research has demonstrated that (1) a fairly large percentage of young people in the general population have signif-icant mental health problems, with about 4–6% having more severe needs and close to 20% having difficulties requiring some form of for-mal mental health supports (Hoagwood & Erwin, 1997); (2) students with EBD and those with mental health needs are underidentified and underserved (Hoagwood & Johnson, 2003; U.S. Department of Health and Human Services, 1999); and (3) these students often demonstrate a constellation of difficulties, many of which are amenable to CBM-based interventions (Mayer, Lochman, & Van Acker, 2005; Polsgrove

& Smith, 2004). Hence, a discussion of CBIs that is singularly tailored to the community of students with EBD within the context of special education would miss the mark. Students with EBD compose a critical subset of a larger group of youth who need a range of mental health and related social intervention supports.

Most theoretical and applied developments in CBM have come from clinical and cognitive psychology. The special education literature on EBD over the decades has dedicated minimal coverage to CBM. It may seem ironic that in view of well-documented needs of students with EBD in the areas of anger/aggression, anxiety, and depression, CBIs developed in other fields for addressing emotional and behavioral needs were not widely adopted within the field of special education. Yet special education researchers interested in academic strategy instruction embraced cognitive-behavioral techniques in the 1980s for the purpose of developing cognitive strategy instruction to support academic needs (Gerber, 1987; Harris, 1982, 1985; Harris & Pressley, 1991; Swanson, 1989; Wong, 1985). We see the fruits of this line of research today in varied writing strategy approaches such as Self-Regulated Strategy Development (Graham & Harris, 2003).

Several factors may help explain the limited adoption of CBIs in the EBD special education community in earlier years: (1) Many researchers heavily influencing EBD during the late 1970s through 1990s maintained a traditional behaviorist orientation, (2) collaboration with clinical psychology was limited, (3) there was reluctance to cross a boundary into interventions that were considered therapeutic and more properly the province of psychiatry and clinical psychology, and (4) university training programs in EBD rarely focused on CBM. More recently, however, there has been movement within special education, in the area of EBD, to focus on CBIs (Mayer et al., 2005; Robinson, Smith, & Miller, 2002).

This chapter begins with an overview of historical developments in CBIs, with attention to key theoretical advances. The remaining sections of the chapter lay the groundwork for the rest of the book, introducing several critical research-to-practice themes: (1) roles of school staff in school-based applications of CBI, with a brief look at programs addressing anger/aggression and depression, and concerns related to school-based CBI programming; (2) special education issues for interventions directed to students with EBD and other disabilities; (3) relative consideration of stand-alone CBIs and those embedded in more complex interventions for use in schools; and (4) adaptation of CBI techniques for day-to-day use in schools by a wide array of education professionals. The chapter closes with a brief discussion with a view toward the future of CBIs.

Historical Development of CBM

Ancient Greek writings suggested that human perception drives one's view of reality. Later Western philosophical writings of the 19th century linked awareness of reality to specific cognitions, suggesting that the world was not directly "knowable" but could be understood through "categories of thinking" or what we would today call *schemas* (Leahy, 1996). The early 20th century witnessed the advent of early forms of behaviorism, as seen in the work of Watson, Rayner, and Jones (Craighead, Kazdin, & Mahoney, 1976). Although there was some behavioral work done from the 1920s to the 1940s, applied behavior interventions did not really gain momentum until the 1950s (Craighead, 1982). Psychoanalytic methods dominated the treatment landscape throughout the 1940s and early 1950s but gradually lost ground in the 1950s and 1960s, with growing criticism of their effectiveness and the emergence of competing theoretical orientations and methodologies (Craighead, 1982; Craighead et al., 1976).

Taking a broad view spanning 60–70 years, one can divide the evolution of CBIs into three successive phases. Early behaviorism, as exemplified by the work of John Watson and colleagues, addressed events within a stimulus–response (S-R) framework using observable behavioral data and avoiding indirect indicators of thoughts and emotion. A second phase that included various mediation models followed, as seen in the work of Hull and Tolman, where the person, or organism (O), had attributes deemed worthy of study. This marked a transition from S-R to S-O-R psychology (Mahoney, 1974). By the 1950s and 1960s, a third phase developed, with increased investment in understanding cognitive processes such as discrimination, generalization, cueing, and labeling, as evidenced by the work of Bolles, Bower, and Neisser (Kazdin, 1978).

Developments in this third phase, from the 1950s to the 1970s, fostered the emergence of a coherent discipline of CBM that can be understood by considering the confluence of several historical currents. First, as suggested by William Dember (1974, p. 161) in his classic statement "Psychology has gone cognitive," there were significant advances in modeling, self-instruction, and problem-solving protocols (Craighead, 1982; Craighead, Meyers, & Craighead, 1985; Hughes, 1988; Meyers, Cohen, & Schleser, 1989). Second, self-regulation research was augmented with cognitive elements, expanding on its traditional contingency-based framework. Third, therapeutic tools were developed to support a more integrated approach to cognitive and behavioral change.

Advances in Cognitive Research

Early modeling effects research by Dollard and Miller (as cited in Kazdin, 1978) established the function of reinforcement through viewing behaviors of others. Piaget (as cited in Bandura, 1977) addressed modeling effects, but more from the perspective of a person's schema. Bandura, in contrast, went beyond the notion of schema, investigating modeling as a function of encoding-related processes including attention, retention, physical reproduction, and motivation. Bandura extended on explicating cognitive components of vicarious reinforcement, attending to the primacy of verbal over visual encoding processes and articulating the notion of *reciprocal determinism,* with dynamic bidirectional interactions among person, behavior, and environment (Bandura, 1977).

Research in self-instruction was predicated in part on earlier work of Luria and Vygotsky on inner speech, as well as perception-driven behavior (Craighead, 1982; Harris, 1982). Studies of children's inner dialogue revealed cognitive processes in effect, including (1) selective attention to environmental cues, (2) attributions to self, (3) evaluative thinking, and (4) perception of coping ability. Meichenbaum, who made major contributions to research in self-instruction, commented on Mahoney's (1974) treatment of perception-based response, saying that *what a person said to himself about events* was much more relevant than simply looking at a situation using an antecedent–behavior–consequence model. Meichenbaum's self-instruction methods included (1) role model enactment, including talking; (2) child duplication of model behavior with external guidance; (3) child enactment with self-guidance; (4) child enactment with faded self-guidance; and (5) child enactment with silent self-guidance.

Problem-solving research emerged in the 1970s, seen primarily in the work of D'Zurilla and Goldfried, Spivak and Shure, and Meichenbaum (Craighead, 1982; Mahoney, 1974). Researchers of this period reported that youth with EBD had problem-solving skill deficits and, as a result of their limited behavioral repertoire, tended toward maladaptive behavioral responses (Mahoney, 1974). Mahoney suggested that problem solving was not historically embraced by behavioral therapists because of its "mediational flavor" and difficulties operationalizing elements of problem solving for measurement (1974, p. 200). Most problem-solving approaches are based on those of D'Zurilla and Goldfried (1971), who articulated a five-step approach: (1) Orient to problem; (2) define problem; (3) generate alternatives to resolve problem; (4) evaluate alternatives, select best, and develop plan; and (5) engage plan and evaluate.

Self-Regulation Research

Self-regulation transcended traditional contingency-based behavior management approaches in which changes in child and adolescent behavior were dependent on external influences (Rosenbaum & Drabman, 1979). Kazdin (2001) argued that self-regulation offers advantages over external control methods: (1) Many problem behaviors do not occur in the presence of adults who might provide guidance, (2) external-only control is associated with limited generalization of behavior change, and (3) there is evidence of improved client investment in behavioral change when it is by choice as opposed to imposition. Three key components of self regulation are self-monitoring, self-evaluation, and self-reinforcement.

Self-monitoring is an intentional focused effort of attending to one's feelings, thoughts, beliefs, or behaviors. Engagement in self-monitoring creates an *expectancy,* which helps drive behavioral change (Bandura, 1969; Karoly, 1993; Mahoney, 1974). *Self-evaluation* is based on applying an internal standard against an external standard (Karoly, 1993; Rosenbaum & Drabman, 1979). Self-evaluation, which is not an automatically maintained behavior, requires some form of activation (external or internal cueing) and forms part of the foundation for individual motivation. Limitations such as cognitive deficiencies, distortions, and biases can influence cognitive processing, interfering with effective self-monitoring (Craighead et al., 1976; Lochman, Whidby, & FitzGerald, 2000).

Self-reinforcement, which has internal and external facets, is the self-dispensing of a favored outcome contingent upon a behavior (Bandura, 1977). Behavioral criteria are typically derived from external sources, often models that have been observed. Internally, a person self-regulates via covert self-reinforcement, employing some form of self-commendation. Consequences driving the effectiveness of self-reinforcement are internal (e.g., satisfaction from heightened self-image) and external (e.g., reinforcement from others). Research has demonstrated effects of self-reinforcement equivalent to those of external reinforcement (Bandura, 1969, 1977; Mahoney, 1974; Rosenbaum & Drabman, 1979).

Cognitive Therapeutic Tools and Procedures

Cognitive-behavioral procedures developed by Meichenbaum and colleagues focused on changing irrational, maladaptive, and dysfunctional thinking. The therapist worked with clients to help them understand trigger events linked to the problem, gain insight into their own thoughts and feelings in response to those triggers, and change their beliefs and thinking about the problem situation. Therapeutic tools included insight-oriented dialogue, behavioral modeling and enactment, and related methods to alter problematic attitudes, beliefs, and expectancies. For example, five areas of cognitive distortion targeted by Beck were (1) arbitrary inference; (2) magnification or exaggeration of the importance of an event;

(3) cognitive deficiency-lacking knowledge/attention to an important facet of life; (4) dichotomous, either–or reasoning; and (5) overgeneralization of events (Meichenbaum, 1977).

With regard to management of anger, anxiety, and related problems, therapists worked in the areas of cognitive reappraisal, behavioral experimentation with adaptive responses, positive and strategic self-statements, and self-instruction. General problem-solving protocols began with identifying the problem, generating alternative behavioral responses, choosing and enacting the optimal response, and evaluating results. Clients were scaffolded into a process of self-guided management of thoughts, feelings, and behaviors using therapeutic tools including discussion, client homework, cognitive practice activities, and behavioral enactment.

As cognitive behavioral science has advanced over the decades, its applications have expanded across many parts of the human services from psychiatry and psychology to social work, juvenile justice, counseling, and education. CBIs have addressed many areas beyond anger, anxiety, and depression, including obsessive–compulsive behavior, obesity and weight management, sexual abuse, and coping with disasters/terrorism. Increasingly complex CBI models have emerged that more fully address ecological and situational contexts. In sum, the field has reached a maturity where currently efficacious methods are being extended and refined to better serve CBI clients.

Provision of School-Based CBI Programs

Linking theory to practice is critical to understanding CBIs, particularly as they are applied in school-based settings. Schools are natural settings for such interventions, given their physical centrality in the community, their availability of space, the time youngsters spend in school, the availability of personnel support, and the ability to create targeted treatment groups based on need. Roles of school staff and organizational factors that may inhibit or facilitate incorporation of CBIs in schools can be understood through an examination of several current school-based CBIs. Lochman's Coping Power Program, the Fast Track-Program, and the Adolescents Coping with Depression Program are used to facilitate this discussion.

Most CBIs are taught through some well-structured curriculum using a combination of lecture, discussion, demonstration/modeling, self-study, role play, rehearsal, and client homework. Sometimes, as in the case of CBIs for anxiety, there is a broad segmentation of the curriculum, with skill-building tasks followed by controlled exposure and subsequent coping practice. Clients are often given workbooks to support improved understanding of areas such as (1) recognizing their own physiological responses to triggers, (2) understanding the thoughts and feelings of themselves and others, (3) addressing their biased beliefs and attributions, (4) learning a problem-solving procedure using self-instruction, and (5) recording data on related experiences at home and at school. The ultimate success of virtually all CBIs (as well as other types of behavioral interventions) depends on the opportunity to practice newly acquired skills addressing authentic life challenges in real-world contexts.

Lochman's *Coping Power Program* is a school-based program for students in fourth through sixth grades employing approximately 34 student sessions and 16 parent sessions and conducted over 1.5 years (Lochman, Powell, Whidby, & FitzGerald, 2006). Research by Lochman and colleagues has shown that reinforcement of learning goals can be more readily achieved in a group setting (in schools or clinics) than in sessions with peer dyads or with adult therapists because of increased opportunities for frequent reinforcement, greater receptivity to peer feedback compared to that of authority figures, and more authentic opportunities for addressing challenging situations and practicing skills. Opportunities exist for direct involvement of school personnel where intervention sessions are codirected by a mental health and school professionals (Lochman, Curry, Dane, & Ellis, 2001). Interestingly, Meyers et al. (1989) commented on the importance of teachers and their potential influence on children in CBI training through instructing and modeling and providing powerful motivation. Thus we can draw several conclusions with regard to CBIs in schools: (1) The school provides a natural setting that can be leveraged to provide effective training, (2) economies of scale can be realized by serving more students more efficiently, and (3) interventions can be offered by well-trained school personnel.

The *Fast Track Program* (Conduct Problems Prevention Research Group, 1999), based on cognitive-behavioral theory, is an ecologically and developmentally oriented multicomponent program to improve antisocial behavior of high-risk youth. The intervention sessions are delivered in teacher-led class sessions in combination with social skills training and peer tutoring, which is provided by paraprofessionals. Other multifacted programs, such as Second Step (Frey, Hirschstein, & Guzzo, 2000), have established the value of using teachers and paraprofessionals in providing CBIs and related interventions. Earlier research by Durlak (1982) reported evidence supporting the utility of paraprofessionals providing components of CBIs in schools.

The *Adolescents Coping with Depression Program* provides a psychoeducational group intervention in schools developed from a multifactor model of depression (negative thoughts, high negative reinforcement and low positive reinforcement, life stressors, minimal protective factors, and many risk factors; Clarke, DeBar, & Lewinsohn, 2003). The 16 semiweekly sessions are delivered by therapists and organized into two primary program stages: (1) behavioral activation (using age-appropriate and fun activities to foster change), and (2) cognitive therapy. School professionals (teachers and paraprofessionals) can offer supportive services with interventions for depression, working with therapists to modify classroom environment, reinforcing appropriate student behaviors, and facilitating communication among stakeholders (student, family, school staff, and therapists).

Regardless of the treatment focus (e.g., anger/aggression, anxiety, depression), concerns exist with regard to providing CBIs in schools (Gerber & Solari, 2005). First, discussion continues over the mission of schools in providing a variety of mental health and associated psychological supports, above and beyond the school's core academic mission (National Research Council, 2004, Chapter 6; Rones & Hoagwood, 2000; Weist, 2005). Concern often focuses on allocations of personnel, staff training, strategic use of funds, and competing academic imperatives (e.g., No Child Left Behind proficiency tests). Second, schools have been struggling to do more with limited financial resources. Limited mental health programs for youth have placed increased demands on schools and allied agencies to provide services. For example, more than 12,000 children entered state child welfare systems or county juvenile justice systems in fiscal year 2001 as a way of obtaining badly needed mental health services (U.S. General Accounting Office, 2003). About one third of school districts in a recent major federal study—*School Mental Health Services in the United States 2002–2003*—that included a nationally representative sample of 83,000 public elementary, middle, and high schools, reported declining mental health funding and reduced services available from outside (the school) providers, and about two thirds reported increased demand for mental health services (Foster et al., 2005). Recent data from the U.S. Department of Education's National Longitudinal Transition Study–2 (NLTS-2) and Special Education Elementary Longitudinal Study (SEELS; discussed below) show striking declines from 2001 to 2005 in mental health services available to students with disabilities and, more specifically, students with EBD.

Third, the increased movement for academic accountability as evidenced by the high-stakes testing movement in the late 1990s and enactment of No Child Left Behind have driven schools to focus mainly on raising test scores. Emerging indicators suggest that nonacademic programs have been reduced in many jurisdictions in favor of more narrow curricula with increased academic programming time in reading and math (Center on Education Policy, 2004; Cole, 2006; Daly et al., 2006).

This suggests that in such a political environment, schools will not be highly receptive to offering mental health and social competency interventions (Mayer, 2006; Paternite, 2005; Weist, 2005). Fourth, fidelity to intervention is critical for effective intervention programming. Yet both general and special educators are typically overworked, with little time for additional training and involvement in supplementary intervention programming (Carlson & Billingsley, 2001; Coleman, 2000; National Center for Education Statistics, 2005; SPENSE, 2002b). Fifth, to be effective, interventions require not only client but allied stakeholder (parent, teacher, school administration) buy in (Hoagwood, Burns, Kiser, Ringeisen, & Shoenwald, 2001; Kratochwill & Stoiber, 2000; Lochman et al., 2000; Stark, Sander, Yancy, Bronik, & Hoke, 2000). Sixth, generalization and maintenance of treatment effects in CBI and related interventions continue to be problematic (Conoley, 1989; Mathur & Rutherford, 1996; Smith, Lochman, & Daunic, 2005). Consideration of critical contextual variables as well as responsiveness to issues of race and ethnicity are also highly relevant to maintenance of treatment gains (Ghafoori, 2001; Guerra, Eron, Huesmann, Tolan, & Van Acker, 1997; Guerra & Jagers, 1999; Vera, Vila, & Alegria, 2003).

There are many challenges to the successful use of CBIs in schools, which can be resistant to change. Yet research has demonstrated the efficacy of school-delivered CBIs in multiple areas of need (Lochman et al., 2006; Stark et al., 2006). Several meta-analyses and reviews of research have pointed to the importance of providing comprehensive school-based programming to address the social, emotional, and behavioral needs of at-risk students (Mytton, DiGuiseppi, Gough, Taylor, & Logan, 2006; J. Wilson, Lipsey, & Derzon, 2003; D. B. Wilson et al., 2001). Yet interestingly, some recent meta-analyses of school-based violence prevention programs have shown negligible effects for multifaceted, comprehensive approaches (Hahn et al., 2007; Wilson & Lipsey, 2007). This suggests a need to continue research into effective means of providing such services in schools, while addressing the constraints and barriers previously discussed.

CBIs for Students in Special Education:
Limited Data and Many Questions

The literature on CBIs and, more generally, mental health service provision, has been very limited with respect to discussing students with disabilities and the special education system per se. The purpose of this section is to articulate a framework and introduce related issues that merit greater attention in future research and publications addressing CBIs.

No one knows what percentage of youth nationally who are receiving formal mental health services are in special education. Hoagwood and Johnson (2003) reported estimates of 16–22% of school-age youth having diagnosable mental health disorders, with 5–9% eligible for classification as seriously emotionally disturbed (compared to a prevalence figure of abut 0.8% in the emotionally disturbed category under the Individuals with Disabilities Education Act). Although these estimates suggest that about 70–80% of youth's mental health services are provided in school, perhaps 20% of students with the greatest mental health needs are receiving services.

Data from the NLTS-2 and SEELS shed light on availability and provision of mental health services for students in special education more generally based on parent reports of services received over the past 12 months. In 2001, approximately 70% of students with emotional disturbance eligible for special education services received mental health services from a recognized provider, with close to 40% receiving these services through the schools. However, the trend in service provision between 2001 and 2005 suggests a serious decline in the provision of mental health services (see Table 1.1). Over this relatively short time span there was an overall decrease in the number of students with disabilities being provided mental health services both within the schools and other service settings. The decline in services was most significant ($p < .001$) for elementary students with emotional disturbance, and for high school students with disabilities overall, receiving services from a provider in or out of the school. These data corroborate reports of funding cutbacks and a decline in mental health service availability in recent years (Foster et al., 2005; U.S. General Accounting Office, 2003) and suggest a different trend than other reported data for the period of 1997–2002 that demonstrated slight increases in the availability of mental health services for youth (Sturm & Andreyeva, 2005).

Consideration of these data set the stage for discussing CBIs in schools. Improved collaboration, including coordinated data collection and reporting, could help mental health and special education professionals develop a better understanding of who they are serving with various types of interventions. There appear to be no extant data on the percentage of students receiving CBIs who are in special education, nor any information on types of interventions provided to different groups of students. Part of the problem relates to the insularity of these disciplines, the widely varied nature of intervention programming, the different service providers, and the many venues in which service is provided. Although we do have national-level data on implementation of some comprehensive prevention programs that include CBM methods (e.g., about

TABLE 1.1. Mental Health Services in School and Elsewhere Provided to Students with Disabilities

Students		Wave 1 (2001)	Wave 3 (2005)	2001–2005 change in p-value	Significance
Students With ED (Emotional Disturbance)					
Elementary (SEELS)	MH from school	.435 (.025)	.338 (.03)	.0065	**
	MH anywhere	.709 (.0229)	.585 (.0312)	.0007	***
Secondary (NLTS-2)	MH from school	.363 (.025)	.223 (.0607)	.0165	*
	MH anywhere	.689 (.024)	.511 (.0729)	.0102	**
Students with Disability					
Elementary (SEELS)	MH from school	.141 (.0089)	.119 (.0102)	.0521	*
	MH anywhere	.229 (.0108)	.23 (.0132)	.4766	
Secondary (NLTS-2)	MH from school	.155 (.012)	.09 (.0217)	.0044	**
	MH anywhere	.316 (.015)	.206 (.0307)	.0006	

Note: Cell values are percentages of the sample whose parents indicated receipt of mental health services. Standard errors are in parentheses. Data from U.S. Department of Education, Office of Special Education Programs' Special Education Elementary Longitudinal Study (SEELS); National Longitudinal Transitional Study–2 (NLTS-2)0. From Mayer and Leone (2007). Copyright 2007 by Love Publishing. Reprinted by permission.
*$p < .05$; **$p < .01$; ***$p < .0010$.

27,000 schools used Second Step in 2006), we lack a coherent national data set on cognitive-behavioral programs.

The special education system poses a number of challenges for CBIs with regard to research and practice, including (1) constraints implementing randomized controlled trials to evaluate interventions, including grouping practices, small sample sizes, and legal prohibitions relative to service delivery; (2) availability of self-contained classes for research across states, due to variation in categorical and noncategorical service delivery systems across states; (3) variability in student class placements during the day across self-contained, resource, and inclusion settings,

making consistent provision of CBI training and follow-up support difficult; (4) limits on certified and well trained special education personnel,
raising concerns about fidelity of implementation; (5) historical tendencies in special education to favor tried and true behavioral approaches;
(6) heavy reliance on exclusion consequences from inclusion classes
when problem behaviors occur, interfering with opportunities to practice
newly learned cognitive-behavioral skills and making students more vulnerable to academic failure and concomitant social, emotional, and behavioral difficulties; (7) limited availability of special education personnel to help deliver CBIs due to work overload (see, e.g., SPENSE,
2002a); (8) competition for service delivery time for CBIs where other
specific goals are already in place in the student's individualized education plan; (9) competition for service delivery time for CBIs where
schools are scheduling more academic remediation for students in special education to raise subgroup scores on the No Child Left Behind Act
adequate yearly progress measures; (10) periodic inaccessibility to high-
risk groups due to school refusal, disciplinary exclusion, and time spent
in psychiatric hospital/incarceration; (11) legal barriers to sharing and
transmission of sensitive student data; and (12) funding stream restric-
tions that may limit provision of services by special education personnel to general education students, interfering with assignment to treatment groups.

Despite these concerns, there is general agreement in the field that a
substantial percentage of students in special education, especially those
identified as emotionally disturbed, are typical candidates for CBIs. Future collaborative research across special education and psychology
holds the promise of developing an improved knowledge base with respect to these issues.

Stand-Alone CBIs and CBIs Embedded
in More Comprehensive Interventions

Examination of training materials from programs such as Second Step
and Incredible Years reveals something that may surprise someone not
familiar with such programming. These comprehensive prevention programs include elements that clearly derive from stand-alone CBIs. Over
the decades, cognitive-behavioral techniques have permeated many types
of interventions. Questions have naturally arisen as to the relative utility
of CBIs as stand-alone techniques compared to their modular and/or embedded use in more comprehensive programs. Several core themes have
emerged as a result of this line of inquiry: (1) results of meta-analyses
and research syntheses on effects of multifaceted interventions, (2) ca-

pacity and fidelity of intervention constraints, (3) comorbidity issues, and (4) research challenges.

There exists a tension between more focused, manageable interventions designed to ameliorate a particular condition and those addressing a more authentic balance of client needs. Several meta-analyses and reviews of research on antisocial behavior prevention programming (Catalano, Arthur, Hawkins, Berglund, & Olson, 1998; Gottfredson, 2001; Hawkins, Farrington, & Catalano, 1998; Lipsey, 1995; Wasserman & Miller, 1998) have pointed to the importance of more comprehensive, multifaceted prevention approaches. Narrowly conceived, one-shot programs are generally of limited use. For example, Catalano and colleagues and others (Lochman, 2000) have discussed the importance of offering more comprehensive interventions that simultaneously work to reduce known risk factors and promote protective factors at multiple ecological levels. Yet this type of comprehensive programming can bring additional challenges relative to units of analysis, as discussed below in the section on research challenges. Gottfredson's research on changing school environments (p. 157) pointed to the advantages of more comprehensive programs but stressed the potential benefits of more singularly focused interventions, particularly in the case where behavioral and cognitive-behavioral methods are used. Several reviews of research have also suggested that increased generalizability may result from the more multifaceted interventions that span the ecologies of the child. In addition, research has established the efficacy of systems change approaches (e.g., Positive Behavioral Supports) as well as contingency-based approaches that manipulate environmental antecedents and consequences. For CBIs that are embedded in more complex interventions, there exist greater possibilities to capitalize on effective practices from these allied literatures in concert with CBI methods.

With any intervention, there are systems capacity issues to consider, along with sequelae of these capacity constraints, including maintaining fidelity of implementation. Although demonstration projects that are supported with university trainers, onsite supervisors, and multiple trained interventionists can demonstrate efficacy, concerns exist with regard to intervention sustainability (Kratochwill & Shernoff, 2004). Research has demonstrated that well-trained interventionists are a prerequisite for effective programs (S. J. Wilson et al., 2003; Gottfredson, 2001), yet current accountability measures in schools nationwide raise concerns as to the availability of time, funds, human resources, and material resources to allow teachers and other education professionals to receive training and implement interventions more widely (Chorpita, 2003; Mayer, 2006). Likewise, constrained school budgets and competing educational priorities can make the large-scale implementation of costly comprehensive interventions more problematic.

Comorbidity is more often the rule rather than the exception when working with high-risk youth. Yet many efficacy studies have often taken an unrealistic approach, tending to treat clients with less severe needs and identified with singularly defined conditions (Kratochwill & Stoiber, 2000; Weisz, Donenberg, Han, & Weiss, 1995; Weisz & Hawley, 1998). Child and adolescent clients in the real world tend to have comorbid conditions of greater intensity. Thus, successfully addressing comorbidities may drive the field in the direction of using more complex interventions. Yet more comprehensive, complex, and well-attuned interventions to address these needs will require greater training for interventionists, take more time to fully implement, and be more costly. Children and adolescents with comorbid disorders, particularly in the areas of anger, aggression, and antisocial behaviors, are often referred to treatment by parents or other adults working with them (Kazdin & Weisz, 1998; Weisz & Hawley, 1998). Research has demonstrated linkages of these comorbid conditions to family problems (Kazdin & Weisz, 1998; Loeber & Stouthamer-Loeber, 1998; Patterson, 2002; Snyder & Stoolmiller, 2002; Zoccolillo et al., 2005), where client acceptability and ability to persevere with treatment participation can be problematic (Chambless & Hollon, 1998; Hoagwood et al., 2001; Kratochwill & Stoiber, 2000). This sets the stage for a dilemma with CBIs and other interventions that necessarily demand more time and energy investment of clients to benefit from more comprehensive interventions that are designed to ameliorate these comorbid conditions. Furthermore, given multicomponent interventions that address multiple problems areas, it can be extremely challenging to determine which aspects of the more comprehensive interventions are relatively more or less effective at ameliorating specific aspects of the clients' needs. A recent surprising finding by Kazdin and Whitley (2006) demonstrated reasonably strong evidence for equivalent treatment outcomes from youth with multiple comorbidities compared to those with more narrowly focused problems. Testing the so-called complexity hypothesis, Kazdin and Whitley found reason for hope in real-world clinical practice addressing more severe client challenges. Interestingly, they also identified certain parental barriers to treatment as key variables associated with differentially low treatment outcomes of youth with more multiple comorbidities compared to others. These issues as a whole point to the need for focused research that identifies where the most "bang for the buck" occurs in designing and delivering more efficient comprehensive interventions to address comorbid disorders that can be used effectively in real-world situations and bringing these interventions to scale in schools and other treatment venues.

Research into CBIs that stand alone or are embedded in more complex interventions poses multiple challenges. As previously suggested, confounds exist that make it difficult to tease out the partial effects of CBI components relative to other aspects of a comprehensive program. Research on mediators and moderators is essential to advancing theory and developing effective interventions (Clingempeel & Henggeler, 2002; Lochman, 2000; Weisz & Hawley, 1998). Yet many researchers do not address the effects of specific treatment components. Weisz and Hawley (1998) provided a surprising example from a 1991 meta-analysis by Durlak of cognitive-behavioral therapy, where differences in cognitions were not significantly correlated with differences in target behaviors, yet cognitive behavioral methods were presumed to alter thinking, which then alters behavior.

Highly specific theoretical models in applied research can complicate matters. For instance, some interventions in psychiatry and psychology are primarily disorder focused, based on a model of pathology (Kratochwill & Stoiber, 2000). These stand in contrast to various hybrid contextual models (e.g., cognitive–ecological approaches to CBIs) that may address some combination of developmental and/or ecological variables. Although a well-focused pathology-based approach may facilitate more discernible intervention results for analysis, it can at the same time preclude the discovery and development of more effective interventions. With CBIs embedded in more comprehensive interventions, mixed units of analysis may pose a threat to the integrity of the findings (Catalano et al., 1998). For example, given an ecological approach, the unit that is randomly assigned may typically be the classroom or school. Yet data are often collected and analyzed on individual students. Variance at multiple levels of the ecological structure that is not properly analyzed can compromise findings. Catalano and colleagues suggested several possible remedies, including appropriate use of hierarchical linear modeling techniques in study design, implementation, and analysis; pre-matching of higher levels in the ecology before performing random selection; use of randomized block and factorial designs; and use of mixed-model analysis of variance. The critical connection of theory to intervention—and the integration of assessment, intervention, and evaluation—were highlighted by Lochman (2000) in the context of a systematic and linked program of scientific inquiry, where basic efficacy is established first and effectiveness and dissemination research is conducted later. These research concerns are but a sample of the many challenges facing the profession. A related area of interest raises questions about adapting CBIs for routine embedded use in schools on a day-to-day basis.

Adapting CBI for Day-to-Day Use in Schools by Education Professionals

Schools have inherited the responsibility of providing various mental health and related social interventions to help address a wide variety of student needs. Although there may be debate over the appropriate role for schools in providing mental health and similar services, along with the many challenges involved, schools currently provide 70–80% of mental health services to those in greatest need (Hoagwood & Johnson, 2003). A significant percentage of students in special and general education demonstrate problems in anger/aggression, anxiety, depression, and related areas of need, all of which have been successfully addressed with CBIs (Kazdin & Weisz, 1998; Ollendick & King, 1998, 2000; Weisz & Hawley, 2002). But questions have been raised as to how CBIs can be used more effectively in schools.

One idea gaining attention is the use of curriculum-embedded interventions in schools (Rones & Hoagwood, 2000; Weist, 2005). For example, a CBI program could leverage local school district curriculum-based materials in a language arts class (e.g., a novel such as *The Outsiders,* in which social conflict and methods of resolution are examined) to teach generalized cognitive-behavioral techniques such as monitoring one's physical level of arousal indicating distress, implementing a relaxation strategy, launching a problem-solving method using self-talk, and so forth. Local school curriculum and classroom learning materials would be adapted for the embedded training. The teacher-delivered training to students could involve three basic components: (1) initial training in general CBI techniques over an 8-week or similar period using authentic situations relevant to students and engagement in modeling and role-playing activities; (2) embedded instruction in the context of classroom language arts materials that relate to interpersonal conflict; and (3) incidental prompting and practicing of newly learned cognitive-behavioral methods by students, seizing on "teachable moments" as related problems crop up in the classroom.

Three conceptual linchpins argue in favor of the field moving toward some type of embedded use of CBIs in schools. First, cognitive-behavioral techniques have been used since the 1970s to address a wide variety of social, emotional, and behavioral needs of youth and adults, including, but not limited to, anger/aggression, anxiety, and depression. In the zeitgeist of evidence-based intervention standards, CBIs fare well, having been one of the few treatments to meet the *probably efficacious* standard (Lonigan, Elbert, & Johnson, 1998; Ollendick & King, 2004) for addressing these needs areas. A substantial research base, independent of the American Psychological Association perspective of well-established and probably efficacious treatment, has demonstrated the efficacy of cognitive-behavioral techniques. Said plainly, we know that CBIs basically work, given appropriate selection of clients, appropriate match of methods to needs, fidelity of implementation, and expert professional support throughout the treatment process.

Second, schools are overburdened with existing academic and related social programming. It is virtually impossible to keep adding on stand-alone interventions, taking time and resources away from the primary academic mission of the school. Implementation of scaled-up school-based therapeutic and social competency interventions has been problematic at the national level. As schools have struggled to meet accountability requirements of No Child Left Behind, do more with marginal financial resources, and respond to a host of special needs of their student populations, they have been stretched to the limit of their capacities. New interventions that may benefit students in the social, emotional, and behavioral realms need to "double dip" (Van Acker, 1993) in terms of protecting teacher time and student engagement in class (e.g., avoiding pull-outs for stand-alone training). This means that to the degree possible and practical, such training needs to be embedded within the natural flow of classroom learning activities. Classes in language arts, social studies, and health education hold the greatest promise in this respect because they often address matters of individual and group conflict. Pilot studies should be developed that begin with language arts classes and utilize local school district curriculum materials as a teaching vehicle, combined with semistructured and incidental learning opportunities for students.

Third, the time has come to begin studying ways in which certain CBT techniques can be embedded into day-to-day classroom practice while also delineating appropriate professional boundaries. We need to ensure that students with serious social, emotional, and behavioral needs are appropriately referred to clinical specialists and not relegated to educators who lack the necessary clinical expertise. Over the past 40 years, the science of applied behavior analysis has relied on basic principles such as (1) stimulus control, (2) positive/negative reinforcement, (3) extinction, and (4) punishment. At a point 30–40 years ago, these principles and techniques were more in the domain of experimental studies and clinic-based treatment. However, over the decades, these fundamental principles have been infused into the educational system and are now part of embedded day-to-day practice in classrooms. Most teachers make purposeful, regular use of techniques based on reinforcement, extinction, and so forth. We are now approaching a historical juncture where a similar transition needs to begin with respect to cognitive-behavioral methods.

When considering embedded CBIs in day-to-day practice in schools, one must address several important research questions as a beginning step in this direction. We will use the target area of anger/aggression management for example purposes. First, to what degree can curriculum-embedded instruction in cognitive-behavioral techniques for students to address anger/aggression and related interpersonal conflict promote academic and social success? Second, what types of embedded methods can provide for a reasonable degree of fidelity of implementation, while also satisfying systemic and local classroom constraints that would tend to limit the implementation of such a student training approach? Third, what factors at the student, teacher, classroom, and school levels appear to influence (facilitate or inhibit) the successful implementation of this type of training? There are other critical research questions as well. This area of research appears promising as a focus for new advances in the field of CBIs.

Looking toward the Future

Students with EBD served by special education as well as those students in general education with difficulties in areas such as anger/aggression, anxiety, and depression can benefit from CBIs. The field has matured over several decades, expanding far beyond its original client treatment foci, and many new techniques have been developed. CBIs are now approaching the status of a mature treatment strategy for a variety of social, emotional, and behavioral needs. New opportunities exist to further advance the knowledge base in CBIs, with the conducting of research on the dissemination of these approaches to schools for embedded use on a day-to-day basis.

Problems and challenges remain with regard to scaling up efficacy studies to provide a stronger foundation of effectiveness and dissemination research. Systemic constraints and barriers to implementation in schools will continue to present challenges to researchers and practitioners. Limits to effective collaboration across disciplines, particularly school psychology, special education, and general education, need to be addressed, fostering improved lines of communication; facilitating shared funding streams; creating systems of data exchange; providing release time for interdepartmental team meetings; and allowing for collaboration in planning, implementing, and evaluating interventions.

Graduate programs in psychology and allied fields need to expand training programs for students to more fully cover CBIs as part of a longer term goal of building a professional infrastructure. Likewise, graduate programs in colleges of education, particularly special education, need to begin to incorporate CBIs in behavior management courses, using resources such as Smith and Daunic (2006), which provides concise training for school-based practitioners in CBM-derived methods. Behavioral consultant training programs should offer more focused training in CBIs as part of their curricula.

Funding organizations, particularly at the federal level, need to recognize the critical importance of maintaining a well-funded research program that builds on the current knowledge base in CBIs. New, promising directions for interventions, such as curriculum-embedded approaches in schools, also need to be supported, especially small-scale pilots and larger demonstration projects. Interdisciplinary research programs offer the promise of new advances in cognitive-behavioral science but require targeted research funding support at the federal level.

Cognitive-behavioral science is growing and maturing, having developed a strong theoretical foundation and an evidence base in varied disciplines demonstrating efficacy over the past four decades. The field can look forward to exciting developments in new ecologically and developmentally driven and curriculum-embedded models aimed at reaching youth clientele more effectively. Students with EBD, as well as those with mental health needs who are not served under special education, are likely to benefit greatly from these developments.

References

Bandura, A. (1969). *Principles of behavior modification.* New York: Holt, Rinehart & Winston.

Bandura, A. (1977). *Social learning theory.* Upper Saddle River, NJ: Prentice Hall.

Carlson, E., & Billingsley, B. (2001, July). *Working conditions in special education: Current research and implications for the field.* Paper presented at the meeting of the Office of Special Education Programs Project Director's Conference, Washington, DC.

Carson, R., Sitlington, P., & Frank, A. (1995). Young adulthood for individuals with behavioral disorders: What does it hold? *Behavioral Disorders, 20,* 127–135.

Catalano, R. F., Arthur, M. W., Hawkins, J. D., Berglund, L., & Olson, J. J. (1998). Comprehensive community- and school-based interventions to prevent antisocial behavior. In R. Loeber & D. P. Farrington (Eds.), *Serious and violent juvenile offenders* (pp. 248–283). Thousand Oaks, CA: Sage.

Center on Education Policy. (2004). *From the Capitol to the classroom: Year two of the No Child Left Behind Act.* Washington, DC. Retrieved January 19, 2007, from *www.cep-dc.org/pubs/nclby2.*

Chambless, D. L., & Hollon, S. D. (1998). Defining empirically supported therapies. *Journal of Consulting and Clinical Psychology, 66,* 7–18.

Chorpita, B. F. (2003). The frontier of evidence-based practice. In A. E. Kazdin & J. R. Weisz (Eds.), *Evidence-based psychotherapies for children and adolescents* (pp. 42–59). New York: Guilford Press.

Clarke, G. N., DeBar, L. L., & Lewinsohn, P. M. (2003). Cognitive-behavioral group treatment for adolescent depression. In A. E. Kazdin & J. R. Weisz (Eds.), *Evidence-based psychotherapies for children and adolescents* (pp. 120–134). New York: Guilford Press.

Clingempeel, W. G., & Henggeler, S. W. (2002). Randomized clinical trials, developmental theory, and antisocial youth: Guidelines for research. *Development and Psychopathology, 14,* 695–711.

Cole, C. (2006). *Closing the achievement gap series Part III: What is the impact of NCLB on the inclusion of students with disabilities?* (Education Policy Brief, Vol. 4, No. 11). Bloomington, IN: Center for Evaluation & Education Policy.

Coleman, M. R. (2000). *Bright futures for exceptional learners: Technical report. Conditions for special education teaching: CEC commission technical report.* Chapel Hill: University of North Carolina, Frank Porter Graham Center. (ERIC Document Reproduction Service No. ED457632)

Conduct Problems Prevention Research Group. (1999). Initial impact of the Fast Track prevention trial for conduct problems: I. The high-risk sample. *Journal of Consulting and Clinical Psychology, 67,* 631–647.

Conoley, J. C. (1989). Cognitive-behavioral approaches and prevention in the schools. In J. N. Hughes & R. J. Hall (Eds.), *Handbook of cognitive-behavioral approaches in educational settings* (pp. 535–568). New York: Guilford Press.

Craighead, W. F. (1982). A brief clinical history of cognitive-behavioral therapy with children. *School Psychology Review, 11,* 5–13.

Craighead, W. E., Kazdin, A. E., & Mahoney, M. J. (Eds.). (1976). *Behavior modification: Principles, issues, and applications.* Boston: Houghton Mifflin.

Craighead, W. E., Meyers, A. W., & Craighead, L. W. (1985). A conceptual model for cognitive behavioral therapy with children. *Journal of Abnormal Child Psychology, 13,* 331–342.

Daly, B. P., Burke, R., Hare, I., Mills, C., Owens, C., Moore, E., et al. (2006). Enhancing No Child Left Behind—School mental health connections. *Journal of School Health, 76,* 446–451.

Dember, W. N. (1974). Motivation and cognitive revolution. *American Psychologist, 29,* 161–168.

Durlak, J. A. (1982). Use of cognitive-behavioral interventions by paraprofessionals in schools. *School Psychology Review, 11,* 64–66.

D'Zurilla, T. J., & Goldfried, M. R. (1971). Problem solving and behavior modification. *Journal of Abnormal Psychology, 78,* 107–126.

Foster, S., Rollefson, M., Doksum, T., Noonan, D., Robinson, G., & Teich, J. (2005). *School mental health services in the United States, 2002–2003* (DHHS Publication No. SMA 05-4068). Rockville, MD: Center for Mental Health Services, Substance Abuse and Mental Health Services Administration.

Frey, K. S., Hirschstein, M. K., & Guzzo, B. A. (2000). Second Step: Preventing aggression by promoting social competence. *Journal of Emotional and Behavioral Disorders, 8,* 102–112.

Gerber, M. M. (1987). Application of cognitive-behavioral training methods to teaching basic skills to mildly handicapped elementary school students. In M. C. Wang, M. C. Reynolds, & H. J. Walberg (Eds.), *Handbook of special education: Research and practice* (Vol. 2, pp. 167–186). Oxford, UK: Pergamon Press.

Gerber, M. M., & Solari, E. (2005). Teaching effort and the future of cognitive-behavior interventions. *Behavior Disorders, 30,* 289–299.

Ghafoori, B. (2001). *Effectiveness of cognitive behavioral therapy in reducing classroom disruptive behaviors: A meta-analysis. Dissertation Abstracts International, 61*(11), 6133B. (UMI No. 9994801)

Gottfredson, D. C. (2001). *Schools and delinquency.* New York: Cambridge University Press.

Graham, S., & Harris, K. R. (2003). Students with learning disabilities and the process of writing: A meta-analysis of SRSD studies. In H. L. Swanson, K. R. Harris, & S. Graham (Eds.), *Handbook of learning disabilities* (pp. 323–344). New York: Guilford Press.

Greenbaum, P. E., Dedrick, R. F., Friedman, R. M., Kutash, K., Brown, E. C., Lardieri, S. P., et al. (1996). National Adolescent and Child Treatment Study (NACTS): Outcomes for children with serious emotional and behavioral disturbance. *Journal of Emotional and Behavioral Disorders, 4,* 130–146.

Guerra, N. G., Eron, L. D., Huesmann, L. R., Tolan, P., & Van Acker, R. (1997). A cognitive-ecological approach to the prevention and mitigation of violence and aggression in inner-city youth. In D. P. Fry & K. Bjorkqvist (Eds.), *Cultural variation in conflict resolution: Alternatives to violence* (pp. 199–214). Mahwah, NJ: Erlbaum.

Guerra, N. G., & Jagers, R. (1999). Ethnic sensitivity in research. In V. McLoyd & L. Steinberg (Eds.), *Methodological issues in the study of minority adolescents and their families* (pp. 167–182). Hillsdale, NJ: Erlbaum.

Hahn, R., Fuqua-Whitley, D., Wethington, H., Lowy, J., Crosby, A., Fullilove, M., et al. (2007). Effectiveness of universal school-based programs to prevent violent and aggressive behavior: A systematic review. *American Journal of Preventive Medicine, 33*(Suppl. 2), S114–S129.

Harris, K. R. (1982). Cognitive behavior modification: Application with exceptional children. *Focus on Exceptional Children, 15*(2), 1–16.

Harris, K. R. (1985). Conceptual, methodological, and clinical issues in cognitive-behavioral assessment. *Journal of Abnormal Child Psychology, 13,* 373–390.

Harris, K., & Pressley, M. (1991). The nature of cognitive strategy instruction: Interactive strategy construction. *Exceptional Children, 57,* 392–404.

Hawkins, J. D., Farrington, D. P., & Catalano, R. F. (1998). Reducing violence through the schools. In D. S. Elliott, B. A. Hamburg, & K. R. Williams (Eds.), *Violence in American schools* (pp. 188–216). New York: Cambridge University Press.

Hoagwood, K., Burns, B. J., Kiser, L., Ringeisen, H., & Schoenwald, S. K. (2001). Evidence-based practice in child and adolescent mental health services. *Psychiatric Services, 52,* 1179–1189.

Hoagwood, K., & Erwin, H. D. (1997). Effectiveness of school-based mental health services for children: A 10-year research review. *Journal of Child and Family Studies, 6,* 435–454.

Hoagwood, K., & Johnson, J. (2003). School psychology: A public health framework. I. From evidence-based practices to evidence-based policies. *Journal of School Psychology, 41,* 3–21.

Hughes, J. N. (1988). *Cognitive behavior therapy with children in schools.* New York: Pergamon Press.

Karoly, P. (1993). Mechanisms of self-regulation: A systems view. *Annual Review of Psychology, 44,* 23–52.

Kazdin, A. E. (1978). *History of behavior modification: Experimental foundations of contemporary research* (pp. 119–185, 307–338). Baltimore: University Park Press.

Kazdin, A. E. (2001). *Behavior modification in applied settings* (6th ed.). Belmont, CA: Wadsworth.

Kazdin, A. E., & Weisz, J. R. (1998). Identifying and developing empirically supported child and adolescent treatments. *Journal of Consulting and Clinical Psychology, 66,* 19–36.

Kazdin, A. E., & Whitley, M. K. (2006). Comorbidity, case complexity, and effects of evidence-based treatment for children referred for disruptive behavior. *Journal of Consulting and Clinical Psychology, 74,* 455–467.

Kendall, P. C. (1993). Cognitive-behavioral therapies with youth: Guiding theory, current status, and emerging developments. *Journal of Consulting and Clinical Psychology, 61,* 235–247.

Kendall, P. C. (Ed.). (2006). *Child and adolescent therapy: Cognitive-behavioral procedures* (3rd ed.). New York: Guilford Press.

Kratochwill, T. R., & Shernoff, E. S. (2004). Evidence-based practice: Promoting evidence-based interventions in school psychology. *School Psychology Quarterly, 18*(4), 1–21.

Kratochwill, T. R., & Stoiber, K. C. (2000). Empirically supported interventions and school psychology: Conceptual and practice issues—Part II. *School Psychology Quarterly, 15,* 233–253.

Leahy, R. L. (1996). Historical context of cognitive therapy. In R. L. Leahy (Ed.), *Cognitive behavioral therapy: Basic principles and applications* (pp. 9–22). Northvale, NJ: Aronson.

Leone, P. E., Mayer, M. J., Malmgren, K., & Meisel, S. M. (2000). School violence and disruption: Rhetoric, reality, and reasonable balance. *Focus on Exceptional Children, 33*(1), 1–20.

Lipsey, M. W. (1995). What do we learn from 400 research studies on the effectiveness of treatment with juvenile delinquents? In J. McGuire (Ed.), *What works? Reducing reoffending* (pp. 63–78). New York: Wiley.

Lochman, J. E. (2000). Theory and empiricism in intervention research: A dialectic to be avoided. *Journal of School Psychology, 38,* 359–368.

Lochman, J. E., Curry, J. F., Dane, H., & Ellis, M. (2001). The Anger Coping Program: An empirically supported treatment for aggressive children. *Residential Treatment for Children and Youth, 18,* 63–73.

Lochman, J. E., Powell, N. R., Whidby, J. M., & FitzGerald, D. P. (2006). Cognitive-behavioral assessment and treatment with aggressive children. In P. C. Kendall (Ed.), *Child and adolescent therapy: Cognitive-behavioral procedures* (3rd ed., pp. 33–81). New York: Guilford Press.

Lochman, J. E., Whidby, J. M., & FitzGerald, D. P. (2000). Cognitive-behavioral assessment and treatment with aggressive children. In P. C. Kendall (Ed.), *Child and adolescent therapy: Cognitive-behavioral procedures* (2nd ed., pp. 31–87). New York: Guilford Press.

Loeber, R., & Stouthamer-Loeber, M. (1998). Juvenile aggression at home and at school. In D. S. Elliott, B. A. Hamburg & K. R. Williams (Eds.), *Violence in American schools: A new perspective* (pp. 94–126). Cambridge, UK: Cambridge University Press.

Lonigan, C. J., Elbert, J. C., & Johnson, S. B. (1998). Empirically supported psychosocial interventions for children: An overview. *Journal of Clinical Child Psychology, 27,* 138–145.

Mahoney, M. J. (1974). *Cognition and behavior modification.* Cambridge, MA: Ballinger.

Malmgren, K., Edgar, E., & Neel, R. S. (1998). Postschool status of youth with behavioral disorders. *Behavioral Disorders, 23,* 257–263.

Mathur, S. R., & Rutherford, R. B., Jr. (1996). Is social skill training effective for students with emotional and behavioral disorders: Research issues and needs. *Behavioral Disorders, 22,* 21–28.

Mayer, M. J. (2006). The current state of methodological knowledge and emerging practice in evidence-based evaluation: Applications to school violence prevention research. In S. Jimerson & M. J. Furlong (Eds.), *Handbook of school violence and school safety: From research to practice* (pp. 171–190). Hillsdale, NJ: Erlbaum.

Mayer, M. J., & Leone, P. E. (2007). School violence and disruption revisited: Establishing equity and safety in the school house. *Focus on Exceptional Children, 40*(1), 1–28.

Mayer, M. J., Lochman, J. E., & Van Acker, R. (2005). Introduction to the special issue: Cognitive-behavioral interventions with students with EBD. *Behavioral Disorders, 30,* 197–212.

Meichenbaum, D. (1977). *Cognitive-behavioral modification: An integrated approach.* New York: Plenum.

Meyers, A. W., Cohen, R., & Schleser, R. (1989). A cognitive behavioral approach to education: Adopting a broad-based perspective. In J. N. Hughes & R. J. Hall (Eds.), *Handbook of cognitive behavioral approaches in educational settings* (pp. 62–84). New York: Guilford Press.

Mytton, J., DiGuiseppi, C., Gough, D., Taylor, R., & Logan, S. (2006). School-based secondary prevention programmes for preventing violence (Art. No. CD004606. DOI: 10.1002/14651858.CD004606.pub2). *Cochrane Database of Systematic Reviews,* Issue 3.

National Center for Education Statistics. (2005). *The condition of education 2005* (NCES 2005–094). Washington, DC: U.S. Government Printing Office.

National Longitudinal Transition Study–2. *NLTS2 data tables.* Retrieved January 12, 2007, from *www.nlts2.org/data_tables/index.html.*

National Research Council. (2004). *Engaging schools: Fostering high school students' motivation to learn.* Washington, DC: National Academies Press.

Ollendick, T. H., & King, N. J. (1998). Empirically supported treatments for children with phobic and anxiety disorders: Current status. *Journal of Clinical Child Psychology, 27,* 156–167.

Ollendick, T. H., & King, N. J. (2000). Empirically supported treatments for children and adolescents. In P. C. Kendall (Ed.), *Child and adolescent therapy: Cognitive behavioral procedures* (2nd ed., pp. 386–425). New York: Guilford Press.

Ollendick, T. H., & King, N. J. (2004). Empirically supported treatments for children and adolescence: Advances toward evidence-based practice. In P. M. Barrett & T. H. Ollendick (Eds.), *Handbook of interventions that work with children and adolescents: Prevention and treatment* (pp. 3–25). New York: Wiley.

Paternite, C. E. (2005). School-based mental health programs and services: Overview and introduction to the special issue. *Journal of Abnormal Child Psychology, 33,* 657–663.

Patterson, G. R. (2002). The early development of coercive family process. In J. B. Reid, G. R. Patterson, & J. Snyder (Eds.), *Antisocial behavior in children and adolescents: A developmental analysis and model for intervention* (pp. 25–44). Washington, DC: American Psychological Association.

Polsgrove, L., & Smith, S. (2004). Informed practice in teaching students self-control. In R. Rutherford, M. Quinn, & S. Mathur (Eds.), *Research in emotional and behavioral disorders* (pp. 399–425). New York: Guilford Press.

Robinson, T. R., Smith, S. W., & Miller, M. D. (2002). Effect of a cognitive behavioral intervention on responses to anger by middle school students with chronic behavior problems. *Behavioral Disorders, 27,* 256–271.

Rones, M., & Hoagwood, K. (2000). School-based mental health services: A research review. *Clinical Child and Family Psychology Review, 3,* 223–241.

Rosenbaum, M. S., & Drabman, R. S. (1979). Self control training in the classroom: A review and critique. *Journal of Applied Behavior Analysis, 12,* 467–485.

Smith, S. W., & Daunic, A. P. (2006). *Behavior management for elementary students: Teaching social problem solving.* Boston: Allyn & Bacon.

Smith, S. W., Lochman, J. E., & Daunic, A. P. (2005). Managing aggression using cognitive-behavioral interventions: State of the practice and future directions. *Behavioral Disorders, 30,* 227–240.

Snyder, J., & Stoolmiller, M. (2002). Reinforcement and coercion mechanisms in the development of antisocial behavior: The family. In J. B. Reid, G. R. Patterson, & J. Snyder

(Eds.), *Antisocial behavior in children and adolescents: A developmental analysis and model for intervention* (pp. 65–100). Washington, DC: American Psychological Association.

Special Education Elementary Longitudinal Study. *SEELS data tables overview.* Retrieved January 12, 2007, from *seels.net/search/datatableOverview.htm.*

SPENSE. (2002a). *Beginning special educator: Characteristics, qualifications, and experiences.* Retrieved August 1, 2002, from *www.spense.org/IHEsummaryfinal. pdf.*

SPENSE. (2002b). *Paperwork in special education.* Retrieved August 1, 2002, from *www. spense.org/Paperwork.pdf.*

Stark, K. D., Hargrave, J., Sander, J., Custer, G., Schnoebelen, S., Simpson, J., et al. (2006). Treatment of childhood depression: The ACTION treatment program. In P. C. Kendall (Ed.), *Child and adolescent therapy: Cognitive-behavioral procedures* (3rd ed., pp. 169–216). New York: Guilford Press.

Stark, K. D., Sander, J. B., Yancy, M. G., Bronik, M. D., & Hoke, J. A. (2000). Treatment of depression in childhood and adolescence: Cognitive behavioral procedures for the individual and family. In P. C. Kendall (Ed.), *Child and adolescent therapy: Cognitive-behavioral procedures* (2nd ed., pp. 173–234). New York: Guilford Press.

Sturm, R., & Andreyeva, T. (2005). Datapoints: Use of mental health care among youths in 1997 and 2002. *Psychiatric Services, 56,* 793.

Swanson, H. L. (1989). Strategy instruction: Overview of principles and procedures for effective use. *Learning Disability Quarterly, 12,* 3–14.

U.S. Department of Health and Human Services. (1999). *Mental health: A report of the Surgeon General.* Rockville, MD: U.S. Department of Health and Human Services, Substance Abuse and Mental Health Services Administration, Center for Mental Health Services, National Institutes of Health, National Institute of Mental Health.

U.S. General Accounting Office. (2003, April). *Federal agencies could play a stronger role in helping states reduce the number of children placed solely to obtain mental health services* (Report No. GAO-03-397). Washington, DC: Author.

Van Acker, R. (1993). Dealing with conflict and aggression in the classroom: What skills do teachers need? *Teacher Education and Special Education, 16*(1), 23–33.

Vera, M., Vila, D., & Alegria, M. (2003). Cognitive behavioral therapy: Concepts, issues, and strategies for practice with racial/ethnic minorities. In G. Bernal, J. Trimble, A. Berlew, & F. Leong (Eds.), *Handbook of racial and ethnic minority psychology* (pp. 521–538). Thousand Oaks, CA: Sage.

Wagner, M. (1995). Outcomes for youth with serious emotional disturbance in secondary school and early adulthood. *Future of Children, 5,* 90–113.

Wasserman, G. A., & Miller, L. S. (1998). The prevention of serious and violent juvenile offending. In R. Loeber & D. P. Farrington (Eds.), *Serious and violent juvenile offenders* (pp. 197–247). Thousand Oaks, CA: Sage.

Weist, M. D. (2005). Fulfilling the promise of school based mental health: Moving towards a public mental health promotion approach. *Journal of Abnormal Child Psychology, 33,* 735–741.

Weisz, J., Donenberg, G., Han, S., & Weiss, B. (1995). Bridging the gap between lab and clinic in child and adolescent psychotherapy. *Journal of Consulting and Clinical Psychology, 63,* 688–701.

Weisz, J. R., & Hawley, K. M. (1998). Finding, evaluating, refining, and applying empirically supported treatments for children and adolescents. *Journal of Clinical Child Psychology, 27,* 206–216.

Weisz, J. R., & Hawley, K. M. (2002). Developmental factors in the treatment of adolescents. *Journal of Consulting and Clinical Psychology, 70,* 21–43.

Wilson, D. B., Gottfredson, D. C., & Najaka, S. S. (2001). School-based prevention of problem behaviors: A meta-analysis. *Journal of Quantitative Criminology, 17,* 247–272.

Wilson, S. J., & Lipsey, M. W. (2007). School-based interventions for aggressive and disruptive behavior: Update of a meta-analysis. *American Journal of Preventive Medicine,
33*(Suppl. 2), S130–S143.

Wilson, S. J., Lipsey, M. W., & Derzon, J. H. (2003). The effects of school-based intervention
programs on aggressive behavior: A meta-analysis. *Journal of Consulting and Clinical
Psychology, 71,* 136–149.

Wong, B. (1985). Issues in cognitive-behavioral interventions in academic skill areas. *Journal
of Abnormal Child Psychology, 13,* 425–442.

Zoccolillo, M., Romano, E., Joubert, D., Mazzarello, T., Côté, S., Boivin, M., et al. (2005).
The intergenerational transmission of aggression and antisocial behavior. In R. E.
Tremblay, W. W. Hartup, & J. Archer (Eds.), *Developmental origins of aggression* (pp.
353–375). New York: Guilford Press.

CHAPTER 2

Intervention Development, Assessment, Planning, and Adaptation

The Importance of Developmental Models

JOHN E. LOCHMAN
FRANK M. GRESHAM

Effective use of cognitive-behavioral interventions (CBIs) in school settings with children with emotional and behavioral disorders requires careful consideration of the developmental model that describes the beginning and the maintenance of the particular form of psychopathology that is being addressed. This chapter describes how developmental models serve an important function in identifying targets for intervention and the mechanisms that can produce change. The chapter further illustrates how the developmental model should be reflected in the assessment model and in the intervention model that is selected. Finally, the chapter emphasizes that interventions that are developed and tested in this way should be delivered in "real-world" school settings with integrity with regard to the intervention model, but also with careful flexibility.

Developmental Models

Developmental models can serve as the foundation for new CBIs by identifying the active mechanisms that can be the targets of the intervention, as indicated below (Lochman, 2006; Lochman, Boxmeyer, & Powell, in press). Therapeutic innovations are more likely to occur when theory is emphasized in treatment research (Jensen, 1999). However, there has been a long-standing neglect of theory and of empirical tests of theory in child and adolescent psychotherapy research until recent years (Kazdin, 1999). Kazdin (1999) believed that Paul's (1967) dictum three decades ago to identify treatments that work with specific types of individuals in specific types of circumstances successfully led the field to move beyond the basic question of "Does therapy work?" to an emphasis on identifying moderators of intervention effects. However, Kazdin believed that this practical focus on moderators contributed to a lack of emphasis on theory and on research examining the mediators of treatment effects, which would contribute to our understanding of why therapy works. *Moderators* affect the relation between two other variables (in this case, the intervention and its outcomes), whereas *mediators* are variables that intervene between two other variables and indicate the mechanism accounting for a given effect between the intervention and its outcomes. Thus, mediation analyses determine whether changes on the presumed active mechanisms targeted by the intervention (e.g., hostile attributions) actually lead to the observed outcome. Moderation analyses, in contrast, determine whether a given intervention has different effects on an outcome for individuals identified by the presumed moderator (e.g., high severity of baseline aggression) versus other individuals (see Chapter 3 for more on moderators and mediators). An active and productive scientific approach to intervention requires reciprocal and lively interaction between empiricism and theory (Hughes, 2000; Lochman, 2000).

Thus, school-based intervention programs should be rooted in clear, well-articulated models for the development and maintenance of particular problem behaviors (Conduct Problems Prevention Research Group, 1992). The conceptual developmental model can indicate how certain characteristics of the child and of the child's social context can influence the child's behavior and adjustment, and how these influences can vary over time. This developmental aspect of the conceptual foundations for interventions has often been deficient, especially for behavioral interventions, but intervention research in recent years has begun to be more focused on developmental trajectories leading up to the expression of the particular form of psychopathology. A clear conceptual model has several key effects on intervention research and intervention application by (1) serving as the framework for the *development of intervention goals and activities* that target multiple active mechanisms that contribute to the development of the disorder (e.g., role-play and game-like tasks designed to amplify anger management or to promote parents' more consistent use of positive consequences for appropriate behavior); (2) permitting the *individualization of the intervention* in a rigorous, non-haphazard manner, when children are assessed and identified to have certain, but not all, of the identified deficits in the conceptual model (e.g., if a particular aggressive child does not have attributional biases, then the intervention should focus on the problem-solving deficits that do exist, and intervention activities addressing attributional biases should be deemphasized); and (3) permitting the *testing of the theory* underlying the intervention, through mediational analyses, as well as the intervention itself. The conceptual, assessment, and intervention models should all be well integrated.

Ecological Models

Developmental models have been heavily influenced by ecological theories of child development (Bronfenbrenner, 1995), which have suggested that a child's behavior is the result of individual characteristics (such as irritable temperament) and of social and contextual influences that radiate out around the child (Lochman, Barry, & Salekin, 2005; see Figure 2.1). Social contexts that are most proximal (microsystems) are those in which the child spends the most time and that are likely to have the most impact on the child's behavior (e.g., family environment, school environment, and peer groups). Children's broader environments (exosystem), such as their neighborhoods, and the medical clinics, social agencies, and recreation centers within their communities, also can impact the children but often in an indirect way. Typically this occurs because the stresses produced by these community and family forces lead to disruptions in the parents' efforts to raise and discipline their children. The ecological model also stresses the importance of understanding how these systems interact with each other (mesosystem) and how these interactions between systems also influence children's behavioral development. For example, parents' abilities to interact in positive, proactive ways with school personnel (crossing the family and school systems) can assist children's positive behavior.

In the following section, an example indicates how existing research findings can provide the framework for an ecologically grounded developmental model. The example model to be used throughout this chapter specifically addresses children's aggressive behavior. Similar models can be formed for other types of behavioral and emotional problems.

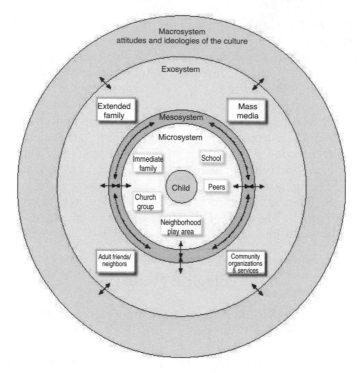

FIGURE 2.1. Bronfenbrenner's ecological model of development. From Lochman, Barry, and Salekin (2005). Copyright 2005 by Sage Publications. Reprinted by permission.

Contextual Social-Cognitive Model: An Example of Aggressive Behavior

As an example of the use of research findings to form a contextual social-cognitive model that serves as the basis of our Coping Power program (Lochman & Wells, 2002a), empirically identified risk factors that predict children's antisocial behavior can be examined (Coie & Dodge, 1998; Lochman, 2006; Pennington, 2002). As children develop, they can experience an accumulating and "stacking" of risk factors, increasing the probability of the children eventually displaying serious antisocial behavior (Loeber, 1990; see Figure 2.2). These risk factors can be conceptualized as falling within five categories: biological and temperamental child factors, family context, neighborhood context, peer context, and later emerging child factors involving social-cognitive processes and emotional regulation (see Figure 2.3).

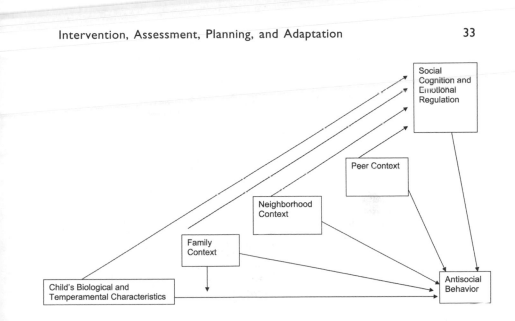

FIGURE 2.2. Developmental sequence of stacking of problem behaviors in children with disruptive behavior disorders. From Lochman (2006). Copyright 2005 by Sage Publications. Reprinted by permission.

Biological and Temperament Factors

With regard to biological and temperamental child factors, some prenatal factors such as maternal exposure to alcohol, methadone, cocaine, and cigarette smoke and severe nutritional deficiencies (Brennan, Grekin, & Mednick, 1999; Delaney-Black et al., 2000) have been found to have direct effects on child aggression. However, it is more commonly found in diathesis–stress models that aggression is the result of interactions between child risk factors and environmental factors (Masten, Best, & Garmezy, 1990). Thus, risk factors such as birth complications, genes, cortisol reactivity, testosterone, abnormal serotonin levels, and temperament all contribute to children's conduct problems, but only when environmental factors such as harsh parenting or low socioeconomic status are present (Arseneault, Tremblay, Boulerice, & Saucier, 2002; Raine, Brennan, & Mednick, 1997; Scarpa, Fikretoglu, & Luscher, 2000). For example, some boys have been found to have a gene that expresses only low levels of MAOA (monoamine oxidase A) enzyme. MAOA metabolizes and gets rid of excess neurotransmitters. Low MAOA leads to violent behavior, but only if children are maltreated—an indicator of diathesis stress (Caspi et al., 2002). School-based personnel have little control over these early distal risk factors, which are thus not

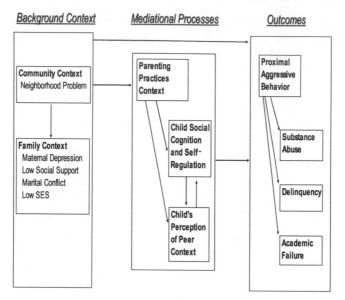

FIGURE 2.3. Contextual social-cognitive model. From Lochman (2006). SES, socio-economic status. Copyright 2006 by Sage Publications. Reprinted by permission.

the direct focus of school-based interventions. However, their presence may moderate the effectiveness of an intervention.

Community and Neighborhood Factors

Neighborhood and school environments have also been found to be risk factors for aggression and delinquency over and above the variance accounted for by family characteristics (Kupersmidt, Griesler, DeRosier, Patterson, & Davis, 1995). High neighborhood crime rates and low social cohesion have been found to predict disruptive and aggressive behavior in children (e.g., Colder, Mott, Levy, & Flay, 2000; Guerra, Huesmann, & Spindler, 2003) and their beliefs about aggression (Guerra et al., 2003). Neighborhood effects begin to create heightened risk during middle childhood (Ingoldsby & Shaw, 2002), as children become more independent in moving around their community. Early onset of aggression and violence has been associated with neighborhood disorganization and poverty partly because some children who live in poor and disorganized neighborhoods are not well supervised and engage in more risk-taking behaviors.

Schools can further exacerbate children's conduct problems because of children's frustration with academic demands and because of peer influences in the school setting. Many children with aggressive behavior problems tend to have conflicted relations with school personnel because of the monitoring and consequences students receive from teachers and other adults at school for their behavior problems. Because of their impulsive behavior and their deteriorating relations with teachers, aggressive children can begin to have lower levels of academic achievement, and this can have reciprocal effects on the students' frustration with school tasks and anger at people associated with school (Larson & Lochman, 2002). Children's peers in the classroom also have powerful effects on their behavior. The density of aggressive children in classroom settings can increase the amount of aggressive behavior emitted by individual students during the course of that school year and, especially for younger children, in subsequent years as well (Barth, Dunlap, Dane, Lochman, & Wells, 2004; Kellam, Xiange, Mersica, Brown, & Ialongo, 1998). A student who is placed in a classroom with a large number of aggressive children is likely to increase his or her own aggression because of modeling of peers' behavior, of reactive frustration with being victimized, and of peer reinforcement of the student's deviant ideas and behaviors, a form of deviancy training.

Family Factors

There is a wide array of factors in the family that can affect child aggression, ranging from poverty to more general stress and discord within the family. Children's aggression has been linked to family background factors such as parent criminality, substance use, and depression (Loeber & Stouthamer-Loeber, 1998); poverty (Dodge, Pettit, & Bates, 1994); stressful life events (Guerra, Huesmann, Tolan, Van Acker, & Eron, 1995); single and teenage parenthood (Nagin, Pogarsky, & Farrington, 1997); and insecure, disorganized attachment (Shaw & Vondra, 1995). All of these family risk factors intercorrelate, especially with socioeconomic status (Luthar, 1999), and can influence child behavior through their effect on parenting processes. For example, marital conflict during the preschool years causes disruptions in parenting, and these disruptions contribute to some children's high levels of stress and consequent aggression (Dadds & Powell, 1992).

Parenting Processes

Parenting processes linked to children's aggression (e.g., Patterson, Reid, & Dishion, 1992; Shaw, Keenan, & Vondra, 1994) include (1) nonresponsive parenting at age 1, with pacing and consistency of parent responses not meeting children's needs; (2) coercive, escalating cycles of harsh parental nattering and child noncompliance starting in the toddler years, especially for children with difficult temperaments; (3) harsh, inconsistent discipline; (4) unclear directions and commands; (5) lack of warmth and involvement; and (6) lack of parental supervision and monitoring as children approach adolescence. The relations between parenting factors and childhood aggression are bidirectional, as child temperament and behavior also affect parenting behavior (Fite, Colder, Lochman, & Wells, 2006).

Peer Factors

Children with disruptive behaviors are at risk for being rejected by their peers (Cillessen, van IJzendoorn, Van Lieshout, & Hartup, 1992). Aggressive children who are also socially rejected exhibit more severe antisocial behavior than children who are either aggressive only or rejected only (Lochman & Wayland, 1994; Miller-Johnson, Coie, Maumary-Gremaud, Bierman, & Conduct Problems Prevention Research Group, 2002). The match between the race of students and their peers in a classroom influences the degree of social rejection that students experience (Jackson, Barth, Powell, & Lochman, 2006), and race and gender appear to moderate the relation between peer rejection and negative adolescent outcomes. For example, Lochman and Wayland (1994) found that peer rejection ratings of African American children within a mixed-race classroom did not predict subsequent externalizing problems in adolescence, whereas peer rejection ratings of Caucasian children were associated with future disruptive behaviors. Similarly, whereas peer rejection can predict serious delinquency in boys, it can fail to do so with girls (Miller-Johnson, Coie, Maumary-Gremaud, Lochman, & Terry, 1999).

As children with conduct problems enter adolescence, many of them tend to associate with deviant peers. Adolescents who have been continually rejected from more prosocial peer groups because they lack appropriate social skills turn to antisocial cliques for social support (Miller-Johnson et al., 1999). The tendency for aggressive children to associate with one another increases the probability that they will escalate the seriousness of their antisocial behavior (e.g., Dishion, Andrews, & Crosby, 1995; Vitaro, Brendgen, Pagani, Tremblay, & McDuff, 1999).

Social Cognition

Based on children's temperament and biological dispositions, and on children's contextual experiences from their family, peers, and community, they can begin to form stable patterns of processing social information and of regulating their emotions. The contextual social-cognitive model (Lochman & Wells, 2002a) stresses the reciprocal interactive relationships between children's initial cognitive appraisal of problem situations, their efforts to think about solutions to the perceived problems, their physiological arousal, and their behavioral response. The level of physiological arousal will depend on the individual's biological predisposition to becoming aroused and will vary depending on the interpretation of the event (Williams, Lochman, Phillips, & Barry, 2003). The level of arousal will further influence the social problem solving, operating either to intensify the fight-or-flight response or to interfere with the generation of solutions. Because of the ongoing and reciprocal nature of interactions, it may be difficult for children to extricate themselves from aggressive behavior patterns.

Some aggressive children, especially those displaying reactive aggressive behavior, have cognitive distortions at the appraisal phases of social-cognitive processing because of difficulties in encoding incoming social information and in accurately interpreting social events and others' intentions. In the appraisal phases of information processing, aggressive children have been found to recall fewer relevant nonhostile cues about events (Lochman & Dodge, 1994), and reactively aggressive children have been found to have a hostile attributional bias, as they excessively infer that others are acting toward them in a provocative and hostile manner (Dodge, Lochman, Harnish, Bates, & Pettit, 1997; Lochman & Dodge, 1994).

Many aggressive children also have cognitive deficiencies at the problem solution phases of social-cognitive processing. They may have dominance- and revenge-oriented social goals (Lochman, Wayland, & White, 1993) that guide the maladaptive action-oriented and nonverbal solutions they generate for perceived problems (Dunn, Lochman, & Colder, 1997; Lochman & Dodge, 1994; Pepler, Craig, & Roberts, 1998). Aggressive children frequently have low verbal skills, and this contributes to their difficulty in accessing and using competent verbal assertion and compromise solutions. At the next processing step they identify consequences for each of the solutions generated and make a decision how to respond to the situation. It is common for aggressive children to evaluate aggressive behavior in a positive way (Crick & Werner, 1998), and they expect that aggressive behavior will lead to positive outcomes for them (Lochman & Dodge, 1994). Deficient beliefs at this stage of information processing are especially characteristic for children with proactive aggressive behavior patterns (Dodge et al., 1997) and for youth who have callous, unemotional traits consistent with early phases of psychopathy (Pardini, Lochman, & Frick, 2003). Children's schematic beliefs and expectations affect each of these information-processing steps (Lochman & Dodge, 1998; Zelli, Dodge, Lochman, Laird, & Conduct Problems Prevention Research Group, 1999).

The Developmental Model Identifies Targets for Intervention

The contextual social-cognitive model (Lochman & Wells, 2002a) that is derived from these research findings indicates that certain family and community background factors (neighborhood problems, maternal depression, low social support, marital conflict, low socioeconomic status) have both a direct effect on children's aggressive behaviors, and an indirect effect through their influence on key mediational processes (parenting practices, children's social cognition and emotional regulation, children's peer relations, see Figure 2.3). This model led to an intervention, the Coping Power Program, which is designed to change these specific mutable, mediating risk factors and thereby reduce children's aggressive behaviors and their subsequent delinquent and substance abuse behavior (Lochman & Wells, 2002a, 2002b, 2003, 2004). Thus, the child component of the Coping Power Program has a series of structured activities designed to produce accurate awareness of anger and feelings related to vulnerability, enhance anger management training, increase perspective taking and attribution retraining, increase social problem-solving skills using a Problem Identification, Choices and Consequences (PICC) model, and increase resistance to peer pressure and involvement with nondeviant peer groups. These Coping Power child component activities are designed to affect children's social-cognitive processes, their self-regulation abilities, and their perceptions of and involvement in their peer context. The parent component of the Coping Power Program is focused on improving a set of appropriate parenting skills (positive attention and rewards for appropriate child behavior; ignoring of minor disruptive behavior; provision of clear commands, rules, and expectations; use of consistent consequences for negative child behavior; and monitoring of children's behavior in the community) along with enhancing the parents' stress management skills and family problem-solving skills. These intervention goals thus follow directly from the mediational processes in the developmental model derived from research on the risk factors.

This example indicates how a model of the development of children's conduct problems can be used to generate the targets for CBIs. In other areas of child psychopathology, an understanding of the developmental model of the disorder can in a very similar way lead to identified intervention targets (Lochman & Pardini, in press). For example, depressed youth have been found to have certain common social-cognitive characteristics. Depressed youth display both cognitive distortions and cognitive deficits evident in their core symptoms of feelings of worthlessness, associated negative beliefs about themselves and their future, attributions of failures, and external locus of control (Gladstone & Kaslow, 1995). Depressed children and adolescents attribute positive events to external causes, rather than perceiving that they have active, internal control over the positive things that happen to them (Kaslow, Rehm, Pollack, & Siegel, 1988; Curry & Craighead, 1990). Garber, Braafladt, and Zeman (1991) found that depressed children had certain problem-solving difficulties as well, evident in their patterns of generating avoidant and aggressive strategies to handle social difficulties. The onset of youth depression is often affected by contextual factors and can be preceded by family conflict, physical illness, the breakup of romantic relationships, low rates of social acceptance, or the loss of a friendship (Weersing & Brent, 2003). Other evidence of contextual effects is evident in depressed children's distorted schemas and internal working models, which have been found to be linked to insecure attachment to parent figures (Cowan, Cohn, Cowan, & Pearson, 1996; Stark, Sander, et al., 2006). Thus, common cognitive-behavioral treatment components directed at these risk factors for childhood depression include (1) self-control skills, self-consequation (reinforcing themselves more, punishing themselves less), self-monitoring (paying attention to positive things they do), self-evaluation (setting less perfectionistic standards for their performance), and assertiveness training; (2) social skills, including methods of initiating interactions, maintaining interactions, handling conflict, and using relaxation and imagery; and (3) cognitive restructuring, involving confronting children about the lack of evidence for their distorted perceptions (Stark, Hargrave, et al., 2006).

Assessment

Conducting a thorough assessment of the factors related to a child's behavioral and emotional tendencies is an extremely important part of designing a comprehensive treatment plan. The assessment model for a particular form of psychopathology should follow from the developmental model for that disorder. In this section, a rationale is provided for evaluating children on a number of behavioral and social-cognitive variables, again using an example of how assessment relates to the developmental model in our work with aggressive children.

We have used a battery of all these types of assessment tools in clinical research with our school-based Anger Coping and Coping Power programs (Lochman, Powell, Whidby, & FitzGerald, 2006). In a clinic-based Conduct Disorders program we have used selected subsets of the measures and have often informally assessed for aspects of the social-cognitive deficiencies and distortions during comprehensive structured and unstructured interviews. We use these assessments to identify which aspects of the developmental model represent problems for the child, and this active assessment can then lead to an adaptive intervention, in which different aspects of an intervention receive greater or lesser stress because of the precise distortions and deficiencies that a child has.

Behavior Presentation of the Child

Typically a first step in the assessment process is to clarify whether the child is displaying abnormally high levels of behavioral or emotional problems. It is important to look at aggression within the context of all other observable behavior problems, interaction styles, and environmental factors. Often these patterns of behavior problems will vary with respect to the environmental context (e.g., location, home vs. school; person involved, peer vs. teacher). Therefore it is important to obtain information from as many sources as possible.

Behavioral Rating Scales

One of the most commonly used behavioral rating scales is the Behavior Assessment System for Children (BASC-2; Reynolds & Kamphaus, 2004). The BASC-2 is appropriate for use with children and adolescents from the ages of 2 years, 6 months, through 18 years, 11 months. Different versions of the BASC are available, including Teacher Rating Scales, Parent Rating Scales, and Self-Report of Personality, allowing information to be gathered from multiple informants. Scoring of the BASC yields both broad-band composite scores (e.g., Externalizing Problems, Internalizing Problems), and narrow-band scale scores (e.g., Aggression, Anxiety). Another advantage of the BASC is that it offers information on adaptive skills (e.g., Leadership, Social Skills) in addition to problem areas. Other useful rating scales include the Child Behavior Checklist (Achenbach, 1991), the Revised Behavior Problem Checklist (Quay & Peterson, 1983), and the Eyberg Child Behavior Inventory (Eyberg, 1980).

Clinical Interviews

Unstructured clinical interviews are important tools for flexibly gathering information about the developmental and behavioral history of the child and for assessing the child's cognitions, perceptions, and expectations about his or her social problems (this will be useful in developing hypotheses about the child's social cognitions, as noted below). Structured clinical interviews are useful for providing diagnostic impressions of specific psychiatric disorders. The Diagnostic Interview Schedule for Children is the most widely used structured interview with children, can be administered in a computerized version, and can be used with multiple informants (youth, parents, teacher; Shaffer, Fisher, Lucas, Dulcan, & Schwab-Stone, 2000). Although structured diagnostic interviews provide rigorously determined diagnoses, they are relatively time consuming and may be of limited use in school settings where the assessment questions are typically not related to psychiatric diagnoses per se.

Behavioral Observations and Peers' Ratings

Behavioral observations may yield some of the most useful information about aggressive children (McMahon & Estes, 1997). Behavioral observation can be collected with structured interval sampling systems (e.g., Breyer & Calchera, 1971) or can be obtained informally during the clinical process. Conducting screenings in a group format with potential group members has the advantage of allowing clinicians to observe peer interactions as well as to obtain a preview of important group composition and cohesion issues. Parent–child interactions also should be observed during the assessment period. The seating behavior that occurs prior to conducting a parent–child interview often informs clinicians about family structure, especially if the child verbally or behaviorally dictates where the parent should sit. Other important behaviors to observe during a parent–child interview include interrupting, withdrawal, and the affective valence of the interaction.

Not surprisingly, many aggressive children have poor peer relations. They are often judged as being less socially competent by parents, teachers, and peers (e.g., Conduct Problems Prevention Research Group, 2004b). Use of peer evaluations may be particularly helpful in identifying the subgroup of aggressive socially rejected children who exhibit a combination of risk factors (e.g., attentional and learning problems, low self-esteem, peer-rejected status) and who are at particular risk for antisocial behavior in adolescence (Coie, Lochman, Terry, & Hyman, 1992). However, other highly aggressive children are more socially accepted and report high general self-esteem (Lochman & Lampron, 1986), or they misperceive their rejection from peers and believe they are better accepted than they really are (Pardini, Barry, Barth, Lochman, & Wells, 2006). Because these groups of children believe they enjoy high social acceptance, they may be less motivated to cooperate with treatment efforts to reduce their aggressive behavior.

Evaluation of Social-Cognitive/Affective Characteristics

As indicated in the contextual social-cognitive model of aggression, the current literature suggests that aggressive children have particular social-cognitive characteristics that differ in meaningful ways from those of nonaggressive children and that these differences can be assessed. We have used a "battery" of assessment techniques for clinical evaluation designed to assess the specific areas of weaknesses or strengths of the child within the developmental model that we described earlier in this chapter. However, although group differences exist on these measures, the measures should be primarily used to examine the social-cognitive profile of individual children in clinical settings in a heuristic manner. Therefore, the following procedures are offered for consideration as a means to obtain relevant clinical information and could be collected along with a clinical interview probing children's social cognitions. Most researchers and clinicians with any experience with highly aggressive children readily agree that these children seem to perceive the social world in a very different manner than nonaggressive children. The goal of a social-cognitive assessment battery is to refine a clinician's understanding of a particular aggressive child's social information processing and to help identify which particular social-cognitive distortions or deficiencies are present.

Social-Cognitive Processes

To answer the question of what a child attends to and encodes when presented with information in a social situation, researchers have developed a number of interesting measures to test a series of related hypotheses about aggressive children's skills for encoding different types of social cues. Dodge and Frame (1982) presented videotaped "hypothetical situations" to children in which a child experiences hostile, benign, or neutral outcomes in a peer interaction. Children's responses to this measure can be used to evaluate their (1) ability to recall cues freely from the interaction, (2) recognition of events that actually occurred, (3) "mistaken" accounts of the event (commission errors, intrusions), and (4) attributions and expectations about a hypothetical peer's intentions of future behavior. In our use of this type of measure (e.g., Lochman & Dodge, 1994), aggressive children tend to attend to and remember hostile and irrelevant cues selectively in interactions with peers, particularly when they are asked to imagine being a participant in the interaction.

Another general question about aggressive children's way of thinking is the following: What kinds of ideas do they have about how to interact in and "solve" social situations? How does their style of information processing influence their strategies (or lack thereof) in social problem solving? In evaluating the actual content of social problem-solving solutions a number of factors need to be considered: (1) the type of social task (e.g., entering peer group, initiating friendships, resolving conflict situations), (2) the persons involved in the hypothetical situation (peers, teachers, parents), and (3) the apparent intentions (hostile, benevolent, ambiguous). Lochman and Lampron (1986) evaluated aggressive children's social problem-solving strategies to two types of situational variables while holding constant a third variable—the type of social task. The Problem Solving Measure for Conflict (PSM-C) presents hypothetical stories involving only interpersonal conflict and systematically varies the type of antagonist (peer, teacher, parent) and the expressed intent of the antagonist (hostile or ambiguous frustration of the protagonist's wishes). On this measure aggressive boys compared to nonaggressive boys had lower rates of "verbal assertion" solutions for conflicts with peers and those involving a hostile antagonist (of any type: peer, parent, teacher). They had higher rates of direct-action solutions for conflicts with teachers and hostile antagonists and a higher rate of physically aggressive solutions in peer conflicts. This measure has been actively used in clinical research on the specific nature of social problem-solving deficits in children with conduct disorder and oppositional defiant disorder (Dunn et al., 1997).

Clearly, aggressive children not only perceive social situations in a different light but tend to generate solutions to problematic situations that are maladaptive. This pattern leads to the question of "Why?" Do aggressive children hold particular beliefs or expectations or goals that are related to, or perhaps lead them to, their unskilled handling of social situations? In addition to assessing for the answers to these questions during the interview, it can be useful to conduct several experimental measures. The Outcome–Expectation Questionnaire and Self-Efficacy Questionnaire (Perry, Perry, & Rasmussen, 1986), measures of beliefs and expectations (Slaby & Guerra, 1988), and a measure of social goals (Lochman et al., 1993) have all been used to distinguish aggressive children and adolescents from less aggressive peers. Assessments of such schematic propositions permit a more detailed and coherent understanding of aggressive children's maladaptive behavior and approaches for intervention with them.

There are a variety of available measures of attributional biases, problem solving, and outcome evaluations and of the other social-cognitive processes described above. One useful resource is the website provided by the Collaborative for Social and Emotional Learning (CASEL; *www.casel.org*). Clicking on this website's Assessment button, then the Tools and Measures button, and then the Needs and Outcome Assessment button leads to a set of measures used by a variety of projects to measure different aspects of social cognition. For example, clicking on the Developmental Studies Center link leads to a useful hypothetical vignette measure of decision making and problem solving. Another useful resource (which can also be accessed through the CASEL website as well) is the Fast Track website (*www.fasttrack project.org*), which contains a variety of measures that have demonstrated good reliability and validity in outcome and developmental research studies with the Fast Track sample (e.g., Conduct Problems Prevention Research Group, 1999, 2002b, 2004a). These measures include hypothetical vignette measures (Home Interview With Child, What Do You Think?, Adolescent Stories) assessing the multiple social information-processing steps of attributions, response generation, and response evaluation, as well as more specialized measures of just certain social information-processing steps (Social Problem Solving Measure). Other measures using other formats, such as video presentation of problem situations, are being developed for dissemination. One example is the Schultz Test of Emotion Processing, which is a video-based assessment tool developed by David Schultz that examines aspects of children's social information processing (*www.umbc. edu/psyc/social%20development%20lab/step.htm*).

Schematic Propositions

A measure of a child's relative evaluation of social goals such as dominance, revenge, avoidance, and affiliation assists clinicians in determining how consistent a child's social behavior is with his or her stated goals. A measure adapted from Lochman et al. (1993) allows clinicians to view a child's relative ranking of these social goals. These rankings can then be placed in context with the child's other social-cognitive characteristics. For example, some aggressive children with a poor ability to manage their arousal may endorse prosocial goals and adequate problem-solving strategies but may be unable to exercise behavior consistent with these goals because of their self-control deficits. The knowledge gained from such an assessment profile has clear treatment indications.

Appraisal of Internal Arousal

Aggressive children often have difficulty differentiating their own negative affect, tending to overlabel negative affective arousal (fear, sadness) as anger. An aggressive child's unstructured self-report of his or her negative affect can provide some insight into the child's feeling identification skills. Of course, these feeling identification skills are a prerequisite for understanding the emotions of others. Social perspective taking and empathy are tapped by Bryant's (1982) Empathy Index for Children and Adolescents. Assessing a child's empathic tendencies can also establish how receptive he or she might be to change in general and to cognitive-behavioral techniques in particular.

Intervention Planning

Use of Assessment in Intervention Planning

For assessment to be useful in intervention planning, the purpose of assessment should be kept in mind. As a result, rather than using a stock assessment battery for all cases, it is useful to modify the assessment battery to meet the nature of the case that has been referred for intervention. Several general assessment strategies are useful to keep in mind. First, general behavioral rating scales can be used in most cases to provide a broad view of the child's behavioral and emotional problems, both in the problem area related to the referral but also in other areas that could represent comorbid or co-occuring conditions. Second, referrals that involve problems with social relations can best be assessed by sociometric measures gathered from peers, but teacher and self-impressions of social acceptance can also be useful and are much easier to obtain. Third, when the clinician expects to be using CBIs, then some assessment of children's social-cognitive functioning is critical, either by using specific social-cognitive measures or by tailoring an unstructured clinical interview to assess children's perceptions of the social problems they encounter, their attributions of others' intentions, their range of solutions that they could consider to resolve the problems, and their expectations that aggressive and competent (e.g., verbal assertion, compromise, bargaining) solutions can resolve their problems. Fourth, in cases where a needed diagnostic formulation is an important aspect of the referral, such as a case that potentially involves attention-deficit/hyperactivity disorder (ADHD) as a primary or comorbid problem, then a structured diagnostic interview would be useful. In this example, referral for medication to treat ADHD may be a critically important part of intervention planning to increase the likelihood that the CBIs can be optimally received and employed by the child.

Another critical issue in the assessment process that has implications for intervention planning has to do with the number and type of sources (self, parent, teacher, behavior observer, peer) that are used to obtain assessments. As a general principle, it is particularly useful to obtain assessment information (such as behavioral rating scales) from others besides the target child when the referral involves externalizing behavior problems. In contrast, it is especially useful to have youth self-report of their symptoms (at least after age 7 or 8) when the referral problem is primarily about internalizing difficulties.

However, all measurement sources have some potential for providing incomplete or biased information, and it is thus often optimal to obtain assessment information from more than one source, no matter what the referral problem is. Although parents have a deep historical perception of the child's functioning, parents' reports can be biased by their own psychopathology or their unrealistic expectations for their child. Teachers' reports have the advantage of being provided in a relative way, because they are able to rate children's behavior based on the range of other children of the same age, but their pre-existing expectations and limited knowledge of children's behavior outside of the classroom can lead to some inaccuracy. Children's self-reports can be strongly affected by their own misperceptions of their social acceptance or of their behavior (as noted previously) or can be influenced to provide socially desirable responses. Thus, augmenting child self-reports with teacher, parent, and peer reports can not only lead to an overall more accurate assessment of the child but can identify patterns of inaccuracy in reporters' ratings that can then become a direct target of intervention (e.g., children's inflated or deflated perceptions of their peer acceptance, which might require additional focus on perspective taking; parents' lack of awareness of some of their children's conduct problems, which might require additional emphasis on parental supervision and monitoring skills).

Individualizing Intervention Based on Assessment

Individualized assessments, derived from an assessment model, can be used in two ways within empirically supported treatments for children with conduct problems, as summarized in reviews such as Brestan and Eyberg's (1998). First, some empirically supported treatments are specifically designed to be individualized from the outset. A central tenet of multisystemic therapy (Henggeler, Schoenwald, Borduin, Rowland, & Cunningham, 1998) is that the youth lives within a set of social contexts, and that individualized assessments are required to determine if intervention will focus on parent training, child skill training, peer interventions, school interventions, marital therapy, or all of these. This approach to empirically supported treatments has the strength of embedding the individualization of intervention into the basic treatment model, requiring the intervention to begin to articulate how assessments can be used through assessment algorithms to make precise prescriptions for the types of interventions to use.

Second, for the more common empirically supported treatments that do rely on standard, structured interventions, intervention developers typically prescribe that some degree of individualization of an intervention is often required. For example, the Coping Power Program should be adapted to particular individuals and groups when used clinically (Lochman et al., 2006). Social-cognitive assessments of children's social problem-solving and cue-processing abilities can be used as standard clinical assessments and, along with focused interviews, can be used to guide intervention planning. Intervention with reactive aggressive children will stress more of the parts of the program addressing attribution retraining, and intervention with proactively aggressive children will emphasize more those aspects of the program that deal with establishing clear consequences for behavior and for children's expectations about whether aggression will be a successful strategy. These more standardized empirically supported interventions still require more research to definitively identify the key components for different types of children, but in the meantime the interventions can and should be adapted for the specific deficiencies of individual children and to address comorbid conditions.

Contextual Factors as Predictors of Individual Responsivity to Interventions

Intervention research can be engaged in the relatively straightforward task of determining if certain baseline risk characteristics predict which children will have better or worse outcomes on defined outcomes, and hence whether these variables predict intervention effects. The prediction literature on parental context risk factors with regard to aggressive children is relatively mixed (Kazdin, 1995), as children of depressed mothers and single parents have been found to have poorer response to intervention in some studies (e.g., Webster-Stratton & Hammond, 1997) but not in others (Holden, Lavigne, & Cameron, 1990). Similarly, children living in families with low socioeconomic status and socioeconomic disadvantage have not benefited as much from intervention in some studies (Holden et al., 1990) but not in others (Serketich & Dumas, 1996). These results indicate that specific parental and family context risk factors are important to assess as potential predictors of intervention outcome, but that the particular risk predictors may vary from one intervention program to another depending on the format and characteristics of the intervention. In addition, a certain risk predictor, such as maternal depression, can predict lack of intervention responsivity on certain outcomes, such as teacher ratings of school behavior, but not on other outcomes within the same intervention, such as parent ratings of children's aggression (Conduct Problems Prevention Research Group, 2002a).

Flexible Adaptation

Clearly, the current status of intervention research does not allow clinicians to take treatment packages and to implement them with all or most of their clients in a simple cookbook manner. Variations in the characteristics of specific children, including the presence of important comorbid conditions, need to be addressed, and individual and group interventions often need to be adapted to meet these specific needs. Treatment manuals from empirically supported treatment programs often do not explicitly indicate what and how much adaptation is permissible. A recent survey of clinical diplomates of the American Board of Professional Psychology found that 44% believed that individual differences were not taken into adequate account in the manuals used in empirically supported treatments (Plante, Andersen, & Boccaccini, 1999). It is often difficult to take an empirically supported intervention off the shelf and apply it to a particular child who has grown up within a specific family and neighborhood.

Psychotherapy with children and adolescents has traditionally been a field in which many empirically unsupported approaches have been used (Lochman & Pardini, in press; Roberts, Lazicki-Puddy, Puddy, & Johnson, 2003). However, in the past decade there has been a tremendous increase in efforts to identify and disseminate evidence-based treatments, many of them based on cognitive-behavioral models (Hawley & Weisz, 2002). Systematic research on the dissemination process of evidence-based interventions for children has only recently begun (Silverman & Kurtines, 2004).

Although intervention developers may often insist on complete adherence to protocols, interventions inevitably change as dissemination proceeds (Berwick, 2003) to adjust program materials to address participants' educational developmental and motivational levels. Arguments can be made for both sides of debates about whether adaptations to evidence-based prevention protocols promote effective use of the programs. On the one hand, careful use of the intervention protocol, with high intervention integrity, would be expected to produce outcomes similar to those obtained in rigorous efficacy trials with that intervention. On the other hand, innovative interventions often need to be adapted to the realities of intervening with children in applied settings (Stirman, Crits-Christoph, & DeRubeis, 2004). When exporting interventions from research labs to clinical practice settings, refinements can be made to fit clinic conditions (Weisz, Donenberg, Han, & Kauneckis, 1995) and to make strategies appropriate for the target audiences. As long as rigid adherence to manuals is avoided, then clinicians may not regard a manual as a "required cookie cutter approach" (Kendall, 2002, p. 215) and be more open to using them. The creative, flexible use of CBI manual-based interventions can permit individualization of intervention and increases the likely transportability of the intervention to new settings. Thus, manuals derived from intervention research may not be expected to be followed word for word in applied practice but could instead provide a *road map* of core skills and concepts to be covered (Connor-Smith & Weisz, 2003).

Despite the likelihood of adaptation of programs over time, and the possibility that rigid, inflexible use of manuals may lead to less effective outcome when interventions are disseminated to applied settings, little research has examined the effects of program adaptations. Research on the overall usefulness of manuals in treatments with adults has had mixed results (Herschell, McNeil, & McNeil, 2004). Although some studies with adults have found the use of a manual to be related to better outcomes (e.g., DeRubeis & Feeley, 1990), other studies of the use of intervention manuals with adult clients have had negative outcomes (e.g., Castonguay, Goldfried, Wiser, Raue, & Hayes, 1996).

Only two studies have directly addressed this issue with child interventions (Harnett & Dadds, 2004; Kendall & Chu, 2000). Harnett and Dadds asked facilitators in a school-based dissemination of a universal prevention program for depression to complete checklists on intervention integrity and on their degree of deviation from the manual's instructions for specific activities. Prior analyses had found that facilitators' ratings on this checklist were generally, though not completely, correlated with the ratings of independent observers ($r = .65$ for changes on activities; $r = .73$ for the percentage of core concepts presented). The program was not found to have an influence on outcomes in this dissemination study, and facilitators' degree of deviation from session activities was not found to be significantly associated with program outcomes.

Kendall and Chu (2000) asked therapists who had used a structured evidence-based CBI manual with 148 children (ages 9–13) who had primary anxiety disorders what kinds of intervention adaptations they had made. Therapists made retrospective ratings using the Flexibility Questionnaire. This measure had 7-point rating scales and assessed the therapists' degree of flexibility in using seven techniques and activities and their flexibility in the scope of material discussed. The Flexibility Questionnaire had strong internal consistency ($\alpha = .83$). Prior research with these samples had found very high treatment integrity, with 100% adherence to session goals. The study found that the therapists' ratings of flexible adaptation of intervention activities were not related to intervention outcome. In addition, flexible adaptation was not found to be related to client characteristics such as their age, sex, race, family income, specific anxiety diagnosis, or comorbid diagnoses. Thus, it appears that the combination of strictly adhering to session goals while permitting careful flexibility in adapting specific activities that are meant to address the session goals can lead to successful implementation of programs in "real-world" settings.

Summary

This chapter has stressed the central importance of firmly rooting CBIs in developmental models that are appropriate for various types of child and adolescent behavioral and emotional problems. It is imperative that we understand the broad range of risk factors that contribute to the development of children's behavior problems, recognizing that these risk factors vary from some that are firmly rooted in the child at the time of birth (i.e., are genetic polymorphisms or are the result of deleterious factors on the pregnancy or the birth process); to some that represent the context around the child; to some that are later developing risk factors in the child that are the result of these genetic, biological, and environmental effects.

Contextual risk factors have powerful effects on children's development and include the effects of (1) general background risk factors (e.g., neighborhood violence and poverty, parental psychopathology) that can moderate intervention effects, determining whether the intervention will work well; and (2) potentially mediating risk factors. These latter risk factors are critically important in intervention planning because they are assumed to be mutable and represent potentially active mechanisms of change. These mediating contextual risk factors include aspects of parenting practices and children's peer relations. Based on their experiences within their families, in schools, and with peer relations, children have evolving internalized social cognitions representing the children's tendencies to perceive other peoples' behaviors and intentions and to think about how they can respond to the social problems they encounter.

Two key clinical functions develop directly out of the consideration of developmental models for disorders. First, the developmental informs the assessment model and identifies the types of measures that should be used to assess the child. Second, the developmental informs the intervention model, and it does so in two key ways. The developmental model of a disorder is very important at the time that an intervention program is being developed because the intervention should clearly target the mediating risk factors that represent the active mechanisms contributing to the disorder. The developmental model also permits an informed, carefully considered approach to treatment planning, as the intervention can be adaptively adjusted to meet the specific risk factors that are evident for a particular child with the disorder being addressed. For example, reactively aggressive children are much more likely than other aggressive children to have notable problems in the beginning stages of information processing and thus to have stronger hostile attribution biases. Thus, when using an evidence-based CBI designed for aggressive children, one should enhance and emphasize the portions of the program directed at hostile attributions. Because of the variability in the presentation of children with specific behavioral and emotional disorders, it is important to flexibly adapt a program to address the most apparent risk factors, and this adaptive use of interventions is a central function treatment planning.

References

Achenbach, T. M. (1991). *Manual for the Child Behavior Checklist/4–18 and 1991 profile.* Burlington: University of Vermont, Department of Psychiatry.

Arseneault, L., Tremblay, R. E., Boulerice, B., & Saucier, J. F. (2002). Obstetric complications and adolescent violent behaviors: Testing two developmental pathways. *Child Development, 73,* 496–508.

Barth, J. M., Dunlap, S. T., Dane, H., Lochman, J. E., & Wells, K. C. (2004). Classroom environment influences on aggression, peer relations, and academic focus. *Journal of School Psychology, 42,* 115–133.

Berwick, D. M. (2003). Disseminating innovations in health care. *Journal of the American Medical Association, 289,* 1969–1975.

Brennan, P. A., Grekin, E. R., & Mednick, S. A. (1999). Maternal smoking during pregnancy and adult male criminal outcomes. *Archives of General Psychiatry, 56,* 215–219.

Brestan, E., & Eyberg, S. (1998). Effective psychosocial treatments for conduct-disordered children and adolescents: 29 years, 82 studies, and 5,272 kids. *Journal of Clinical Child Psychology, 27,* 180–189.

Breyer, N. L., & Calchera, D. J. (1971). A behavioral observation schedule for pupils and teachers. *Psychology in the Schools, 8,* 330–337.

Bronfenbrenner, U. (1995). Developmental ecology through space and time: A future perspective. In P. Moen, G. H. Elder, & K. Luescher (Eds.), *Examining lives in context: Perspectives on the ecology of human development* (pp. 619–647). Washington, DC: American Psychiatric Association.

Bryant, B. K. (1982). An index of empathy for children and adolescents. *Child Development, 53,* 413–425.

Caspi, A., McClay, J., Moffitt, T., Mill, J., Martin, J., Craig, I. W., et al. (2002, August 2). Role of genotype in the cycle of violence in maltreated children. *Science, 297,* 851–854.

Castonguay, L. G., Goldfried, M. R., Wiser, S., Raue, P. J., & Hayes, A. M. (1996). Predicting the effects of cognitive therapy for depression: A study of unique and common factors. *Journal of Consulting and Clinical Psychology, 64,* 497–504.

Cillessen, A. H., van IJzendoorn, H. W., Van Lieshout, C. F., & Hartup, W. W. (1992). Heterogeneity among peer-rejected boys: Subtypes and stabilities. *Child Development, 63,* 893–905.

Coie, J. D., & Dodge, K. A. (1998). Aggression and antisocial behavior. In W. Damon (Series Ed.) & N. Eisenberg (Vol. Ed.), *Handbook of child psychology: Vol. 3. Social, emotional and personality development* (5th ed., pp. 779–862). New York: Wiley.

Coie, J. D., Lochman, J. E., Terry, R., & Hyman, C. (1992). Predicting early adolescent disorders from childhood aggression and peer rejection. *Journal of Consulting and Clinical Psychology, 60,* 783–792.

Colder, C. R., Mott, J., Levy, S., & Flay, B. (2000). The relation of perceived neighborhood danger to childhood aggression: A test of mediating mechanisms. *American Journal of Community Psychology, 28,* 83–103.

Conduct Problems Prevention Research Group. (1992). A developmental and clinical model for the prevention of conduct disorder: The Fast Track Program. *Development and Psychopathology, 4,* 509–527.

Conduct Problems Prevention Research Group. (1999). Initial impact of the Fast Track prevention trial for conduct problems: I. The high-risk sample. *Journal of Consulting and Clinical Psychology, 67,* 631–647.

Conduct Problems Prevention Research Group. (2002a). Predictor variables associated with positive Fast Track outcomes at the end of third grade. *Journal of Abnormal Child Psychology, 30,* 37–52.

Conduct Problems Prevention Research Group. (2002b). Evaluation of the first three years of the Fast Track prevention trial with children at high risk of adolescent conduct problems. *Journal of Abnormal Child Psychology, 30,* 19–35.

Conduct Problems Prevention Research Group. (2004a). The effects of the Fast Track program on serious problem outcomes at the end of elementary school. *Journal of Clinical Child and Adolescent Psychology, 33,* 650–661.

Conduct Problems Prevention Research Group. (2004b). The Fast Track experiment: Translating the developmental model into a prevention design. In J. B. Kupersmidt & K. A. Dodge (Eds.), *Children's peer relations: From development to intervention* (pp. 181–208). Washington, DC: American Psychological Association.

Connor-Smith, J. K., & Weisz, J. R. (2003). Applying treatment outcome research in clinical practice: Techniques for adapting interventions to the real world. *Child and Adolescent Mental Health, 8,* 3–10.

Cowan, P. A., Cohn, D. A., Cowan, C. P., & Pearson, J. L. (1996). Parents' attachment histories and children's externalizing and internalizing behaviors: Exploring family systems models of linkage. *Journal of Consulting and Clinical Psychology, 64,* 53–63.

Crick, N. R., & Werner, N. E. (1998). Response decision processes in relational and overt aggression. *Child Development, 69,* 1630–1639.

Curry, J. F., & Craighead, W. E. (1990). Attributional style in clinic depressed and conduct disordered adolescents. *Journal of Consulting and Clinical Psychology, 58,* 109–116.

Dadds, M. R., & Powell, M. B. (1992). The relationship of interparental conflict and global marital adjustment to aggression, anxiety, and immaturity in aggressive and nonclinic children. *Journal of Abnormal Child Psychology, 19,* 553–567.

Delaney-Black, V., Covington, C., Templin, T., Ager, J., Nordstrom-Klee, B., Martier, S., et al. (2000). Teacher-assessed behavior of children prenatally exposed to cocaine. *Pediatrics, 106,* 782–791.

DeRubeis, R. J., & Feeley, M. J. V. (1990). Determinants of change in cognitive therapy for depression. *Cognitive Therapy and Research, 14,* 469–482.

Dishion, T. J., Andrews, D. W., & Crosby, L. (1995). Antisocial boys and their friends in early adolescence: Relationship characteristics, quality, and interactional process. *Child Development, 66,* 139–151.

Dodge, K. A., & Frame, C. L. (1982). Social cognitive biases and deficits in aggressive boys. *Child Development, 53,* 620–635.

Dodge, K. A., Pettit, G. S., & Bates, J. E. (1994). Socialization mediators of the between socioeconomic status and child conduct problems. *Child Development, 65,* 649–665.

Dodge, K. A., Lochman, J. E., Harnish, J. D., Bates, J. E., & Pettit, G. S. (1997). Reactive and proactive aggression in school children and psychiatrically impaired chronically assaultive youth. *Journal of Abnormal Psychology, 106,* 37–51.

Dunn, S. E., Lochman, J. E., & Colder, C. R. (1997). Social problem-solving skills in boys with conduct and oppositional disorders. *Aggressive Behavior, 23,* 457–469.

Eyberg, S. M. (1980). Eyberg Child Behavior Inventory. *Journal of Clinical Child Psychology, 9,* 29–40.

Fite, P. J., Colder, C. R., Lochman, J. E., & Wells, K. C. (2006). The mutual influence of parenting and boys' externalizing behavior problems. *Journal of Applied Developmental Psychology, 27,* 151–164.

Garber, J., Braafladt, N., & Zeman, J. (1991). The regulation of sad affect: An information-processing perspective. In J. Garber & K. Dodge (Eds.), *The development of emotional regulation and dysregulation* (pp. 208–240). New York: Cambridge University Press.

Gladstone, T. R. G., & Kaslow, N. J. (1995). Depression and attributions in children and adolescents: A meta-analytic review. *Journal of Abnormal Child Psychology, 23,* 597–606.

Guerra, N. G., Huesmann, L. R., & Spindler, A. (2003). Community violence exposure, social cognition, and aggression among urban elementary school children. *Child Development, 74,* 1561–1576.

Guerra, N. G., Huesmann, L. R., Tolan, P. H., VanAcker, R., & Eron, L. D. (1995). Stressful events and individual beliefs as correlates of economic disadvantage and aggression among urban children. *Journal of Consulting and Clinical Psychology, 63,* 513–528.

Harnett, P. H., & Dadds, M. R. (2004). Training school personnel to implement a universal school-based prevention of depression program under real-world conditions. *Journal of School Psychology, 42,* 343–357.

Hawley, K. M., & Weisz, J. R. (2002). Increasing the relevance of evidence-based treatment review to practitioners and consumers. *Clinical Psychology: Science and Practice, 9,* 225–230.

Henggeler, S. W., Schoenwald, S. K., Borduin, C. M., Rowland, M. D., & Cunningham, P. B. (1998). *Multisystemic treatment of antisocial behavior in children and adolescents.* New York: Guilford Press.

Herschell, A. D., McNeil, C. B., & McNeil, D. W. (2004). Clinical child psychology's progress in disseminating empirically supported treatments. *Clinical Psychology: Science and Practice, 11,* 267–288.

Holden, G. W., Lavigne, V. V., & Cameron, A. M. (1990). Probing the continuum of effectiveness of parent training: Characteristics of parents and preschoolers. *Journal of Clinical Child Psychology, 19,* 2–8.

Hughes, J. H. (2000). The essential role of theory in the science of teaching children: Beyond empirically supported treatments. *Journal of School Psychology, 38,* 301–330.

Ingoldsby, E. M., & Shaw, D. S. (2002). Neighborhood contextual factors and early-starting antisocial pathways. *Clinical Child and Family Psychology Review, 5,* 21–55.

Jackson, M. F., Barth, J. M., Powell, N., & Lochman, J. E. (2006). Classroom contextual effects of race on children's peer nominations. *Child Development, 77,* 1325–1337.

Jensen, P. S. (1999). Links among theory, research and practice: Cornerstones of clinical scientific progress. *Journal of Clinical Child Psychology, 28,* 553–557.

Kaslow, N. J., Rehm, L. P., Pollack, S. L., & Siegel, A. W. (1988). Attributional style and self-control behavior in depressed and non-depressed children and their parents. *Journal of Abnormal Child Psychology, 16,* 163–175.

Kazdin, A. E. (1995). Child, parent and family dysfunction as predictors of outcome in cognitive-behavioral treatment of antisocial children. *Behaviour Research and Therapy, 33,* 271–281.

Kazdin, A. E. (1999). Current (lack of) status of theory in child and adolescent psychotherapy research. *Journal of Clinical Child Psychology, 28,* 533–543.

Kellam, S. G., Xiange, L., Mersica, R., Brown, C. H., & Ialongo, N. (1998). The effect of the level of aggression in the first grade classroom on the course of malleability of aggressive behavior into middle school. *Development and Psychopathology, 10,* 165–185.

Kendall, P. (2002). Toward a research-practice-community partnership: Goin' fishing and showing slides. *Clinical Psychology: Science and Practice, 9,* 214–216.

Kendall, P. C., & Chu, B. C. (2000). Retrospective self-reports of therapist flexibility in a manual-based treatment for youths with anxiety disorders. *Journal of Clinical Child Psychology, 29,* 209–220.

Kupersmidt, J. B., Griesler, P. C., DeRosier, M. E., Patterson, C. J., & Davis, P. W. (1995). Childhood aggression and peer relations in the context of family and neighborhood factors. *Child Development, 66,* 360–375.

Larson, J., & Lochman, J. E. (2002). *Helping school children cope with anger: A cognitive-behavioral intervention.* New York: Guilford Press.

Lochman, J. E. (2000). Theory and empiricism in intervention research: A dialectic to be avoided. *Journal of School Psychology, 38,* 359–368.

Lochman, J. E. (2006). Translation of research into interventions. *International Journal of Behavioral Development, 31,* 31–38.

Lochman, J. E., Barry, T. D., & Salekin, K. (2005). Aggressive/oppositional behaviors (oppositional defiant and conduct disorders). In L. Osborn, T. DeWitt, & L. R. First (Eds.), *Pediatrics* (pp. 1577–1585). Philadelphia: Elsevier.

Lochman, J. E., Boxmeyer, C., & Powell, N. (in press). Contributions of developmental psychopathology. In C. R. Reynolds & T. B. Gutkin (Eds.), *Handbook of school psychology* (4th ed.). New York: Wiley.

Lochman, J. E., & Dodge, K. A. (1994). Social-cognitive processes of severely violent, moderately aggressive, and nonaggressive boys. *Journal of Consulting and Clinical Psychology, 62,* 366–374.

Lochman, J. E., & Dodge, K. A. (1998). Distorted perceptions in dyadic interactions of aggressive and nonaggressive boys: Effects of prior expectations, context, and boys' age. *Development and Psychopathology, 10,* 495–512.

Lochman, J. E., & Lampron, L. B. (1986). Situational social problem-solving skills and self-esteem of aggressive and nonaggressive boys. *Journal of Abnormal Child Psychology, 14,* 605–617.

Lochman, J. E., & Pardini, D.A. (in press). Cognitive behavioral therapies. In M. Rutter, D. Bishop, D. Pine, S. Scott, J. Stevenson, E. Taylor, et al. (Eds.), *Rutter's child and adolescent psychiatry* (5th ed.). London: Blackwell.

Lochman, J. E., Powell, N. R., Whidby, J. M., & FitzGerald, D. P. (2006). Cognitive-behavioral assessment and treatment with aggressive children. In P. C. Kendall (Ed.), *Child and adolescent therapy: Cognitive-behavioral procedures* (3rd ed., pp. 33–81). New York: Guilford Press.

Lochman, J. E., & Wayland, K. K. (1994). Aggression, social acceptance and race as predictors of negative adolescent outcomes. *Journal of the American Academy of Child and Adolescent Psychiatry, 33,* 1026–1035.

Lochman, J. E., Wayland, K. K., & White, K. J. (1993). Social goals: Relationship to adolescent adjustment and to social problem solving. *Journal of Abnormal Child Psychology, 21,* 135–151.

Lochman, J. E., & Wells, K. C. (2002a). Contextual social-cognitive mediators and child outcome: A test of the theoretical model in the Coping Power Program. *Development and Psychopathology, 14,* 971–993.

Lochman, J. E., & Wells, K. C. (2002b). The Coping Power Program at the middle school transition: Universal and indicated prevention effects. *Psychology of Addictive Behaviors, 16,* S40–S54.

Lochman, J. E., & Wells, K. C. (2003). Effectiveness study of Coping Power and classroom intervention with aggressive children: Outcomes at a one-year follow-up. *Behavior Therapy, 34,* 493–515.

Lochman, J. E., & Wells, K. C. (2004). The Coping Power Program for preadolescent aggressive boys and their parents: Outcome effects at the one-year follow-up. *Journal of Consulting and Clinical Psychology, 72,* 571–578.

Loeber, R. (1990). Development and risk factors of juvenile antisocial behavior and delinquency. *Clinical Psychology Review, 10,* 1–42.

Loeber, R., & Stouthamer-Loeber, M. (1998). Development of juvenile aggression and violence: Some common misconceptions and controversies. *American Psychologist, 53,* 242–259.

Luthar, S. S. (1999). *Children in poverty: Risk and protective factors in adjustment.* Thousand Oaks, CA: Sage.

Masten, A. S., Best, K. M., & Garmezy, N. (1990). Resilience and development: Contributions from the study of children who overcome adversity. *Development and Psychopathology, 2,* 425–444.

McMahon, R. J., & Estes, A. M. (1997). Conduct problems. In E. J. Mash & L. G. Terdal (Eds.), *Assessment of childhood disorders* (3rd ed., pp. 130–193). New York: Guilford Press.

Miller-Johnson, S., Coie, J. D., Maumary-Gremaud, A., Bierman, K., & Conduct Problems Prevention Research Group. (2002). Peer rejection and aggression and early starter models of conduct disorder. *Journal of Abnormal Child Psychology, 30,* 217–230.

Miller-Johnson, S., Coie, J. D., Maumary-Gremaud, A., Lochman, J. E., & Terry, R. (1999). Relationship between childhood peer rejection and aggression and adolescent delinquency severity and type among African American youth. *Journal of Emotional and Behavioral Disorders, 7,* 137–146.

Nagin, D., Pogarsky, G., & Farrington, D. (1997). Adolescent mothers and the criminal behavior of their children. *Law and Society, 31,* 137–162.

Pardini, D. A., Barry, T. D., Barth, J. M., Lochman, J. E., & Wells, K. C. (2006). Self-perceived social acceptance and peer social standing in children with aggressive–disruptive behaviors. *Social Development, 15,* 46–64.

Pardini, D. A., Lochman, J. E., & Frick, P. J. (2003). Callous/unemotional traits and social cognitive processes in adjudicated youth. *Journal of the American Academy of Child and Adolescent Psychiatry, 42,* 364–371.

Patterson, G. R., Reid, J. B., & Dishion, T. J. (1992). *Antisocial boys.* Eugene, OR: Castalia.

Paul, G. L. (1967). Outcome research in psychotherapy. *Journal of Consulting Psychology, 31,* 109–118.

Pennington, B. F. (2002). *The development of psychopathology: Nature and nurture.* New York: Guilford Press.

Pepler, D. J., Craig, W. M., & Roberts, W. I. (1998). Observations of aggressive and nonaggressive children on the school playground. *Merrill–Palmer Quarterly, 44,* 55–76.

Perry, D. G., Perry, L. C., & Rasmussen, P. (1986). Cognitive social learning mediators of aggression. *Child Development, 57,* 700–711.

Plante, T. G., Andersen, E. N., & Boccaccini, M. T. (1999). Empirically supported treatments and related contemporary changes in psychotherapy practice: What do clinical ABPPs think. *Clinical Psychologist, 52,* 23–31.

Quay, H. C., & Peterson, D. R. (1983). *Interim manual for the Revised Behavior Problem Checklist.* Unpublished manuscript, University of Miami, FL.

Raine, A., Brennan, P., & Mednick, S. A. (1997). Interactions between birth complications and early maternal rejection in predisposing individuals to adult violence: Specificity to serious, early onset violence. *American Journal of Psychiatry, 154,* 1265–1271.

Reynolds, C. R., & Kamphaus, R. W. (2004). *Behavior Assessment System for Children* (2nd ed.). Circle Pines, MN: American Guidance Service.

Roberts, M. C., Lazicki-Puddy, T. A., Puddy, R. W., & Johnson, R. J. (2003). The outcomes of psychotherapy with adolescents: A practitioner-friendly research review. *Journal of Clinical Psychology, 59,* 1177–1191.

Scarpa, A., Fikretoglu, D., & Luscher, K. (2000). Community violence exposure in a young adult sample: II. Psychophysiology and aggressive behavior. *Journal of Community Psychology, 28,* 417–425.

Serketich, W. J., & Dumas, J. E. (1996). The effectiveness of behavioral parent training to modify antisocial behavior in children: A meta-analysis. *Behavior Therapy, 27,* 171–186.

Shaffer, D., Fisher, P., Lucas, C., Dulcan, M., & Schwab-Stone, M. (2000). NIMH Diagnostic Interview Schedule for Children version IV (NIMH DISC-IV): Description, differences from previous versions, and reliability of some common diagnoses. *Journal of the American Academy of Child and Adolescent Psychiatry, 39,* 28–38.

Shaw, D. S., Keenan, K., & Vondra, J. I. (1994). The developmental precursors of antisocial behavior: Ages 1–3. *Developmental Psychology, 30,* 355–364.

Shaw, D. S., & Vondra, J. I. (1995). Infant attachment security and maternal predictors of early behavior problems: A longitudinal study of low-income families. *Journal of Abnormal Child Psychology, 26,* 407–414.

Silverman, W. K., & Kurtines, W. M. (2004). Research progress on effectiveness, transportability, and dissemination of empirically supported treatments: Integrating theory and research. *Clinical Psychology: Science and Practice, 11,* 295–299.

Slaby, R. G., & Guerra, N. G. (1988). Cognitive mediators of aggression in adolescent offenders: I. Assessment. *Developmental Psychology, 24,* 580–588.

Stark, K., Hargrave, J., Sander, J., Custer, G., Schnoebelen, S., Simpson, J., et al. (2006). Treatment of childhood depression: The ACTION treatment program. In P. C. Kendall (Ed.), *Child and adolescent therapy: Cognitive-behavioral procedures* (3rd ed., pp. 169–216). New York: Guilford Press.

Stark, K. D., Sander, J., Hauser, M., Simpson, J., Schoebelen, S., Glenn, R., et al. (2006). Depressive disorders during adolescence. In E. J. Mash & R. A. Barkley (Eds.), *Treatment of childhood disorders* (3rd ed., pp. 336–407). New York: Guilford Press.

Stirman, S. W., Crits-Christoph, P., & DeRubeis, R. J. (2004). Achieving successful dissemination of empirically supported psychotherapies: A synthesis of dissemination theory. *Clinical Psychology: Science and Practice, 11,* 343–359.

Vitaro, F., Brendgen, M., Pagani, L., Tremblay, R. E., & McDuff, P. (1999). Disruptive behavior, peer association, and conduct disorder: Testing the developmental links through early intervention. *Development and Psychopathology, 11,* 287–304.

Webster-Stratton, C., & Hammond, M. (1997). Treating children with early-onset conduct problems: A comparison of child and parent training interventions. *Journal of Consulting and Clinical Psychology, 65,* 93–109.

Weersing, V. R., & Brent, D. A. (2003). Cognitive-behavioral therapy for adolescent depression: Comparative efficacy, mediation, moderation, and effectiveness. In A. E. Kazdin & J. R. Weisz (Eds.), *Evidence-based psychotherapies for children and adolescents* (pp. 135–147). New York: Guilford Press.

Weisz, J. R., Donenberg, G. R., Han, S. S., & Kauneckis, D. (1995). Child and adolescent psychotherapy outcomes in experiments versus clinics: Why the disparity? *Journal of Abnormal Child Psychology, 23,* 83–106.

Williams, S. C., Lochman, J. E., Phillips, N. C., & Barry, T. D. (2003). Aggressive and nonaggressive boys' physiological and cognitive processes in response to peer provocations. *Journal of Clinical Child and Adolescent Psychology, 32,* 568–576.

Zelli, A., Dodge, K. A., Lochman, J. F., Laird, R. D., & Conduct Problems Prevention Research Group. (1999). The distinction between beliefs legitimizing aggression and deviant processing of social cues: Testing measurement validity and the hypothesis that biased processing mediates the effects of beliefs on aggression. *Journal of Personality and Social Psychology, 77,* 150–166.

CHAPTER 3

Methodological Issues
in Research Using
Cognitive-Behavioral Interventions

FRANK M. GRESHAM
JOHN E. LOCHMAN

Almost all areas of applied psychology and special education that utilize interventions to deliver services have embraced the notion of *evidence-based practice* to bridge the research-to-practice gap in these areas (Gersten et al., 2005; Kratochwill & Stoiber, 2000; Kazdin & Weisz, 2003; Stoiber & Kratochwill, 2000). It is quite clear that any scientific field cannot progress without considering proper research methodologies to establish what is and is not known about phenomena of interest. The primary goal of research methodology is to allow professionals to draw *valid inferences* from controlled research that are not confounded or otherwise disconfirmed by plausible rival hypotheses. A report by the National Research Council (Shavelson & Towne, 2002) on scientific research in education suggested that educational research can and should be subjected to the same standards of scientific research as other disciplines such as physics, biology, or chemistry. Although the National Research Council report indicated that all research methods should be used (correlational/regression, survey, and qualitative), the *gold standard* for controlling for most threats to valid inference making is the randomized clinical trial. This same sentiment was expressed in the now classic text by Campbell and Stanley (1966) more than 40 years ago.

The purpose of the current chapter is to describe and discuss methodological considerations and issues in research using cognitive-behavioral interventions (CBIs) for children and youth. Criteria for evidence-based interventions are used to evaluate the *efficacy* and *effectiveness* of CBIs for various types of emotional and behavioral disorders. Consideration is given to threats of valid inference making, mediators and moderators of treatment effects, power analysis, experimental and quasi-experimental design options, and use of appropriate data analytic strategies. Before discussing these methodological issues, we give a brief overview of cognitive behavioral theory to provide a context for the points made in this chapter.

Overview of Cognitive-Behavioral Theory

CBIs are based on the premise that thoughts, emotions, and behaviors are reciprocally linked and that changing one of these will necessarily result in changes in the others. These reciprocal relationships between thoughts, emotions, and behaviors serve as the fundamental basis of all CBIs. Kendall (2000) maintained that CBIs for child and adolescent problems emphasize both the influence of external contingencies (e.g., reinforcement and punishment) as well as the individual's mediating or information-processing style in resolving adjustment difficulties. In a cognitive-behavioral approach, cognitions, emotions, perceptions, and information processing all play a central role in the development and remediation of behavioral and adjustment difficulties.

A variation of cognitive-behavioral theory includes *social-cognitive theory*, deriving primarily from the work of Bandura (1977, 1986). This approach utilizes the concept of vicarious learning and the role of cognitive-mediational processes in determining which environmental events are attended to, retained, and subsequently performed, given exposure to modeling stimuli (Gresham, 2004). Bandura (1986) used the notion of *reciprocal determinism* that describes the role an individual's behavior has on producing changes in the environment and vice versa. Social-cognitive theory is based on reciprocal relationships between the person, behavior, and the environment whereby producing a change in one will produce changes in the others or what is known as *person–behavior–environment reciprocality*.

In CBIs, *cognitions* may be defined as sets of skills that include problem solving, coping strategies, regulation of affect, and interpersonal skills (Weimer, 1977). A central assumption in all CBIs is that adaptive and maladaptive behavior cannot be separated from the social context in which cognitions occur (Kendall & Hollon, 1979; Lochman, Whidby, & FitzGerald, 2000). A fundamental tenet of CBIs is that one cannot successfully intervene with children and adolescents without incorporating the home and peer group at some level in the intervention process (Reinecke, Dattilio, & Freeman, 2003).

A good example of the above principle can be found in the literature on the cognitive and attributional processes of aggressive children. Dodge and colleagues conducted seminal research on how aggressive, rejected children process social information, interpret interpersonal cues, and make decisions based on this information (Dodge, 1985, 1986). Aggressive children frequently make errors in evaluating the motives and intent underlying the social behavior directed toward them by peers and adults. They are likely to attribute hostile intentions to accidental or ambiguous behavior from others, and they respond inappropriately as a result (Dodge & Crick, 1990).

Aggressive, rejected children seem to have quite abnormal standards and expectations regarding their own behavior, and these beliefs, in turn, "legitimize" much of their deviant, aversive behavior. These hostile attributional biases prevent these children from accurately decoding negative and disapproving feedback about their behavior (Walker, Ramsay, & Gresham, 2004). Smith, Lochman, and Daunic (2005) provided an in-depth analysis of CBIs with problems of anger/aggression of children with emotional and behavioral disorders.

Evidence-Based Interventions (EBIs)

There have been major advances over the past 10 years in the development and implementation of evidence-based practices for children's and adolescents' emotional and behavioral difficulties (Lonigan, Elbert, & Johnson, 1998; Stoiber & Kratochwill, 2000; Walker et al., 2004). For example, various meta-analyses of the clinical child/adolescent psychotherapy literature involving more than 300 studies published between 1952 and 1993 showed that children and adolescents receiving intervention scored higher on outcome measures than about 80% of individuals in control groups (Casey & Berman, 1985; Weisz, Weiss, Alicke, & Klotz, 1987; Weisz, Weiss, Han, Granger, & Morton, 1995). School- and clinic-based interventions having a strong base of empirical support include social skills training (Gresham, Cook, Crews, & Kern, 2004), teacher consultation (Hoagwood & Erwin, 1997), parent training (Brestan & Eyberg, 1998), and CBIs (Kendall, 2000). These EBIs have been empirically supported across a wide array of clinical diagnostic categories including attention-deficit/hyperactivity disorder (ADHD; Pelham, Wheeler, & Chronis, 1998), anxiety/phobia disorders (Ollendick & King, 1998), and conduct disorder/oppositional defiant disorder (Brestan & Eyberg, 1998).

There has been a great deal of debate concerning the level of evidence necessary for determining if particular interventions are effective with specific problems. Barlow (1996) suggested that there are increasing pressures from outside agencies such as managed care organization, governmental agencies, funding agencies, and professional organizations to demonstrate the efficacy and effectiveness of interventions with children and adolescents. Professional organizations such as several divisions within the American Psychological Association (i.e., child clinical/adolescent psychology, school psychology, and pediatric psychology) have published guidelines for evaluating whether a given intervention has a sufficient evidence base to be considered empirically supported (Kratochwill & Stoiber, 2000; Lonigan et al., 1998; Stoiber & Kratochwill, 2000). The field of special education in general (Gersten et al., 2005; Thompson, Diamond, McWilliam, Synder, & Syder, 2005) and behavioral disorders in particular has also called for the use of evidence-based interventions (Walker, 2004; Walker et al., 2004).

Determining EBIs

Several characteristics distinguish EBIs from other types of interventions. First, EBIs have a sound theoretical basis. Intervention procedures deriving from cognitive-behavior theory have a strong theoretical basis in areas of cognitive theory, social learning theory, attribution theory, and applied behavior analysis (Kendall, 2000; Reinecke, 2003).

Second, EBIs have empirical support that is based on appropriate experimental design features using either group- or single-case experimental designs. Studies using group experimental designs *must* randomly assign participants to experimental and control conditions to be considered evidence based, because this procedure provides statistically unbiased estimates of treatment effects. Studies using single-case experimental designs must use designs that adequately control for threats to internal validity (e.g., multiple baseline, withdrawal, or multielement designs).

Third, studies must be subject to criteria-based analyses of treatment effects. Kazdin (2003) described several methods that can be used to determine criteria-based outcome analyses, such as peer comparisons, absolute change form pretest to posttest, complete elimination of behavior problems, and whether the individual no longer meets diagnostic criteria for a psychological disorder. All of the above criteria for EBIs are discussed later in this chapter.

Efficacy versus Effectiveness of Interventions

An important distinction one has to make in evaluating EBIs is between efficacy research and effectiveness research. *Efficacy research* involves measurable behavioral or symptom reduction and increased adaptive functioning demonstrated under tightly controlled experimental conditions. The randomized clinical trial, in which participants are randomly assigned to treatment and control or comparison groups (e.g., no treatment, wait list, or placebo), represents the prototypical efficacy study (Nathan, Stuart, & Dolan, 2000). Efficacy studies typically use participants who are homogenous on a particular diagnostic category (e.g., ADHD, anxiety disorder, oppositional defiant disorder) and use therapists who are well trained in the delivery of the intervention procedures. Outcomes in efficacy research usually involve short-term focused assessments of changes in the behavioral symptoms or characteristics of the disorder being studied rather than global assessments of changes in quality of life (Nathan et al., 2000). For example, an efficacy study of treatment of ADHD might use assessments of reductions in core ADHD symptoms such as hyperactivity, impulsivity, and inattention rather than global measures of school and home adjustment. In short, efficacy research is concerned with the *internal validity* of experimental designs: Was the intervention, and not extraneous factors, responsible for changes in the outcome measures?

Effectiveness research refers to the clinical or educational utility of a particular intervention in the natural environment or in "real-world" settings such as schools, home, and the community. Effectiveness studies typically use treatment agents who may not be highly trained in a particular treatment protocol and participants who may not meet diagnostic criteria for a particular disorder or who may be comorbid for several psychological disorders (Nathan et al., 2000). Outcome measures in effectiveness research focus on broad or global measures of quality of life or adaptive functioning rather than focused, short-term measures of behavioral symptomology. In short, effectiveness research focuses on the *external validity* of research designs: Will the findings of the study generalize to other participants and across other settings not included in the study?

Methodological Considerations in Efficacy and Effectiveness Research

A number of methodological variables characterize both efficacy and effectiveness research studies. Efficacy studies emphasize replication of research studies so other researchers can conduct similar studies in similar settings with similar participants to validate treatment effects (Nathan et al., 2000). This emphasis on replication requires the use of appropriate control groups against which the experimental conditions can be compared. As such, *random assignment* to experimental and control groups becomes an essential methodological component of efficacy studies. Randomization to experimental and control conditions is also an important component of effectiveness studies, however the focus is on the *generality* of findings (external validity) rather than tight experimental control (internal validity). The following methodological variables are described below due to their importance to both efficacy and effectiveness research: (1) control groups, (2) random assignment, (3) treatment integrity, and (4) homogeneity/heterogeneity of samples.

Types of Control Conditions

A number of control condition options exist in experimental efficacy and effectiveness research. These include no-treatment controls, placebo controls, alternative treatment controls, and delayed treatment controls. Some have raised ethical objections to the use of certain types of control conditions. For example, Parloff (1986) argued that an experimental condition should be compared to another treatment that has demonstrated effectiveness and not to an inert or placebo control condition. Seligman (1995) further argued that participants who actively seek treatment in the community differ fundamentally from those who are randomly assigned to experimental and comparison group conditions.

Nathan et al. (2000) suggested that placebo control conditions may be either completely inert or theoretically inert. A classic example of a completely inert treatment in psychopharmacological research is the use of a sugar pill compared to an active psychopharmacological agent under double-blind conditions. Such an experimental arrangement is not plausible in CBI interventions given the impossibility of double blinding and the difficulty in removing therapist attention effects in the placebo control condition. Theoretically inert placebo control conditions are those that intentionally do not include the presumed causal mechanisms of cognitive and/or behavior change. For example, a theoretically inert control condition for the treatment of anxiety in children would not include teaching of cognitive strategies, self-instruction training, correction of maladaptive self-talk, or problem solving. Instead, a theoretically inert control condition in this case could be an intervention involving various types of physical exercises.

Another type of control condition that is often used is the treatment-as-usual control conditions in which participants are randomly assigned to treatments available in the community or to an experimental condition. This type of control condition is particularly important in effectiveness research (Nathan et al., 2000). The question to be answered in this arrangement is whether the experimental treatment is more effective than a treatment provided in the community for the same problem. A good example of the use of this type of control group can be found in the National Institute of Mental Health collaborative Multisite MTA study (MTA Cooperative Group, 1999), which was the first major clinical trial focusing on a childhood disorder (i.e., ADHD). Participants in this study were randomly assigned to one of four conditions: (1) medication alone, (2) behavior modification alone, (3) combined medication management + behavior modification, or (4) community comparison. Children in the community comparison condition received no intervention from the MTA staff but sought treatment typically provided in the community. Approximately two thirds of the participants in the community comparison condition received medication for ADHD; however, their medications were not as closely titrated as those of participants in the medication alone condition (Barkley, 2006).

A final type of control condition that is often used is a wait-list control group, in which participants are randomly assigned to experimental or wait-list control groups. The major limitation of a wait-list control condition is that the long-term effects of history, maturation, repeated testing, and other influences cannot be evaluated (Kazdin, 1992). Also, depending on the severity of the problem, a wait-list control group may pose some ethical concerns. Despite these limitations, the use of wait-list controls provides a viable alternative to no-treatment and placebo control group experimental arrangements.

Random Assignment

Random assignment is an essential aspect of all group experimental designs when researchers want do draw unequivocal conclusions regarding the efficacy or effectiveness of treatments. *Random assignment* is a process in which units are assigned to conditions by chance and each unit has a nonzero probability of being assigned to a given condition (Shadish, Cook, & Campbell, 2002). It is important to note the distinction between random assignment and random sampling. Random sampling is often used in consumer opinion polls or political election polls and estimates what might be obtained if a researcher had administered the poll to everyone in the population. Random assignment allows for causal inferences by making *samples* similar to one another, and random sampling allows for inferences by making *samples* similar to a *population* (Shadish et al., 2002).

Shadish et al. (2002) listed five reasons and conceptual explanations of why random sampling works. These are as follows: (1) It ensures that alternative causes or explanations are not confounded with a unit's treatment condition, (2) it diminishes the plausibility of threats to valid inference making by distributing these threats randomly across conditions, (3) it equates groups on expected values of all variables at prior to treatment whether they are measured or not, (4) it allows researchers to know and model the selection process correctly, and (5) it allows for the computation of error variance that is unrelated to treatment. No other research procedure can accomplish this or controls as many threats to valid inference making as random assignment to conditions. Other methods attempt to mimic control of extraneous variables by matching, blocking, or using statistics (e.g., analysis of covariance), but none can accomplish a "true" nonzero probability of being assigned to a condition.

Treatment Integrity

A fundamental goal of all intervention research is the demonstration that change in a dependent variable is related to systematic, manipulated changes in an independent variable and is not due to extraneous factors. An independent variable in intervention research means an active, manipulated treatment variable designed to produce a change in behavior. *Treatment integrity* (or fidelity) refers to the degree to which a treatment is implemented as planned or intended (Gresham, 1989; Yeaton & Sechrest, 1981). Treatment integrity is concerned with the *accuracy* and *consistency* with which treatments are implemented based on an established treatment protocol. Deviations from an established treatment protocol produce lapses in treatment integrity and may dilute the effects of treatment. It is quite likely that the ineffectiveness of many treatments delivered in clinical or school settings is due to the poor integrity with which these treatments are implemented. This is particularly true of treatments delivered by teachers and parents who may not be familiar with a given treatment protocol (Gresham, 1989; Peterson, Homer, & Wonderlich, 1982).

Many published reports of school-based and clinical interventions for child and adolescent behavior problems do not assess or report the integrity with which these interventions were implemented (Gresham, 2005a; Gresham, Gansle, & Noell, 1993; Gresham, Gansle, Noell, Cohen, & Rosenblum, 1993; Perepletchikova & Kazdin, 2005). A similar lack of integrity data was noted in a meta-analytic review of the cognitive-behavior therapy literature with children and adolescents (Durlak, Fuhrman, & Lampman, 1991).

Many CBI researchers construct treatment manuals written with detailed step-by-step procedures, activities, and topics that are involved in delivering a given treatment (Moncher & Prinz, 1991). Treatment manuals are advantageous because those responsible for implementing the treatment can be trained in the use of the treatment and can consult the treatment manual while delivering a particular treatment. Kiesler (1994) suggested that efficacy studies using treatment manuals have the following three components: (1) a clear description of the techniques specific to the therapy being tested; (2) a unambiguous statement in concrete, observable terms of the operations the therapist is to conduct; and (3) a measure of the degree to which the therapist adheres to the prescribed techniques. Meta-analytic work in this area has shown that treatment manuals reduced therapist differences to 4% of the outcome variance compared to 13% in investigations that did not use treatment manuals (Crits-Christoph, 1996).

A major drawback of manualized treatments is that many investigations do not use a direct measure or monitoring of therapist adherence to the treatment protocol (Gresham, 2005a). Treatment manuals maybe a necessary but insufficient method for ensuring the integrity of CBI treatments. Another criticism of treatment manuals is that they may unnecessarily constrain therapists by preventing them from tailoring a given treatment for a particular participant (Nathan et al., 2000). Others have argued that psychotherapy is more of an "art" than a "science," and the use of treatment manuals violates the nature of the psychotherapeutic process (Edelson, 1994).

Homogeneity/Heterogeneity of Samples

Samples of participants who are selected to be homogenous on a variable of interest (e.g., diagnostic category) will produce smaller variances on outcomes measures of interest than heterogeneous samples (Shadish et al., 2002). Efficacy studies typically utilize homogenous samples, thereby controlling for a major threat to statistical conclusion validity based on interactions between participant characteristics and a particular treatment. This homogenous selection of participants enhances the replicability and internal validity of a particular study but at the same time limits the external validity or generalizibility of the findings (Nathan et al., 2000). Effectiveness studies, in contrast, utilize heterogeneous samples that pose threats to statistical conclusion validity but enhance the generality of the findings in terms of external validity.

The issue of homogeneity/heterogeneity of samples can affect the outcomes and interpretation of findings in CBIs. For example, some CBIs may only be effective with older, more verbal children than with younger, less verbal children, the latter of whom may be at a maturational disadvantage. CBIs may be effective with normally developing children and adolescents but ineffective with developmentally disabled participants. The issue of homogeneity/heterogeneity of samples also creates threats to the external validity of findings in the sense of interactions of the causal relationship with participants (Shadish et al., 2002).

Mediators and Moderators of EBIs

An important consideration in evaluating the effects of CBIs is the specification of those variables that moderate treatment effects and those variables that mediate treatment effects. *Moderator variables* affect the relationship between two variables such that the level of one variable (the moderator) affects the level or value of another variable (i.e., the criterion or outcome variable; Holmbeck, 1997). Baron and Kenny (1986) defined a moderator variable as a qualitative or quantitative variable that changes the strength or direction of a relationship between a predictor variable and a criterion variable. Moderator variables can be qualitative or nominal (e.g., age, sex, race, diagnostic category) and/or quantitative or interval (e.g., IQ, level of depression, verbal skills). *Mediator variables* specify how or by which mechanism a given effect occurs (Holmbeck, 1997). Baron and Kenny characterized mediator variables as generative mechanisms through which focal independent variables influence or thereby "cause" changes in a dependent variable.

A number of variables have been shown to moderate the effects or outcomes in the child psychotherapy literature. For example, Weisz et al.'s (1995) meta-analysis found that age, sex, and the Age × Sex interaction moderated treatment effects on various outcome measures. In terms of mediator variables, it has been demonstrated that poor parenting practices, coercive parent-child interactions, and explosive discipline mediate or cause the development of antisocial behavior in children (Patterson, Reid, & Dishion, 1992).

Baron and Kenny (1986) specified that four conditions must be met for a variable to be considered a mediator: (1) A predictor variable must be associated with a mediator, (2) a predictor must be associated with a dependent variable, (3) a mediator must be associated with a dependent variable, and (4) the effect of a predictor variable on a dependent variable must be *less* after controlling for the mediator. Holmbeck (1997) described two types of analytic procedures that can be used to test for mediated effects: regression approaches and structural equation modeling (SEM) approaches. In multiple regression, one could test the relationship between the predictor and the mediator (A-B), the predictor and the dependent variable (A-C), and the mediator and the dependent variable (B-C) in a series of three multiple regression analyses to test Baron and

Kenny's four conditions. Condition (4) would be tested by the A-C (controlling for B) regression analysis.

SEM approaches examine the relationships between one or more predictor variables (continuous or discrete) and one or more dependent variables (continuous or discrete). SEM or causal modeling analyzes the effects of latent predictor variables on latent dependent or outcome variables. Latent variables are operationalized by measured variables or indicators and are analyzed using multiple regression analyses. Unlike multiple regression analyses, however, SEM requires that the investigator specify and test various models and decide which model provides the best "fit" to the data. The last step in a SEM analysis is to test the fit of a model under two conditions: (1) when the predictor–outcome path (A-C) is constrained to zero, and (2) when the A-C path is not constrained to zero (Holmbeck, 1997). If the second model fits the data better than the first model (comparison of two chi-square tests), then that model is selected as the best mediational model.

CBIs are based on the assumption that cognition *mediates* or causes changes in the behavior of the dependent variable. Hence, changes in cognition are necessary to produce changes in behavior. However, the meta-analysis by Durlak et al. (1991) of the CBI literature with children did not find a significant relationship between changes in cognitive processes and behavior. Theoretically, effective CBIs are brought about by changing cognitions and cognitive processes that, in turn, produce changes in behavior. Thus, it is unclear what the underlying mechanisms of change (i.e., mediators) are in CBIs, although recent research in specific areas of psychopathology has explored putative mediational processes.

Validity Considerations in CBI Research

The purpose of research methodology is to design studies that uncover relations among variables that might not be readily apparent by casual observation. Research design assists in simplifying a situation in which many variables are operating simultaneously and in helping the researcher to isolate the variables of interest (Kazdin, 1992). Research designs thus help the researcher to rule out alternative explanations for the data that are collected. The extent to which any given research design is successful in ruling out plausible rival hypotheses is not absolute but rather a matter of degree. Specifically, researchers use validity arguments to assist them in ruling out alternative explanations for their data. Four types of validity are typically considered: internal validity, external validity, construct validity, and statistical conclusion validity (Campbell &

Stanley, 1966; Shadish et al., 2002). Each of these is briefly described in the following sections.

Internal Validity

Internal validity refers to the degree to which a researcher can attribute changes in a dependent variable to an independent variable while simultaneously ruling out alternative explanations (Campbell & Stanley, 1966). An experiment or study that does not have adequate internal validity suffers from competing rival hypotheses that could explain the obtained results of the study. Internal validity is the key consideration in *efficacy studies* described earlier in this chapter. Shadish et al. (2002) discussed a number of potential threats to the internal validity of research studies. These threats include history, maturation, instrumentation, statistical regression, selection biases, attrition, and interaction of selection biases with other threats to internal validity (e.g., Selection × Maturation or Statistical Regression × Attrition).

A true randomized experiment or randomized clinical trial is the best way to control for these threats to internal validity. In this arrangement, experimental units are randomly assigned to treatment and control groups and compared on a dependent measure. An alternative would be to use intact groups in which the researcher would match experimental units on relevant variables (e.g., sex and age). This arrangement, however, would be a quasi-experimental design and would not control for threats to internal validity as well as a randomized clinical trial would.

External Validity

External validity refers to the *generalizability* of the results of a research study. It asks the following question: To what extent can the results of a study be generalized to other populations, settings, treatment variables, and measurement variables (Campbell & Stanley, 1966)? The issue of external validity is about the boundary conditions or limits of research findings (Kazdin, 1992). As such, external validity is of utmost concern in *effectiveness studies* described earlier. Whereas internal validity is concerned with attributing changes in a dependent variable to an independent variable, external validity is concerned with demonstrating the extent to which that same effect would be observed with other participants, in other settings, using other treatments, and measuring outcomes using other methods.

External validity concerns the interactions between a treatment and other conditions (e.g., testing, selection, setting, history). Several threats to external validity have been identified and can be grouped into four broad categories: sample characteristics, stimulus characteristics, contextual characteristics, and assessment characteristics (Bracht & Glass, 1968). Sample characteristics may limit the generalizability of research findings to other samples that may differ on key variables. For example, a CBI shown to be effective in reducing symptoms of depression in highly verbal, intelligent adolescents might not show the same effects with less verbal and less intelligent adolescents. In this case, the CBI treatment for depression would be considered efficacious but not effective.

Another major threat to the external validity of research studies is *multiple treatment interference,* which refers to interpreting the results of a particular treatment within the context of other treatments (Kazdin, 1992). Multiple treatment interference can be particularly problematic for someone interpreting the outcomes of CBIs, because these interventions often utilize multiple treatment components such as self-instruction, problem solving, self-monitoring, and verbal reinforcement from the therapist (Durlak et al., 1991; Kendall, 2000). Few if any CBIs have systematically isolated the unique contributions of multiple treatment components in CBIs, thereby posing threats to the external validity of these interventions.

Construct Validity

Construct validity refers to the basis for interpreting a causal relation between an independent variable and a dependent variable. Whereas internal validity is concerned with whether an independent variable is responsible for a change in the dependent variable, construct validity focuses on the *reason, interpretation,* or *explanation* for the change in the dependent variable. Several aspects in an experiment may interfere with or compromise the interpretation of findings. These can be described as *confounds* because it might be possible that a particular factor covaries with an intervention that could be responsible for changes in the dependent variable (Kazdin, 1992).

An example illustrates confounds that might exist in interpreting the effects of a CBI. Suppose a number of cognitive-behavior therapists are randomly assigned to Treatment Method A (self-statement modification) and other therapists are randomly assigned to Treatment Method B (problem solving). At the conclusion of the study, it is shown that Method B is superior to Method A in producing behavior change. However, because therapists are nested within method (A and B), one cannot separate the therapy method from therapist effects because therapists are nested within each method. It may well be the case that therapists in

Method B were simply better therapists than therapists in Method A (a Therapist × Method confound).

Kazdin (1992) characterized the construct validity of an experiment based on two questions: What is the intervention? And, what explains the causal mechanism for change in the dependent variable? Many CBIs are embedded within other conditions that might account for changes in the dependent variable. For example, CBIs are embedded or confounded by the skill and knowledge of the consultant as well as the social influence the therapist has on clients. It is difficult in cases like this to disentangle the effects of therapist expertise from the social influences of the therapist to determine the most important mechanisms of change. Construct validity is important because it affects the field's interpretation of the reasons for behavior change produced by CBIs.

Statistical Conclusion Validity

Statistical conclusion validity refers to threats to drawing valid inferences that result from random error and the inappropriate selection of statistical procedures (Kirk, 1995). In short, statistical conclusion validity deals with those aspects of the statistical evaluation of a study that affect the conclusions drawn from the experimental conditions and their effect on the dependent variable. There are several threats to statistical conclusion validity. These include low statistical power, reliability of treatment implementation, reliability of dependent variables, random irrelevancies in the experimental setting, and random heterogeneity of respondents (Kirk, 1995).

Statistical power refers to the probability of rejecting the null hypothesis when the null hypothesis is false. Power is a function of four variables: (1) sample size, (2) significance level, (3) effect size, and (4) power level (Cohen, 1992). A power analysis specifies the sample size (N) that is required to obtain a given level of significance (α) for a given effect size (small, medium, or large) at a given power level (typically .80). Many studies in both psychology and education produce either nonsignificant or weak effects because of low statistical power (Maxwell, 2000).

The most straightforward way to increase power is to increase sample size; however, this may be difficult to accomplish or economically unfeasible for many researchers. Other ways to increase statistical power are to adopt a higher significance level ($\alpha = .10$), use a lower power level (< .80), or employ a higher effect size (.80). Cohen (1988) has published power tables for a variety of statistical procedures, and many power software programs are available online and are either free or available for purchase.

Another threat to statistical conclusion validity is the *unreliability of treatment implementation* or what was described earlier as lapses in treatment integrity. Failure to implement an intervention as planned or intended may lead to inaccurate conclusions regarding the effects of the intervention. For example, a CBI can produce null results because the intervention was implemented without integrity rather than because the intervention itself was ineffective. Statistically, in this case, the researcher would commit a Type II error by concluding the intervention was ineffective when it was potentially effective but its effectiveness was compromised by poor integrity.

Another threat to statistical conclusion validity is the *unreliability of dependent measures* used to assess intervention outcomes. Measures with low reliability inflate error variance and reduce the effect size, thereby leading to Type II error rates (Kirk, 1995). Researcher-constructed measures that are not subjected to reliability analyses are likely to suffer from this threat to statistical conclusion validity.

Finally, the *random heterogeneity of respondents* poses a threat to statistical conclusion validity. This was described earlier "Homogeneity/ Heterogeneity of Samples"). Differing characteristics of participants as well as therapists may inflate error variance, leading to Type II errors. For example, some clients are brighter and easier to work with than other clients. Some therapists may be more experienced and better trained than other therapists in delivering CBIs. Comparisons of the effectiveness of CBIs can be compromised by the characteristics of both clients and therapists that lead to Type II errors (inaccurate retention of a false null hypothesis).

Defining Empirical Support

Defining what is meant by *empirical support*, although seemingly simple, involves some complex theoretical and measurement issues (Weisz & Hawley, 1998). If a particular treatment produces changes in the core features of a behavior disorder, does that mean it has empirical support? For example, recall the MTA study of ADHD that showed that medication management was more effective than behavioral modification and community comparisons in reducing the core features of ADHD and that there was no added benefit of combined medication + behavior modification (MTA Cooperative Group, 1999). However, a different pattern of results was observed among the four groups when considering secondary or ancillary dependent measures (e.g., social skills, internalizing problems, academic achievement). Based on these findings, can one state that medication treatment of ADHD has unequivocal empirical support? In studies such as the MTA study using multiple outcome measures, it is unclear what the standard should be for judging whether a treatment has adequate empirical support. Should studies be required to produce significant changes on the majority of outcome measures (50%) or on all outcome measures?

Another possibly is that a treatment may produce significant changes on associated characteristics for a behavioral disorder but no changes on the core features of the disorder. For instance, if a CBI treatment for depression produced changes in social skills functioning but did not produce clinically significant changes in hopelessness, concentration, or self-esteem, would that constitute empirical support? What if a treatment produced changes immediately after the conclusion of treatment (immediate posttest), but not at 1-month, 2-month, or 3-month follow-up? Would that be an empirically supported treatment? The answer to this question might be yes and no. Yes, it would be an evidence-based short-term treatment; but no, it would not be an evidence-based long-term treatment.

A related issue is the nature of the outcome measures used to determine empirical support. CBI interventions may produce changes on "soft" outcome measures (e.g., self-reports) but not on more objective "hard" outcome measures (e.g., direct observations). A good example of this is the early research on using CBI to decrease impulsivity in children with ADHD (Meichenbaum & Goodman, 1971). A popular outcome measure used in this line of research was the Matching Familiar Figures Test (Kagan, 1966), which is a measure of conceptual tempo. Impulsive children tended to respond rapidly and incorrectly on this task, which involved matching a figure from an array of figures to a standard figure. Training children to be less impulsive and more accurate on the Matching Familiar Figures Test, however, did not generalize to changes on hard measures of impulsivity in the natural environment such as direct observations or informant ratings (DuPaul & Stoner, 2003).

This same problem with the ecological validity of outcome measures can be found in the social skills training literature that has used CBI-based interventions (Gresham et al., 2004). Various meta-analyses using social problem-solving strategies and other CBI interventions have shown the greatest changes on social problem-solving measures and various indices of social cognition, but little change on more ecologically valid indices of social competence (e.g., direct observations of prosocial behavior, peer acceptance, informant ratings). Many outcome measures used in CBI-based social skills training studies have lacked social validity and often include measures having a great deal of construct-irrelevant variance (Gresham et al., 2004).

Statistical Significance and Clinical Significance

Statistical Significance

Statistical significance deals with issues of reliability of change and group differences as well as the magnitude of effects expressed as effect sizes. Perhaps the simplest expression of an effect is the difference between two group means of which the null value is set at zero (Kelley & Rausch, 2006). The behavioral and social sciences (unlike the physical and biological sciences) use units of measurement that are arbitrary and that are placed on different scales of measurement. To correct for this, researchers often convert mean scores into standardized units of measurement so that effects of various studies can be placed on comparable scales of measurement. The most common statistical conversion is to express group mean differences as *effect sizes* or a standardized mean difference. Cohen's d (Cohen, 1988) is commonly used and is based on the following formula: $(M_1 - M_2)/[SD_1 + SD_2/2]$ where M_1 is the mean for the experimental group, M_2 is the mean for the control group, and $(SD_1 + SD_2)/2$ is the pooled standard deviation of the experimental and control groups. This standardized mean difference can be interpreted as a z score with a mean of 0 and a standard deviation of 1. Cohen (1988) provided guidelines for interpreting effect sizes as small (.2), medium (.5), and large (.8).

Perhaps a more useful way of expressing an effect size that can be used to determine significance is using the binomial effect size display (BESD) developed by Rosenthal and Rubin (1982), who suggested that labeling effect sizes as small, medium, and large might provide misleading interpretation of results. Effect sizes expressed as BESD show the effects of group membership (treatment vs. control) on the success rate on a given outcome (improved vs. not improved). Calculation of BESD is straightforward when effect sizes are expressed as correlation coefficients (Pearson's r) and the improved/not improved statuses for the treatment and control groups are specified. The BESD is calculated as follows: $.50 + (r/2)$. For example, the average effect size of CBI studies with children expressed as Pearson's r is about .30 (Durlak et al., 1991; Dush, Hirt, & Schoeder, 1989; Weisz et al., 1995). The BESD for this shows that approximately 65% of individuals receiving CBIs improved compared to only 35% of controls [BESD = $.50 + (.30/2) = .65$]. Effect sizes in terms of Cohen's d can be easily converted to Pearson's r by the following formula: $r = d/(\sqrt{d^2 + 4})$.

Clinical Significance

Whereas statistical significance deals with the reliability of change based on group differences, clinical significance involves the determination of whether the quantity and quality of behavior change make a difference in an *individual's* functioning. Did the intervention produce socially important effects (Wolf, 1978)? Does the change in behavior have "habilitative validity" (Hawkins, 1991)? Kazdin (2003) defined *clinical significance* in terms of whether an intervention makes a real, genuine, palpable, practical, or noticeable difference in everyday life to the individual and the people with whom that person interacts.

Kazdin (2003) reviewed several indices of clinical significance, each of which has strengths and weaknesses. Perhaps the most ubiquitous index of clinical significance is the *amount or degree of behavior change*. Large changes on outcomes measures are more likely to be clinically significant than small changes. However, it is possible for an individual to demonstrate moderate or small changes in behavior and for these changes to be clinically significant (Abelson, 1985; Rosenthal & Rosnow, 1991). For example, children may continue to meet diagnostic criteria for conduct disorder but show substantial changes in anger control and intensity of aggressive outbursts.

The amount of behavior change can be operationalized in several ways. First, one can calculate the *absolute* level of behavior change without reference to a normative sample. Kazdin (2003) suggested three ways of doing this: (1) calculating the amount of change from pretreatment to posttreatment (e.g., a change of two standard deviations), (2) determining whether the individual continues to meet classification criteria for a psychiatric diagnosis, and (3) completely eliminating behavioral difficulties.

Another method of demonstrating clinical significance is comparing an individual's scores to normative criteria before and after treatment. An intervention that moves an individual's score at pretest from the 98th percentile (+2 standard deviations above the mean) on a problem behavior measure to the 55th percentile at posttest would be considered clinically significant. Pelham et al. (1998) used this logic in their review of the ADHD intervention literature and showed that even after treatment (medication or psychosocial), individuals were still functioning +1 standard deviation of the mean (84th percentile) on behavioral measures of ADHD.

Clinically significant change is rarely cast in terms of a dichotomy in the sense of symptom-free versus not symptom-free, but rather these changes are perhaps best thought of on a continuum (Kazdin, 2003). Conceptualizing change on a continuum requires the researcher to adopt reasonable cut scores that will identify whether individuals show marked changes in behavior. Depending on the cut score adopted, four possible outcomes are possible: true-positive, true-negative, false-positive, and false-negative decisions. *True positives* are cases that are correctly identified as having made clinically significant change, and *true negatives* are cases that are correctly identified as not having made clinically significant change. *False positives* are cases that are incorrectly identified as having made clinically significant change, and *false negatives* are cases that are incorrectly identified as not having made clinically significant change. Cut scores (based on tests or other assessments) that yield low false-negative rates have high *sensitivity*, and cut scores that yield low false-positive rates have high *specificity*.

It should be noted that adopting a cut score that reduces the false-positive rate will necessarily increase the false-negative rate and vice versa (Meehl & Rosen, 1955). A useful procedure that systematically considers all possible cut scores and graphs true-positive rates against false-positive rates is the *receiver operating curve* (McFall & Treat, 1999). Receiver operating curve methods have been widely adopted in the physical, medical, and psychological sciences and have been proven to identify to most valid cut scores for accurate decision making (Swets, Dawes, & Jonathan, 2000) and screening (Hill, Lochman, Coie, Greenberg, & Conduct Problems Prevention Research Group, 2004).

Conclusion

CBIs have been shown to be efficacious interventions for a variety of behavioral difficulties of children and adolescents. Meta-analyses of the CBI literature consistently show that approximately 65% of individuals receiving CBIs improve and 35% do not improve with these interventions. This chapter described a number of methodological considerations involved in evaluating the evidence base for CBIs. One important distinction we described in EBIs is between *efficacy* and *effectiveness* of CBIs. Efficacy research is concerned primarily with internal validity and the demonstration of behavior changes under tightly controlled conditions, whereas effectiveness is concerned primarily with external validity and the demonstration of the generality of behavior change across settings, populations, and therapists.

Another important methodological consideration discussed was the issue of treatment integrity (or fidelity), which describes the extent to which interventions are implemented as planned or intended. Although the issue of treatment integrity has received increased attention in recent years (see Gresham, 2005a; Perepletchikova & Kazdin, 2005), it remains an understudied phenomenon in intervention research. Future CBI research should systematically address the effect of treatment integrity on treatment outcome.

This chapter also addressed the analysis of moderating and mediating variables on outcomes produced by CBIs. Several meta-analyses have identified significant moderators of treatment outcomes in CBI research such as sex, age, and Sex × Age interaction effects; however, these types of analyses are sparse in the literature. Few if any studies have tested mediational models in treatment outcome research using CBIs. There is a great need in future research to expand statistical analyses beyond mean difference comparisons to hierarchical regression-based analyses and SEM of moderators and mediators, respectively.

This chapter concluded with a discussion of how best to define statistical and clinical significance in CBIs. Statistical significance is typically reflected in group mean differences based on analysis of variance models and adopting an arbitrary criterion for significance ($p < .05$). Statistical significance, however, does not express the importance of an effect and is greatly affected by sample size. A useful metric is Cohen's d, which is a standardized mean difference between groups that can be characterized as small, medium, or large depending on the magnitude of the effect size (.2, .5, and .8, respectively). An even more useful metric is the BESD, which characterizes an effect size (expressed in terms of Pearson's r) as the proportion of individuals in each group (treatment and control) who improve and who do not improve. It would be useful to the field if all future CBI studies used measures of effect size expressed in terms of the BESD so consumers can gauge how many individuals are likely to improve with which interventions.

Clinical significance, unlike statistical significance, deals with the issue of the quality of behavior change on real-world outcome measures. Clinical significance is closely related to the concept of external validity and captures the notion of whether an intervention produced a genuine or noticeable change in how a person deals with everyday life issues and circumstances. Although there are several methods of indexing clinical significance (e.g., absolute level of change, elimination of clinical-level symptoms, functioning in normative range), there are advantages and disadvantages of each method. Another useful way of expressing clinical significance is using a specified cut score for improvement (improved or not improved) and contrasting the proportion of correct decisions (true positives and true negatives) against the proportion of incorrect decisions (false positives and false negatives). These cut scores reflect the sensitivity (low false-negative rates) and specificity (low false-positive rates) of judging the effectiveness of CBIs. Receiver operating curve analyses are recommended to enhance the accuracy of decision making and identify the most valid cut scores for gauging improvement in CBIs.

References

Abelson, R. (1985). A variance explanation paradox: When a little is a lot. *Psychological Bulletin, 97,* 129–133.

Bandura, A. (1977). *Social learning theory.* Englewood Cliffs, NJ: Prentice Hall.

Bandura, A. (1986). *Social foundations of thought and action: A social cognitive theory.* Upper Saddle, NJ: Prentice Hall.

Barkley, R. (2006). *Attention-deficit hyperactivity disorder: A handbook for diagnosis and treatment* (3rd ed.). New York: Guilford Press.

Barlow, D. (1996). Health care policy, psychotherapy research, and the future of psychotherapy. *American Psychologist, 51,* 1050–1058.

Baron, R., & Kenny, D. (1986). The moderator–mediator variable distinction in social psychology research: Conceptual, strategic, and statistical considerations. *Journal of Personality and Social Psychology, 51,* 1173–1182.

Bracht, G., & Glass, G. (1968). The external validity of experiments. *American Educational Research Journal, 5,* 437–474.

Brestan, E., & Eyberg, S. (1998). Effective psychosocial treatments for conduct-disordered children and adolescents: 29 years, 82 studies, and 5,272 kids. *Journal of Clinical Child Psychology, 27,* 180–189.

Campbell, D., & Stanley, J. (1966). *Experimental and quasi-experimental designs for research.* Chicago: Rand McNally.

Casey, R., & Berman, J. (1985). The outcome of psychotherapy with children. *Psychological Bulletin, 98,* 388–400.

Cohen, J. (1988). *Statistical power analysis for the behavioral sciences* (2nd ed.). Hillsdale, NJ: Erlbaum.

Cohen, J. (1992). A power primer. *Psychological Bulletin, 112,* 155–159.

Crits-Christoph, P. (1996). The dissemination of efficacious psychological treatments. *Clinical Psychology: Science and Practice, 3,* 260–263.

Dodge, K. (1985). Attributional bias in aggressive children. In P. Kendall (Ed.), *Advances in cognitive-behavioral research and therapy* (Vol. 4, pp. 75–110). New York: Academic Press.

Dodge, K. (1986). A social-information processing model of social competence in children. In M. Perlmutter (Ed.), *The Minnesota Symposia on Child Psychology: Vol. 18. Cognitive perspectives on children's social and behavioral development* (pp. 77–125). Hillsdale, NJ: Erlbaum.

Dodge, K., & Crick, N. (1990). Social-information processing bases of aggressive behavior in children. *Personality and Social Psychology Bulletin, 16,* 8–22.

DuPaul, G., & Stoner, G. (2003). *ADHD in the schools: Assessment and intervention strategies* (2nd ed.). New York: Guilford Press.

Durlak, J., Fuhrman, T., & Lampman, C. (1991). Effectiveness of cognitive-behavior therapy for maladapting children: A meta-analysis. *Psychological Bulletin, 110,* 204–214.

Dush, D., Hirt, M., & Schoeder, H. (1989). Self-statement modification in the treatment of child behavior disorders: A meta-analysis. *Psychological Bulletin, 106,* 97–106.

Edelson, M. (1994). Can psychotherapy research answer this psychotherapist's questions? In P. Talley, H. Strupp, & S. Butler (Eds.), *Psychotherapy research and practice: Bridging the gap* (pp. 60–87). New York: Basic Books.

Gersten, R., Fuchs, D., Compton, D., Coyne, M., Greenwood, C., & Innocenti, M. (2005). Quality indicators for group experimental and quasi-experimental research in special education. *Exceptional Children, 71,* 149–164.

Gresham, F. M. (1989). Assessment of treatment integrity in school consultation and prereferral intervention. *School Psychology Review, 18,* 37–50.

Gresham, F. M. (2004). Current status and future directions of school-based behavioral interventions. *School Psychology Review, 33,* 326–343.

Gresham, F. M. (2005a). Methodological issues in evaluating cognitive-behavioral treatments for students with behavioral disorders. *Behavioral Disorders, 30,* 213–225.

Gresham, F. M. (2005b). Treatment integrity and therapeutic change: Commentary on Perepletchikova and Kazdin. *Clinical Psychology: Science and Practice, 12,* 391–394

Gresham, F. M., Cook, C., Crews, S. D., & Kern, L. (2004). Social skills training for children and youth with emotional and behavioral disorders: Validity considerations and future directions. *Behavioral Disorders, 30,* 19–33.

Gresham, F. M., Gansle, K., & Noell, G. (1993). Treatment integrity in applied behavior analysis with children. *Journal of Applied Behavior Analysis, 26,* 257–263.

Gresham, F. M., Gansle, K., Noell, G., Cohen, S., & Rosenblum, S. (1993). Treatment integrity in school-based consultation studies: 1980–1990. *School Psychology Review, 22,* 254–272.

Hawkins, R. (1991). Is social validity what we are interested in? Argument for a functional approach. *Journal of Applied Behavior Analysis, 24,* 205–213.

Hill, L. G., Lochman, J. E., Coie, J. D., Greenberg, M. T., & Conduct Problems Prevention Research Group. (2004). Effectiveness of early screening for externalizing problems: Issues of screening accuracy and utility. *Journal of Consulting and Clinical Psychology, 72,* 809–820.

Hoagwood, K., & Erwin, H. (1997). Effectiveness of school-based mental health services for children: A 10-year research review. *Journal of Child and Family Studies, 6,* 435–451.

Holmbeck, G. (1997). Toward terminological, conceptual, and statistical clarity in the study of mediators and moderators: Examples from the child-clinical and pediatric psychology literatures. *Journal of Consulting and Clinical Psychology, 65,* 599–610.

Kagan, J. (1966). Reflection–impulsivity: The generality and dynamics of conceptual tempo. *Journal of Abnormal Psychology, 71,* 17–24.

Kazdin, A. (1992). *Research design in clinical psychology* (2nd ed.). New York: Macmillan.

Kazdin, A. (2003). Clinical significance: Measuring whether interventions make a difference. In A. Kazdin & J. Weisz (Eds.), *Methodological issues and strategies in clinical research* (3rd ed., pp. 691–710). Washington, DC: American Psychological Association.

Kazdin, A., & Weisz, J. (Eds.) (2003). *Evidence-based psychotherapies for children and adolescents.* New York: Guilford.

Kelley, K., & Rausch, J. (2006). Sample size planning for the standardized mean difference: Accuracy in parameter estimation via narrow confidence intervals. *Psychological Methods, 11,* 363–385.

Kendall, P. C. (Ed.). (2000). *Child and adolescent therapy* (2nd ed.). New York: Guilford Press.

Kendall, P. C., & Hollon, S. (1979). Cognitive-behavioral interventions: Overview and current status. In P. Kendall & S. Hollon (Eds.), *Cognitive-behavioral interventions: Theory, research, and procedures* (pp. 1–9). New York: Academic Press.

Kiesler, D. (1994). Standardization of intervention: The tie that binds psychotherapy research and practice. In P. Talley, H. Strupp, & S. Butler (Eds.), *Psychotherapy research and practice: Bridging the gap* (pp. 143–153). New York: Basic Books.

Kirk, R. (1995). *Experimental design: Procedures for the behavioral sciences* (3rd ed.). Pacific Grove, CA: Brooks/Cole.

Kratochwill, T. R., & Stoiber, K. (2000). Empirically supported interventions and school psychology: Conceptual and practice issues—Part II. *School Psychology Quarterly, 15,* 233–253.

Lochman, J., Whidby, J., & FitzGerald, D. (2000). Cognitive-behavioral assessment and treatment with aggressive children. In P. Kendall (Ed.), *Child and adolescent therapy: Cognitive-behavioral procedures* (2nd ed., pp. 31–87). New York: Guilford Press.

Lonigan, J., Elbert, J., & Johnson, S. (1998). Empirically supported psychosocial interventions for children: An overview. *Journal of Clinical Child Psychology, 27,* 138–145.

Maxwell, S. (2000). Sample size and multiple regression analysis. *Psychological Methods, 5*, 434–458.

McFall, R. M., & Treat, T. A. (1999). Quantifying the information value of clinical assessments with signal detection theory. *Annual Review of Psychology, 50*, 215–241.

Meehl, P., & Rosen, A. (1955). Antecedent probability and the efficiency of psychometric signs, patterns, or cutting scores. *Psychological Bulletin, 52*, 194–216.

Meichenbaum, D., & Goodman, J. (1971). Training impulsive children to talk to themselves: A means of developing self-control. *Journal of Abnormal Psychology, 77*, 115–126.

Moncher, F., & Prinz, R. (1991). Treatment fidelity in outcome studies. *Clinical Psychology Review, 11*, 247–266.

MTA Cooperative Group. (1999). A 14-month randomized clinical trial of treatment strategies for attention-deficit/hyperactivity disorder. *Archives of General Psychiatry, 56*, 1073–1086.

Nathan, P., Stuart, S., & Dolan, S. (2000). Research on psychotherapy efficacy and effectiveness: Between Scylla and Charybdis? *Psychological Bulletin, 126*, 964–981.

Parloff, M. B. (1996). Placebo controls in psychotherapy research a sine qua non or a placebo for research problems? *Journal of Consulting and Clinical Psychology, 54*, 79–87.

Patterson, G., Reid, J., & Dishion, T. (1992). *A social interactional approach: Vol. 4. Antisocial boys*. Eugene, OR: Castalia.

Pelham, W., Wheeler, T., & Chronis, A. (1998). Empirically supported psychosocial treatments for attention deficit hyperactivity disorder. *Journal of Clinical Child Psychology, 27*, 190–205.

Perepletchikova, F., & Kazdin, A. (2005). Treatment integrity and therapeutic change: Issues and research recommendations. *Clinical Psychology: Science and Practice, 12*, 365–383.

Peterson, L., Homer, A., & Wonderlich, S. (1982). The integrity of independent variables in behavior analysis. *Journal of Applied Behavior Analysis, 15*, 477–492.

Reinecke, M., Dattilio, F., & Freeman, A. (Eds.). (2003). *Cognitive therapy with children and adolescents*. New York: Guilford Press.

Rosenthal, R., & Rosnow, R. (1991). *Essentials of behavioral research: Methods and data analysis* (2nd ed.). New York: McGraw-Hill.

Rosenthal, R., & Rubin, D. (1982). A simple general purpose display of magnitude of experimental effect. *Journal of Educational Psychology, 74*, 166–169.

Seligman, M. (1995). The effectiveness of psychotherapy. The *Consumer Reports* study. *American Psychologist, 50*, 965–974.

Shadish, W., Cook, T., & Campbell, D. (2002). *Experimental and quasi-experimental designs for generalized causal inference*. New York: Houghton Mifflin.

Shavelson, R., & Towne, I. (2002). *Scientific research in education*. Washington, DC: National Academy Press.

Smith, S., Lochman, J., & Daunic, A. (2005). Managing aggression using cognitive-behavioral interventions: State of the practice and future directions. *Behavioral Disorders, 30*, 227–240.

Stoiber, K., & Kratochwill, T. R. (2000). Empirically supported interventions and school psychology: Rationale and methodological issues—Part I. *School Psychology Quarterly, 15*, 75–105.

Swets, J., Dawes, R., & Monahan, J. (2000). Psychological science can improve diagnostic decisions. *Psychological Science in the Public Interest, 1*, 1–26.

Thompson, B., Diamond, K., McWilliam, R., Snyder, P., & Snyder, S. (2005). Evaluating the quality of evidence from correlational research for evidence-based practice. *Exceptional Children, 71*, 181–194.

Walker, H. M. (2004). Commentary: Use of evidence-based interventions in schools: Where we've been, where we are, and where we need to go. *School Psychology Review, 33,* 398–407.

Walker, H. M., Ramsay, E., & Gresham, F. M. (2004). *Antisocial behavior at school: Evidence-based practices* (2nd ed.). Belmont, CA: Wadsworth.

Weimer, W. (1977). A conceptual framework for cognitive psychology: Motor theories of mind. In R. Shaw & J. Bransford (Eds.), *Perceiving, acting, and knowing* (pp. 267–311). Hillsdale, NJ: Erlbaum.

Weisz, J., & Hawley, K. (1998). Finding, evaluating, and applying empirically supported treatments for children and adolescents. *Journal of Clinical Child Psychology, 27,* 206–216.

Weisz, J., Weiss, B., Alicke, M., & Klotz, M. (1987). Effectiveness of psychotherapy with children and adolescents: A meta-analysis for clinicians. *Journal of Consulting and Clinical Psychology, 55,* 542–549.

Weisz, J., Weiss, B., Han, S., Granger, D., & Morton, T. (1995). Effects of psychotherapy with children and adolescents revisited: A meta-analysis of treatment outcomes studies. *Psychological Bulletin, 117,* 450–468.

Wolf, M. M. (1978). Social validity: The case for subjective measurement or how applied behavior analysis is finding its heart. *Journal of Applied Behavior Analysis, 11,* 211–226.

Yeaton, W., & Sechrest, L. (1981). Critical dimensions in the choice of successful treatments: Strength, integrity, and effectiveness. *Journal of Consulting and Clinical Psychology, 49,* 156–167.

CHAPTER 4

Cognitive-Behavioral Interventions and the Social Context of the School

A Stranger in a Strange Land

RICHARD VAN ACKER
MATTHEW J. MAYER

The school represents a rather unique social environment for most children and youth. Society does not invite children to participate within the social context of the school; their attendance is mandated by law. Once at school, these children are required to conform to specific behavioral expectations and to engage in a variety of activities designed to promote academic, social, and emotional development. Most children can readily adapt to the expectations of the school setting. Others, however, appear ill prepared to meet the demands placed upon them in this setting. For these students the school day can be characterized by relatively high levels of verbal reprimand, ridicule, social rejection, and academic failure (Furlong, Morrison, & Jimerson, 2004; Leone & Mayer, 2004; Reinke & Walker, 2006). Nevertheless, these students are expected to return the next day "enthusiastically" prepared to start anew, only to face another day of failure from which they cannot escape.

Children and youth who are at risk for the development of, or who display, emotional and mental health disorders are particularly vulnerable within the school setting. Research supports the fact that this population often experiences a social context within the school that differs significantly from that of the typical student. Students with emotional disorders, with mental health problems, and/or who display antisocial behavior experience significantly more verbal reprimand and less praise from their teachers (Gunter, Denny, Jack, Shores, & Nelson, 1993); praise, when given, is often noncontingent, making it impossible for students to understand how praise is related to desired behavior (Nelson & Roberts, 2000; Shores & Wehby, 1999; Van Acker, Grant, & Henry, 1996). Additionally, these students are at greater risk for poor grades and grade retention (Armstrong, Dedrick, & Greenbaum, 2003) and school suspension and expulsion (Duchnowski, 1994; Wagner, 1995) and are more likely than their typical peers to drop out of school (Wagner, 1995). Overall, the social context of the school is not particularly supportive of these students.

Educators are often quite concerned about the challenging behaviors these at-risk youth display (e.g., aggression, bullying, social withdrawal, depression, anxiety). Many schools implement school-based intervention efforts (Gottfredson et al., 2000) yet fail to address aspects of the social context (e.g., peer group affiliation) and aspects of the school climate (e.g., autocratic and punitive discipline policies) that might serve to promote student disaffection and the display of challenging behaviors (Skiba & Peterson, 1999; Peterson & Skiba, 2000). Often, too little attention is paid to the social context in which these children must function and to the role that the social context plays in the development and maintenance of these challenging behaviors (Dodge, 1993; Guerra, Huesmann, Tolan, Van Acker, & Eron, 1990; Tolan & Guerra, 1994). Frequently school personnel, with the hopes of reducing problem behaviors, implement prevention and intervention programs employing strategies that exacerbate the problems. For example, many schools provide intervention services (e.g., anger management classes, self-contained classrooms for students with behavioral disorders) that are designed to reduce antisocial behavior by aggregating "problem children" in small self-contained groups. More and more research suggests that such groupings may actually support the display and maintenance of antisocial behavior by providing a type of "deviance training" where peers provide a positive reaction to rule-breaking behavior (e.g., Cho, Hallfors, Dion, & Sanchez, 2005; Dishion, McCord, & Poulin, 1999; Moos, 2005; Werch & Owen, 2002). These iatrogenic effects are more pronounced for groups of younger adolescents (ages 10–16), as older adolescents appear less affected (Eggert et al., 1994). These results may be significant for schools as common discipline practices (e.g., detention and in-school suspension programs) typically cluster high-risk youth together (Reinke & Walker, 2006).

Schools are constantly asked (and sometimes mandated) to provide another program or another initiative to address the learning, behavioral, and/or emotional needs of their students. Currently, there is increasing pressure placed on schools to provide mental health services for their students. This will undoubtedly involve the implementation of a variety of social learning interventions, and cognitive-behavioral interventions (CBIs). An overarching question must be asked: To what extent can schools be asked to take on a greater responsibility for children's mental health services?

In this chapter, we examine the school as the setting for the delivery of mental health services for children and the increased integration of CBIs to address the social and emotional needs of at-risk youth. We examine the history of CBIs in schools, service delivery models and issues, and barriers to increased efforts to address the mental health needs of students and the acceptance and use of CBIs in the school. Finally, suggestions are offered that may help address some of the challenges discussed.

High Numbers of Youth at Risk for Emotional and Mental Disorders

Historically, the nation has failed to adequately address the emotional and mental health needs of our children (U.S. Department of Health and Human Services, 1999). Approximately 20% of children and youth in the United States have a diagnosable mental health disorder (Hoagwood & Johnson, 2003), and 5–9% of these children meet the criteria for classification as seriously emotionally disturbed (Merrell & Walker, 2004). Hoagwood and Johnson suggested that of children and adolescents with the most severe mental health needs, only one fifth are receiving mental health services. Yet interestingly, according to recent data, close to one fifth of youth nationally have received some type of mental-health-related service through the schools (Foster, Rollefson, Doksum, Noonan, & Robinson, 2005). Research data have provided varied and possibly conflicting information regarding mental health services. For example, whereas some indicators have suggested slight improvement in the availability of mental health services for youth more generally (Sturm, Andreyeva, Pincus, & Tanielian, 2005), other data have demonstrated statistically significant declines in mental health supports (according to parent reports) for students with disabilities, and particularly students with emotional disturbance served by special education (Mayer & Van Acker, Chapter 1, this volume).

Additionally, a large number of youth display emotional and behavioral disorders that may not meet symptom criteria for a mental health disorder, but these youth experience significant problems as they attempt to function within their family, school, and community. Some of these children (less that 1% of the total population) are provided educational support and related services through special education (U.S. Office of Special Education Programs, 2001). The Surgeon General's 1999 report on mental health, however, estimated that as many as 70% of children with emotional and mental health needs in the United States are not getting the services they need, and as many as 6 to 9 million youth are getting no services at all (U.S. Department of Health and Human Services, 1999). This problem is even more serious for children and youth of color, as they generally have less access to mental health services. When mental health services are available to minority youth, they are often inadequate or of a significantly poorer quality than those obtainable by nonminority youth (President's New Freedom Commission on Mental Health, 2003, p. 49). Surgeon General David Satcher made the following statement:

> Growing numbers of children are suffering needlessly because their emotional, behavioral, and developmental needs are not being met by those very institutions which were explicitly created to take care of them. It is time that we as a Nation took seriously the task of preventing mental health problems and treating mental illnesses in youth. (U.S. Department of Health and Human Services, 2000, p. 15)

Alarmingly, the situation appears to be getting worse. By 2020, childhood neuropsychiatric disorders are predicted to rise by more than 50% internationally to become one of the five most common causes of morbidity, mortality, and disability (U.S. Department of Health and Human Services, 2000). Yet there are some recent indicators of a decline in the level of mental health services available to address the current need, notwithstanding the expected rise in childhood emotional and mental disorders (Mayer & Van Acker, Chapter 1, this volume; Foster et al., 2005). Despite national calls for increased attention and increased funding for children's mental health services (e.g., President's New Freedom Commission on Mental Health, 2003), there have been few signs of improvement. In fact, the vast majority of children and youth receiving mental health treatment do so within the school setting (Rones & Hoagwood, 2000; U.S. Department of Health and Human Services, 2000, 2001). Thus, schools have become the de facto mental health system for children and youth in the United States.

School systems, however, are not responsible for meeting the mental health needs of every student. Only when the emotional or mental health disorder displayed by a student formally served by the special education system adversely affects his or her academic performance must the school address the issue. This explains the fact that school-based mental health services have historically been provided primarily to students who have qualified for special education (Foster et al., 2005). However, in recent years, students in the general population have also been regular recipients of mental health supports in schools (Weist, Rubin, Moore, Adelsheim, & Wrobel, 2007). Policymakers are looking to the school as the "location of choice" for the delivery of children's mental health services. The rationale for targeting the school is discussed below.

The Public School as the Setting
for Children's Mental Health Services

Over the past 50 years there has been increasing support for more comprehensive school mental health (SMH) programs (e.g., Evans, 1999; Flaherty & Osher, 2003; Lambert & Bower, 1967; U.S. Department of Health and Human Services, 2000; Weist & Paternite, 2006). Federal initiatives such as the *No Child Left Behind Act* (2002) and the *President's New Freedom Commission on Mental Health* (2003) have acknowledged the potential of SMH as a potentially powerful new approach to address the mental health needs of the nation's youth. School-based systems of care would greatly improve the early identification of and intervention for children at risk for and displaying emotional and mental health disorders. The goal is to promote a collaborative effort between schools and community service providers to design a system of care in which an informed and well-trained group of professionals in concert with educators can provide preventive and intervention services delivered within one community setting—the school. There appears to be a growing realization that the piecemeal approach of providing children's mental health through a series of disjointed service providers has little hope of providing the system of care that is called for by the increasing numbers of children in need of services.

The President's New Freedom Commission on Mental Health (2003) highlighted the need to close the gap between needs and effective services. This report strongly supported the adoption of an epidemiological approach to children's mental health. For example, in every school, three types of students can be identified: (1) typical students who are not at risk, (2) students with an elevated risk for the development of serious emotional problems, and (3) students who have already developed emotional and/or mental health disorders. A three-tiered strategy of prevention and intervention recognizes this and is the most efficient way to head off potential problems and address existing ones (see also World Health Organization, 2001). This epidemiological model posed the following:

- *Primary prevention:* Schoolwide activities targeting all students to prevent the risk of developing emotional problems. These programs would serve to improve school learning environments and broadly promote good mental health (e.g., programs to address anxiety, aggression, etc.) and academic success.
- *Secondary prevention:* Activities and programs aimed at early identification and targeting at-risk students for small-group and more individualized prevention activities.
- *Tertiary prevention/intervention:* Long-term, intensive services for students with serious and/or chronic disorders.

The report went on to support the development of a nationwide system of SMH programs.

The literature cites several reasons schools have been identified as the location of choice for the delivery of children's mental health services. First and foremost, schools are "where the children are located." About 48.5 million students in grades pre-K to 12 attended approximately 95,000 U.S. public schools during the 2003–2004 school year (Snyder, Tan, & Hoffman, 2006). Given that close to 20% of these students may have a diagnosable mental health issue, this suggests that just under 10 million students may need mental health supports. These children and adolescents do not leave their emotional and mental health issues "at the door" as they enter the school building; they bring them into the school and the classroom. Thus, schools must address the mental health issues presented by their students.

Onsite school mental health professionals can serve as a resource for administrators struggling with difficult discipline issues. Likewise, SMH providers may give direct guidance to teachers in meeting student classroom needs (e.g., helping teachers understand how symptoms of attention-deficit/hyperactivity disorder or bipolar disorder can best be accommodated given the demands of the classroom curriculum and structure). School-based programs can potentially target elements in the social ecology that serve as risk factors that exacerbate the development and/or display of mental health problems (e.g., school climate, student and teacher interactions, peer relations, the specific nature of the academic demand (Greenberg, Domitrovich, Graczyk, & Zins, 2005; Leone & Mayer, 2004).

Interestingly, the economic and racial segregation in schools enables the targeting of those populations with the greatest need. Schools in communities with high numbers of students exposed to known risk factors for the development of emotional and mental health disorders (e.g., poverty and low social cohesion) could provide a greater variety of and more intensive secondary and tertiary programming. Schools serving those populations of students traditionally denied quality services (e.g., those predominantly serving minority students) could be targeted as priority sites for empirically validated SMH programs.

Schools are generally conveniently located and reduce issues related to the cost and/or availability of transportation. School-based services provide improved potential for the coordination of interventions around the "whole child" and family. Families report greater levels of comfort when receiving services through school-based programs versus community mental health centers (Weist, Myers, Hastings, Ghuman, & Han, 1999). Receiving services within the school is thought to reduce the stigma often related to accessing mental health services (Foster et al., 2005).

A strong collaboration between mental health providers within the school and educators would allow for the early identification of students often missed by traditional referral procedures (e.g., those youth with internalizing disorders such as anxiety, depression, and suicide ideation; Weist et al., 2007). SMH programs have been associated with a decrease in inappropriate referrals to special education (Bruns, Walrath, Glass-Siegel, & Weist, 2004) and could play a critical role in evaluation, recommendations, interventions, and the development of individualized education programs (IEPs) for students who are eligible for special education services.

Finally, the school represents an ideal social context for the prevention of and the intervention for children's emotional and mental health disorders. Educators have the ability to engage children and youth in an array of programmed and real-world activities and to employ a variety of strategies that can help identify and simultaneously address children's academic, social, emotional, behavioral, and developmental needs (Van Acker, 1993; Weist et al., 1999). Schools provide a social context in which children and youth are provided the opportunity to obtain feedback from both significant adults and peers related to children's effective use of prosocial problem-solving strategies (Lochman, Curry, Dane, & Ellis, 2001). One of the most promising approaches available to both mental health professionals and educators involves the use of CBIs within the school.

History of CBIs in the Schools

CBIs have been used to address a myriad of academic and social-emotional skills since their introduction in the early 1970s. Over the past three decades, CBIs have been shown to demonstrate the ability to reduce serious emotional and mental health disorders and to promote and strengthen prosocial behavior (Kazdin & Weisz, 1998; Kendall, 2000, 2006; Ollendick & King, 2004). Cognitive-behavior modification is a model of teaching and learning that incorporates many of the tenets of operant, social, and cognitive learning theories and posits that cognitive behaviors (self-talk, attitudes, and beliefs) can be changed to observable behaviors, and that changing these cognitive behaviors will, in fact, result in changes in observable behaviors (Harris, 1985). Cognitive-behavioral approaches do not reject more traditional classical and operant perspectives on learning; rather, they suggest that cognitive mediation plays a role in interpreting stimuli and directing one's actions. Interventions to impact the cognitive supports underlying behavior were anticipated to improve maintenance and generalization. By the late 1960s and early 1970s, emerging forms of CBIs were waiting in the wings to appear while more strictly behavioral approaches were starting to diminish somewhat.

Behavioral modification approaches became a fairly regular part of the educational landscape throughout the 1960s, but over time resistance to these approaches grew. This was in part due to high expectations for remarkable results that did not appear, limited training of teachers in these techniques, intrusion of techniques into teaching time and activities, limited generalizability and durability, and overall contextual limitations of using such an objectified approach (Hughes, 1988; Meichenbaum, 1980). Attention gradually turned in the direction of CBIs. Cognitive-behavioral approaches offered the promise of ecological utility that seemed lacking with applied behavioral analysis (Meyers, Cohen, & Schleser, 1989). As a result of these and other factors, a number of efforts to offer CBIs in schools emerged in the 1970s. The following discussion briefly outlines school-based CBI developments over the past 35–40 years, addressing three historical periods: (1) *formative* (early 1970s to mid-1980s); (2) *maturation* (mid-1980s to late 1990s), and (3) *established* (late 1990s to present). These historical periods are identified so as to aid conceptualization, but the choices of names and time periods reflect our own points of view and do not necessarily represent consensus in the field.

The *formative* period for school-based CBIs saw wide-ranging interest and activity across academic and social, emotional, and behavioral domains. For example, a subset of researchers in the learning disabilities community moved forward with academic strategy research, some of which was targeted at the writing process (Harris & Graham, 1985), whereas other early work related to learning disabilities was more generalized, addressing self-monitoring (Hallahan et al., 1983). Related research targeted attributions related to academic achievement for students, including those with disabilities (Pearl, 1985). Additional research on students with disabilities was done in academic areas of reading, writing, and math, and also in attention, impulsivity motivation, problem solving, self-monitoring, and self-regulation (Harris, 1982; Meichenbaum & Asarnow, 1979). Other broader school-related research addressed nonacademic factors, including generalized problem solving (D'Zurilla & Goldfried, 1971) and interpersonal social problem solving and communication (Shure & Spivack, 1979). Additionally, there was more school-based research in areas of anger/aggression (Lochman, Nelson, & Sims, 1981), self-control (Kendall & Braswell, 1982), anxiety and coping skills training (Stevens & Pihl, 1983, as cited in Hughes, 1988), and depression (Butler, Miezitis, Friedman, & Cole, 1980).

Several key developments from the formative period stand out as contributing to our modern foundations in school-based CBIs. First, firm foundations for academic strategy development, especially in writing, were developed during this era. Second, research was able to focus on cognitive-behavioral and metacognitive strategy development that directly addressed skills and tasks essential for academic and social-emotional success as opposed to invisible and hypothesized underlying general deficits (Meichenbaum & Asarnow, 1979, p. 30). Third, broader school-based prevention programming was recognized as an essential long-term national priority, as evidenced in the 1987 statement of the Commission on the Prevention of Mental–Emotional Disabilities (Hughes, 1988, p. 196). Fourth, extensive school-based research in interpersonal cognitive problem solving brought focused attention to several critical skill areas that were subsequently refined: (1) alternative solution generation, (2) reflection on the consequences of one's actions, (3) fostering social-causal cognition, (4) means–end thinking, (5) awareness of sensitivity to interpersonal problems, and (6) orientation to unobservable human dynamics (Hughes, 1988). However, some research syntheses of CBIs for social problem solving demonstrated minimal benefits, especially with lack of generalization (Conoley, 1989; Gresham, 1985). Fifth, as with developments in interpersonal cognitive problem-solving skills, related progress was made in CBIs addressing anger/aggression, anxiety, and depression that provided foundations for next-generation interventions that demonstrated efficacy in the 1980s and early 1990s. Sixth, emerging evidence pointed to the efficacy of paraprofessionals working with teachers and clinical experts to support CBIs (Durlak, 1982; Glenwick & Jason, 1984).

The *maturation period* (mid-1980s to the late 1990s) saw more widespread use of cognitive-behavioral approaches in schools; further development of underlying theory, particularly in social information processing; refinement of interventions, especially in treating anger/aggression, anxiety, and depression; and more consistent research demonstrating the efficacy of these procedures. Although explication of theory refinement of this period (e.g., Lochman's social-cognitive model of anger and aggression) is beyond the scope of this chapter, the larger school-based developments can be considered through a brief discussion of exemplars in the academic and social, emotional, and behavioral realms. It is important to note that several of these exemplars span the *maturation* and *established* periods, attesting to their success and more general use over time. We do not provide a separate discussion of the *established* period in this chapter as much of the text content is focused on current developments.

Educators have readily adopted cognitive-behavioral approaches to enhance their teaching of various academic skills. For example, Deshler, Schumaker, and their associates at the University of Kansas Institute for Research in Learning Disabilities employed CBI strategies in the learning strategies intervention model (Deshler & Schumaker, 1986) to promote the academic achievement of students with learning disabilities. This teaching model relies heavily upon guided modeling, self-instruction, self-evaluation and self-regulation. An example of a specific learning strategy is MULTIPASS (Schumaker, Deshler, Alley, Warner, & Denton, 1982). Using MULTIPASS, students are taught to master content from textbooks by making a series of three passes over the text while performing different substrategies during each pass (i.e., Survey, Size-up, and Sort-out).

Clearly, cognitive-behavioral strategies play an important role in the teaching and learning of academic skills within the public schools of this nation. Almost every classroom posts charts and diagrams designed to identify the steps involved in various academic skills (e.g., math computation, writing, editing, reading comprehension). These visual aids are designed to promote self-regulation, self-talk, and reflective thinking. Successful school-based CBIs have been developed to address almost every curricular area, with an incredible array of strategies targeting reading, writing, and mathematics (e.g., Kymes, 2005; Ruddell & Unrau, 2004; Winstead, 2004).

Implementation of some type of CBI designed to assist children and youth with their interpersonal problem-solving and social skill development is also common within many of the schools and classrooms throughout the United States (e.g., Gottfredson et al., 2000). One example involves a social cognitive problem-solving strategy with the acronym FAST (Vaughn & Lancelotta, 1990; see Figure 4.1). The purpose of FAST is to teach students to consider problems carefully before responding and to consider various alternative responses and their consequences before acting. FAST employs socially rejected students paired with same-sex popular classmates to serve as the social skill trainers for the various classrooms in a schoolwide universal intervention. These trainers are provided direct instruction in the use of the strategies and then teach these skills to others and help monitor their use throughout the school. This provides added opportunities for practice, monitoring, and evaluation of self and others.

Freeze and Think! What is the problem?

Alternatives? What are my possible solutions?

Solution Evaluation. Choose the best solution. Is it safe? Is it fair?

Try It! Slowly and carefully. Does it work?

FIGURE 4.1. FAST: An interpersonal problem-solving strategy. Data from Vaughn, Lancelotta, and Minnis (1988).

CBIs have been shown to be effective in addressing a variety of challenging behaviors across multiple target populations within the school setting (e.g., Lochman, Powell, Whidby, & FitzGerald, 2006). For example, there is evidence supporting the effectiveness of CBI in addressing anger and aggression in children and youth with emotional and behavioral disorders (Etscheidt, 1991; Larson & Lochman, 2005; Robinson, Smith, & Miller, 2002), interpersonal problem solving and social interaction for children with autism (Bauminger, 2002), drug use by inner city youth (Scheier & Botvin, 1996), attention and learning problems in at-risk youth (Argulewicz, 1982), impulsivity in students with attention-deficit/hyperactivity disorder (Fiore, 1992), and impulse control and social problem solving in delinquent youth (Hains & Haines, 1988).

Given the general effectiveness of CBIs and the common use of these strategies in academic instruction, why are some educators and school personnel reluctant to systematically apply these strategies to address the social and emotional needs of their students? A number of service delivery issues have been discussed and multiple barriers to using CBIs have been identified.

CBI Service Delivery Issues and Barriers to Implementation in Schools

Perhaps the greatest issue and barrier to the use of CBIs within the school results from the opinion held by some that addressing the emotional and mental health needs of youth goes beyond the purview of the public school. Some feel that even if public education could allow the time and had the necessary resources (barriers discussed below), the school is not in the mental health business. They suggest that educators should address the academic needs of youth and that concern for youth's mental health falls to others. Unfortunately, children bring their emotional and mental health needs with them to school. Regardless of whether educators wish to address the emotional and mental health needs of their students, these needs arise and interfere with learning.

Another barrier to the increased implementation of CBIs to address the emotional and mental health needs of children and youth within the school setting results from concern for the overall effectiveness, maintenance, and generalizability of these interventions (Coleman, 2000). Although initial gains are often reported during intervention, some follow-up assessments fail to support the continued improvement for key problem behaviors (e.g., depression, aggression; e.g., Spence, Sheffield, & Donovan, 2005; Weisz, McCarthy, & Valeri, 2006). There also are concerns that interventions found effective in clinical trials conducted in university or clinical mental health research centers will not necessarily transfer well to the public school, where staff are overworked and confronted with multiple and often competing priorities (Hoagwood et al., 2001). Much of what passes for research on evidence-based practice might more aptly be described as clinical treatment efficacy research. The central problem is that treatments that have been validated in efficacy studies cannot be assumed to be effective when implemented within the day-to-day operation of the school.

However, a growing body of research supports the premise that CBIs can be effective when delivered within the school (Lochman et al., 2006) and that addressing a child's mental health can result in improved school performance. For example, Wood (2006) found that participation in a CBI to reduce anxiety resulted in improved academic and social functioning over the course of the intervention. Likewise, the Anger Coping Program (Larson & Lochman, 2005) has demonstrated improvements in student academic performance, social competence, and classroom behavior concomitant with reductions in aggression. Thus, the involvement of teachers and other related service personnel within the school setting to employ CBIs in an effort to reduce the risk for and effects of emotional and mental health disorders need not detract from the scholastic goals of the school and very well may enhance the potential to achieve these goals within schools where risk for serious emotional and mental health disorders are the greatest.

Although CBIs have been found to be generally effective in addressing many of the emotional and mental health concerns of children and youth, we lack the needed understanding of the moderators and mediators that may impact the effective use of these prevention and intervention strategies within the school (Lochman, 2000). As mentioned in the introduction to this chapter, the school represents a very challenging social context. Schools are responsible for the education of all children. Race, ethnicity, nature of the child's disability, age, and gender all may prove to impact the efficacy of treatment (Ghafoori, 2001; Guerra, Eron, Huesmann, Tolan, & Van Acker, 1998; Guerra & Jagers, 1999; Weisz, Weiss, Han, Granger, & Morton, 1995). The responsiveness of the teacher and other factors related to the climate of the school (e.g., punitive discipline practices, lack of resources) and/or the classroom (e.g., amount of time and effort expended to practice skills, level of praise or reprimand delivered by the teacher) may serve as important mediators or moderators to the effectiveness of an intervention. The social ecology of many schools can itself represent a risk factor for the development of emotional and mental health disorders, with coercive teacher and student interactions, the presence of peers willing to support antisocial behavior, and significant risk for academic failure on the part of many at-risk youth (Barth, Dunlap, Dane, Lochman, & Wells, 2004; Grant & Van Acker, 2000). As schools are mandated to employ scientifically based interventions (No Child Left Behind, 2002), some feel additional research is needed prior to any wholesale adoption of CBIs and increased involvement in the development of SMHs.

Schools, especially those serving economically depressed urban neighborhoods, are characterized by high rates of student mobility and rapid turnover among administrators, teachers, and other school personnel (Guarino, Santibanez, Daily, & Brewer, 2004; Harry & Klingner, 2006). Thus, the school represents a "moving target" where continued support and repeated professional development are needed to keep school personnel prepared to implement programs that have been established. High turnover of school personnel makes it difficult to sustain existing initiatives and the necessary relationships between school and community entities. Site-based management employed by many public school districts impedes the development and maintenance of the working agreements regarding roles, functions, and communication between community mental health agencies and the schools, as they must be negotiated on a school-by-school basis (Weist & Paternite, 2006).

Lack of time is another serious barrier to the effective use of CBIs within the schools. Numerous reports have identified problems experienced by school personnel at all levels related to the identification of the time necessary to complete their current work assignments (e.g., Odden & Archibald, 2000). Time constraints imposed by work schedules, union contracts, the length of the school day, and the length of the academic year impose significant limits on the time available for collaboration with peers, program development, implementation and evaluation, and professional development. For example, in one study, McLoone (2004, as cited in McLoone, Hudson, & Rapee, 2006) trained 11 school counselors to deliver an anxiety management program in their school, however only 3 of the counselors were able to deliver the program as planned due to the excessive and competing demands of their school positions. Likewise, Stark, Best, and Sellstrom (1989) cautioned about working collaboratively with school personnel to avoid problems related to pull outs and other modifications to school practices.

The effective and efficient implementation of SMH programs requires increased knowledge and awareness of the mental health needs of children and their families, the implementation of assessment, early identification and screening procedures, the development and implementation of prevention and intervention services on three levels (including universal, selective, and indicated), and procedures to evaluate program effectiveness. The idea of adding another level of necessary collaboration with community mental health workers to guide and support the delivery of additional mental health services would require a paradigm shift and system change within the schools of this nation.

Addressing the mental health needs of children and youth within the school cannot remain an add-on responsibility that continues to be marginalized—desirable, but not primary to the role of the school. Doing so ensures the continued proliferation of health and psychological programming with little or no concern for planning and coordination. Moreover, when viewed as nothing more than a desirable support service, mental health services can be easily abandoned by school administrators strapped for financial resources. Schools must work to develop comprehensive, multifaceted approaches designed to ensure that schools represent caring and supportive settings that can foster the learning and well-being of the students, families, and neighborhoods they serve.

Generally schools do not fail their communities unless the community fails the school. That is, schools cannot take responsibility for supporting the academic, social, and emotional development of the nation's youth alone. Without overt community support, schools will be unable to meet the expanding demands of public education. They need the financial support and the active participation of members of their surrounding community. Tax caps and failed referendums result in schools that are less and less capable of meeting their academic mandates, much less able to mount new initiatives to address the mental health needs of the students (Owings & Kaplan, 2004; Parrish & Wolman, 2004; Weist et al., 2007). New models of resource allocation and shared fiscal responsibility between schools and community agencies for youth services are sorely needed.

Educators often lack the knowledge and clinical experience necessary to take responsibility for the implementation of many CBIs designed to address significant emotional and mental health disorders. The goal of SMHs would not involve community mental health agencies abandoning children's mental health services to school personnel. Rather, the aim is to develop effective collaborative systems of care delivered within the school setting. Clinical personnel would serve to direct prevention and intervention plans, while educators and other school per sonnel would play a greater role in the delivery and monitoring of services within their day-to-day interactions with the students. Nevertheless, systematic efforts to increase the use of CBIs and the development of SMH programs will require increased efforts to educate teachers, administrators, school staff, students, and families about children's mental health issues and their impact on education. The success of any initiative focused on improved mental health services within the school will depend on the wide involvement and continued education of all school personnel.

There is increasing support for the implementation of CBIs by educators and paraeducators; a number of studies have reported positive outcomes when these strategies are applied by nonclinical personnel. For example, teachers have been shown to be effective in the instruction of a number CBIs designed to address aggression (Larson & Lochman, 2005), depression (Mufson, Dorta, Olfson, Weissman, & Hoagwood, 2004), anxiety (McLoone et al., 2006), trauma (Saltzman, Pynoos, Layne, Steinberg, & Aisenberg, 2001), and antisocial behavior (Guerra et al., 1998). In fact, Durlak (1982) reported the effective delivery of instruction and prompted use of CBI strategies by paraprofessionals within the school. Nevertheless, we strongly urge that educators seeking to employ CBIs seek the appropriate instruction, support, and monitoring needed to ensure the ethical and effective use of these intervention strategies.

Issues of "turf," licensing, credentialing, and certification will undoubtedly surface and require careful negotiation. Collaboration and coordination between school personnel and community mental health providers is critical. The roles of all onsite providers, including school health professionals, must be clear and agreed upon by all involved.

Communication and confidentiality issues must be directly addressed. Concerns related to student and family privacy must be addressed in a manner that ensures their rights while supporting transdisciplinary involvement in student care. Systems to meet the bureaucratic requirements involved in providing student mental health services (e.g., third-party payment requirements), resource coordination, and data collection and record keeping systems must be developed and coordinated in a manner that displays an acceptable level of "goodness of fit" with the school and the community agencies involved. How then should educators proceed to overcome the barriers identified and develop a comprehensive school-based system of care to promote the academic and emotional development of all children and youth?

The Future Promise of SMH Programs and CBIs

As mentioned above, currently most schools are engaged in a variety of activities in an effort to address the academic and emotional needs of their students (see Figure 4.2). The proliferation of service delivery pro-

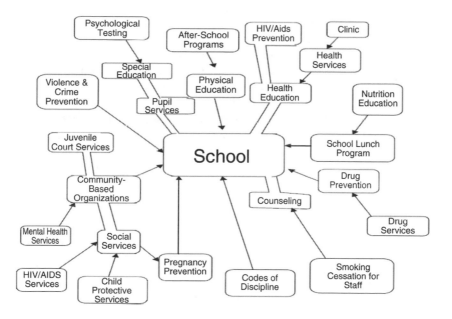

FIGURE 4.2. Fragmented services available in many schools. Adapted from Marx and Wooley with Northrop (1998). Copyright 1998 by Teachers College Press. Adapted by permission.

grams within the school tends to occur with little planning and/or coordination. Yet taken together, these activities appear to represent considerable effort and the expenditure of substantial resources. However, the resulting system of care is highly fragmented, often displaying significant gaps in service and considerable overlap of effort and services (Center for Mental Health in Schools, 2005). Obviously there is a need to actively address the current state of affairs. There are precious few resources available within the school setting. There is little hope of implementing new initiatives without first removing some current programs, projects, or initiatives. Schools must explore current efforts and make every effort to shift, adapt, or abandon piecemeal efforts and fragmented services toward efforts to develop a unified and cohesive approach to enhance the coordination and delivery of services.

Despite the numerous challenges confronting the process of developing effective and efficient SMH programs, a number of model programs have been identified (see Weist & Paternite, 2006). The Center for Mental Health in Schools (2002) at the University of California–Los Angeles has proposed a framework to assist schools in the development of school-based and school-linked programs. They propose a systemic restructuring of all student support programming and the development of a unified three-prong approach that combines a learning component, a governance and resource management component, and what they term an *enabling or learning supports component* to address the needs of the entire child within the school (see Figure 4.3).

There appear to be four trends in the delivery of SMH programs (Center for Mental Health in Schools, 2002). These involve a move away from (1) narrowly focused interventions to comprehensive approaches; (2) fragmentation to coordinated/integrated interventions; (3) problem-specific and discipline-oriented services to less categorical, transdisciplinary services; and (4) a view of health and mental health services as supplementary services to policy that recognizes the central and essential role services play in learning and development.

A number of states (e.g., Hawaii, Maryland, New York, New Mexico, Ohio, and South Carolina) and various major cities (e.g., Baltimore, Dallas, Los Angeles, and Memphis) have embraced the development of SMH programs. To further these efforts, proponents for SMHs (e.g., Center for Mental Health in Schools, Center for School-based Mental Health, Ohio Mental Health Network for School Success) have made a number of sweeping recommendations. They call for the following:

- The creation of a joint health and education agency at the federal level (e.g., the Office of School Health/Mental Health) that would

Needed: Revised Policy to Establish an Umbrella for School Improvement Planning Related to Addressing Barriers to Learning and Promoting Healthy Development

Direct Facilitation of Learning
(Instructional Component)

Addressing Barriers to Learning & Teaching
(Enabling or Learning Supports Component—an umbrella for ending marginalization by unifying the many fragmented efforts and evolving a comprehensive approach)

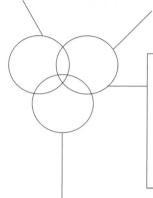

Examples of initiatives, programs, and services

- positive behavioral supports
- full service community schools & Family Resource Centers
- Safe Schools/Healthy Students
- School-Based Health Center movement
- Coordinated School Health Program
- bilingual, cultural, and other diversity programs
- compensatory education programs
- special education programs
- mandates stemming from the No Child Left Behind Act
- many more activities by student support staff

Governance and Resource Management
(Management Component)

FIGURE 4.3. Unified three-prong approach for restructuring student support services in the school context. From Center for Mental Health in Schools. (2002). Copyright 2002 by School Mental Health Project, University of California, Los Angeles. Reprinted by permission.

pool funds from multiple agencies and distribute these monies to school–community collaboratives.

- The development of state-level infrastructure for mental health service system delivery between mental health and education systems.
- The creation of closer partnerships between the schools and community mental health agencies and a greater focus on services for adolescents making a transition into adulthood.
- The expansion of incentives to increase the numbers of child-trained mental health providers and the requirement of a school-based component to their preservice education.
- The funding of SMH demonstration sites and dissemination of the most effective models.
- An improvement in the quality of services through increased attention to the recruitment, retention, and education of staff.
- A greater use of evidence-based practices, the expansion of provider networks, and the establishment of professional standards.
- Greater public education efforts to reduce stigma and increase support for children's mental health.

Current efforts to develop SMH programs rely on funding from a number of rather limited local, state, and federal programs (e.g., state and local grants and contracts; federal and foundation grants and contracts; Medicaid fee-for-service; Medicaid managed care; Medicaid in the Schools; and/or allocations from schools, special education services, and departments of education). However, there is a need for a greater level of federal and state support. The President's New Freedom Commission on Mental Health (2003) called for the creation of specific funding for SMH services in school-based health centers and as a part of federally funded mental health and education programs.

The development of a comprehensive system of care recognizing that physical and mental health services play an essential element in enabling learning will require a significant paradigm shift within schools and communities. These types of programs will not result from simply asking more of existing school personnel. Greenberg (2004) identified a number of characteristics found in effective SMH programs. These include (1) delivering comprehensive, evidence-based interventions while remaining flexible and responsive to the needs of the youth being served; (2) viewing children in the context of broader ecologies—families, schools, neighborhoods, churches, and communities; (3) linking with other systems of support and intervention to ensure they can produce and sustain their impacts over time; (4) involving people with a commitment and intensity to their work and a clear sense of mission; and (5) basing services upon quality staff with effective models of training and ongoing technical assistance.

Effective SMH programs result in a number of desirable outcomes: diverse stakeholder satisfaction (Nabors, Reynolds, & Weist, 2000); improved student emotional and behavioral functioning (Armbruster & Lichtman, 1999; Nabors & Reynolds, 2000); and improved student outcomes such as reduced levels of bullying (Zins, Weissberg, Wang, & Walberg, 2004), reductions in school suspensions (Sugai et al., 2000), and reduced referrals to special education (Bruns et al., 2004). They are also associated with improved school climate, a reduction in school dropouts (Schargel & Smink, 2001), and a significant reduction in school violence and aggression (U.S. Department of Health and Human Services, 2001).

A Bottom-Line View

There exists in this nation a serious need to better meet the emotional and mental health concerns of children and youth. A significant number of children and youth display emotional or mental health disorders, yet the majority of these children go untreated. There is little disagreement that these emotional disorders impact the academic and social functioning of these children. There is sufficient evidence to suggest that a variety of prevention and intervention strategies exist that could effectively address these needs. Some of the more promising approaches call for the implementation of cognitive-behavioral strategies within the school setting. Although educators have considerable expertise in the delivery of CBIs designed to enhance academic learning, there is reluctance on the part of educators to employ these strategies to address the emotional and mental health needs of children. Indeed, there exist a number of serious barriers to the school becoming the setting of choice for the delivery of children's mental health services, despite a number of very compelling reasons that this should indeed be the location of choice.

The education system is at a crossroads. Educators are beyond weary as they face the added demands of recent legislation calling for greater academic accountability. Educators are angry—they cannot be all things to the children and communities they serve. There is no "free energy" available to tap into efforts to promote the delivery of needed mental health services within schools. In order to develop SMH programs and to support teachers in their efforts to employ effective CBIs to address the emotional needs of their students, we must promote a significant paradigm shift within the educational setting. This will call for a serious shift in attitudes toward the role of the school and community agencies in the delivery of children's mental health services. We will need to adopt a public health perspective related to children's mental health similar to that held for immunizations. All children will need to be screened for emotional and mental health concerns early and on a regular basis. Financial resources and personnel, equal to that provided for adult programs, must be made available for prevention and early identification. The federal government, state governments, and local communities will need to willingly share the fiscal responsibility for quality services. Personnel preparation in the fields of education, mental health, social services, and medicine must prioritize children's services. Additional funds will be required to conduct the necessary research related to prevention and intervention services within the school setting and the identification of mediators and moderators of treatment effects.

The need exists. The potential solutions have been identified, and the route has been mapped. What is needed is commitment on the part of all involved to make the necessary effort to move to a better tomorrow, one in which the academic, social, and emotional needs of all children are addressed with effective prevention and intervention efforts.

References

Argulewicz, E. N. (1982). Application of a cognitive-behavioral intervention for improving classroom attention. *School Psychology Review, 11*(1), 90–95.

Armbruster, P., & Lichtman, J. (1999). Are school-based mental health services effective? *Community Mental Health Journal, 35*, 493–504.

Armstrong, K. H., Dedrick, R. F., & Greenbaum, P. E. (2003). Factors associated with community adjustment of young adults with serious emotional disturbance: A longitudinal analysis. *Journal of Emotional and Behavioral Disorders, 11*(2), 66–76.

Barth, J. M., Dunlap, S. T., Dane, H., Lochman, J. E., & Wells, K. C. (2004). Classroom environment influences on aggression, peer relations, and academic focus. *Journal of School Psychology, 42*, 115–133.

Bauminger, N. (2002). The facilitation of social-emotional understanding and social interaction in high-functioning children with autism: Intervention outcomes. *Journal of Autism and Developmental Disorders, 32*(4), 283–298.

Bruns, E. J., Walrath, C., Glass-Siegel, M., & Weist, M. D. (2004). School-based mental health services in Baltimore: Association with school climate and special education referrals. *Behavior Modification, 28*(4), 491–512.

Butler, L., Miezitis, S., Friedman, R., & Cole, E. (1980). The effects of two school-based intervention programs on depressive symptoms in preadolescents. *American Educational Research Journal, 17*, 111–119.

Center for Mental Health in Schools. (2002). *About mental health in schools: An introductory packet.* Los Angeles: UCLA Department of Psychology. Available at *smhp.psych. ucla.edu.*

Center for Mental Health in Schools. (2005). *Another initiative? Where does it fit? A unifying framework and an integrated infrastructure for schools to address barriers in learning and promote healthy development.* Available at *smhp.psych. ucla.edu.*

Cho, H., Hallfors, D. D., Dion, D., & Sanchez, V. (2005). Evaluation of a high school peer group intervention for at-risk youth. *Journal of Abnormal Child Psychology, 33*(3), 363–374.

Coleman, M. R. (2000). *Bright futures for exceptional learners: Technical report. Conditions for special education teaching: CEC Commission technical report.* Chapel Hill, NC: University of North Carolina, Frank Porter Graham Center.

Conoley, J. C. (1989). Cognitive-behavioral approaches and prevention in the schools. In J. N. Hughes & R. J. Hall (Eds.), *Handbook of cognitive-behavioral approaches in educational settings* (pp. 535–568). New York: Guilford Press.

Deshler, D. D., & Shumaker, J. B. (1986). Learning strategies: An instructional alternative for low-achieving adolescents. *Exceptional Children, 52*(6), 583–590.

Dishion, T. J., McCord, J., & Poulin, F. (1999). When interventions harm: Peer groups and problem behavior. *American Psychologist, 54*, 755–764.

Dodge, K. (1993). The future research on conduct disorder. *Development and Psychopathology, 5*, 311–320.

Duchnowski, A. J. (1994). Innovative service models: Education. *Journal of Clinical Child Psychology, 23*, 13–18.

Durlak, J. A. (1982). Use of cognitive-behavioral interventions by paraprofessionals in schools. *School Psychology Review, 11*, 64–66.

D'Zurilla, T. J., & Goldfried, M. R. (1971). Problem solving and behavior modification. *Journal of Abnormal Psychology, 78*, 107–126.

Eggert, L. L., Thompson, E. A., Herting, J. R., Nicholas, L. J., & Dicker, B. G. (1994). Preventing adolescent drug abuse and high school drop-out through an intensive school-based social network development program. *American Journal of Health Promotion, 8,* 202–215.

Etscheidt, S. (1991). Reducing aggressive behavior and improving self-control: A cognitive-behavioral training program for behaviorally disordered adolescents. *Behavioral Disorders, 16*(2), 107–115.

Evans, S. W. (1999). Mental health services in the schools: Utilization, effectiveness and consent. *Clinical Psychological Review, 19,* 165–178.

Fiore, T. A. (1992). *Research synthesis on educational interventions for students with attention deficit disorder: Education of children with attention deficit disorder.* Research Triangle Park, NC: Research Triangle Institute.

Flaherty, L. T., & Osher, D. (2003). History of school-based mental health services. In M. D. Weist, S. W. Evans, & N. A. Lever (Eds.), *Handbook of school mental health: Advancing practice and research* (pp. 11–22). New York: Kluwer Academic/Plenum.

Foster, S., Rollefson, M., Doksum, T., Noonan, D., & Robinson, G. (2005). *School mental health services in the United States, 2002–2003.* Rockville, MD: Center for Mental Health Services, Substance Abuse and Mental Health Services Administration.

Furlong, M. J., Morrison, G. M., & Jimerson, S. R. (2004). Externalizing behaviors of aggression and violence and the school context. In R. B. Rutherford, M. M. Quinn, & S. R. Mathur (Eds.), *Handbook of research in emotional and behavioral disorders* (pp. 243–261). New York: Guilford Press.

Ghafoori, B. (2001). Effectiveness of cognitive-behavioral therapy in reducing classroom disruptive behaviors: A meta-analysis. *Dissertation Abstracts International, 61*(11), 6133B. (UMI No. 9994801)

Glenwick, D. S., & Jason, C. A. (1984). Locus of intervention in child cognitive behavior therapy: Implications of a behavioral community perspective. In A. W. Meyers & W. E. Craighead (Eds.), *Cognitive behavior therapy with children* (pp. 129–162). New York: Plenum.

Gottfredson, G. D., Gottfredson, D. C., Czeh, E. R., Cantor, D., Crosse, S. B., & Hantman, I. (2000). *National Survey of Delinquency Prevention in Schools: Final report.* Elliot City, MD: Gottfredson Associates.

Grant, S. H., & Van Acker, R. (2000). Do schools teach aggression? Recognizing and re-tooling the interactions that lead students to aggression. *Reaching Today's Youth, 5*(1), 27–32.

Greenberg, M. T. (2004). Current and future challenges in school-based prevention: The researcher perspective. *Prevention Science, 5*(1), 5–13.

Greenberg, M. T., Domitrovich, C. E., Graczyk, P. A., & Zins, J. E. (2005). *The study of implementation in school-based preventive interventions: Theory, research, and practice* (Vol. 3). Rockville, MD: Center for Mental Health Services, Substance Abuse and Mental Health Services Administration.

Gresham, F. M. (1985). Utility of cognitive-behavioral procedures for social skills training with children: A critical review. *Journal of Abnormal Child Psychology, 13,* 411–423.

Guarino, C., Santibanez, L., Daily, G., & Brewer, D. (2004). A review of the research literature on teacher recruitment and retention. *Rand Education Technical Report prepared for the Education Commission of the States,* 1–252.

Guerra, N. G., Eron, L. D., Huesmann, L. R., Tolan, P., & Van Acker, R. (1997). A cognitive-ecological approach to the prevention and mitigation of violence and aggression in inner-city youth. In D. P. Fry & K. Bjorkqvist (Eds.), *Cultural variation in conflict resolution: Alternatives to violence* (pp. 199–214). Mahwah, NJ: Erlbaum.

Guerra, N. G., Eron, L. D., Huesmann, L. R., Tolan, P., & Van Acker, R. (1998). A cognitive/ecological approach to the prevention and mitigation of violence and aggression in inner-city youth. In K. Bjorkguist & D. P. Fry (Eds.), *Styles of conflict resolution: Models and applications from around the world.* New York: Academic Press.

Guerra, N. G., Huesmann, L. R., Tolan, P. H., Van Acker, R., & Eron, L. D. (1995). Stressful events and individual beliefs as correlates of economic disadvantage and aggression among urban children. *Journal of Consulting and Clinical Psychology, 63*, 518–528.

Guerra, N. G., & Jagers, R. (1999). Ethnic sensitivity in research. In V. McLoyd & L. Steinberg (Eds.), *Methodological issues in the study of minority adolescents and their families* (pp. 167–182). Hillsdale, NJ: Erlbaum.

Gunter, P. L., Denny, R. K., Jack, S. L., Shores, R. E., & Nelson, C. M. (1993). Aversive stimuli in academic interactions between students with serious emotional disturbance and their teachers. *Behavioral Disorders, 18*, 265–274.

Hains, A. A., & Haines, A. H. (1988). Cognitive-behavioral training of problem-solving and impulse-control with delinquent adolescents. *Journal of Offender Counseling, Services, and Rehabilitation, 12*(2), 95–113.

Hallahan, D. P., Hall, R. J., Ianna, S. O., Kneedler, R. D., Lloyd, J. W., Loper, A. B., et al. (1983). Summary of research findings at the University of Virginia Learning Disabilities Research Institute. *Exceptional Education Quarterly, 4*(1), 95–114.

Harris, K. R. (1982). Cognitive behavior modification: Application with exceptional children. *Focus on Exceptional Children, 15*(2), 1–16.

Harris, K. R. (1985). Cognitive behavior modification: Application with exceptional children. *Focus on Exceptional Children, 15*(2), 1–16.

Harris, K. R., & Graham, S. (1985). Improving learning disabled students' composition skills: Self-control strategy training. *Learning Disability Quarterly, 8*, 27–36.

Harry, B., & Klingner, J. (2006). *Why are so many minority students in special education?* New York: Teachers College Press.

Hoagwood, K., Burns, B. J., Kiser, L., Ringeisen, H., & Schoenwald, S. K. (2001). Evidence-based practice in child and adolescent mental health services. *Psychiatric Services, 52*, 1179–1189.

Hoagwood, K., & Johnson, J. (2003). School psychology: A public health framework: From evidence-based practices to evidence-based policies. *Journal of School Psychology, 41*, 3–21.

Hughes, J. N. (1988). *Cognitive behavior therapy with children in schools.* New York: Pergamon Press.

Kazdin, A. E., & Weisz, J. R. (1998). Identifying and developing empirically supported child and adolescent treatments. *Journal of Consulting and Clinical Psychology, 66*, 19–36.

Kendall, P. C. (2000). *Child and adolescent therapy: Cognitive-behavioral procedures* (2nd ed.). New York: Guilford Press.

Kendall, P. C. (Ed.). (2006). *Child and adolescent therapy: Cognitive-behavioral procedures* (3rd ed.). New York: Guilford Press.

Kendall, P. C., & Braswell, L. (1982). Cognitive-behavioral self-control therapy for children: A components analysis. *Journal of Consulting and Clinical Psychology, 50*, 672–689.

Kymes, A. (2005). *Teaching online comprehension strategies using think-alouds.* Newark, DE: International Reading Association.

Lambert, N. M., & Bower, E. M. (1967). *The protection and promotion of mental health in the schools.* Washington, DC: U.S. Government Printing Office.

Larson, J., & Lochman, J. E. (2005). *Helping school children cope with anger: A cognitive-behavioral intervention.* New York: Guilford Press.

Leone, P. E., & Mayer, M. J. (2004). Safety, diversity, and disability: "Goodness of fit" and the complexities of the school environment. In M. J. Furlong, M. P. Bates, & P. Kingery (Eds.), *Best practices in school-based threat assessment* (pp. 135–163). Hauppauge, NY: Nova Science.

Lochman, J. E. (2000). Theory and empiricism in intervention research: A dialectic to be avoided. *Journal of School Psychology, 38,* 359–368.

Lochman, J. E., Curry, J. F., Dane, H., & Ellis, M. (2001). The Anger Coping Program: An empirically-supported treatment for aggressive children. *Residential Treatment for Children and Youth, 18,* 63–73.

Lochman, J. E., Nelson, W. M., & Sims, J. P. (1981). A cognitive behavioral program for use with aggressive children. *Journal of Clinical Child Psychology, 13,* 146–148.

Lochman, J. E., Powell, N. R., Whidby, J. M., & FitzGerald, D. P. (2006). Cognitive-behavioral assessment and treatment with aggressive children. In P. C. Kendall (Ed.), *Child and adolescent therapy: Cognitive-behavioral procedures* (3rd ed., pp. 33–81). New York: Guilford Press.

Marx, E., & Wooley, S. F., with Northrop, D. (Eds.). (1998). *Health is academic: A guide to coordinated school health programs.* New York: Teachers College Press.

McLoone, J., Hudson, J. L., & Rapee, R. M. (2006). Treating anxiety disorders in a school setting. *Education and Treatment of Children, 29*(2), 219–242.

Meichenbaum, D. (1980). Cognitive behavioral modification with exceptional children: A promise yet unfulfilled. *Exceptional Education Quarterly, 1*(1), 83–88.

Meichenbaum, D., & Asarnow, J. (1979). Cognitive-behavioral modification and metacognitive development: Implications for the classroom. In P. C. Kendall & S. D. Hollon (Eds.), *Cognitive-behavioral interventions* (pp. 11–35). New York: Academic Press.

Merrell, K. W., & Walker, H. M. (2004). Deconstructing a definition: Social maladjustment versus emotional disturbance and moving the EBD field forward. *Psychology in the Schools, 41*(8), 899–910.

Meyers, A. W., Cohen, R., & Schleser, R. (1989). A cognitive behavioral approach to education: Adopting a broad-based perspective. In J. N. Hughes & R. J. Hall (Eds.), *Handbook of cognitive-behavioral approaches in educational settings* (pp. 62–84). New York: Guilford Press.

Moos, R. H. (2005). Iatrogenic effects of psychosocial interventions for substance use disorders: Prevalence, predictors, and prevention. *Addiction, 100*(5), 595–604.

Mufson, L. H., Dorta, K. P., Olfson, M., Weissman, M. M., & Hoagwood, K. (2004). Effectiveness research: Transporting interpersonal psychotherapy for depressed adolescents (IPT-A) from the lab to school-based health clinics. *Clinical Child & Family Psychology Review, 7,* 251–261.

Nabors, L. A., & Reynolds, M. W. (2000). Program evaluation activities: Outcomes related to treatment for adolescents receiving school-based mental health services. *Children's Services: Social Policy, Research, and Practice, 3,* 175–189.

Nabors, L. A., Reynolds, M. W., & Weist, M. D. (2000). Qualitative evaluation of a high school mental health program. *Journal of Youth and Adolescence, 29,* 1–14.

Nelson, J. R., & Roberts, M. L. (2000). Ongoing reciprocal teacher-student interactions involving disruptive behaviors in general education classrooms. *Journal of Emotional and Behavioral Disorders, 8*(1), 27–37.

No Child Left Behind Act of 2001, Public Law 107-110, 115 Stat. 1425 (2002).

Odden, A., & Archibald, S. (2000). *A case study of resource reallocation to reduce class size, enhance teacher planning time, and strengthen literacy: Clayton Elementary School.* Madison: Wisconsin Center for Education Research.

Ollendick, T. H., & King, N. J. (2004). Empirically supported treatments for children and adolescence: Advances toward evidence-based practice. In P. M. Barrett & T. H. Ollendick (Eds.), *Handbook of interventions that work with children and adolescents: Prevention and treatment* (pp. 3–25). New York: Wiley.

Owings, W. A., & Kaplan, L. S. (2004). *School finance as investment in human capital.* Thousand Oaks, CA: Sage.

Parrish, T. B., & Wolman, J. (2004). *How is special education funded?: Issues and implications for school administrators.* Thousand Oaks, CA: Sage.

Pearl, R. (1985). Cognitive-behavioral interventions for increasing motivation. *Journal of Abnormal Child Psychology, 13,* 443–454.

Peterson, R. L., & Skiba, R. (2000). Creating school climates that prevent school violence. *Preventing School Failure, 44*(3), 122–129.

President's New Freedom Commission on Mental Health. (2003). *Achieving the promise: Transforming mental health care in America. Final report* (DHHS Publication No. SMA-03-3832). Rockville, MD: U.S. Department of Health and Human Services.

Reinke, W. M., & Walker, H. M. (2006). Deviant peer effects in education. In K. A. Dodge, T. J. Dishion, & J. E. Lansford (Eds.), *Deviant peer influences in programs for youth* (pp. 122–140). New York: Guilford Press.

Robinson, T. R., Smith, S. W., & Miller, M. D. (2002). Effect of a cognitive-behavioral intervention on responses to anger by middle school students with chronic behavior problems. *Behavioral Disorders, 27*(3), 256–271.

Rones, M., & Hoagwood, K. (2000). School-based mental health services: A research review. *Clinical Child and Family Psychological Review, 3*(4), 223–241.

Ruddell, R. B., & Unrau, N. J. (2004). *Theoretical models and processes of reading* (5th ed.). Newark, DE: International Reading Association.

Saltzman, W. R., Pynoos, R. S., Layne, C. M., Steinberg, A. M., & Aisenberg, E. (2001). Trauma- and grief-focused intervention for adolescents exposed to community violence: Results of a school-based screening and group treatment protocol. *Group Dynamics: Theory, Research, and Practice, 5,* 291–303.

Schargel, F. P., & Smink, J. (2001). *Strategies to help solve our drop-out problem.* Larchmont, NY: Eye on Education.

Scheier, L. M., & Botvin, G. J. (1996). Purpose in life: Cognitive efficacy, and general deviance as determinants of drug abuse in urban black youth. *Journal of Child and Adolescent Substance Abuse, 5*(1), 1–26.

Schumaker, J. B., Deshler, D. D., Alley, G. R., Warner, M. M., & Denton, P. H. (1982). Multipass: A learning strategy for improving reading comprehension. *Learning Disability Quarterly, 5*(3), 295–304.

Shores, R. E., & Wehby, J. H. (1999). Analyzing the classroom social behavior of students with EDB. *Journal of Emotional and Behavioral Disorders, 7*(4), 194–199.

Shure, M., & Spivack, G. (1979). Interpersonal cognitive problem-solving and primary prevention: Programming for preschool and kindergarten children. *Journal of Clinical Psychology, 8,* 89–94.

Skiba, R., & Peterson, R. L. (1999). The dark side of zero tolerance: Can punishment lead to safe schools? *Phi Delta Kappan, 80*(5), 381–382.

Snyder, T. D., Tan, A. G., & Hoffman, C. M. (2006). *Digest of education statistics 2005* (NCES 2006–030). Washington, DC: U.S. Government Printing Office.

Spence, S. H., Sheffield, J. K., & Donovan, C. L. (2005). Long-term outcome of a school-based, universal approach to prevention of depression in adolescents. *Journal of Consulting and Clinical Psychology, 73,* 160–167.

Stark, K. D., Best, L. R., & Sellstrom, E. A. (1989). A cognitive-behavioral approach to the treatment of childhood depression. In J. N. Hughes & R. J. Hall (Eds.), *Handbook of cognitive-behavioral approaches in educational settings* (pp. 389–433). New York: Guilford Press.

Sturm, R., Adreyeva, T., Pincus, H. A., & Tanielian, T. L. (2005). Datapoints: Use of mental health care among youths in 1997 and 2002. *Psychiatric Services, 56,* 793.

Sugai, G., Homer, R. H., Dunlap, G., Hieneman, M., Lewis, T., Nelson, C. M., et al. (2000). Applying positive behavior support and functional behavioral assessment in schools. *Journal of Positive Behavior Interventions, 3,* 131–143.

Tolan, P. H., & Guerra, N. (1994). *What works in reducing adolescent violence: An empirical review of the field.* Boulder, CO: Institute for Behavioral Science.

U.S. Department of Health and Human Services. (1999). *Mental health: A report of the Surgeon General—Executive summary.* Rockville, MD: U.S. Department of Health and Human Services, Substance Abuse and Mental Health Services Administration, Center for Mental Health Services, National Institutes of Health, National Institute of Mental Health.

U.S. Department of Health and Human Services. (2000). *Report of the Surgeon General's conference on children's mental health: A national action agenda.* Rockville, MD: U.S. Department of Health and Human Services, Substance Abuse and Mental Health Services Administration, Center for Mental Health Services, National Institutes of Health, National Institute of Mental Health.

U.S. Department of Health and Human Services. (2001). *Youth violence: A report of the Surgeon General.* Rockville, MD: U.S. Department of Health and Human Services, Substance Abuse and Mental Health Services Administration, Center for Mental Health Services, National Institutes of Health, National Institute of Mental Health.

U.S. Office of Special Education Programs. (2001). *Twenty-third annual report to Congress on the implementation of the Individuals with Disabilities Education Act: Results.* U.S. Department of Education, Office of Special Education Programs (OSEP).

Van Acker, R. (1993). Dealing with conflict and aggression in the classroom: What skills do teachers need? *Teacher Education and Special Education, 16*(1), 23–33.

Van Acker, R., Grant, S. H., & Henry, D. (1996). Teacher and student behavior as a function of risk for aggression. *Education and Treatment of Children, 19,* 316–334.

Vaughn, S., & Lancelotta, G. X. (1990). Teaching interpersonal skills to poorly accepted students: Peer-pairing versus non-peer-pairing. *Journal of School Psychology, 28*(3), 181–188.

Vaughn, S., Lancelotta, G. X., & Minnis, S. (1988). Social strategy training and peer involvement: Increasing peer acceptance of a female, LD student. *Learning Disabilities Focus, 4*(1), 32–37.

Wagner, M. (1995). Outcomes for youth with serious emotional disturbance in secondary school and early adulthood. *Future of Children: Critical Issues for Children and Youth, 5,* 90–112.

Weist, M. D., Myers, C. P., Hastings, E., Ghuman, H., & Han, Y. (1999). Psychosocial functioning of youth receiving mental health services in schools and mental health centers. *Community Mental Health Journal, 35*(5), 69–81.

Weist, M. D., & Paternite, C. E. (2006). Building an interconnected policy-training practice-research agenda to advance school mental health. *Education and Treatment of Children, 29*(2), 173–196.

Weist, M. D., Rubin, M., Moore, E., Adelsheim, S., & Wrobel, G. (2007). Mental health screening in schools. *Journal of School Health, 77*(2), 53–58.

Weisz, J. R., McCarthy, C. A., & Valeri, S. M. (2006). Effects of psychotherapy for depression in children and adolescents: A meta-analysis. *Psychological Bulletin, 132,* 132–149.

Weisz, J. R., Weiss, B., Han, S. S., Granger, D. A., & Morton, T. (1995). Effects of psychotherapy with children and adolescents revisited: A meta-analysis of treatment outcome studies. *Psychological Bulletin, 117,* 450–468.

Werch, C. E., & Owen, D. M. (2002). Iatrogenic effects of alcohol and drug prevention programs. *Journal of Studies on Alcohol, 63*(5), 581–590.

Winstead, L. (2004). Increasing academic motivation and cognition in reading, writing, and mathematics: Meaning-making strategies. *Educational Research Quarterly, 28*(2), 29–47.

Wood, J. (2006). Effect of anxiety reduction on children's school performance and social adjustment. *Developmental Psychology, 42,* 345–349.

World Health Organization. (2001). *The World Health Report 2001, mental health: New understanding, new hope.* Geneva, Switzerland: Author.

Zins, J. E., Weissberg, R. P., Wang, M. C., & Walberg, H. J. (2004). *Building academic success on social and emotional learning: What does the research say?* New York: Teachers College Press.

PART II

COGNITIVE-BEHAVIORAL INTERVENTIONS FOR ANGER/AGGRESSION

CHAPTER 5

Review of Research and
Research-to-Practice Issues

STEPHEN W. SMITH
JULIA A. GRABER
ANN P. DAUNIC

Children and youth in schools are challenged by normative expectations for well-behaved, socially appropriate behavior. Demands for appropriate behavior range from following simple adult directions and rules to more complex social behaviors, such as working cooperatively in groups and successfully negotiating conflicts with peers and adults. For most school professionals, sporadic incidents of inappropriate, maladaptive, and sometimes unpleasant behavior during teacher-controlled instruction and in peer-controlled free play are viewed as normal, and even expected, for many children and adolescents. With effective instruction, strategic guidance, and the appropriate amount of empathy from teachers, administrators, and other caregivers, children and youth can maneuver through the often subtle and complex behavioral landscape to emerge as socially competent individuals who succeed in life.

For children and youth who display significant and chronic behavioral problems, however, difficulties adhering to the demands of the school day often engender harsh rebukes from school professionals who rely on a variety of punitive actions to decrease the occurrence of these problems (Kauffman, 2005). Such a pattern of persistent maladaptive student behavior and punitive reactions from adults can result in an escalating spiral of negativity, hostility, and social conflict at school and in the family (Patterson & Capaldi, 1991). Moreover, recurring undesirable social interactions can contribute to unproductive peer group relationships, limiting opportunities to garner social acceptance (Bierman, 2004). Generally, children and youth who lack the requisite skill repertoire to control their behavior and respond appropriately to school demands are most at risk for school failure (Kauffman, 2005) and a lifetime of difficulties, including delinquency, substance abuse, depression, low self-esteem, antisocial behavior, general adult adjustment problems, unemployment, and possible institutionalization (Walker, Colvin, & Ramsey, 1995; Wolf, Braukmann, & Ramp, 1987). Clearly, school personnel need empirically validated strategies that are compatible with the school environment and demonstrate effectiveness in ameliorating harmful behavior patterns, increasing prosocial skills, and altering the trajectory of students at risk of school failure and peer rejection.

Fortunately, schools are a natural point of entry for intervention and remediation, as evidenced by the myriad academic programs necessary to serve increasingly diverse school populations. Interestingly, schools provide 70–80% of the mental health services received by children (Burns et al., 1995). However, providing specialized services, such as special education and alternative education programs to remediate significant behavioral problems, can be expensive in both time and effort because of the need for specialized staff training, continuous monitoring of treatment protocols, and ongoing evaluation. Despite these barriers, students who exhibit significant behavioral problems may be better served in school settings because of the increasing number of promising school-based programs for preventing and reducing anger, aggression, and associated destructive behaviors.

In this chapter, we (1) provide a context for using school-based programs in the form of promising cognitive-behavioral interventions (CBIs) to address anger and aggression in school settings, (2) describe anger and aggression through a unifying theoretical framework, (3) review research studies on four selected school-based CBIs designed to prevent or reduce anger and aggression (i.e., PATHS, Tools for Getting Along, Second Step, Coping Power), and (4) discuss the research-to-practice issues relevant to successfully implementing CBIs in schools.

CBIs for Students with Emotional and Behavioral Disorders (EBD)

For some students, long-term and significant negative behavior patterns in school provide the impetus for their referral and subsequent placement in programs for students with EBD. Prevalence studies consistently estimate that from 3–10% of the school-age population have EBD and require ongoing services (Kauffman, 2005; U.S. Department of Health and Human Services, 2000). Compared to typical peers, children with EBD exhibit maladaptive behavior patterns, including aggression, that are stable over time and highly predictive of detrimental outcomes into adolescence and adulthood (e.g., Lochman, Dunn, & Klimes-Dougan, 1993). Aggression, often preceded by anger, is one of the most common forms of childhood disorder (e.g., Averill, 1982). Aggressive behavior patterns approach a level of stability that, according to Loeber and Hay (1997), is comparable to that of IQ and highly correlated at all ages with negative peer status (Coie, Underwood, & Lochman, 1991).

Kauffman (2005) noted several disconcerting facts about the placement of students with EBD following referral: An increasing percentage of students with EBD are served in separate facilities, students with EBD constituted slightly more than half of the total population of students with disabilities placed in separate residential schools and approximately 48% of those in day schools, and 44% of those in residential schools carried a primary diagnosis of serious conduct/behavior disorders. What is clear from these statistics is that (1) children with EBD constitute a significant percentage of those isolated from the mainstream of education; and (2) despite the emphasis in education for increased general classroom placements, providing students with EBD opportunities to interact with their typical peers in regular education is difficult. Even though some behavior patterns such as aggression are highly resistant to intervention, it is the professional ethic of education communities to continue a search for effective school-based strategies that advance the treatment for students with high-risk profiles and those who exhibit EBD. CBIs offer one such approach.

The proponents of CBI believe that use of verbal self-statements can regulate and maintain adaptive behavior. Verbal self-regulation occurs when a person uses language as an internal control on thought processes that, in turn, regulate overt behavior. Verbal self-regulation is simply talking to oneself to guide problem solving or some other behavior (Mahoney, 1974; Mahoney & Kazdin, 1979; Meichenbaum, 1977). According to Smith and Daunic (2006a), most CBIs include some forms of modeling, role playing, feedback, and reinforcement, along with cognitive components such as think-alouds (i.e., cognitive modeling) and explicit teaching, to promote the understanding and use of self-talk to achieve self-control.

Deficient or maladaptive self-statements can contribute to behavior problems such as aggression and anger, and conversely, adaptive self-statements help foster self-control (Bandura, 1986). Research reviews and meta-analyses have revealed that CBIs can remediate aggression and disruption (e.g., Abikoff, 1991; Dush, Hirt, & Schroeder, 1989; Robinson, Smith, Miller, & Brownell, 1999), and subsequent studies (see Conduct Problems Prevention Research Group [CPPRG], 1999, 2002; Daunic, Smith, Brank, & Penfield, 2006; Lochman & Wells, 2004; Robinson, Smith, & Miller, 2002) have substantiated the value of teaching cognitive strategies to decrease disruption/aggression and strengthen prosocial behavior.

Several meta-analyses conducted over the past several years to explore the effects of CBI on the anger, aggression, antisocial behavior, and hyperactivity/impulsivity of children and youth have shown promising results. In 1999, Robinson et al. examined the outcomes of 23 school-based studies using CBI with nonpsychotic children (K–12). The mean effect size across all studies was 0.89, and 89% of the studies had participants who experienced greater gains on posttest and maintenance measures when exposed to treatment with a cognitive component. Beck and Fernandez (1998) found an overall CBI effect size of 0.70 across 50 anger treatment studies (1,640 subjects) of mostly clinical samples (e.g., prison inmates, abusive parents and spouses, college students with anger problems) that also included juvenile delinquents, adolescents in residential settings, and children with aggressive behavior in schools. More specific to school-age populations, Sukhodolsky, Kassinove, and Gorman (2004) found an overall mean effect size of 0.67 for CBI on anger-related problems in children across 21 published and 19 unpublished studies. Using a meta-analysis of participants 18 years old and younger who exhibited antisocial behavior (e.g., physical or verbal aggression, delinquency), McCart, Priester, Davies, and Azen (2006) found that behavioral parent training had a stronger effect for preschool and school-age youth, whereas CBI had a stronger effect for adolescents. Thus, there is current and consistent evidence that CBIs are effective for the treatment of chronic problematic behaviors such as anger, aggression, antisocial behavior, and hyperactivity/impulsivity in school-age populations.

Along with the consistent evidence for the effectiveness of CBIs for anger and aggression, CBIs are easily adaptable for whole-class regular education instruction (universal prevention); small-group pull-out instruction (selected or secondary intervention) taught by school counselors, school psychologists, or behavioral resource teachers; or more restrictive venues such as self-contained special education programs for students with EBD.

Aggression and Anger

There is little doubt that aggression in childhood and adolescence poses challenges for teachers and school administrators, as well as peers and parents. One of the first steps in understanding how to offset aggression is to consider what constitutes aggression. One of the most widely accepted definitions is that *aggression* comprises acts intended to cause harm to others (Dodge, Coie, & Lynam, 2006; Parke & Slaby, 1983). Such acts include physical (e.g., hitting) and verbal (e.g., yelling, name calling) aggression, as well as social aggression designed to injure someone's reputation with peers (e.g., exclusion from a group, gossip). In addition, a distinction has been made between *reactive aggression,* which occurs in response to the thwarting of one's goals or direct provocation, and *proactive or instrumental aggression,* which occurs without provocation as a means to achieve a desired goal (Dodge, 1991). Aggressive behaviors, in particular physical aggression, frequently co-occur with antisocial behaviors such as oppositional behavior in childhood and adolescence (e.g., noncompliance, irritability) and delinquent behaviors (e.g., theft, vandalism) that typically have higher rates during adolescence. Hence, examinations of aggression frequently focus on antisocial behavior and can also include more serious behavioral problems such as oppositional defiant disorder, conduct disorder, and EBD. To provide a developmental context for those children who compose the EBD population in schools, our discussion of aggression focuses predominantly on physical aggression and its developmental course over childhood and adolescence. We also emphasize cognitive-behavioral processes, with attention to emotion processes—specifically anger—and emotion regulation, as these targets of intervention are the focus of several programs with demonstrated effectiveness.

Anger plays a central role in many aggressive behaviors. Humans generally experience anger when they are frustrated or provoked or their goals are blocked. According to cognitive arousal theories (e.g., Nelson & Finch, 2000; Schacter & Singer, 1962), frustrating or provocative experiences produce autonomic arousal. During their early development, toddlers learn that this arousal is labeled *anger.* Notably, the highest rates of physical aggression are observed in preschoolers ages 2–3, with more than 70% engaging in hitting (Keenan & Shaw, 2003). This behavior declines dramatically during ages 4–5 (down to 20%), with progressive declines over the ensuing school years, such that only about 12% of third graders engage in physical aggression. The rapid extinction of hitting during the preschool years has been linked to several factors, including brain and cognitive development associated with acquisition of language skills (Dionne, Boivin, Tremblay, Laplante, & Perusse, 2003). Improved language skills afford different methods for asserting oneself and expressing or attaining goals. Moreover, the ability to regulate emotion, especially anger, becomes a primary developmental goal. Young children learn how to label and regulate their emotions via interactions with or direct instruction from parents or other adult caregivers (Cole, Teti, & Zahn-Waxler, 2003).

When regulated, anger may stimulate effective behaviors such as being able to assert oneself and develop autonomy (Chaplin & Cole, 2005). However, when caregivers engage in mutually angry interactions, children often fail to learn appropriate responses. Moreover, a pattern of coercive parenting may develop that leads to aggression problems in children (Patterson & Capaldi, 1991). As with language development, brain development during early childhood promotes better anger regulation. Finally, research suggests that peer input influences declines in physical aggression and inappropriate displays of anger during the preschool years, as a result of peers providing feedback on poor behavioral regulation. That is, other children, as well as adults, let the child know that physically aggressive behavior is not acceptable in social interactions (Dodge et al., 2006). Over time, many peers actively reject children who fail to regulate anger and aggression (Bierman, 2004; Rodkin, Farmer, Pearl, & Van Acker, 2000).

Although physical aggression typically declines during childhood, some children, albeit a minority, persist in exhibiting problematic aggressive behaviors throughout childhood and into adulthood. In fact, several cross-national and longitudinal studies have identified an "early-starter" or "life-course-persistent" group of children who are consistently aggressive during childhood and adolescence (Broidy et al., 2003) and as adults (e.g., Dodge et al., 2006; Moffitt, Caspi, Rutter, & Silva, 2001). Numerous recent studies have identified genetic, neurological, cognitive, parental, and peer factors that differentiate early starters from other children (e.g., Dodge et al., 2006; Moffitt, 1993). In particular, attention deficits and hyperactivity among early starters are highly comorbid with conduct problems (Campbell, 2000). The school years, then, are particularly important to intervention efforts that would improve outcomes for these children.

Early starters are not the only children, however, who engage in serious aggressive or antisocial problems during the school years. Additional children begin to engage in or escalate to more serious forms of aggressive or antisocial behavior in late childhood and early adolescence. Moffitt (1993) referred to these individuals as having "adolescent-limited" problems, in that they begin to join a deviant peer culture and exhibit aggressive or delinquent behaviors, but these behaviors desist as the youth enter adulthood. Whereas this conceptualization of pathways of antisocial behavior has a reasonable fit with data on crime during adolescence and young adulthood, as well as with longitudinal studies of aggression and delinquent behaviors (Moffitt et al., 2001), there has been considerable debate about the emergence and desistance of aggressive problems in adolescence. In particular, researchers such as Farrington (2004) and Pajer (1998) have argued that many adolescents who experience serious problems continue their antisocial behavior into adulthood. In addition, in a cross-study comparison, Broidy et al. (2003) reported that not all studies find a late-starter group. Finally, at least one longitudinal study identified a late-starter group that experienced serious problems during the transition to adulthood. The boys in this study had moderate antisocial behaviors in adolescence, including difficulties at school (e.g., Graber, Seeley, Brooks-Gunn, & Lewinsohn, 2004). As such, much less attention has been given to identifying unique developmental pathways for late starters, with the consequence that specific intervention initiatives for aggression in adolescence may not be appropriately matched to the needs of this group or groups of youth.

Person-in-Context Interactions in the Development of Aggression

Numerous explanations for the development of aggression have been proposed, ranging from functionalist or evolutionary theories that emphasize the adaptive value of aggression (e.g., Cairns & Cairns, 2000) to social-cognitive models (e.g., Bandura, 1977) that emphasize the importance of environmental influences—in particular, parents, peers and the media—in children's acquisition of aggressive behaviors. Several models for aggression, as well as intervention programs that target aggression such as we describe later in the chapter, draw upon Bronfenbrenner's (1979) ecological theory. The ecological model emphasizes the importance of context and person–context interactions (Bronfenbrenner, 1989). That is, not only do contexts influence individuals, but also individual characteristics influence and often form the contexts in which individuals interact. This is true in peer and school contexts, as well as within the family (Sameroff & Chandler, 1975).

One of the challenges for developmental scientists is to explain and integrate the factors associated with the development of aggressive behaviors. One critique of Bronfenbrenner's model is that it does not include "person" factors with the same specificity that describes person–context interactions. Hence, although the ecological model is a useful rubric, Lochman and colleagues (e.g., Lochman, Whidby, & FitzGerald, 2000) have proposed a contextual social-cognitive model that elaborates on social-cognitive processes and key contextual factors that are most salient to the development of aggression. Across studies of aggression, important person factors include (1) genetic factors; (2) neuropsychological factors like hyperactive, impulsive, and attention problems along with brain development and executive control functions (e.g., planning); (3) temperament or personality traits such as negative emotionality, low inhibitory control, fearlessness, and stimulation seeking; (4) cognitive processing and attribution bias as well as emotion processing and the interconnection with cognition; and (5) physiological functioning, including autonomic nervous system functioning and pubertal hormones (e.g., testosterone and adrenal androgens). Contextual factors include (1) parenting, including early attachment, warmth, coercive parenting practices, physical abuse, and, particularly in adolescence, parental monitoring of behavior; (2) poor peer relationships typified by peer rejection and/or socializing with peers who also engage in aggressive or antisocial behavior; (3) family context variables such as father absence, poverty, low parental education, or unemployment; (4) neighborhood context and community norms for violence and antisocial behaviors; and (5) broader societal influences such as state and federal regulations for schools and juvenile justice, and media depictions of behaviors and images that reward antisocial behaviors. From this list, it is clear that aggression develops via multiple person and contextual factors, many of which are associated. Delineating the influence of each of these factors on pathways of aggression at specific developmental periods is beyond the scope of this chapter (see Dodge et al., 2006, for a comprehensive review).

Contextual Social-Cognitive Models

Many of the prevention and intervention programs we highlight in the following section of this chapter target these person–context interactions and focus on influencing (1) children's cognitive and emotional processing and (2) teacher and parent behaviors that help regulate or prevent aggression. In particular, contextual social-cognitive models (e.g., Lochman et al., 2000) speak directly to identifying both intra- and interindividual targets for intervention while accounting for developmental periods. For example, programs may focus on person-level factors, such as anger management or self-control training, to help children learn individual regulation skills that offset high emotionality or low impulse control. Other programs may target person-in-context protective factors such as parenting practices that decrease use of coercion and increase consistency, warmth, and monitoring. Or programs may focus on groups of children at high risk for aggressive problems as identified by particular environmental conditions (e.g., underresourced schools in low-income communities) and thus use known risk factors to determine who will be targeted for intervention or prevention.

In addition, contextual social-cognitive models have proven useful for identifying mechanisms or developmental processes of aggression that are essential for deciding which behaviors or processes might be the best targets for prevention and intervention. The social information-processing model (Crick & Dodge, 1994) and the social-cognitive model (Lochman et al., 2000) specify cognitive processes and decision making that lead to aggressive behaviors. For example, in the social information-processing model, Crick and Dodge outline the series of steps taken in processing information and making decisions in social interactions. These steps include encoding cues, interpreting cues, identifying or clarifying one's goals in the situation (e.g., standing up for oneself or maintaining relationships), generating responses, deciding on a response, and, ultimately, enacting the response. Tests of the model have shown that children with aggression problems process social information differently at several of the steps. For example, aggressive children often have biased interpretation of cues with which they evaluate the cause or intent of others as aggressive or provoking (see Orobio de Castro, Veerman, Koops, Bosch, & Monshouwer, 2002, for a meta-analysis). In addition, such children and adolescents often generate fewer possible responses to social problems with fewer nonaggressive possibilities in their repertoires (Dodge, McClaskey, & Feldman, 1985; Guerra & Slaby, 1990).

Lemerise and Arsenio (2000) elaborated on the Crick and Dodge (1994) model to explain how emotion processes impact cognitive processing during decision making. In particular, they noted that many decisions in social situations happen very quickly and that emotional memories and cues may serve to prioritize information and alternatives, making some cues more salient to the situation than others (Damasio, 1994; Lemerise & Arsenio, 2000). For example, children with high impulsivity or emotionality may experience emotional arousal that makes escalating or retaliatory responses a high priority.

Such integrated models are useful for identifying targets of intervention and have been cornerstones of CBIs. Whereas these cognitive-emotional models focus on the development of children's competent versus maladaptive behavior, they apply equally well to cognitive processes at any particular stage of development. The CBI programs we discuss in this chapter specifically target emotion regulation (e.g., anger management and impulse control) along with social problem-solving and decision-making processes. As such, they effectively draw on contextual social-cognitive models to provide universal prevention with children (e.g., Second Step) and emerging adolescents (e.g., Tools for Getting Along, PATHS) as well as selected children at high risk (e.g., Coping Power).

The Role of Gender

We have discussed children and adolescents as a group in the description of pathways of aggressive problems. However, research has shown that boys are much more likely than girls to exhibit physical aggression and related problems (Zahn-Waxler, 1993). For example, in cross-national studies (e.g., Broidy et al., 2003), boys consistently exhibit higher rates of physical aggression than girls, and boys are much more likely to be identified as early starters and have serious aggression problems in childhood than are girls (Moffitt et al., 2001). There are some concerns about the attention given to the gender difference, especially the predominance of boys in the early starter group. First, many studies of aggression, as well as prevention and intervention programs targeting aggression, have included only boys (Nichols, Graber, Brooks-Gunn, & Botvin, 2006). Specific tests of gender differences in the effects of vulnerability, risk, and protective factors on the development of aggression have not been conducted extensively. In one of the few studies to test this issue, Moffitt and colleagues did not find substantial differences in the risk factors for antisocial problems between boys and girls, indicating that underlying developmental processes may be similar. Although more tests are needed, such findings indicate that CBI programs effectively address person factors (e.g., cognition and emotion processing) and contextual factors (e.g., parenting and teacher skills) for both boys and girls.

Second, youth who meet criteria for adolescent onset of conduct disorder are more likely to be girls. Although girls have less risk for antisocial problems during childhood (Lahey et al., 1998), new risks emerge with the transition into adolescence (Graber, Brooks-Gunn, & Archibald, 2005). It should be noted that Lahey and colleagues found that adolescent girls with conduct disorder had lower reports of physical aggression than individuals who had earlier onset of the disorder. Several investigators have suggested that individuals with adolescent- or later onset conduct disorder, especially girls, are less likely to have longer term consequences, such as adult criminal behavior. Researchers who have followed girls into adulthood who were delinquent or had conduct disorder as adolescents have, in fact, found evidence of continued serious difficulties, including increased mortality rates, higher rates of adult criminal activity, psychiatric difficulties including substance abuse and suicidal behavior, dysfunctional interpersonal relationships (e.g., marriage to abusive spouses), and higher rates of impaired parenting (e.g., children removed from mother's care) in comparison to the general population and, often, in comparison to psychiatric controls (Pajer, 1998). It is noteworthy that serious impairments in parenting are known risk factors for the development of aggression in children. Thus, long-term consequences of adolescent aggression problems may differ for boys and girls, but potential outcomes are still serious for both genders. Again, the need for programming that continues into adolescence and includes both girls and boys is apparent.

Third, there may be important contexts or subgroups of individuals in which gender differences are less pronounced. In a study of urban minority middle school students, both boys and girls increased in aggression from sixth to seventh grade, but girls increased more than boys, such that there was no gender difference by seventh grade (Nichols et al., 2006). Boys still had higher rates of delinquency in this study at both years in school. Notably, girls and boys reported similar rates of anger and self-control in sixth grade, but girls had greater increases in their reports of anger from sixth to seventh grade, resulting in girls having significantly higher reports of being angry. Unfortunately, regulation skills did not change over time. Both anger and regulation were associated with changes in aggression and delinquency in middle-school students. Overall, it seems that girls in metropolitan environments may have higher risks or fewer protective factors for aggression than girls in suburban or middle-class communities. Such possibilities merit greater attention and would have implications for the generalizability of prevention initiatives. In addition, gender differences in anger during adolescence may be experienced more broadly than what was measured in this study, but few researchers have examined this issue. CBI efforts for regulating anger may become more salient for girls during early adolescence. Hence, programs originally designed to target anger regulation in boys, such as Coping Power, have also proven useful with girls with aggressive problems (see subsequent discussion).

Finally, it has been asserted that other types of aggression (e.g., relational) may be more common among girls than boys (e.g., Crick & Bigbee, 1998; Underwood, 2003). To date, there is not a definitive answer as to whether there is a gender difference in relational or social aggression (see Dodge et al., 2006, for a review). Several studies of relational aggression included only girls, and in studies of both boys and girls, findings have been mixed. Regardless, it should be noted that children may engage in several types of aggression. Crick, Ostrov, and Werner

(2006) reported large correlations between relational and physical aggression in middle childhood (specifically, $r = .80$ for boys and $r = .64$ for girls). In addition, children who engaged in both types of aggression were more likely to have future aggressive and delinquent problems in the next year. In conclusion, we believe that greater inclusion of girls in studies of aggression and examination of gender-specific prevention and intervention program effects are warranted.

Based on the extensive literature on the development of aggression, CBI approaches are well suited for school-based prevention and intervention programming that can target at least a part of the developmental process. In particular, theoretical models of social-cognitive processing (e.g., Lemerise & Arsenio, 2000; Lochman et al., 2000) provide specific emotion and cognitive targets of intervention in terms of regulation skills, decision making, and related processes. At the same time, developmental studies point to the need to expand attention beyond one pattern of aggressive behavior, the early starters, and consider how prevention efforts could offset the development of other pathways of aggression, especially for girls and adolescents.

Research on School-Based CBIs

Not all interventions to reduce anger and aggression can be considered CBIs. Whereas some CBIs focus exclusively on teaching the use of internal dialogue (e.g., the steps of social problem solving), such as I Can Problem Solve (Shure, 2001) and Tools for Getting Along (TFGA; see Smith, Lochman, & Daunic, 2005), there are those that are integrated within comprehensive interventions or programs. Programs such as Fast Track, a comprehensive, multi-site prevention intervention (see CPPRG, 2004); Coping Power, which includes a child and parent component (Lochman & Wells, 2002a); The Incredible Years, a multicomponent behavior program (Webster-Stratton, 2001; see Nelson & Schultz, Chapter 6, this volume, for a description of these interventions); and Linking the Interests of Families and Teachers, a school-based prevention program with a parent and teacher component (Reid, Eddy, Fetrow, & Stoolmiller, 1999) all contain multiple types of training. These programs include components reflecting a cognitive approach (e.g., social competence, emotional literacy, problem solving, stress reduction, coping skills, anger management, goal setting) and multiple treatment modalities (e.g., family intervention, academic tutoring, classroom supports, systematic parent/teacher communication). As such, when investigating the effects of CBIs on behavior, it is necessary to focus on interventions that use a cognitive framework for the salient components of instruction.

Thus, in this section, we have chosen to concentrate on four empirically based interventions that have a major cognitive training component focused on the use of self-talk to help children and youth regulate their own behavior. Each incorporates CBI components that comprise appropriate universal or selected prevention/intervention for children who have problems managing anger and aggression and indicated interventions for students with EBD in special education settings. From our perspective, these four curricula/programs are representative of the diverse types of CBIs available and demonstrate the applicability of the approach across grade levels, especially during the elementary years. Moreover, these programs draw upon developmental models of aggression and target multiple risk factors that include individual child and context (e.g., peer and parent) components.

Promoting Alternative THinking Strategies (PATHS; see CPPRG, 1999), is a universally applied curriculum that can be systematically taught throughout the K–6 school years. TFGA, a universal CBI curriculum focused on social problem solving, has a more specific focus on upper elementary students. Second Step (Committee for Children, 1997) is a universal prevention program for the elementary and middle grades designed to reduce aggressive behavior and increase social competence. Finally, Coping Power, which targets upper elementary school boys, is a multicomponent intervention that includes small-group and individual student instruction, parent group sessions, and periodic home visits to promote generalization of learned skills.

PATHS

As the universal component of the Fast Track prevention study (see CPPRG, 1992), PATHS was designed as a prevention curriculum for use in the regular education classroom. The program is to be implemented in conjunction with the existing school curriculum. Designed to teach individual problem-solving skills and enhance social competence, PATHS also promotes student empathy and openness, factors that potentially influence the classroom atmosphere and help prevent or reduce behavioral and emotional problems.

The PATHS curriculum was developed for students in grades K–6. The components that can be taught throughout the elementary school years include readiness and self-control (one volume), feelings and relationships (three volumes), a problem-solving unit (the CBI component; one volume), and supplementary lessons (one volume). Taught three times per week for a minimum of 20–30 minutes per day, PATHS can provide teachers with lessons, materials, and instructions for systematically teaching students emotional literacy, self-control, social competence, positive peer relations, and interpersonal problem-solving skills. Instruction in specific areas includes feelings identification and labeling; assessing, expressing, and managing the intensity of feelings; delaying gratification; understanding the difference between feelings and behaviors; impulse control; stress reduction; problem solving and decision making; positive attitude instruction; self-awareness; and nonverbal and verbal communication skills, all of which are potentially important for children at risk for anger and aggression.

Outcome Research for PATHS

PATHS has been researched and field-tested in general education classrooms that contained diverse student populations (e.g., white, black, Asian) and a variety of special education students, including those with EBD. The CPPRG (1999), as part of the multicomponent Fast Track program, assessed the impact of the PATHS curriculum as a separate intervention on students' social competence using three distinct outcome measures: (1) teacher reports (two structured interviews with each participating teacher), (2) individual sociometric interviews with all children with parental consent, and (3) observer ratings of the classroom atmosphere as a whole on a scale of 1 to 5. In addition, they analyzed the effects of dosage and quality of implementation. Thousands of first-grade students composed the sample in participating schools (i.e., 198 intervention classrooms and 180 comparison classrooms) from four areas of the country. Hierarchical and general linear modeling were used to control for various differences among individual students and to compare the social competencies of students in the treatment and control classrooms using peer ratings of behavior, teacher-rated aggression and conduct problems, and classroom atmosphere.

The CPPRG (1999) found significant effects of intervention on peer-rated aggression and hyperactive–disruptive behavior. Also, intervention classrooms were rated as having a more positive classroom atmosphere than control classrooms, with significant effects on 4 of the 10 subscales: students' ability to follow rules, students' ability to express feelings appropriately, classroom level of interest and enthusiasm, and classrooms' ability to stay focused and on task. There were no main intervention or interaction effects on any teacher ratings.

In another study, Kam, Greenberg, and Kusché (2004) examined the long-term effectiveness of PATHS for special education students. Using a randomized, controlled clinical trial, they tracked changes in students' externalizing and internalizing behaviors, social competence, self-reported depression, affective vocabulary, and problem-solving skills. Kam et al. found that compared to a control group, special education students who were taught PATHS showed more positive, long-term trends in rates of externalizing and internalizing behavior, including a sustained 3-year reduction in rate of self-reported depression. They did not find differences, however, between treatment and control students in overall social competence levels, growth in affective vocabulary, or social problem solving skills. Kam et al. suggested that the lack of an observable treatment effect on overall social competence and problem-solving may have resulted from (1) a single-year exposure to PATHS, (2) use of an early version of PATHS that lacked specific lessons on positive approaches to difficult peer relations, and (3) a teacher-rated measure of social competence with questionable sensitivity to detect change.

TFGA: Teaching Students to Problem Solve

Similar to the PATHS component of the Fast Track program, TFGA was developed, piloted, and investigated as a universal, cognitive-behavioral social problem-solving curriculum. The purpose of its development was to determine whether a CBI implemented by classroom teachers (i.e., universal prevention) could sustain positive outcomes, particularly for students targeted as at risk for disruptive and/or aggressive behavior (i. e., selected intervention; Smith & Daunic, 2004). The initial version of TFGA was adapted from a cognitive-behavioral curriculum developed by Robinson et al. (2002) to investigate the effects of CBI on middle school special education students' inappropriate responses to anger. To engage the relationship between internal cognitive events (the problem-solving process) and overt behavior, the intervention incorporated role-plays and teacher modeling to teach the cognitive processes involved in problem solving. Students' personal experiences were frequently incorporated to illustrate problem situations and help generalize learned skills to daily life. Following the 10 instructional lessons were five review sessions that provided practice and additional exposure to problem-solving concepts.

The initial version of TFGA was adapted to be age appropriate for upper elementary students (fourth and fifth grades) in regular or special education classrooms. As recommended for the teaching of cognitive skills (Lochman et al., 1993), the adapted curriculum focuses on a specific domain: understanding and dealing with frustration and anger, frequent correlates of disruptive and aggressive behavior (Averill, 1982). Its intent is to provide cognitive problem-solving skills, enhance their use as self-statements to guide decision making, and, ultimately, to foster automaticity in challenging social situations at school and elsewhere. Skills are organized in a six-step problem-solving framework, and the 20 core lessons incorporate direct instruction, modeling, guided practice, and independent practice for skill development and generalization. Lessons are designed for teaching one to three times per week, with each lesson lasting approximately 25–35 minutes. Fifteen content lessons cover six problem-solving steps, and five strategically placed role-play lessons provide opportunities to practice steps as they are learned. Following the 20 core lessons, six booster lessons are implemented less frequently (e.g., one every other week), providing additional review and opportunities for generalization.

Outcome Research for TFGA

TFGA has been implemented with more than 2,300 students (approximately 400 target students) in more than 100 elementary classrooms and is currently undergoing randomized field trials (Smith & Daunic, 2006b). In a preliminary study, Smith and Daunic (2004) found that TFGA was effective in increasing student knowledge of problem-solving strategies, whether implemented in classwide or pull-out settings, and that students retained knowledge gains approximately 5 months after instruction was terminated. Moreover, TFGA positively influenced teacher ratings of aggressive behavior but apparently did not change student self-reports of behavior or sociometric ratings.

Building on this preliminary work, Daunic et al. (2006) conducted a randomized efficacy trial involving 165 fourth- and fifth-grade target students (i.e., those nominated by teachers as at risk for problems with anger and aggression) from a total of 35 classrooms and used multilevel modeling to assess TFGA's effects on measures of knowledge and behavior. Schools were matched on risk status and randomly assigned to one of three experimental conditions: 20-lesson curriculum, 20-lesson curriculum plus booster lessons, or no-treatment control. Significant positive treatment effects were found on student knowledge of problem-solving concepts, teacher ratings of student aggression, and student reports of anger suppression. Outcomes differed, however, across teachers/classrooms, and the addition of booster lessons did not significantly affect treatment efficacy. Randomized field trials are currently underway that will aggregate findings from a larger group of students over a 3-year period and incorporate direct observations of classrooms and teachers to help explain classroom-level sources of variance in student outcome measures.

Second Step

The Second Step curriculum is a universal prevention program designed to reduce aggression and promote social competence. The program is designed to develop skills central to children's healthy social and emotional development, such as empathy, impulse control, problem solving, and anger management. The curriculum is designed with preschool through fifth-grade and sixth- through ninth-grade groupings. There are five teaching kits within each group, and lessons build sequentially at each grade level. Each Second Step lesson is based on a story that demonstrates an important peer relations skill. This format makes it easier for children to discuss feelings and gives them concrete ways to understand complex social skills concepts. The stories are used to teach affective, cognitive, and behavioral social skills in a developmental sequence. The middle school curriculum includes three levels wherein teachers use discussion, role play, homework, and a video. There are between 20 and 25 lessons per year for the elementary curriculum, and the middle school curriculum contains 15 lessons in year 1 and 8 lessons in years 2 and 3.

Outcome Research for Second Step

In one large research study, Grossman et al. (1997) randomly assigned 12 elementary schools matched on socioeconomic and ethnic makeup to control or experimental conditions. In the experimental condition, trained second- and third-grade classroom teachers taught Second Step. Trained coders blind to condition observed students in their classrooms, lunchrooms, and on the playground. Each child was observed prior to the intervention, 2 weeks following completion of the program, and again 6 months later for a total of 45–60 minutes. Teacher and parent ratings of prosocial and aggressive behavior were also assessed.

Grossman et al. (1997) found that observed physical aggression and hostile and aggressive comments decreased during the school year among students in the Second Step classrooms, whereas these same behaviors increased in control classrooms. Students in treatment classrooms continued to show lower levels of observed aggression 6 months later. Prosocial and neutral interactions (i.e., friendly behavior) increased during the school year in Second Step classrooms but did not change in control classrooms. Six months following Second Step instruction, students in treatment classes maintained the higher levels of positive interaction. There were, however, no significant differences between treatment and control conditions in teacher or parent ratings of aggressive and prosocial behaviors. Grossman et al. concluded that teaching Second Step could decrease aggression and increase neutral and prosocial student behavior in schools. Conversely, without the Second Step curriculum, students' school behavior deteriorated as the year progressed, showing more physical and verbal aggression.

In 2005, Frey, Nolen, Van Schoiack-Edstrom, and Hirschstein studied the effects of Second Step in 15 schools assigned to either treatment

(n = 462) or control conditions (n = 436). As part of a larger 2-year study on Second Step, Frey et al. used teacher ratings, self-report, and observations of children involved in two structured conflicts (i.e., contrived situations designed to elicit competition or cooperation over the distribution of available resources) to assess effects. Frey et al. found that participation in the Second Step program demonstrated significant benefits in student behavior, goals, and social reasoning for the sample as a whole and for the smaller, randomly assigned subsample. When observed during the structured conflicts, children in the intervention group displayed less aggression than control children, and teacher ratings of behavior showed improvement over time.

Coping Power Program (CCP)

The CPP (Lochman & Wells, 2002a) is a lengthier, multicomponent version of the Anger Coping Program (ACP) intervention designed to maximize outcome effects and maintenance of gains over time. ACP is a structured 18-session group intervention for aggressive children that has been developed over a period of 20 years and evolved from the earlier 12-session ACP (Lochman, Nelson, & Sims, 1981). The ACP has been used in school settings for both prevention and early intervention. Groups of four to six children typically meet for 45–60 minutes in school-based settings; outpatient sessions can last 60–90 minutes. This model was designed for use with elementary and middle school children and has been used primarily with children in the fourth to sixth grades, although the program can be adapted for children several years older or younger. The goals for group sessions include (1) introduction and establishment of the group rules and reinforcement systems, (2) goal-setting, (3) anger management training, (4) perspective-taking, (5) awareness of physiological arousal and anger, and (6) social problem-solving. A detailed session-by-session outline of the ACP can be found elsewhere (Larson & Lochman, 2002; Lochman, FitzGerald, & Whidby, 1999). Built on the ACP, the child component of the CPP includes additional sessions that address such areas as emotional awareness, relaxation training, social skills enhancement, positive social and personal goals, and dealing with peer pressure. The parent component of the CPP can be delivered during the same 15–18 month period.

Outcome Research for CPP

The CPP was derived from earlier research on the ACP that demonstrated intervention effects at a 3-year follow-up (Lochman, 1992). In an initial efficacy study of CPP, Lochman and Wells (2002a, 2004) randomly assigned 183 aggressive boys to one of three conditions: a cognitive-behavioral CPP child component, combined CPP child and behavioral parent training components, or a no-treatment group. The two intervention conditions took place during Grades Four and Five or Five and Six, and intervention lasted for 1.5 school years. Screening of risk status took place in 11 elementary schools and was based on a multiple-gating approach using teacher and parent ratings of children's aggressive behavior. The at-risk boys were in the top 20% on aggression according to teacher ratings of their classrooms.

Analyses of outcomes at 1-year follow-up indicated that intervention groups (child component only, child plus parent components) produced reductions in children's self-reported delinquent behavior and parent reports of the child's alcohol and marijuana use, and improvements in teacher-rated functioning at school, in comparison to the high-risk control condition (Lochman & Wells, 2004). Results also indicated that the effects on delinquent behavior and substance use were most apparent for children and parents who received CPP with both child and parent components. In contrast, the improvements in teacher-rated functioning for boys, specifically, during the follow-up year appeared to be influenced primarily by the CPP child component. Path analytic techniques indicated that all intervention effects were mediated by intervention-produced improvements in children's internal locus of control, perceptions of parental consistency, attributional biases, person perception, and expectations that aggression would not work for them (Lochman & Wells, 2002a).

Given these positive findings, researchers then examined whether CPP had similar positive effects in other settings and with personnel more equivalent to typical school and agency staff providing services to youth with disabilities. Studies have indicated intervention effects on children's aggressive behavior and problem-solving skills, specifically, among aggressive deaf children (Lochman et al., 2001) and children with conduct disorder and oppositional defiant disorder in Dutch outpatient clinics (van de Wiel, Matthys, Cohen-Kettenis, & van Engeland, 2003).

Lochman and Wells (2002b), in an extensive effectiveness study, examined the effects of (1) CPP (combined child and parent components) as an indicated preventive intervention for high-risk children and (2) a universal, classroom-level preventive intervention. A total of 245 male and female aggressive fourth-grade students were randomly assigned to one of four conditions. Children were selected from 17 primarily inner city, high-poverty elementary schools with intervention beginning in the fall of the fifth-grade year. At post-intervention, the three intervention conditions (CPP alone, CPP plus classroom intervention, classroom intervention alone) produced lower rates of substance use than did the control condition (Lochman & Wells, 2002b). Children who received both intervention components displayed improvements in their social competence with peers, and their teachers rated these children as having the greatest increases in problem-solving and anger-coping skills. CPP also produced reductions in parent-rated and teacher-rated proactive aggressive behavior and improvements in teacher-rated behavior. A 1-year follow-up of this sample replicated the findings of the prior efficacy study. CPP children were found to have lower rates of self-reported substance use and delinquency and lower levels of teacher-rated aggressive social behavior at school in comparison to control children (Lochman & Wells, 2003).

CBIs for Anger and Aggression: Research to Practice

Variability in Outcomes

Although researchers and developers have identified several efficacious programs that target anger and aggression and work in particular environments under defined conditions, there is still significant variability in the student outcomes reported across individual studies and in meta-analyses (Gerber & Solari, 2005). There are many potential reasons for such variability, particularly because most CBIs are multifaceted; require a level of conceptual sophistication on the part of practitioners; and address differing constellations of student risk and protective factors at the individual student, classroom, family, and community levels. Moreover, these challenges are not unique to intervention research aimed at aggression but apply as well to CBI studies that target a range of inappropriate or maladaptive behaviors. It is no wonder, then, that attempts to replicate findings and compare studies across diverse settings and implementation conditions do not always yield consistent results. Along with varying levels of treatment fidelity and the complex task of teasing out critical intervention components, measurement is a significant concern.

Measurement Issues

One of the most challenging aspects in weighing the current evidence about the efficacy of CBIs for addressing anger and aggression is outcome measurement (Mayer, Lochman, & Van Acker, 2005). Use of different measures across studies makes comparisons difficult, and the instruments used often lack adequate reliability and validity or are only loosely tied to theoretically based constructs (Gresham, 2005). For example, teachers might report that elementary students' levels of aggression are lower following treatment, but student responses to questions on anger or aggression scales might not change. This discrepancy could result from teacher bias (e.g., teachers were involved in treatment implementation), inadequate test–retest reliability for student-report measures, or behavior changes not recognized by students with limited self-awareness. Such differences among respondents are difficult to resolve. Moreover, the same measure may be more or less sensitive or accurate at different developmental stages.

Use of indirect or self-report measures to assess effects of CBIs for students with or at risk for EBD raises concerns about response bias due to social desirability effects. CBI researchers, however, are dependent on indirect or self-report measures to connect changes in thought processes to proximal or distal behavioral outcomes. A viable alternative, or supplement, to traditional paper-and-pencil surveys may be a method developed by Davison and colleagues (see Eckhardt, Barbour, & Davison, 1998) to study naturalistic "on-line cognitive activity" during emotion activation. The articulated thoughts in simulated situations paradigm provides open-ended verbal reporting of participants' thoughts as they listen to an audiotaped social interaction scenario and imagine they are actively involved. Thoughts are articulated at frequent intervals (e.g., every 30 seconds) rather than after participants were exposed to an entire scenario and questioned about their responses. Use of such measures could be part of studies about the efficacy of CBI for altering cognitive responses to anger-provoking social stimuli.

Not only do measures differ across studies for assessing an array of risk factors, such as student aggression, student response to problem-solving scenarios, or overall classroom climate, researchers also measure a variety of outcome variables at different time points following intervention. As part of the Fast Track multicomponent intervention, the CPPRG (2004) tracked students over a period of years and attempted to tie proximal changes with more successful long-term outcomes, whereas others (Daunic et al., 2006; Van Schoiack, 2002) focused on whether CBIs positively affected students in a classroom setting within the course of a school year. In addition, many CBIs include multiple treatment components, and relatively few researchers have conducted component analyses to identify which are most salient in producing short- or long-term gains (Gerber & Solari, 2005). Most programmatic research is resource intensive, and researchers should consider cost–benefit ratios in light of the immediate need for effective programming.

In sum, if researchers are to establish "evidence-based practices," there will have to be a specificity of criteria about measurement reliability and validity; proximal versus distal outcomes; and symptom reduction versus more practically significant changes, such as peer group affiliation or drug use. Further complicating measurement challenges is the complexity of issues involved in disseminating research-based interventions that are, or will be, deemed efficacious in particular contexts into the diverse world of practice, specifically schools.

Research to School-Based Practice

According to Aber, Brown, and Jones (2003), most rigorous evaluations of school-based universal interventions to lower violence and aggression can be classified as efficacy studies that maximize internal validity to detect causal influences. The need for rigor in design, measurement, treatment integrity, and statistical analyses in such studies is self-evident. The issue, then, becomes the degree to which different personnel, for different student populations, and in different contexts, can implement interventions with positive outcomes under controlled conditions with integrity. There may always be some tension between rigorous scientific control (i.e., internal validity) and generalizability (i.e., external validity) in applied science, but in the case of school-based CBIs, this tension presents a particularly thorny conundrum. The complexity of CBI itself interacts with the complexity of schools and classrooms as intervention settings, such that disseminating research into practice becomes a process worthy of its own research (Gerber & Solari, 2005; Greenberg, 2004). In fact, Silverman, Kurtines, and Hoagwood (2004) suggested that efficacy and effectiveness, as related to study characteristics, are not dichotomous but represent a continuum. Thus, aspects of each can take on varying degrees of importance within a given study. Simply put, it will not serve parents, students, and education professionals well to simply identify prevention and intervention strategies that are effective only under clinical conditions by trained researchers. The ultimate goal is the generation of effective strategies that can be sustained in the complex and unpredictable arenas of classrooms and schools.

Feasibility and Sustainability

First, the multifaceted components and multiple implementers of many research-based CBIs can compromise the sustainability of the intervention in the absence of substantial external sources of support (Smith & Daunic, 2004). Interventions tested under rigorous implementation constraints, even in school settings, may require extensive initial training; incentives to teachers, parents, and/or peers involved in program components; and ongoing support and feedback from members of the research team. Even under the best of circumstances, there is evidence that many such programs are not continued after research funding has ended

(Sindelar & Brownell, 2001). Many multicomponent intervention studies are in schools where there are large percentages of students at risk for school failure because of poverty, minority status, and/or academic or social difficulties and where aggression and violence are major concerns. Such schools are often the least equipped to provide needed supports for sustaining multicomponent interventions because of lack of resources, lack of teacher expertise, and competing priorities (Greenberg, 2004).

Further complicating the sustainability of CBIs for countering student aggression is the emphasis on teaching accountability and high-stakes testing, which can eclipse a focus on social–emotional learning (Greenberg et al., 2003). Gerber and Solari (2005) pointed out that even tried and true, and relatively easily implemented, forms of behavior management like contingent reinforcement are not used with high frequency, given their solid research base and comparatively straightforward delivery mechanisms. It would be logical to assume that teachers would be highly motivated to implement universal interventions that could provide for more efficient learning—by influencing level of student disruption in the classroom, time on task, or classroom climate, for example—but that expected implementation is apparently not the case. Thus, Gerber and Solari noted that (1) CBIs may present even greater challenges for moving research to practice and going to scale because of their complexity, (2) there is a need to examine more fully the contextual variables that influence how teachers make instructional decisions, and, ultimately, (3) professional educators cannot expect to address the needs of students with EBD effectively without also addressing the "baseline" of teaching practice that profoundly affects all students.

Teacher as Interventionist

To date, the majority of researchers who assess CBIs have not used the teacher as the primary interventionist (Gerber & Solari, 2005). Therefore, how specific teacher characteristics such as use of contingent praise, instructional arrangements, instructional delivery (e.g., opportunities to respond), attitudes toward students with disabilities (particularly EBD), and management style (i.e., authoritarian vs. democratic) and how support for social–emotional learning interact with intervention components to affect student outcomes is yet to be explored. In an investigation of Second Step, Van Schoiack (2002) found that such characteristics could outweigh the impact of treatment. Similarly, Greenberg (2004) noted that the quality of implementation is critical, suggesting that a "science of implementation" be focused on delivery factors themselves as outcome variables.

As part of implementation studies, teacher characteristics, as well as school leadership, structure, and curriculum, would be of paramount interest. In a discussion of the issues of implementation at scale (i.e., research to practice), Gerber and Solari (2005) argued that an explicit part of CBI research agendas should include not only teacher characteristics that may facilitate or impede the efficacy of CBI, but factors located in school organization, administration, and leadership as well. Particularly with complex interventions that may require ongoing teacher feedback and support from guidance or other behavior resource personnel, teacher buy in, attitudes toward implementation, and skill in intervention delivery could be influenced significantly by the degree to which the school principal is committed to effective social–emotional programming. Moreover, researchers have demonstrated that children's levels of aggression tend to covary within classrooms such that entire classrooms may be considered to be more or less aggressive (Guerra, Boxer, & Kim, 2005). Although Guerra and colleagues pointed out that peer group influence may be partly responsible for this covariance, they argued that factors such as teacher expectations and attitudes toward their students serve as socializing influences that may shape social preferences and peer culture. Teacher expectations and their attitudes could substantially enhance or offset the effects of CBI.

Aligned with issues of research to practice and, specifically, the teacher as interventionist, treatment fidelity merits considerable attention (Smith, Daunic, & Taylor, 2007). Treatment fidelity is considered an essential aspect of ensuring adequate internal validity and thus of establishing efficacy, but it becomes an especially important consideration when viewed through the lens of research to school-based practice and the effectiveness of CBI when going to scale.

Treatment Fidelity

The Behavior Change Consortium, in addressing rigorous testing of behavioral interventions for specific health outcomes (Bellg et al., 2004), suggested that strict adherence to treatment fidelity occur at five stages in clinical trials: study design, provider training, delivery of treatment, receipt of treatment, and enactment of treatment skills. *Fidelity* is defined as meeting a specified standard of successful implementation of change at each of these stages. Although emanating from the health behavior field, the recommendations of Bellg et al. are applicable to CBIs implemented in school settings. In the case of testing TFGA, a cognitive-behavioral social problem-solving curriculum, adequate treatment fidelity could not occur, according to the Behavior Change Consortium, unless the efficacy study (1) were well designed (e.g., random assignment to experimental conditions, use of reliable and valid outcome measures),

(2) included sufficiently rigorous provider training with an evaluation of resultant knowledge and skills, (3) ensured that the curriculum was delivered as planned through manualization or other means of standardizing delivery, (4) measured student knowledge of problem solving as a result of receiving the curriculum, and (5) measured student enactment of a problem-solving sequence when faced with anger- or emotion-provoking situations. Although this last stage/domain could be confused with *treatment efficacy* (i.e., improvement on outcome measures), a student could indeed use or enact problem-solving steps when angry but still respond aggressively. Bellg et al. would thus suggest that enactment is demonstrated, but efficacy, as indicated by measures of aggression, is not.

Researchers might agree that such a rigorous approach to defining treatment fidelity is optimal for particular stages of research, such as establishing the promise of a newly developed intervention to be tested under more varied conditions. When studies of CBI take place in school settings, questions arise about whether the treatment requirements such as those outlined by Bellg et al. (2004) are either realistic or beneficial. In a comment on Bellg et al., Leventhal and Friedman (2004) argued that even in pharmacological intervention research, it is often difficult to apply treatment protocols in real-world conditions. Thus, there is an "efficacy–effectiveness" gap (Leventhal & Friedman, 2004, p. 453) that calls for studies designed specifically to address the processes by which practitioners (1) receive information through training and (2) apply or adapt that information to deliver interventions to a variety of clients in a variety of settings. It may be that some components of treatment are not necessary to achieve desired behavioral change (e.g., lower student aggression), but researchers cannot determine essential versus nonessential treatment components unless they study systematic variations and associated outcomes (Smith, Daunic, & Taylor, 2007).

Indeed, in the case of CBI delivered in classroom settings, teachers may intuitively adapt treatment protocols based on how students respond, making these interventions more, or less, effective or efficient. Requiring rigorous adherence to treatment fidelity at every step outlined by the Behavior Change Consortium would inhibit research designed to determine critical or active (Leventhal & Friedman, 2004) treatment components and how they can or should be modified to be maximally useful for particular student populations. Any researcher who has observed effective teachers deviate from strict curricular protocol to connect their students with challenging content or, conversely, ineffective teachers who follow scripted lessons but do not model the behaviors they are "teaching," knows that defining treatment fidelity is not a simple task. Leventhal and Friedman argued that varying procedures will often be essential to meet "conceptual fidelity" (p. 454).

A further complication that relates to treatment fidelity in school-based studies of CBI for reducing aggression is the fact that practically all schools and classrooms are addressing social or behavioral problems in some form or fashion, such that there are no readily available, pure control groups for assessing the differential impact of treatment (Greenberg, 2004). Although this situation has little bearing on whether an intervention is delivered as designed in treatment condition classrooms, it does have an impact on experimental outcomes. The presence of social educational content in control or comparison conditions similar to the content included in intervention components could confound treatment effects by obfuscating between-group differences in outcome measures. Thus, intervention researchers need to document social–emotional programming in control group classrooms to the extent possible when attempting to determine the efficacy of a CBI for the prevention or amelioration of anger and aggression. Some of these moderating or confounding variables, such as teacher discipline style or explicit lessons in problem solving, could be operationalized and potentially included in statistical models to control partially for their impact on study findings.

Conclusion

It is important that education professionals have access to highly effective prevention and intervention programming to reduce the disruptive and aggressive behaviors of students who exhibit, or are at risk for, EBD while increasing their adaptive, prosocial skills. To this end, prevention and intervention research on CBIs directed at anger and aggression has shown substantial student benefits through multi-informant studies. From what is known about the developmental trajectory of anger and aggression, social–emotional processes, particularly emotion regulation, are likely to constitute the focus of much of the applied research on CBIs in school settings. Although most CBIs are not easily delivered and require a relatively long-term commitment from teachers and other education professionals, there is an increasing body of evidence that these interventions can help students regulate their own behavior in positive ways.

Even as the research base continues to expand, however, issues related to feasibility and sustainability of comprehensive programming, behavioral and cognitive outcome measurement, documentation of treatment fidelity, and the progression from efficacy to effectiveness research (research to practice) warrant concentrated, sustained, and collaborative efforts among researchers and education professionals. Moreover, Polsgrove and Smith (2004) asserted that teacher training in the use of CBIs for students who engage in significant aggressive behavior deserves serious consideration. Whether working with students at risk for or those with significant behavioral disorders, teachers may be unfamiliar with CBIs as a classroom-based approach and with the conceptual underpinnings that provide the requisite context for skill acquisition. Thus, despite emerging evidence that CBIs can positively affect student behavior (Smith et al., 2005), there is still much to be done in continuing to examine their efficacy and effectiveness in improving outcomes for students with anger- and aggression-related problems within the framework of research to classroom-based practice.

References

Aber, J. L., Brown, J. L., & Jones, S. M. (2003). Developmental trajectories toward violence in middle childhood: Course, demographic differences, and response to school-based intervention. *Developmental Psychology, 39,* 324–348.

Abikoff, H. (1991). Cognitive training in ADHD children: Less to it than meets the eye. *Journal of Learning Disabilities, 24,* 205–209.

Averill, J. R. (1982). *Anger and aggression: An essay on emotion.* New York: Springer-Verlag.

Bandura, A. (1977). *Social learning theory.* Englewood Cliffs, NJ: Prentice Hall.

Bandura, A. (1986). *Social foundations of thought and action: A social cognitive theory.* Upper Saddle River, NJ: Pearson.

Beck, R., & Fernandez, E. (1998). Cognitive-behavioral therapy in the treatment of anger: A meta-analysis. *Cognitive Therapy and Research, 22,* 63–74.

Bellg, A. J., Borrelli, B., Resnick, B., Hecht, J., Minicucci, D. S., Ory, M., et al. (2004). Enhancing treatment fidelity in health behavior change studies: Best practices and recommendations from the NIH behavior change consortium. *Health Psychology, 23,* 443–451.

Bierman, K. L. (2004). *Peer rejection: Developmental processes and intervention strategies.* New York: Guilford Press.

Broidy, L. M., Nagin, D. S., Tremblay, R. E., Bates, J. E., Brame, B., Dodge, K. A., et al. (2003). Developmental trajectories of childhood disruptive behaviors and adolescent delinquency: A six-site, cross-national study. *Developmental Psychology, 39*(2), 222–245.

Bronfenbrenner, U. (1979). *The ecology of human development.* Cambridge, MA: Harvard University Press.

Bronfenbrenner, U. (1989). Ecological systems theory. In R. Vasta (Ed.), *Annals of child development—Six theories of child development: Revised formulations and current issues* (pp. 187–250). Greenwich, CT: JAI Press.

Burns, B. J., Costello, E. J., Angold, A., Tweed, D., Stangl, D., Farmer, E., et al. (1995). Children's mental health service use across service sectors. *Health Affairs, 14,* 147–159.

Cairns, R. B., & Cairns, B. D. (2000). The natural history of developmental functions of aggression. In A. J. Sameroff, M. Lewis, & S. M. Miller (Eds.), *Handbook of developmental psychopathology* (2nd ed., pp. 403–429). New York: Plenum Press.

Campbell, S. (2000). Attention deficit/hyperactivity disorder. In A. J. Sameroff, M. Lewis, &

S. M. Miller (Eds.), *Handbook of developmental psychopathology* (2nd ed., pp. 383–401). New York: Plenum Press.

Chaplin, T. M., & Cole, P. M. (2005). The role of emotion regulation in the development of psychopathology. In B. L. Hankin & J. R. Z. Abela (Eds.), *Development of psychopathology: A vulnerability-stress perspective* (pp. 49–74). Thousand Oaks, CA: Sage.

Coie, J. D., Underwood, M., & Lochman, J. E. (1991). Programmatic intervention with aggressive children in the school setting. In D. J. Pepler & K. H. Rubin (Eds.), *Development and treatment of childhood aggression* (pp. 389–410). Hillsdale, NJ: Erlbaum.

Cole, P. M., Teti, L. O., & Zahn-Waxler, C. (2003). Mutual emotion regulation and the stability of conduct problems between preschool and early school age. *Development and Psychopathology, 15,* 1–18.

Committee for Children. (1997). *Second Step: A violence prevention curriculum.* Seattle, WA: Author.

Conduct Problems Prevention Research Group. (1992). A developmental and clinical model for the prevention of conduct disorders: The Fast Track program. *Development and Psychopathology, 4,* 509–527.

Conduct Problems Prevention Research Group. (1999). Initial impact of the Fast Track prevention trial for conduct problems: II. Classroom effects. *Journal of Consulting and Clinical Psychology, 67,* 648–657.

Conduct Problems Prevention Research Group. (2002). Predictor variables associated with positive Fast Track outcomes at the end of third grade. *Journal of Abnormal Child Psychology, 30,* 37–52.

Conduct Problems Prevention Research Group. (2004). The effects of the Fast Track program on serious problem outcomes at the end of elementary school. *Journal of Clinical Child and Adolescent Psychology, 33,* 650–661.

Crick, N. R., & Bigbee, M. A. (1998). Relational and overt forms of peer victimization: A multiinformant approach. *Journal of Consulting and Clinical Psychology, 66,* 337–347.

Crick, N. R., & Dodge, K. A. (1994). A review and reformulation of social information-processing mechanisms in children's social adjustment. *Psychological Bulletin, 115,* 74–101.

Crick, N. R., Ostrov, J. M., & Werner, N. E. (2006). A longitudinal study of relational aggression, physical aggression, and children's social-psychological adjustment. *Journal of Abnormal Child Psychology, 34,* 131–142.

Damasio, A. R. (1994). *Descartes' error: Emotion, reason, and the human brain.* New York: Avon Books.

Daunic, A. P., Smith, S. W., Brank, E. M., & Penfield, R. D. (2006). Classroom based cognitive-behavioral intervention to prevent aggression: Efficacy and social validity. *Journal of School Psychology, 44,* 123–139.

Dionne, G., Boivin, M., Tremblay, R., Laplante, D., & Perusse, D. (2003). Physical aggression and expressive vocabulary in 19-month-old twins. *Developmental Psychology, 39,* 261–273.

Dodge, K. A. (1991). The structure and function of reactive and proactive aggression. In K. H. Rubin & D. J. Pepler (Eds.), *Development and treatment of childhood aggression* (pp. 201–218). Hillsdale, NJ: Erlbaum.

Dodge, K. A., Coie, J. D., & Lynam, D. (2006). Aggression and antisocial behavior in youth. In W. Damon & R. M. Lerner (Series Eds.) & N. Eisenberg (Vol. Ed.), *Handbook of child psychology: Vol. 3. Social, emotional, and personality development* (6th ed., pp. 719–788). New York: Wiley.

Dodge, K. A., McClaskey, C. L., & Feldman, E. (1985). A situational approach to the assessment of social competence in children. *Journal of Consulting and Clinical Psychology,* 53, 344–353.

Dush, D. M., Hirt, M. L., & Schroeder, H. E. (1989). Self-statement modification in the treatment of child behavior disorders: A meta-analysis. *Psychological Bulletin, 106,* 97–106.

Eckhardt, C. I., Barbour, K. A., & Davison, G. C. (1998). Articulated thoughts of maritally violent and nonviolent men during anger arousal. *Journal of Consulting and Clinical Psychology, 66,* 259–269.

Farrington, D. P. (2004). Conduct disorder, aggression, and delinquency. In R. M. Lerner & L. Steinberg (Eds.), *Handbook of adolescent psychology* (2nd ed., pp. 627–664). New York: Wiley.

Frey, K. S., Nolen, S. B., Van Schoiack-Edstrom, L., & Hirschstein, M. (2005). Effects of a school-based social-emotional competence program: Linking children's goals, attributions, and behavior. *Journal of Applied Developmental Psychology, 26,* 171–200.

Gerber, M. M., & Solari, E. J. (2005). Teaching effort and the future of cognitive-behavioral interventions. *Behavioral Disorders, 30,* 289–299.

Graber, J. A., Brooks-Gunn, J., & Archibald, A. B. (2005). Links between puberty and externalizing and internalizing behaviors in girls: Moving from demonstrating effects to identifying pathways. In D. M. Stoff & E. J. Susman (Eds.), *Developmental psychobiology of aggression* (pp. 87–113). New York: Cambridge University Press.

Graber, J. A., Seeley, J. R., Brooks-Gunn, J., & Lewinsohn, P. M. (2004). Is pubertal timing associated with psychopathology in young adulthood? *Journal of the American Academy of Child and Adolescent Psychiatry, 43,* 718–726.

Greenberg, M. T. (2004). Current and future challenges in school-based prevention: The researcher perspective. *Prevention Science, 5,* 5–13.

Greenberg, M. T., Weissberg, R. P., O'Brien, M. U., Zins, J. E., Fredericks, L., Resnik, H., et al. (2003). Enhancing school-based prevention and youth development through coordinated social, emotional, and academic learning. *American Psychologist, 58,* 466–474.

Gresham, F. M. (2005). Methodological issues in evaluating cognitive-behavioral treatments for students with behavioral disorders. *Behavioral Disorders, 30,* 213–225.

Grossman, D. C., Neckerman, H. J., Koepsell, T. D., Liu, P. Y., Asher, K. N., Beland, K., et al. (1997). Effectiveness of a violence prevention curriculum among children in elementary school: A randomized controlled trial. *Journal of the American Medical Association, 277,* 1605–1611.

Guerra, N. G., Boxer, P., & Kim, T. E. (2005). A cognitive–ecological approach to serving students with emotional and behavioral disorders: Application to aggressive behavior. *Behavioral Disorders, 30,* 277–288.

Guerra, N. G., & Slaby, R. G. (1990). Cognitive mediators of aggression in adolescent offenders: II. Intervention. *Developmental Psychology, 26,* 269–277.

Kam, C., Greenberg, M. T., & Kusché, C. A. (2004). Sustained effects of the PATHS curriculum on the social and psychological adjustment of children in special education. *Journal of Emotional and Behavioral Disorders, 12,* 66–78.

Kauffman, J. M. (2005). *Characteristics of emotional and behavioral disorders of children and youth* (8th ed.). Upper Saddle River, NJ: Pearson.

Keenan, K., & Shaw, D. S. (2003). Starting at the beginning: Exploring the etiology of antisocial behavior in the first years of life. In B. B. Lahey, T. E. Moffitt, & A. Caspi (Eds.), *Causes of conduct disorder and juvenile delinquency* (pp. 153–181). New York: Guilford Press.

Lahey, B. B., Loeber, R., Quay, H. C., Applegate, B., Shaffer, D., Waldman, I., et al. (1998). Validity of DSM-IV subtypes of conduct disorder based on age of onset. *Journal of the American Academy of Child & Adolescent Psychiatry, 37,* 435–442.

Larson, J., & Lochman, J. E. (2002). *Helping schoolchildren cope with anger: A cognitive-behavioral intervention.* New York: Guilford Press.

Lemerise, E. A., & Arsenio, W. F. (2000). An integrated model of emotion processes and cognition in social information processing. *Child Development, 71,* 107–118.

Leventhal, H., & Friedman, M. A. (2004). Does establishing fidelity of treatment help in understanding treatment efficacy? Comment on Bellg et al. (2004). *Health Psychology, 23,* 452–456.

Lochman, J. E. (1992). Cognitive-behavioral interventions with aggressive boys: Three-year follow-up and preventive effects. *Journal of Consulting and Clinical Psychology, 60,* 426–432.

Lochman, J. E., Dunn, S. E., & Klimes-Dougan, B. (1993). An intervention and consultation model from a social cognitive perspective: A description of the Anger Coping Program. *School Psychology Review, 22,* 458–471.

Lochman, J. E., FitzGerald, D. P., Gage, S., Kanaly, K., Whidby, J., Barry, T. D., et al. (2001). Effects of a social-cognitive intervention for aggressive deaf children: The Coping Power Program. *Journal of the American Deafness and Rehabilitation Association, 35,* 39–61.

Lochman, J. E., FitzGerald, D. P., & Whidby, J. M. (1999). Anger management with aggressive children. In C. Schaefer (Ed.), *Short-term psychotherapy groups for children* (pp. 301–349). Northvale, NJ: Aronson.

Lochman, J. E., Nelson, W. M., & Sims, J. P. (1981). A cognitive behavioral program for use with aggressive children. *Journal of Clinical Child Psychology, 10,* 146–148.

Lochman, J. E., & Wells, K. C. (2002a). Contextual social-cognitive mediators and child outcome: A test of the theoretical model in the Coping Power Program. *Development and Psychopathology, 14,* 971–993.

Lochman, J. E., & Wells, K. C. (2002b). The *Coping Power Program* at the middle school transition: Universal and indicated prevention effects. *Psychology of Addictive Behaviors, 16 (Supplement),* S40–54.

Lochman, J. E., & Wells, K. C. (2003). Effectiveness study of Coping Power and classroom intervention with aggressive children: Outcomes at a one-year follow-up. *Behavior Therapy, 34,* 493–515.

Lochman, J. E., & Wells, K. C. (2004). The Coping Power Program for preadolescent aggressive boys and their parents: Outcome effects at the one-year follow-up. *Journal of Consulting and Clinical Psychology, 72,* 571–578.

Lochman, J., Whidby, J., & FitzGerald, D. (2000). Cognitive-behavioral assessment and treatment with aggressive children. In P. C. Kendall (Ed.), *Child and adolescent therapy: Cognitive-behavioral procedures* (2nd ed., pp. 31–87). New York: Guilford Press.

Loeber, R., & Hay, D. (1997). Key issues in the development of aggression and violence from childhood to early adulthood. *Annual Review of Psychology, 48,* 371–410.

Mahoney, M. J. (1974). *Cognition and behavior modification.* Cambridge, MA: Ballinger.

Mahoney, M. J., & Kazdin, A. E. (1979). Cognitive behavior modification: Misconceptions and premature evacuation. *Psychological Bulletin, 86,* 1044–1049.

Mayer, M. J., Lochman, J., & Van Acker, R. (2005). Introduction to the special issue: Cognitive-behavioral interventions with students with EBD. *Behavioral Disorders, 30,* 197–212.

McCart, M. R., Priester, P. E., Davies, W. H., & Azen, R. (2006). Differential effectiveness of behavioral parent-training and cognitive-behavioral therapy for antisocial youth: A meta analysis. *Journal of Abnormal Child Psychology, 34,* 527–543.

Meichenbaum, D. H. (1977). *Cognitive-behavior modification: An integrative approach.* New York: Plenum Press.

Moffitt, T. E. (1993). Adolescence-limited and life-course persistent antisocial behavior: A developmental taxonomy. *Psychological Review, 100,* 674–701.

Moffitt, T. E., Caspi, A., Rutter, M., & Silva, P. A. (2001). *Sex differences in antisocial behavior: Conduct disorder, delinquency, and violence in the Dunedin Longitudinal Study.* Cambridge, UK: Cambridge University Press.

Nelson, W. M., III, & Finch, A. J., Jr. (2000). Managing anger in youth: A cognitive-behavioral intervention approach. In P. C. Kendall (Ed.) *Child and adolescent therapy: Cognitive-behavioral procedures* (2nd ed., pp. 129–170). New York: Guilford Press.

Nichols, T. R., Graber, J. A., Brooks-Gunn, J., & Botvin, G. J. (2006). Sex differences in overt aggression and delinquency among urban minority middle school students. *Journal of Applied Developmental Psychology, 27,* 78–91.

Orobio de Castro, B., Veerman, J. W., Koops, W., Bosch, J. D., & Monshouwer, H. J. (2002). Hostile attribution of intent and aggressive behavior: A meta-analysis. *Child Development, 73,* 916–934.

Pajer, K. A. (1998). What happens to "bad" girls? A review of the adult outcomes of antisocial adolescent girls. *American Journal of Psychiatry, 155,* 862–870.

Parke, R. D., & Slaby, R. G. (1983). The development of aggression. In P. Mussen (Series Ed.) & E. M. Hetherington (Vol. Ed.), *Handbook of child psychology: Vol. 4. Socialization, personality, and social development* (4th ed., pp. 547–641). New York: Wiley.

Patterson, G. R., & Capaldi, D. M. (1991). Antisocial parents: Unskilled and vulnerable. In P. A. Cowan & E. M. Hetherington (Eds.), *Family transitions* (pp. 195–218). Hillsdale, NJ: Erlbaum.

Polsgrove, L., & Smith, S. W. (2004). Informed practice in teaching self-control to children with emotional and behavioral disorders. In R. B. Rutherford, M. M. Quinn, & S. R. Mathur (Eds.), *Handbook of research in emotional and behavioral disorders* (pp. 399–425). New York: Guilford Press.

Reid, J. B., Eddy, J. M., Fetrow, R. A., & Stoolmiller, M. (1999). Description and immediate impacts of a preventive intervention for conduct problems. *American Journal of Community Psychology, 27,* 483–517.

Robinson, T. R., Smith, S. W., & Miller, M. D. (2002). Effect of a cognitive-behavioral intervention on responses to anger by middle school students with chronic behavior problems. *Behavioral Disorders, 27,* 256–271.

Robinson, T. R., Smith, S. W., Miller, M. D., & Brownell, M. T. (1999). Cognitive behavior modification of hyperactivity-impulsivity and aggression: A meta-analysis of school-based studies. *Journal of Educational Psychology, 91,* 195–203.

Rodkin, P., Farmer, T. W., Pearl, R., & Van Acker, R. (2000). Heterogeneity of popular boys: Antisocial and prosocial configurations. *Developmental Psychology, 36,* 14–24.

Sameroff, A. J., & Chandler, M. J. (1975). Reproductive risk and the continuum of caretaking casualty. In F. D. Horowitz (Ed.), *Review of child development research* (Vol. 4, pp. 187–244). Chicago: University of Chicago Press.

Schacter, S., & Singer, J. E. (1962). Cognitive, social, and physiological determinants of emotional state. *Psychological Review, 69,* 379–399.

Shure, M. B. (2001). *I Can Problem Solve: An interpersonal cognitive problem-solving program.* Champaign, IL: Research Press.

Silverman, W. K., Kurtines, W. M., & Hoagwood, K. (2004). Research progress on effectiveness, transportability, and dissemination of empirically supported treatments: Integrating theory and research. *Clinical Psychology: Science and Practice, 11*(3), 295–299.

Sindelar, P. T., & Brownell, M. T. (2001). Research to practice dissemination, scale, and context: We can do it, but can we afford it? *Teacher Education and Special Education, 24,* 348–355.

Smith. S. W., & Daunic, A. P. (2004). Research on preventing behavior problems using a cognitive-behavioral intervention: Preliminary findings, challenges and future directions. *Behavioral Disorders, 30,* 72–76.

Smith, S. W., & Daunic, A. P. (2006a). *Managing difficult behavior through problem solving instruction: Strategies for the elementary classroom.* Boston: Allyn & Bacon.

Smith, S. W., & Daunic, A. P. (2006b, June). *Universal cognitive-behavioral intervention for elementary students to reduce disruptive/aggressive behavior: Preliminary findings and future research.* Poster session presented at the U.S. Department of Education Institute of Education Sciences Research Conference, Washington, DC.

Smith, S. W., Daunic, A. P., & Taylor, G. (2007). Treatment fidelity in applied educational research: Expanding the adoption and application of measures to ensure evidence-based practice. *Education and Treatment of Children, 30,* 121–134.

Smith, S. W., Lochman, J. E., & Daunic, A. P. (2005). Managing aggression using cognitive-behavioral interventions: State of the practice and future directions. *Behavioral Disorders, 30,* 227–240.

Sukhodolsky, D. G., Kassinove, H., & Gorman, B. S. (2004). Cognitive-behavioral therapy for anger in children and adolescents: A meta-analysis. *Aggression and Violent Behavior, 9,* 247–269.

Underwood, M. K. (2003). *Social aggression among girls.* New York: Guilford Press.

U.S. Department of Health and Human Services. (2000). *Report of the Surgeon General's conference on children's mental health: A national action agenda.* Rockville, MD: Author.

Van Schoiack, L. (2002). Changing adolescents' attitudes about relational and physical aggression: An early evaluation of a school-based intervention. *School Psychology Review, 31,* 201–216.

van de Wiel, N. M. H., Matthys, W., Cohen-Kettenis, P., & van Engeland, H. (2003). Cost effectiveness of the Coping Power Program with conduct disorder and oppositional defiant disorder children. *Behavior Therapy, 34,* 421–436.

Walker, H. M., Colvin, G., & Ramsey, E. (1995). *Antisocial behavior in school: Strategies and best practices.* Pacific Grove, CA: Brooks/Cole.

Webster-Stratton, C. (2001). The incredible years: Parents, teachers, and children training series. In S. I. Pfeiffer & L. A. Reddy (Eds.), *Innovative mental health interventions for children: Programs that work* (pp. 31–45). New York: Haworth Press.

Wolf, M. M., Braukmann, C. J., & Ramp, K. A. (1987). Serious delinquent behavior as part of a significantly handicapping condition: Cures and supportive environments. *Journal of Applied Behavior Analysis, 20,* 347–359.

Zahn-Waxler, C. (1993). Warriors and worriers: Gender and psychopathology. *Development and Psychopathology, 5,* 79–89.

CHAPTER 6

Managing Anger and Aggression in Students with Externalizing Behavior Problems

Focus on Exemplary Programs

W. M. NELSON III
JANET R. SCHULTZ

Youth aggression and violence in the United States surged in the 1980s and early 1990s, then leveled off and decreased (Fagan, Zimring, & Kim, 1998; Fingerhut & Kleinman, 1990; Snyder & Sickmund, 1995). The adverse impact of aggression and violence is reflected in several facts:

- Prevalence rates for conduct disorder range from 2 to 6% or approximately 1.4 to 4.2 million children in the United States.
- A third to half of youth who severely act out are referred for outpatient treatment. Almost three quarters of all mental health services received by children are provided by the schools (B. J. Burns et al., 1995).

- Disruptive, aggressive, and delinquent child and adolescent behavior accounts for almost a quarter of all special services in school and almost half of all juvenile referrals to community mental health agencies (Stewart, deBlois, Meardon, & Cummings, 1980; Stouthamer-Loeber, Loeber, & Thomas, 1992).
- Approximately 80% of disruptive and aggressive youngsters are likely to meet the criteria for some type of psychiatric disorder in the future, particularly other externalizing or disruptive disorders (e.g., oppositional defiant disorder, conduct disorder, attention-deficit/hyperactivity disorder) but also, to a lesser extent, internalizing disorders (e.g., anxiety disorders, mood disorders). Youth with a history of severe aggressive behavior often continue to perform such acts as they grow up (Farrington, Loeber, & Van Kamman, 1990; Kazdin, 1995).
- From 20 to 40% of school-age children are at risk of school failure and dropping out because of chronic exposure to various conditions of risk in their families and society (Lyon, 2002).
- Other people in the environment (including parents, siblings, peers, teachers, and strangers) who are the targets of aggressive and antisocial behavior experience a variety of consequences including injury, property loss, and disruption. Twelve percent of teachers have reported they were threatened with injury and more felt intimidated by the students in their schools (Kaufman et al., 2001).
- Enormous monetary costs are incurred as these youth are placed in special education classes, receive mental health services, are involved in the juvenile justice system, and receive various social services over the course of their lives. In fact, the staggering cost borne by such systems in this country makes this disorder the most costly mental health problem in North America (Cohen, Miller, & Rossman, 1994; Lipsey, 1992).

Schools have typically been viewed as the primary vehicle for accessing youth who need a range of services, supports, and interventions that impact both their physical and mental health (e.g., Smith, Boutte, Zigler, & Finn-Stephenson, 2004). Schools have been increasingly asked to assume the role of socializing agent, protector, and caregiver for diverse youngsters who manifest very different belief systems, learning capabilities, and behavioral styles, reflecting diversity in society. All this is being asked of schools at the same time there is increased pressure that students meet higher academic standards.

Boys and ethnic minority youth in general are at elevated risk for involvement in aggressive and violent behavior, especially in inner cities

(Hawkins, Laub, & Lauritsen, 1998). Boys in general are far more likely to engage in physically aggressive behaviors and other antisocial behaviors compared to girls, whose infrequent severely aggressive behaviors are often related to abuse and violence in their homes and relationships (Chesney-Lind & Brown, 1999).

Two developmental courses of aggression in youngsters have been identified: (1) life-course persistent and (2) adolescent limited (Loeber & Stouthamer-Loeber, 1998; Moffit, 1993; Moffit, Caspi, Dickson, Silva, & Stanton, 1996). In the life-course-persistent path, youngsters who engage in highly aggressive behavior at an early age continue to do so into adulthood. Although only a small percentage of youth are classified as life-course-persistent offenders, early aggression seems to foreshadow severe acting out problems in adulthood (Farrington, 1991, 1994; Kazdin, 1987; Mash & Wolfe, 2005; Sanford et al., 1999; Stattin & Magnusson, 1989). Even though such behavior decreases with age (e.g., Loeber & Stouthamer-Loeber, 1998), severe aggressive acting-out in children (e.g., persistent physical fighting) is highly stable. In fact, the strongest single predictor of a child's engaging in violent behavior as an adolescent is a history of behaving aggressively as a child (Eron & Slaby, 1994). Such children account for the largest proportion of highly aggressive persons identified in later life.

In contrast, youngsters on the adolescent-limited path begin aggressively acting out around puberty and continue through adolescence until the pattern changes during young adulthood (Farrington, 1986). Aggressive acting out among this group is typically limited to the teenage years, and the behaviors of this group are less extreme by comparison. Such youngsters appear to have stronger ties to family and school and are less likely to become school dropouts. Some youngsters on the adolescent-limited path, however, continue to exhibit aggressive and antisocial behavior well into their 20s before such behavior diminishes.

Aggressive behavior is, however, susceptible to change with systematic interventions (Southam-Gerow & Kendall, 1997; Tate, Reppucci, & Mulvey, 1995; Wasserman & Miller, 1998). A number of effective intervention programs have been developed that appear to have the potential to divert aggressive youths from a trajectory leading to a host of negative outcomes. Intervention works best when it is delivered early in the development of aggressive patterns and through multiple settings: (1) at home by parents, (2) in the classroom by teachers and staff, and (3) in the neighborhood and on the playground involving peers (Dodge, 1993; J. B. Reid, 1993). There is evidence that with effective interventions, at-risk youth will not only learn alternatives to aggression and violence, but also lead productive lives. *Youth Violence: A Report of the Surgeon*

General (U.S. Department of Health and Human Services, 2001) provided an analysis of risk factors and societal conditions that are associated with severe acting out in children and adolescents. The report provided a useful blueprint for addressing this problem through policy and empirically based interventions. Much is now known about evidence-based interventions for dealing with serious acting out (Greenberg, Domitrovich, & Bumbarger, 2001; Loeber & Farrington, 1998, 2001; J. B. Reid, Patterson, & Snyder, 2002). Thus, the progression of early-onset and stable aggression during childhood and adolescence into enduring personality traits is not inevitable.

Early-onset patterns of aggression are often noted when the child enters school and is faced with two major categories of demands: (1) teacher-related adjustment, through which typical students learn to meet the minimal behavioral demands and expectations required by the majority of teachers; and (2) peer-related adjustments, in which children learn to develop satisfactory relationships and friendships with peers (Dodge, 1993; Patterson, Reid, & Dishion, 1992). As early as preschool and kindergarten, teachers can reliably identify the children who have trouble remaining quiet at appropriate times, staying seated, complying with teacher requests/directions, and transitioning between activities (Loeber & Farrington, 2001; Walker, Irvin, Noell, & Singer, 1992). In late childhood and early adolescence, self-regulated adjustment is expected, in which the management of emotions and regulation of behavior is learned. Learning to assert oneself and protect one's reputation is also part of the process (Williams, Walker, Holmes, Todis, & Fabre, 1989). Highly aggressive youngsters are at risk for failure in both teacher- and peer-related adjustment due to behavioral, academic, and social problems. As a result, social adjustment never fully develops and such individuals remain at risk, sometimes throughout their lives.

Schools have been active in attempting to manage and prevent aggressive behaviors in students. Traditionally, schools have dealt with aggression and violence by suspending offenders, increasing police presence on campuses, teaching students alternative ways of handling conflict, and setting up separate schools for disruptive students (National School Boards Association, 1993). Unfortunately, many schools have approached this issue with a "get tough" attitude often consisting of "zero tolerance" toward aggressive behaviors. Although such policy-based programs may have face validity, they do not appear to change the behavior of youngsters who are prone to aggressively acting out (Christner, Friedberg, & Sharp, 2006). Classroom teachers are not trained to deal with the youngsters who moderately to severely act out, nor do they have the resources to do so. Therefore, the task of doing so is often relegated to special education programs or counseling. Counseling/intervention programs within the schools are varied and often involve (1) teaching social skills designed to improve students' social acceptance and/or (2) teaching anger management and conflict resolution strategies. Other commonly used methods for dealing with such youngsters are based on the notion of "catharsis," where students are taught to "get their aggression out" by venting their anger, punching pillows, using a stress ball, yelling, and so on. Such methods not only are generally ineffective in reducing aggression but may actually increase levels of aggression in children and adolescents (e.g., Goldstein, Glick, & Gibbs, 1998). Still other intervention strategies that have been evaluated for children who more seriously act out include medication, home-, and community-based programs, as well as hospital and residential treatment (for reviews, see Brandt & Zlotnick, 1988; Dumas, 1989; Eyberg, Boggs, & Algina, 1995; Kazdin, 2003; L. S. Miller, 1994; Nelson, Finch, & Hart, 2006; Pepler & Rubin, 1991; Stoff, Breiling, & Maser, 1997). Before examining several best practices intervention programs, however, we address assessment issues as the first step in any such program. The goal of assessment is to identify the youth that most need, and may be efficaciously impacted by, intervention strategies.

Assessment

Over the past several decades, psychologists have proposed more than 200 different definitions of aggression (Underwood, 2003). However, the majority of these definitions have typically included two characteristics—the perpetrator must intend to harm someone, and the victim must feel as though he or she has been hurt in some way. In general, there are two major categories of aggression (Hawker & Boulton, 2000): physical (e.g., pushing, kicking, being physically intimidating) and indirect (e.g., spreading nasty rumors, "getting even," damaging another's possessions, attempting to alienate others). It is also useful to evaluate aggression as to whether it is more emotionally (reactive) or instrumentally (proactive) driven (Dodge, 1991). Reactively aggressive children are typically viewed as having "hot tempers" and being prone to becoming angry and aggressive, even at the slightest provocation. Such aggression is targeted to inflict harm on someone else who is viewed as the source of the problems. These children are often disliked and rejected by peers. In contrast, instrumentally aggressive youngsters are motivated more by the desire to acquire things or power. Hence, this type of aggression is exhibited in an attempt to obtain material rewards (e.g., taking someone's lunch money, stealing someone's cell phone) or nonmaterial reinforcement through bullying or other dominant behaviors and may not be associated with anger. These children tend to show serious conduct problems or be bullies at school, and although they may be disliked by their peers, they often have leadership qualities (Dodge, 1991).

Whereas some programs provide universal interventions that target all children in a grade or school, others are delivered only to a subset of high-risk students or are combined with a universal approach. Any program targeting high-risk children needs a method of deciding which children to include. Assessment strategies include the clinical interview, self-monitoring, behavior observation, standardized testing, rating forms from significant others (e.g., teachers, parents, peers), and/or self-report measures, all of which may be worthwhile and desirable. Whenever possible, assessment of children who act out should be multimethod, multiperson, and multisetting. Assessment also needs to be developmentally based, with attention to normal developmental processes and normative comparisons. Such assessment procedures may involve multiple gating (e.g., Loeber, Dishion, & Patterson, 1984). The Systematic Screening for Behavior Disorders (SSBD) procedure (Walker & Severson, 1990) is a multiple gating screening device for identifying children with significant behavior disorders in grades 1–6. It utilizes a combination of teacher nominations (Gate 1), teacher rating scales (Gate 2), and direct observations of classroom and playground behavior by school professionals (e.g., school psychologist, guidance counselor; Gate 3). In Gate 1, teachers identify three students in their classes who match each of two profiles for two types of behavior patterns: externalizing (acting out/aggressive) and internalizing (depressed, anxious, socially withdrawn). Gate 2 involves teacher ratings of three children ranked highest each on the externalizing and internalizing dimensions, as well as a Critical Events Index or formal checklist of problem behaviors. In Gate 3, school professionals directly observe identified students on two measures of school adjustment—working on academic assignments and interacting during recess periods on the playground. A downward extension of the SSBD, the Early Screening Project, has been developed for use with children in preschool and day care settings (Feil, Walker, & Severson, 1995). The process is the same gating procedure as used in the SSBD except that it incorporates parent ratings of problem behaviors at Gate 3.

Overall, understanding and evaluating aggressive behavior can be rather complex, although teachers who spend a significant amount of time with children can readily identify which children have problems with anger and aggression and which do not. The four exemplary programs highlighted in this chapter typically use simple teacher nominations as criteria for inclusion in targeted interventions. Teacher nominations made after time has elapsed in the school year have both ecological and face validity. Another method that holds promise in assessment is the Student Risk Screening Scale (Drummond, 1993). Students are rated from 0 to 3 (0 = never, 1 = occasionally, 2 = sometimes, and 3 = frequently) on seven items—stealing, lying/cheating/sneaking, peer rejection, behavior problems, low academic achievement, negative attitude, and aggressive behavior. Total scores range from 0 to 21, where scores between 9 and 21 suggest further assessment and possible intervention. This empirically supported instrument can accommodate up to 30 students and is highly cost effective. In contrast, some exemplary programs use a simple three-item Likert-type scale asking the teacher's opinion of the child's behaviors, still resulting in clear differentiation from more typical children. However, because programs also typically include universal interventions, teacher ratings are commonly used for baseline and outcome measures. Specific rating scales with known psychometric properties that focus on overt aggression include the Child Behavior Checklist (Achenbach, 1991), Eyberg Child Behavior Inventory (Robinson, Eyberg, & Ross, 1980), and Teacher Observation of Classroom Adaptation—Revised (Werthamer-Larsson, Kellam, & Overson-McGregor, 1990). All three scales bear directly on the question of overt aggression. The Child Behavior Checklist Teacher Report Form includes Aggression, Delinquent or Rule Breaking Behavior, and Social Problems subscales as well as a composite externalizing behavior score. The Eyberg Child Behavior Inventory, which was designed to focus on behavior problems, addresses three subscales: Oppositional Defiant to Adults, Inattentive Behavior, and Conduct Problem Behaviors (L. Burns & Patterson, 2000). The Teacher Observation of Classroom Adaptation—Revised comprises three subscales: Social Contact (relates to withdrawal), Authority Problem (relates to externalizing behavior problems), and Cognitive Concentration (relates to both behavioral and academic difficulties).

Although such assessment strategies focus on overt aggression, it is important to note that aggression and anger are not the same. *Aggression* is an overt behavioral response that may be mediated by *anger*, a subjective emotional state not directly observable by others. Aggressive behavior represents only one of several options in dealing with the subjective experience of anger (i.e., others may include passive aggression, withdrawal, submission/resignation, assertion). Anger is composed of three interrelated domains that include affective/physiological, cognitive, and behavioral components (Nelson & Finch, 2008). A number of assessment instruments tap into these dimensions of anger, although not are all assessed even in the exemplary programs described in this chapter. One such instrument, the Children's Inventory of Anger (Nelson & Finch, 2000), is a self-reported measure assessing intensity of anger across a range of potentially frustrating daily events. The cognitive component of anger involves a set of beliefs about anger-provoking events and, more specifically, how others are viewed as instigators of anger re-actions. The Children's Hostility Inventory (Furlong & Smith, 1994) at-tempts to assess negative thought patterns (such as resentment or jeal-ousy) and corresponding behavioral patterns using parent ratings rather than self-report. Although this three-dimensional model is the basis for a number of anger management interventions, affect/physiological and cognitive components are not typically thoroughly assessed, as the pri-mary focus is on altering aggressive behavior. Nevertheless, professionals planning or conducting treatment interventions need to be aware of such distinctions.

Once children are identified as participants, exemplary programs typically provide intervention in several parts of the children's lives, es-pecially in the classroom and at home. Some provide universal interven-tions for all children in a school or grade, whereas others are more spe-cifically targeted. All four exemplary programs described in this chapter focus on aggression in the school setting as a major outcome measure.

Exemplary Programs

Kazdin (1993) described several criteria in evaluating promising inter-vention programs, including (1) a theoretical conceptualization of the dis-order guides treatment, (2) the conceptualization is supported from re-search, (3) outcome research supports the treatment's efficacy, and (4) outcome is related to processes identified in the conceptualization of the disorder. Currently, there are no programs for aggressive youth that per-fectly meet all of those criteria, although two types appear promising—the family-parent-focused therapies derived from social-learning theory and the child-focused cognitive-behavioral interventions (Kazdin, 2003; G. E. Miller & Prinz, 1990; Southam-Gerow & Kendall, 1997). How-ever, maximizing and measuring the effectiveness or clinical utility of such interventions certainly requires more work (Christopherson & Mortweet, 2003; Kazdin, 2003). The specific programs identified as ex-emplary for this chapter represent notable efforts to meet those require-ments: (1) The Incredible Years, (2) Early Risers: Skills for Success, (3) Fast Track, and (4) Coping Power. Additionally, these programs have all been included in the National Registry of Evidence Based Programs and Practices of the Substance Abuse and Mental Health Services Adminis-tration (SAMHSA; see *www.modelprograms.samhsa.gov*) and have re-ceived at least one other such recognition from an organization such as the Office of Juvenile Justice and Delinquency Prevention (OJJDP; see *www.OJJDP.gov*), Centers for Disease Control and Prevention Best Practices in Youth Violence Prevention, or Blueprints for Violence Prevention. Although other programs might have been selected, together these are representative of best practice approaches that span the youth population from preschool through high school.

The Incredible Years

The Incredible Years: Parents, Teachers, and Children Training series was developed by Carolyn Webster-Stratton (2001) for a target population of children ages 3–10 who would be classified as "early starters" on a risky trajectory. The training materials for the three audiences (parents, teachers, children) are coordinated to prevent or treat aggressive behavior and conduct problems, especially noncompliance, while increasing prosocial behaviors and overall social competence. The program design is consistent with Patterson's social-learning model, which focuses on multiple risk factors including harsh parenting and coercive behavior in the development of either oppositional defiant disorder or conduct disorder (Webster-Stratton, 1990).

Program Description

The parent training series has both BASIC and ADVANCE programs. BASIC level, requiring 12 to 14 sessions 2 hours in length, emphasizes parenting skills known to promote social competence and reduce behavior problems. These skills include knowing how to help children learn and being able to play with them in a developmentally appropriate way. Behavioral change skills covered in the groups include effective use of praise and incentives to promote desirable behaviors, limit setting, ignoring, use of time out, and use of natural consequences to decrease undesirable behaviors. Videotaped vignettes demonstrate the methods and provide material for problem-solving discussions. The ADVANCE level, requiring 10 to 12 weekly sessions 2 hours in length, is designed for parents who have successfully completed BASIC. ADVANCE emphasizes parents' interpersonal skills, including communication, anger management, problem solving with other adults, and support seeking. A third series, Supporting Your Child's Education, which also follows BASIC, is designed to teach parents to help their children with reading and homework and to work collaboratively with school staff members. It also requires 10 to 12 weekly sessions 2 hours in length.

Teacher training concentrates on managing the classroom, promoting children's prosocial behavior, reducing classroom aggression, increasing cooperation with teachers and other students, as well as developing academic skills. Videotapes of teachers interacting with children either effectively or ineffectively in classrooms are used to illustrate important concepts and facilitate discussion. Teachers rehearse new skills in role-playing exercises and homework assignments. Teacher training can be delivered in a 6-day intensive format, in increments of a day a month, or in 18–20 weekly inservice sessions of 2 hours length.

The cognitive-behavioral program for children, focusing primarily on 4- to 7-year-olds, is known as Dinosaur School or Dina Dinosaur's Social Skills and Problem-Solving Curriculum. The curriculum can be delivered as small-group therapy to an identified target group or preventively to whole classes. Treatment groups meet for 18–22 sessions of 2 hours length, usually held weekly. When used for whole classes, the curriculum is delivered in 45-minute class periods that total about 60 lessons. This training series, taught by the Dina Dinosaur character, addresses emotional literacy, perspective taking, friendship, anger management, and interpersonal problem solving. There is also material addressing school rules and BASIC skills contributing to success in school. This series is also video based, with the tapes available in American or British English and Spanish. Puppets and multiethnic characters model the skills. Groups are designed to be fun, with entertaining books, detective home activities, and games. Handouts for parent use at home are available.

A well-developed set of Incredible Years materials is available through Webster-Stratton at the University of Washington. This includes videotapes for the three parent groups, a guide for self-administering BASIC when no groups are available, leader manuals that include discussion questions, homework options, and guidance for using the videotapes. In addition, a book for parents called *The Incredible Years: A Trouble-Shooting Guide for Parents of Children Ages 3–8,* "refrigerator notes" for parents (brief reminders of key concepts), and visual aids are available. Practical aspects of having successful groups for parents such as child care, timing, and space are discussed in the training materials. Training resources for the teacher series include videotapes made in large classes with one teacher and smaller, special education classes with several teachers or aides. The vignettes are used to prompt discussion and group problem solving and sharing. Last, the Dina Dinosaur curriculum (Webster-Stratton, 2000) consists of videotapes for modeling, two child-size puppets who get help from the children for problems and allow for role playing, practice activities, games, books, and the detective club activity book that stars one of the puppets.

Outcome Research

There is strong empirical support for this prevention and treatment package and its components. Incredible Years has been designated a

Model Program by SAMHSA and was rated exemplary by the OJJDP. An American Psychological Association commission found it to be one of the few evidence-based programs shown to reduce aggression in children who are 4 to 8 years old. Similarly, Blueprints for Violence Prevention recognized the program as having a strong evidence base.

The parent, teacher, and child components have been evaluated in randomized trials with control groups. Outcome measures included observations of behavior at home and school, responses to the parent and teacher forms of the Child Behavior Checklist (Achenbach, 1991), and related standardized measures. Webster-Stratton and her colleagues have carried out multiple studies of treatment outcomes and their persistence. In a laudable research decision, Webster-Stratton removed herself from activities such as recruiting, obtaining consent, managing and analyzing data, which her colleagues and the University of Washington have arranged to carry out, so that outcome findings to support the program she developed and sells are not biased (M. J. Reid, Webster-Stratton, & Hammond, 2003). The first component developed, parent training, was shown to significantly improve the at-home behaviors of 75% of treated children compared to controls, with outcomes measured immediately after groups completed training (Webster-Stratton, 1990). More significantly, the improvements were maintained at 1- and 2-year follow-ups (Webster-Stratton & Hammond, 1997; Webster-Stratton, Reid, & Hammond, 2004). The addition of the teacher and child programs helped to target at-school conduct problems as well as those occurring at home (Webster-Stratton & Hammond, 1997; Webster-Stratton et al., 2004).

In 2003, M. J. Reid et al. published a study examining the relative importance of each component and combinations of components. They studied 159 children who were 4 to 7 years old and who were diagnosed with oppositional defiant disorder. Children were randomly assigned to parent training only, parent and teacher training, child training, child plus teacher training, all three components, or a wait-list control. Outcome measures included (1) parent reports of child behavior and independent observations of parent and child interactions at home, (2) teacher reports of child behavior and independent observations of interactions in the classroom, and (3) observations of children with peers in a structured playroom situation. Follow-up outcome measures included parent and teacher reports. Following the intervention (about 6 months in duration), all treatment groups showed significantly fewer problems with conduct with teachers and mothers on all measures relative to the wait-list controls. Children who had been in the Dinosaur School condition (or in combinations that included that child component) showed more prosocial skills with peers than did the controls. Interestingly, teachers and parents employed fewer negative behavior management actions for children in the intervention group. All parent training conditions, whether alone or in combination, resulted in more positive and less negative parenting by mothers. Teacher training improved behavior management strategies and teacher reports of conduct problem behaviors in target children. Results persisted at the 1- and 2-year follow-up with a few exceptions. At that 2-year follow-up, 75% of the children were seen as functioning in the "normal" range on parent and teacher questionnaires. Teacher training was especially beneficial for children who had shown conduct problems at home and at school prior to treatment. Mothers who were rated as highly critical at the end of treatment had children with the least gains in home and school behavior ratings (M. J. Reid et al., 2003).

Early Risers: Skills for Success

Early Risers: Skills for Success was developed at the University of Minnesota and initially applied with semirural, low- to middle-income Caucasian children at high risk because of their aggressive behavior (August, Realmuto, Hektner, & Bloomquist, 2001). Later it was extended to African American and other minority children in low-income urban areas. The program was designed to be implemented in schools, although later a community service organization aspect was added. The Early Risers program was geared toward children ages 6–10 who would be classified as "early starters" on the pathway to antisocial behavior, especially those with high levels of aggression. Multiple risk factors are conceptualized as contributing to the further development of undesirable and aggressive behaviors, with the accumulation of disruptive behavior and poor skill acquisition leading ultimately to academic failure, peer rejection, alienation from school, and experimentation with more serious conduct problem behaviors. The program also attends to protective factors that could help to alter the child's developmental trajectory.

Program Description

Gerald August and colleagues (2001; August, Hektner, Egan, Realmuto, & Bloomquist, 2002), the program developers, described the Early Risers program as multicomponent and high intensity. The two main components of the program are the CORE and FLEX interventions. CORE activities are those addressing the child level by improving competence in areas of school, peers, and family. Interventionists monitor children's behavior and use the information in weekly consultations with classroom teachers, typically beginning in first grade. In the Early Risers program, teachers are not expected to deliver program curriculum or use a particular classroom management method. An evening program for families, with concurrent parent training and child skills groups, is also part of the CORE program. These groups use the Webster-Stratton BASIC and ADVANCE curriculum for parents and the Dinosaur School curriculum for the children (see the Incredible Years section for more detail). The other CORE component is a summer program beginning soon after children are identified, between kindergarten and first grade, offered four full days a week for 6 weeks and modeled after Pelham's Summer Treatment Program (Pelham & Hoza, 1996). Basic academic skills and enrichment activities are offered daily along with social skills training, creative arts, and physical activities. It follows Pelham's model, which uses a highly structured token system and daily report card. In urban settings, there is an optional program for after school.

The FLEX interventions focus on the parents and siblings of the identified children and are individually tailored by case managers. Based in the social ecological perspective of Bronfenbrenner (1979), the goal is to ensure parental investment in promoting the child's development along a healthy trajectory rather than one characterized by conduct problems. Three areas of parenting competence are emphasized: behavioral control, emotional relatedness, and involvement in education (August, Realmuto, Winters, & Hektner, 2001). An important aspect of the program is to assist school staff and community members to move from seeing parents as part of the problem to being part of the solution. Continuing the ecological orientation, FLEX home visitors, known as "family advocates," attempt to provide support similar to that offered by informal social networks. Families are assisted in becoming more well integrated into various community institutions, including the school. Often family advocates serve as liaisons and "service brokers," first building a relationship with the family and then bridging gaps between the families and services that families might not know about or decline without assistance. The intensity of services varies with the level of need of the family (August, Egan, Realmuto, & Hektner, 2003).

Five-day training programs and further phone and e-mail technical assistance are offered. A training manual, video, and other resources are also available for purchase. The program recommends that screening and recruiting children begin during the middle of the kindergarten year so that identification is finished in time to invite target children to the summer program. Family advocates require training but also time (3–6 months) to develop referral sources and relationships within the community. The family program staff can be the same trained staff already described. With trained supervisors, the summer program staff training can be carried out the week prior to the arrival of the children.

Outcome Research

There is excellent empirical support for this treatment package and its components. Both Early Risers overall and its Incredible Years components have been designated Model Programs by SAMHSA and rated as exemplary by the OJJDP. Evaluation of the program included 3-year follow-up, for which more than 80% of the target children were tracked. A control group of the next year's kindergartners who did not receive services was employed for comparison. Participants in the Early Riser: Skills for Success program showed significant improvement in academic achievement relative to controls. The largest gains were in basic reading skills. Children also made significant gains in social skills and leadership over the 3 years relative to controls. In an unexpected finding, both target and control children improved in self-regulation over the 3 years (August et al., 2002). However, the children who as kindergartners had the highest aggression scores on the Child Behavior Checklist made significant gains relative to high-aggression control children, demonstrating a large effect size (August, Realmuto, Hektner, et al., 2001). Participation in the family program of the CORE interventions was associated with improved parent behavior management and gains in child social skills (August et al., 2002). A dose effect was found for the FLEX component, with families receiving higher proportions of those services reporting greater investment in their children's development and less psychological distress (August, Realmuto, Hektner, et al., 2001; August, Lee, Bloomquist, Realmuto, & Hektner, 2003).

Fast Track

Fast Track, a comprehensive prevention and remediation strategy for chronic and severe conduct problems, was developed by the Conduct Problems Prevention Research Group (CPPRG; 1992) for at-risk children identified in kindergarten and extending through the 10th grade. The program was derived from longitudinal research on the development of serious adolescent conduct problems, similar to the underpinnings of the Incredible Years. This body of literature suggests that such problems develop from a combination of child, family, and community risk factors that interact across the period from childhood through adolescence. Because risk is related to developmental deficits that accrue across significant periods of childhood, the CPPRG argued that interventions should be expected to take time and must facilitate development of social and self-regulation skills. According to the CPPRG (1992), "The interventions should not only focus on building behavioral and cognitive skills in the school and family environments, but also focus specifically on changing the patterns of interaction among members of the child's social fields (family, school, and peer) to promote consistent expectations for the child's performance" (p. 511). Besides a focused program for children identified as being at high risk for developing serious conduct problems, Fast Track also provides a program of universal prevention education based on the Promoting Alternative THinking Strategies (PATHS) curriculum (Greenberg & Kusche, 1998; Greenberg, Kusche, Cook, & Quamma, 1995). The most intensive activities are in the earliest grades and then again during the transition to middle school.

Program Description

Fast Track involves five integrated component activities for the children designated at risk. The first is parent training, using a social-learning-based approach, well established as a useful way of intervening to alter the responses to a child. Parents of first graders meet for 22 sessions to address the development of a more positive relationship between the school and the family and to learn specific skills to diminish coercive interactions and to make parent–child relationships more positive. Sessions early in the year focus on helping children succeed in school by setting up organized learning times at home and by helping parents become involved in the educational process. Parents are introduced to the PATHS (Kusche & Greenberg, 1994) curriculum the children learn and are taught ways to coach their children in implementing the anger control and problem-solving strategies. Parents are taught the skills for their own use as well. The remaining sessions are spent on developing positive parent–child interactions and decreasing the frequency of problem behaviors, especially noncompliance and aggression.

The second component is home visiting. Home visits or phone calls are used biweekly to practice skills taught in groups, apply concepts to the actual family environment, and respond to difficulties parents are having implementing the skills. Additionally, the home visits are designed to teach parents problem-solving skills, to promote parental feelings of efficacy, and to increase and enhance family organization to provide a safe and supportive environment for the children. The approach during visits is to ask parents a series of questions and work collaboratively with parents to solve problems in their current lives. The questions help structure the parents' information processing and ultimately contribute to their confidence as parents. Home visits continue during the summer after first grade.

The third component is social skills training for the child with the intention of improving peer relations, including reducing aggressive interchanges. Fast Track includes previously tested approaches that focus on friendship and play skills. Methods addressing self-control and anger management as well as interpersonal problem-solving skills are included in a developmental sequence. The concept and skills of reciprocity are included in the friendship maintenance sessions. Sessions begin with presentation of a specific skill or concept using videotapes, stories, puppets, and role plays by group coaches. The coaches then encourage practice through fun activities such as board games, puppet shows, and dramatic play to provide opportunities to give feedback on the use of the target skills. To enhance generalization, each group member has a half-hour guided play session with a typical classmate (rotating throughout the year). These structured sessions provide mutually rewarding experiences for the children and allow the peer a different view of the target child than may have been the case in the past.

The fourth component of the intervention is academic tutoring related primarily to reading. Coie and Krehbiel (1984) found that academic tutoring with socially rejected children with achievement difficulties improved test scores, classroom behavior, and peer ratings. Fast Track uses phonics program suitable for implementation by paraprofessionals that has been shown to boost readiness of children from poor urban backgrounds. The tutor meets with the child twice during the week and once on Saturday with parents present in order to demonstrate the child-paced aspects of the program but also to help parents see progress in their children's learning. The joint sessions also allow for further collaboration between parents and school staff.

The fifth component is classroom intervention to increase reinforcement for positive behaviors and improve contingencies for behavior management. Teachers are also trained by the Fast Track staff in the use of the PATHS curriculum. This curriculum is designed developmentally for first through fifth graders to enhance self-control, interpersonal problem solving, and emotional awareness. It is based on the affective–behavioral–cognitive–dynamic model of development, which holds that a child's coping (reflected in behavior and internal regulation) is directly related to emotional awareness, self-control, behavioral skills, and understanding of the social system on a cognitive level (Greenberg, Kusche, & Speltz, 1990). PATHS has been field-tested in general classrooms with children of diverse backgrounds and with a variety of special-needs students (Kam, Greenberg, & Kusche, 2004). Classroom teachers present the PATHS material to all the students in their classes three times a week with didactic instruction, modeling, and role playing, providing a universal prevention strategy and helping create a positive peer climate. Generalization is an essential element of PATHS, so the concepts are used to solve problems during the course of the school day. Additionally, the parent updates in group and on handouts suggest ways they can promote the new competence through reinforcement and home activities.

Outcome Research

The Fast Track program has been rated as exemplary by the OJJDP, and the PATHS program has been designated a Model Program by SAMHSA. The multisite evaluation involved schools in four areas of the country all selected as high risk on the basis of local neighborhood crime and poverty statistics (CPPRG, 1999, 2002). Across all sites, the participant sample, primarily boys (69%), was 51% African American, 47% European American, and 2% Hispanic or Pacific Islander. Children were assigned to intervention or control groups on the basis of school attended, as Fast Track is whole-school based. A total of 54 elementary schools were randomly assigned to intervention or control, with a resulting 445 children in the intervention condition and 446 in the control condition. These numbers do not include those children only involved in the universal prevention in the intervention schools.

At the end of the first-grade year, behavioral observations carried out by independent raters indicated lower rates of problem behavior among target children in the intervention schools. Fewer intervention group children spent time in special education, and peer relations were better. Evaluation of the universal intervention found significant effects on peer ratings of aggression and hyperactive–disruptive behavior. Independent observers rated the classroom as being more positive. Quality of implementation of PATHS by classroom teachers predicted variation in assessments of classroom functioning. Similarly, results at the end of the first 3 years indicated that significantly more intervention group children were rated as free of conduct problems than children in the control group. Parent ratings provided added support for those findings and extended the improvement to behavior at home. Effect sizes were moderate but clear. Larger and more varied effects were noted at the end of the third year than the first. An exception was for peer relations, which was attributed to the mixing of class groups within schools so that there were new acquaintanceships without the support of the peer play sessions used in the first grade.

Coping Power

The Coping Power Program evolved from expansion of and improvements to its empirically validated predecessor, Anger Coping. Coping Power is a multicomponent program designed to prevent and address aggressive behavior in 9- to 11-year-old boys at a time when they are reaching puberty and junior high. Rooted in the contextual social-cognitive model, it holds that aggressive children make judgments based on distorted perception of both social events and the intentions of others. Aggressive children have also been shown to have limited or maladaptive problem solving when conflicts arise. The model also stresses the importance of parent–child processes in the development and maintenance of aggressive behaviors.

Program Description

The Coping Power Program is composed of activities for parents and children. During the first half of an academic year, boys are identified on the basis of teacher nomination and responses to a three-item Likert-type scale regarding aggressive and disruptive behaviors. In the second half of the academic year, students are involved in eight group sessions of the child program, developed from the Anger Coping Program. The programming continues the entire next academic year, with 25 group sessions, each requiring 40–60 minutes. Groups are small, with four to six boys; a leader trained at the master's or doctoral level in psychology, social work, or related field; and one of the school counselors. The child program includes behavioral goal setting, awareness of emotions and associated arousal, techniques for handling anger and provocation, perspective taking and attribution training, social problem-solving skills, refusal training to deal with peer pressures, and academic organization and study skills. These goals are addressed in an atmosphere where group rules have been set and are clear to all. Puppets are used for role play, allowing at least one step of distance to expedite coping self-talk, which is then rewarded. The children also create videotapes to demonstrate skills through writing their own scripts and acting out skill-based skits.

The parent program calls for 16 group sessions over the same time period delivered in groups of four to six parents, usually at the boys' school. Efforts are made to include both mothers and fathers whenever possible. Parents learn to discriminate between prosocial and disruptive behaviors, give clear commands, and establish age-appropriate rules. Rules of behavior management, including use of rewards and negative consequences, are presented, modeled, and monitored. Family communication is encouraged, and parents are taught to support the Coping Power child component at home. Last, parents are taught stress management skills to help them remain calm and in control, especially during disciplinary acts. Educational video segments are under development to facilitate building skills taught in this program (W. M. Nelson & J. Lochman, personal communication, March 22, 2007). Lochman and his colleagues have published detailed guidelines for running the groups (Larson & Lochman, 2002), allowing close replication of the program with fidelity.

Outcome Research

Many studies have confirmed the utility of the program and its components, contributing to its exemplary status in the OJJDP Model Programs Guide. In 1986, Lochman and Curry reported that anger coping groups were effective in reducing disruptive–aggressive classroom behaviors, increased on-task time in school, and reduced parental reports of aggressive behaviors at home. In 1992, Lochman published data indicating that at 3-year follow-up, boys who had had the anger coping intervention were no longer distinguishable from previously nonaggressive comparison children on measures of aggression and social skills, whereas untreated boys had higher rates of substance use and poorer problem-solving skills. Lochman and Wells (2002) described statistically equivalent groups of identified middle school boys who were randomly assigned to one of four conditions: a universal intervention, Coping Power, universal intervention plus Coping Power, or a control condition. Substance use rates were significantly lower in children who participated in the interventions. Social competence and emotional and aggressive behaviors in the boys and parenting skills of family members all improved.

At 1-year follow-up, Coping Power participation resulted in lower rates of problem behaviors and substance abuse. The best outcomes came from the combination of parent and child components. All configurations of Coping Power participation improved teacher ratings of school behaviors. The universal intervention particularly enhanced the effects of the Coping Power Program on disruptive behaviors at school (Lochman & Wells, 2003).

Additional Implementation Considerations

Anyone undertaking a therapeutic intervention does so with the hopes of achieving intended outcomes. Programs that are more successful in treating youth in school who severely act out and are aggressive share several features: (1) evidence-based practices implemented with a high degree of fidelity, (2) principal's support, (3) high-quality training to staff, (4) supervised prevention activities, (5) structured materials and plans, and (6) programs integrated into normal school routines. Thus, effective interventions within the schools are ones that forge a strong relationship between research-supported intervention programs and best practices while reshaping school systems in ways that support their use and maintain their effects over time (Walker, Ramsey, & Gresham, 2004).

The therapeutic relationship necessary for any treatment program is an important factor in program implementation, although it is not often discussed. The counselor's skills are essential in his or her ability to motivate individuals to change and to facilitate and maintain strong working relationships among youngsters and other significant individuals within the school and home settings. Such relationships involve clinician–child relationships, clinician–group relationships (if group treatment is utilized), clinician–school personnel relationships, and clinician–parent/caregiver relationships (Lochman, Powell, Jackson, & Czopp, 2006). These are essential for recruiting family involvement and retaining participants in programs. Even the best practices will not help those who refuse to participate or quit.

Multicultural competence is another critical aspect of the therapeutic relationship. Service delivery and working relationships are not usually dependent upon any unique or culturally specific set of prescriptions or guidelines. Rather, it is important for the leaders implementing therapeutic programs to demonstrate sensitivity to the participants' circumstances, resources, beliefs, worldviews, parenting traditions, or distinctive stressors, as well as the meanings they assign to intervention activities. As always, being familiar with or belonging to a particular culture does not necessarily result in a true ability to understand the manner in which a therapeutic technique or intervention within a specific program is experienced by any particular culture or individual (Ortiz, 2006). It is not enough to know either the intervention manual or the culture alone. Most probably, the exemplary programs were successful for children and teens from differing socioeconomic backgrounds and ethnic heritage in part because of the care that was demonstrated in forming relationships in participants' homes, schools, and communities. Future research will need to address the tailoring of manualized treatments to ensure that they are not only attractive, but also effective for the many diverse cultures represented in school systems. Although it is a topic beyond the scope of this chapter, several writers have proposed frameworks for adapting programs when evidence-based treatments are applied to individuals dissimilar to those who participated in the foundational research that produced the initial empirical support (e.g., Barrera & Castro, 2006; Lau, 2006).

Adolescents with histories of delinquency also pose unique challenges for interventions targeting anger and aggression. Dishion, McCord, and Poulin (1999) presented evidence that delinquent youth who associate with other antisocial peers are at risk of developing more serious delinquent behaviors. These researchers called for avoiding such association in prevention and treatment programs. This effect has not been found for preadolescents, and it appears that those at risk but not seriously involved in violent delinquency can benefit from group interventions (Greene, 2005). Approaches that focus on strengths and collaboration may be less vulnerable to negative socialization forces within the groups (Eccles & Goodman, 2002).

Evidence-Based Practices and Fidelity to Treatment Protocols

All of the reviewed intervention programs are "manual based." As such, they are all more structured than most psychological interventions conducted within school settings. The four exemplary programs selected, however, would all be referred to as "evidence-based practices in psychology" (APA [American Psychological Association] Presidential Task Force on Evidence-Based Practice, 2006). The term *evidence-based practice,* however, requires clarification, as it is not always understood or agreed upon (Chorpita, 2003). We strongly argue that it is critical to clearly define the criteria that need to be met before a program can be called "evidence based." In fact, a number of definitions of evidence-based practice have been proposed recently (e.g., Barrett & Ollendick, 2004; Kazdin & Weisz, 2003; Weisz, 2004). The term *evidence-based practices* regarding the four selected programs does not imply that they, in their current state, represent perfect interventions. Rather, there are no treatments for children and adolescents that are so effective and well validated that the use of them is a closed question. Additionally, even evidence-based treatments vary in terms of their standardization. Some programs delineate a precise session-by-session curriculum, whereas others provide a general structure for conceptualizing problems and some general techniques. In the former therapists "follow the script," and in the latter they have a great deal of latitude in conducting treatment.

The reviewed treatment programs vary to some extent in the degree of latitude for those implementing them. These programs were in part designed to facilitate "transportability" (see Kendall, 1998; Stirman, Crits-Christoph, & De Rubeis, 2004), in the sense that it makes such interventions "user friendly" for both therapist and clients by providing a structured, manual-based format for working with clients. It provides an overall framework that outlines treatment sessions and goals, supplies strategies that aid the therapist from different theoretical orientations in achieving their goals, and guides the therapist as he or she tries to tailor interventions to the particular client over the course of treatment. It provides a blueprint for practitioners who need to breathe life into the manual (Kendall, Chu, Gifford, Hayes, & Nauta, 1998). Webster-Stratton (2006) identified five important elements to aid in implementing programs to prevent and treat conduct problems. She listed standardized treatment materials; standardized high-quality training for those delivering the services; supervision and consultation for those delivering the services; ongoing fidelity monitoring, including evaluation of participating clinicians; and administrative support for the program and its staff.

Despite the proliferation of a variety of empirically evaluated treatment programs/manuals, the impact of these interventions on actual clinical practice has been modest at best (Addis & Krasnow, 2000; Chorpita & Nakamura, 2004). A major challenge still lies ahead—how to not only increase the availability of the latest knowledge about psychological treatments to deliverers and consumers of mental health services, but also actively facilitate the use of such treatments in actual practice (Stirman et al., 2004; Weisz, Sandler, Durlak, & Anton, 2005). Although the topic is beyond the scope of this chapter, various models have been proposed to bridge the gulf between empirically based interventions and everyday treatment (e.g., diffusion of innovations models—Gotham, 2004; deployment-focused model—Weisz, Jensen, & McLeod, 2005).

Some readers may find the resource demands or the time required to carry out the exemplary programs according to protocol to be too great for their settings. Although choosing pieces of a program to employ will probably not result in the same outcome as a full replication, there is still much to be gained from the strategies, techniques, and approaches of these empirically based practices. Using the best possible therapeutic approaches and continuing the empirical evaluation of interventions is the best hope for being better able to assist aggressive children and adolescents who act out to develop into adults who are healthy, productive members of society.

References

Achenbach, T. M. (1991). *Manual for the Child Behavior Checklist and Revised Child Behavior Profile*. Burlington: University of Vermont.
Addis, M. E., & Krasnow, A. D. (2000). A rational survey of practicing psychologists' attitudes toward psychotherapy treatment manuals. *Journal of Consulting and Clinical Psychology, 68,* 331–339.
APA Presidential Task Force on Evidence-Based Practice. (2006). Evidence-based practice in psychology. *American Psychologist, 61,* 271–285.
August, G. J., Egan, E. A., Realmuto, G. M., & Hektner, J. M. (2003). Parceling component

effects of a multifaceted prevention program for disruptive elementary school children. *Journal of Abnormal Child Psychology, 31,* 515–527.

August, G. J., Hektner, J. M., Egan, F. A., Realmuto, G. M., & Bloomquist, M. L. (2002). The Early Risers longitudinal prevention trial: Examination of 3-year outcomes in aggressive children with intent-to-treat and as-intended analyses. *Psychology of Addictive Behaviors, 16,* 527–539.

August, G. J., Lee, S. S., Bloomquist, M. L., Realmuto, G. M., & Hektner, J. M. (2003). Dissemination of an evidence-based prevention innovation for aggressive children living in culturally diverse, urban neighborhoods: The Early Risers effectiveness study. *Prevention Science, 4,* 271–286.

August, G. J., Realmuto, G. M., Hektner, J. M., & Bloomquist, M. L. (2001). An integrated components preventive intervention for aggressive elementary school children: The "Early Risers" program. *Journal of Clinical and Consulting Psychology, 69,* 614–626.

August, G. J., Realmuto, G. M., Winters, K. C., & Hektner, J. M. (2001). Prevention of adolescent drug abuse: Targeting high-risk children with a multifaceted intervention model—The Early Risers "Skills for Success" program. *Applied and Preventive Psychology, 10,* 135–154.

Barrera, M., Jr., & Castro, F. G. (2006). A heuristic framework for the cultural adaptation of interventions. *Clinical Psychology: Science and Practice, 13,* 311–316.

Barrett, P. M., & Ollendick, T. H. (Eds.). (2004). *Handbook of interventions that work with children and adolescents: Prevention and treatment.* New York: Wiley.

Brandt, E. E., & Zlotnick, S. J. (1988). *The psychology and treatment of the youthful offender.* Springfield, IL: Charles C Thomas.

Bronfenbrenner, U. (1979). *The ecology of human development: Experiences by nature and design.* Cambridge, MA: Harvard University Press.

Burns, B. J., Costello, E. J., Angold, A., Tweed, D., Stangl, D., Farmer, E., et al. (1995). Children's mental health service use across service sectors. *Health Affairs, 14,* 147–159.

Burns, L., & Patterson, D. R. (2000). Factor structure of the Eyberg Child Behavior Inventory: A parent rating scale of oppositional defiant behavior toward adults, inattentive behavior, and conduct problem behavior. *Journal of Clinical Child Psychology, 29,* 569–577.

Chesney-Lind, M., & Brown. M. (1999). Girls and violence: An overview. In D. J. Flannery & C. R. Huff (Eds.), *Youth violence: Prevention, intervention, and social policy* (pp. 171–199). Washington, DC: American Psychiatric Press.

Chorpita, B. F. (2003). The frontier of evidence-based practice. In A. E. Kazdin & J. R. Weisz (Eds.), *Evidence-based psychotherapies for children and adolescents* (pp. 42–59). New York: Guilford Press.

Chorpita, B. F., & Nakamura, B. J. (2004). Four considerations for dissemination of intervention innovations. *Clinical Psychology: Science and Practice, 11,* 364–367.

Christner, R. W., Friedberg, R. D., & Sharp, L. (2006). Working with angry and aggressive youth. In R. B. Menotti, A. Freeman, & R. W. Christner (Eds.), *Cognitive behavioral interventions in education settings: A handbook for practice* (pp. 203–220). New York: Routledge.

Christopherson, E. R., & Mortweet, S. L. (2003). *Treatments that work with children: Empirically suggested strategies for managing problems.* Washington, DC: American Psychological Association.

Cohen, M., Miller, T., & Rossman, S. (1994). The costs and consequences of violent behavior in the United States. In A. J. Reiss & J. A. Roth (Eds.), *Understanding and preventing violence: Vol. 4. Consequences and control* (pp. 67–167). Washington, DC: National Academy Press.

Coie, J. D., & Krehbiel, G. K. (1984). Effects of academic tutoring on the social status of low-achieving, socially rejected children. *Child Development, 55,* 1465–1478.

Conduct Problems Prevention Research Group. (1992). A developmental and clinical model for the prevention of conduct disorder: The FAST Track program. *Development and Psychopathology, 4,* 509–527.

Conduct Problems Prevention Research Group. (1999). Initial impact of the Fast Track prevention trial for conduct problems: I. The high-risk sample. *Journal of Consulting and Clinical Psychology, 67,* 648–657.

Conduct Problems Prevention Research Group. (2002). Evaluation of the first 3 years of Fast Track prevention trial with children at high risk for adolescent conduct problems. *Journal of Abnormal Child Psychology, 30,* 19–35.

Dishion, T. J., McCord, J., & Poulin, F. (1999). When interventions harm: Peer groups and problem behavior. *American Psychologist, 54,* 755–764.

Dodge, K. A. (1991). The structure and function of reactive and proactive aggression. In D. J. Pepler & K. H. Rubin (Eds.), *Development and treatment of childhood aggression* (pp. 201–218). Hillsdale, NJ: Erlbaum.

Dodge, K. (1993). The future research on conduct disorder. *Development and Psychopathology, 5,* 311–320.

Drummond, T. (1993). *The Student Risk Screening Scale (SRSS).* Grants Pass, OR: Josephine County Mental Health Program.

Dumas, J. E. (1989). Treating antisocial behavior in children: Child and family approaches. *Clinical Psychology Review, 9,* 197–222.

Eccles, J. S., & Goodman, J. (2002). *Community programs to promote youth development.* Washington, DC: National Academy Press.

Eron, L. D., & Slaby, R. G. (1994). Introduction. In L. D. Eron, J. H. Gentry, & P. Schlegel (Eds.), *Reason to hope: A psychological perspective on violence and youth* (pp. 1–22). Washington, DC: American Psychological Association.

Eyberg, S. M., Boggs, J. R., & Algina, J. (1995). New developments in psychosocial, pharmacological, and combined treatments of conduct disorders in aggressive children. *Psychopharmacology Bulletin, 31,* 83–91.

Fagan, J., Zimring, F. E., & Kim, J. (1998). Declining homicide in New York City: A tale of two trends. *Journal of Criminal Law and Criminology, 88,* 1277–1323.

Farrington, D. P. (1986). The application of stress theory to the study of family violence: Principles, problems, and prospects. *Journal of Family Violence, 1,* 131–147.

Farrington, D. P. (1991). Childhood aggression and adult violence: Early precursors and life outcomes. In D. J. Pepler & K. H. Rubin (Eds.), *Development and treatment of childhood aggression* (pp. 5–29). Hillsdale, NJ: Erlbaum.

Farrington, D. P. (1994). Childhood, adolescent, and adult features of violent males. In L. R. Huesmann (Ed.), *Aggressive behavior: Current perspectives* (pp. 215–240). New York: Plenum.

Farrington, D. P., Loeber, R., & Van Kamman, W. B. (1990). Long-term clinical outcomes of hyperactivity–impulsivity–attention deficit and conduct problems in childhood. In L. N. Robins & M. Rutter (Eds.), *Straight and devious pathways from childhood to adulthood* (pp. 62–81). Cambridge, UK: Cambridge University Press.

Feil, E. G., Walker, H. M., & Severson, H. H. (1995). The Early Screening Project for young children with behavior problems. *Journal of Emotional and Behavioral Disorders, 4,* 194–202.

Fingerhut, L. A., & Kleinman, J. C. (1990). International and interstate comparisons of homicide among young males. *Journal of the American Medical Association, 263,* 3292–3295.

Furlong, M. J., & Smith, D. C. (1994). Assessment of youth's anger, hostility and aggression, using self-report and rating scales. In M. J. Furlong & D. C. Smith (Eds.), *Anger, hostility and aggression: Assessment, prevention, and intervention strategies for youth* (pp. 167–244). New York: Wiley.

Goldstein, A. P., Glick, B., & Gibbs, J. C. (1998). *Aggression replacement training: A comprehensive intervention for aggressive youth* (rev. ed.). Champaign, IL: Research Press.

Gotham, H. J. (2004). Differences of mental health and substance abuse treatments: Development, dissemination, and implementation. *Clinical Psychology: Service and Practice, 11,* 160–176.

Greenberg, M. T., Domitrovich, C., & Bumbarger, B. (2001). *Preventing mental disorders in school-age children: A review of the effectiveness of prevention programs.* Available from the Prevention Research Center for the Promotion of Human Development, College of Health and Human Development, Pennsylvania State University, State College.

Greenberg, M. T., & Kusche, C. A. (1998). *Promoting social and emotional development in deaf children: The PATHS Project.* Seattle: University of Washington Press.

Greenberg, M. T., Kusche, C. A., Cook, E. T., & Quamma, J. P. (1995). Promoting emotional competence in school-aged children: The effects of the PATHS curriculum. *Development and Psychopathology, 7,* 117–136.

Greenberg, M. T., Kusche, C. A., & Speltz, M. (1990). Emotional regulation, self-control and psychopathology: The role of relationships in early childhood. In D. Cicchetti & S. Toth (Eds.), *Rochester Symposium on Developmental Psychopathology* (Vol. 2, pp. 21–56). New York: Cambridge University Press.

Greene, M. B. (2004). *Implications of research showing harmful effects of group activities with anti-social adolescents, Persistently Safe Schools 2004: Proceedings of the National Conference of the Hamilton Fish Institute on School and Community Violence.* Washington, DC: Hamilton Fish Institute.

Hawker, D. S. J., & Boulton, M. J. (2000). Twenty years' research on peer victimization and psychosocial adjustment: A meta-analytic review of cross-sectional studies. *Journal of Child Psychology and Psychiatry, 41,* 441–455.

Hawkins, D. F., Laub, J. H., & Lauritsen, J. L. (1998). Race, ethnicity, and serious juvenile offending. In R. Loeber & D. P. Farrington (Eds.), *Serious and violent juvenile offenders: Risk factors and successful interventions* (pp. 30–46). Thousand Oaks, CA: Sage.

Kam, C., Greenberg, M. T., & Kusche, C. A. (2004). Sustained effects of the PATHS curriculum on the social and psychological adjustment of children in special education. *Journal of Emotional and Behavioral Disorders, 12,* 66–78.

Kaufman, P., Chen, X., Choy, S. P., Peter, K., Ruddy, S. A., Miller, A. K., et al. (2001). *Indicators of school crime and safety: 2001* (NCES 2002-113/NCJ-190075). Washington, DC: U.S. Departments of Education and Justice.

Kazdin, A. E. (1987). Treatment of antisocial behavior in children: Current status and future directions. *Psychological Bulletin, 102,* 187–203.

Kazdin, A. E. (1993). Treatment of conduct disorder: Progress and directions in psychotherapy research. *Development and Psychopathology, 5,* 277–310.

Kazdin, A. E. (1995). *Conduct disorder in childhood and adolescence* (2nd ed.). Thousand Oaks, CA: Sage.

Kazdin, A. E. (2003). Problem-solving skills training and parent management training for conduct disorder. In A. E. Kazdin & J. R. Weisz (Eds.), *Evidence-based psychotherapies for children and adolescents* (pp. 241–262). New York: Guilford Press.

Kazdin, A. E., & Weisz, J. R. (Eds.). (2003). *Evidence-based psychotherapies for children and adolescents.* New York: Guilford Press.

Kendall, P. C. (1998). Empirically-supported psychological therapies. *Journal of Consulting and Clinical Psychology, 66,* 3–6.

Kendall, P. C., Chu, B., Gifford, A., Hayes, C., & Nauta, M. (1998). Breathing life into a manual: Flexibility and creativity with manual-based treatments. *Cognitive and Behavioral Practice, 5,* 177–198.

Kusche, C. A., & Greenberg, M. T. (1994). *The PATHS curriculum.* Seattle, WA: Developmental Research and Programs.

Larson, J., & Lochman, J. E. (2002). *Helping schoolchildren cope with anger.* New York: Guilford Press.

Lau, A. S. (2006). Making the case for selective and directed cultural adaptations of evidence-based treatments: Examples from parent training. *Clinical Psychology: Science and Practice, 13,* 295–310.

Lipsey, M. W. (1992). The effects of treatment on juvenile delinquents: Results from meta-analysis. In F. Loesel, D. Bender, & T. Bliesener (Eds.), *Psychology and the law: International perspectives* (pp. 131–143). Berlin, NY: Walter de Gruyter.

Lochman, J. E. (1992). Cognitive-behavioral intervention with aggressive boys: Three-year follow-up and preventive effects. *Journal of Consulting and Clinical Psychology, 60,* 426–432.

Lochman, J. E., & Curry, J. F. (1986). Effects of problem-solving training and self-instruction training with aggressive boys. *Journal of Clinical Child Psychology, 15,* 159–164.

Lochman, J. E., Powell, N. R., Jackson, M. F., & Czopp, W. (2006). Cognitive-behavior psychotherapy for conduct disorder: The Coping Power Program. In W. M. Nelson, III, A. J. Finch, Jr., & K. J. Hart (Eds.), *Conduct disorders: A practical guide to comparative treatments* (pp. 177–215). New York: Springer.

Lochman, J. E., & Wells, K. C. (2002). The Coping Power Program at the middle school transition: Universal and indicated prevention effects. *Psychology of Addictive Behaviors, 16,* S40–S54.

Lochman, J. E., & Wells, K. C. (2003). Effectiveness of the Coping Power Program and of classroom intervention with aggressive children: Outcomes at a 1-year follow-up. *Behavior Therapy, 34,* 493–515.

Loeber, R., Dishion, T., & Patterson, G. (1984). Multiple-gating: A multistage assessment procedure for identifying youths at risk for delinquency. *Journal of Research in Crime and Delinquency, 21,* 7–32.

Loeber, R., & Farrington, D. P. (Eds.). (1998). *Serious and violent juvenile offenders: Risk factors and successful interventions.* Thousand Oaks, CA: Sage.

Loeber, R., & Farrington, D. (Eds.). (2001). *Child delinquents.* Thousand Oaks, CA: Sage.

Loeber, R., & Stouthamer, M. (1998). Development of juvenile aggression and violence: Some common misconceptions and controversies. *American Psychologist, 53,* 242–259.

Lyon, R. (2002, November). *The current status and impact of U.S. reading research.* Keynote address to the National Association of University Centers for Excellence in Developmental Disabilities, Bethesda, MD.

Mash, E. J., & Wolfe, D. A. (2005). *Abnormal child psychology* (3rd ed.). Belmont, CA: Thomson Wadsworth.

Miller, G. E., & Prinz, R. J. (1990). Enhancement of social learning family intervention for childhood conduct disorder. *Psychological Bulletin, 108,* 291–307.

Miller, L. S. (1994). Preventive interventions for conduct disorders: A review. *Child and Adolescent Psychiatric Clinics of North America, 3,* 405–420.

Moffitt, T. E. (1993). Adolescence-limited and life-course-persistent antisocial behavior: A developmental taxonomy. *Psychology Review, 100,* 674–701.

Moffitt, T. E., Caspi, A., Dickson, N., Silva, P., & Stanton, W. (1996). Childhood-onset versus adolescent-onset antisocial conduct problems in males: Natural history from ages 3 to 18 years. *Development and Psychopathology, 8,* 399–424.

National School Boards Association. (1993, January). Report of the National School Boards Association on violence in schools. *Los Angeles Times.*

Nelson, W. M., III, & Finch, A. J., Jr. (2008). *"Keeping your cool": The anger management workbook* (2nd ed.). Cincinatti, OH: LochNels Productions, Inc..

Nelson, W. M., III, & Finch, A. J., Jr. (2000). *Children's Inventory of Anger: Manual.* Los Angeles: Western Psychological Services.

Nelson, W. M., III, Finch, A. J., Jr., & Hart, K. J. (2006). *Conduct disorders: A practitioner's guide to comparative treatments.* New York: Springer.

Ortiz, S. O. (2006). Multicultural issues in working with children and families: Responsive intervention in the educational setting. In R. B. Mennuti, A. Freeman, & R. W. Christner (Eds.), *Cognitive-behavioral interventions in educational settings: A handbook for practice* (pp. 21–36). New York: Routledge.

Patterson, G., Reid, J. B., & Dishion, T. J. (1992). *Antisocial boys.* Eugene, OR: Castalia.

Pelham, W. E., & Hoza, B. (1996). Intensive treatment: A summer treatment program for children with ADHD. In *Psychosocial treatments for child and adolescent disorders: Empirically based strategies for clinical practice* (pp. 311–340). Washington, DC: American Psychological Association.

Pepler, D. J., & Rubin, K. H. (Eds.). (1991). *The development and treatment of childhood aggression.* Hillsdale, NJ: Erlbaum.

Reid, J. B. (1993). Prevention of conduct disorder before and after school entry: Relating interventions to developmental findings. *Development & Psychopathology, 5,* 311–219.

Reid, J. B., Patterson, G. R., & Snyder, J. J. (Eds.). (2002). *Antisocial behavior in children and adolescents: A developmental analysis and the Oregon model for intervention.* Washington, DC: American Psychological Association.

Reid, M. J., Webster Stratton, C., & Hammond, M. (2003). Follow-up of children who received the Incredible Years intervention for oppositional-defiant disorder: Maintenance and prediction of 2-year outcome. *Behavior Therapy, 34,* 471–491.

Robinson, E. A., Eyberg, S. M., & Ross, A. W. (1980). The standardization of an inventory of child conduct problem behaviors. *Journal of Clinical Child Psychology, 9,* 22–28.

Sanford, M., Boyles, M. H., Szatmari, P., Offord, D. R., Jamieson, E., & Spinner, M. (1999). Age-of-onset classification of conduct disorder: Reliability and validity in a prospective cohort study. *Journal of the American Academy of Child and Adolescent Psychiatry, 38,* 992–999.

Smith, E. P., Boutte, G. S., Zigler, E., & Finn-Stephenson, M. (2004). Opportunities for schools to promote resilience in children and youth. In K. Maton (Ed.), *Investing in children, youth, families and communities* (pp. 213–233). Washington, DC: American Psychological Association.

Snyder, H. N., & Sickmund, M. (1995). *Juvenile offenders and victims: A national report* (Document No. NCJ-153569). Washington, DC: U.S. Department of Justice, Office of Juvenile Justice and Delinquency Prevention.

Southam-Gerow, M. A., & Kendall, P. C. (1997). Parent-focused and cognitive-behavioral treatments of antisocial youth. In D. M. Stoff, J. Breiling, & J. D. Moser (Eds.), *Handbook of antisocial behavior* (pp. 384–394). New York: Wiley.

Stattin, H., & Magnusson, D. (1989). The role of early aggressive behavior in the frequency, seriousness, and types of later crime. *Journal of Consulting and Clinical Psychology, 57,* 710–718.

Stewart, M. A., deBlois, S., Meardon, J., & Cummings, C. (1980). Aggressive conduct disorder of children: The clinical picture. *Journal of Nervous and Mental Disease, 168,* 604–615.

Stirman, S. W., Crits-Christoph, P., & De Rubeis, R. J. (2004). Achieving successful dissemination of empirically-supported psychotherapies: A synthesis of dissemination theory. *Clinical Psychology: Science and Practice, 11,* 343–359.

Stoff, D. M., Breiling, J., & Maser, J. D. (Eds.). (1997). *Handbook of antisocial behavior.* New York: Wiley.

Stouthamer-Loeber, M., Loeber, R., & Thomas, C. (1992). Caretakers seeking help for boys with disruptive and delinquent behavior. *Comprehensive Mental Health Care, 2,* 159–178.

Tate, D. C., Reppucci, N. D., & Mulvey, E. P. (1995). Violent juvenile delinquents: Treatment effectiveness and implications for future action. *American Psychologist, 50,* 777–781.

Underwood, M. K. (2003). *Social aggression among girls.* New York: Guilford Press.

U.S. Department of Health and Human Services. (2001). *Youth violence: A report of the Surgeon General.* Rockville, MD: Author.

Walker, H., Irvin, L., Noell, J., & Singer, G. (1992). A construct score approach to the assessment of social competence: Rationale, technological considerations, and anticipated outcomes. *Behavior Modification, 16,* 448–474.

Walker, H. M., Ramsey, E., & Gresham, F. M. (2004). *Antisocial behavior in school* (2nd ed.). Belmont, CA: Wadsworth/Thomson Learning.

Walker, H., & Severson, H. (1990). *Systematic Screening for Behavior Disorders.* Longmont, CO: Sopris West.

Wasserman, G. A., & Miller, L. S. (1998). The prevention of serious and violent juvenile offending. In R. Loeber & D. P. Farrington (Eds.), *Serious and violent juvenile offenders: Risk factors and successful interventions* (pp. 197–247). Thousand Oaks, CA: Sage.

Webster-Stratton, C. (1990). Long-term follow-up of families with young conduct-problem children: From preschool to grade school. *Journal of Consulting and Clinical Psychology, 19,* 1344–1349.

Webster-Stratton, C. (2000). *Dina Dinosaur's social skills and problem-solving curriculum: Leaders guide.* Seattle, WA: Incredible Years.

Webster-Stratton, C. (2001). The Incredible Years: Parents, teachers, and children training series. In S. I. Pfeiffer & L. A. Reddy (Eds.), *Innovative mental health interventions for children: Programs that work* (pp. 31–45). New York: Haworth Press.

Webster-Stratton, C. (2006). Treating children with early-onset conduct problems: Key ingredients to implementing the Incredible Years with fidelity. In T. K. Neill (Ed.), *Helping others help children: Clinical supervision of child psychotherapy* (pp. 161–175). Washington, DC: American Psychological Association.

Webster-Stratton, C., & Hammond, M. (1997). Treating children with early-onset conduct problems: A comparison of child and parenting training interventions. *Journal of Consulting and Clinical Psychology, 65,* 93–109.

Webster-Stratton, C., Reid, M. J., & Hammond, M. (2004). Treating children with early-onset conduct problems: Intervention outcomes for parent, child, and teacher training. *Journal of Clinical Child and Adolescent Psychology, 33,* 105–124.

Weisz, J. R. (2004). *Psychotherapy for children and adolescents: Evidenced-based treatment and case examples.* London: Cambridge University Press.

Weisz, J. R., Jensen, A. L., & McLeod, B. D. (2005). Development and dissemination of child and adolescent psychotherapies: Milestones, methods, and a new development-focused model. In E. D. Hibbs & P. S. Jensen (Eds.), *Psychosocial treatments for child and adolescent disorders: Empirically based strategies for clinical practice* (2nd ed., pp. 9–39). Washington, DC: American Psychological Association.

Weisz, J. R., Sandler, I. N., Durlak, J. A., & Anton, B. S. (2005). Promoting and protecting youth mental health through evidence-based prevention and treatment. *American Psychologist, 60,* 628–648.

Werthamer-Larsson, L., Kellam, S. G., & Overson-McGregor, K. E. (Eds.). (1990). *Teacher interview: Teacher Observation of Classroom Adaptation—Revised (TOCA-R).* Baltimore: Johns Hopkins University Press.

Williams, S. L., Walker, H. M., Holmes, D., Todis, B., & Fabre, T. R. (1989). Social validation of adolescent social skills by teachers and students. *Remedial and Special Education, 10,* 18–27, 37.

PART III

COGNITIVE-BEHAVIORAL INTERVENTIONS FOR ANXIETY/PHOBIC DISORDERS

CHAPTER 7

Cognitive-Behavioral Therapy for Anxious Youth in School Settings

Advances and Challenges

ADAM S. WEISSMAN
DIANA ANTINORO
BRIAN C. CHU

*A*nxiety is a multidimensional construct featuring symptoms of physiological, cognitive, and emotional distress (Roblek & Piacentini, 2005; Kendall, Aschenbrand, & Hudson, 2003). Recent epidemiological reviews have identified anxiety as one of the most prevalent psychiatric problems affecting children and adolescents today. Including generalized anxiety disorder, separation anxiety, social phobia, and specific phobias, anxiety as a class of clinical diagnoses has been estimated to affect between 6 and 18% of youth (Woodward & Fergusson, 2001). These same reports have indicated the persistence of anxiety-based symptoms into adulthood and overall poor prognosis if left untreated.

The emergence of natural anxiety and fear in childhood commonly coincides with normative age-based milestones (e.g., separation anxiety as children enter preschool, social evaluations as expectations around performance and peer associations increase; Silverman & Ollendick, 2005). However, it is only when such developmentally normative experiences result in pervasive, uncontrollable, or interfering distress or avoidance that anxiety is considered a clinical problem (Barlow, Allen, & Choate, 2004). Although it continues to be overlooked, clinically significant anxiety is linked to a number of serious and long-lasting impairments. Anxious youth experience difficulties in social (e.g., limited or unrewarding social networks), familial (e.g., sibling/parental conflict, accommodation around anxiety), and academic (e.g., poor performance, school refusal, limited extracurricular activities; Kendall et al., 2003; Van Ameringen, Mancini, & Farvolden, 2003; Woodward & Fergusson, 2001) domains. Over time, children and adolescents with anxiety disorders experience higher rates of mood disturbances, drug and alcohol abuse, suicidal behavior, and early parenthood during their adult lives relative to nonanxious youth (Kendall et al., 2003; Woodward & Fergusson, 2001). Anxious children are also more likely to experience poor academic and professional achievement, often resulting from higher school dropout rates than their nonanxious peers (Woodward & Fergusson, 2001; Van Ameringen et al., 2003).

In addition, anxiety disorders are linked to high rates of comorbidity with other psychiatric diagnoses, suggesting a more complicated clinical picture than is often attributed to anxiety alone. A meta-analytic review by Angold and colleagues examined comorbidity rates across 21 empirical studies (Angold, Costello, & Erkanli, 1999). Findings revealed that for individuals with a primary anxiety diagnosis, rates of co-occurrence with other disorders were high, including attention-deficit/hyperactivity disorder (ADHD; 4.0–23.7%), conduct disorders (5.9–69.2%), and depression (4.4–69.2%). Additionally, the prevalence of anxiety as a secondary impairment ranged from 12.8–50.8% for ADHD, 4.8–55.3% for behavioral disorders, and 15.4–75.0% for depression.

Because youth spend the majority of their waking lives in school and because of the significance that the school setting has on a child's emotional, intellectual, and social development, there is justifiable concern about any interference that anxiety contributes to school functioning. The subjective distress, cognitive impairments, and behavioral avoidance associated with anxiety can all have direct school-related consequences, including test anxiety, poor academic achievement, sporadic attendance, difficulty with school transitions, poor social networks, and possible dropping out (Van Ameringen et al., 2003; Wood, 2006). Fortunately, substantial research has tracked the development of cognitive-behavioral and skills-building programs aimed at ameliorating anxiety symptoms and disorders. Furthermore, there have been a number of significant attempts to transport cognitive-behavioral therapy (CBT) into school-based settings where access to youth is greatest. This chapter reviews the phenomenology of anxiety, theories of its development, specific negative outcomes related to school functioning, methods for assessing anxiety, and the CBT programs designed to address these concerns. A special emphasis is placed on treatments that have been transported to school settings and the hurdles that challenge successful implementation.

The Development and Maintenance of Anxiety

The origins of anxiety are commonly conceptualized within a diathesis-stress model. Anxious individuals are thought to have a pre-existing temperament, tendency, or vulnerability that increases their susceptibility to anxious arousal, biased interpretation, or sensitivity (Lonigan & Phillips, 2001; Rapee, 2002) in the presence of a disturbing situation. Vulnerability to anxiety is conceptualized as multifactorial, including information-processing biases, personality styles, early learning histories, genetic disposition, and behavioral inhibition, among others (Mineka & Zinbarg, 2006; Hudson & Rapee, 2002; Kendall, 2000; Southam-Gerow, Henin, Chu, Marrs, & Kendall, 1997).

Predisposing individual characteristics often influence and are influenced by factors that contribute to the exacerbation and maintenance of anxiety. These include past experiences with similar events or stimuli, the individual's perceived ability to control a scenario (e.g., escape from the fearful object), future expectations with similar contexts, parental psychopathology, current and future reinforcement or punishment contingencies, and vicarious learning. Parental styles and practices also influence youth anxiety and have received much attention. Negative parenting styles that include harsh or critical parenting or overinvolvement have been associated with increased anxiety in youth (Barrett, Shortt, & Healy, 2002; Hudson & Rapee, 2002). Specific parenting practices, such as modeling of anxious behaviors and information transfer regarding potential threats, have also been shown to contribute to anxiety (Wood, McLeod, Sigman, Hwang, & Chu, 2003).

In cognitive-behavioral theories, the aforementioned factors contribute to the cognitive triad in which cognitions, behaviors, and emotions interact to create the individual's experience of the world. Within this cognitive-behavioral framework, the anxiety temperament or sensitivity manifests as, and is maintained by, behavioral avoidance, rumination or excessive worrying, and intense emotional distress that may be accompanied by physiological distress (increased heartbeat, hyperventilation, shaking, and stomach butterflies; Kendall, 2000). After an anxious individual avoids a fearful stimulus, cognitive biases are confirmed; the individual is unable to handle an unpredictable or uncontrollable situation. In the future, the individual is more likely to fear and avoid a similar situation. Each emotional component (behavioral, physiological, cognitive) is bidirectionally related to one another and serves to maintain an overall anxious response in the presence of a stimulus perceived as threatening by the individual. This relationship between avoidance, threat-sensitive cognitive styles, and increased anxiety is consistently supported by basic research and in treatment studies with anxious individuals (Craske & Mystkowski, 2006).

School Refusal

School refusal, previously known as *school phobia,* is one of the principal referral questions associated with clinical anxiety in youth. *School refusal* is often described as a child-motivated behavior in which the youth refuses to attend school, has trouble remaining in classes, or simply "skips school." School-refusal behavior typically includes emotional distress associated with attending or remaining in school. This distress may manifest in youth as difficulty waking in the morning, asking to stay home to catch up on work, feigning illness, having temper tantrums, skipping classes, frequently visiting the nurse's office, or calling parents during school to get picked up early. When refusal is infrequent and sporadic, this behavior may be benign. Chronic refusal, however, results in a number of secondary difficulties, such as falling behind in academic work, loss of contact with friends, increased dependency on parents, and long-term familial relationship difficulties. A meta-analytic study by Valles and Oddy (1984) revealed that school refusers who did not successfully return to school were later found to have less friends, engage less in social activities, experience criticism with greater sensitivity, be convicted of more crimes, and report relationships of friction with parents and other family members more so than those who returned to school quickly and successfully.

Lifetime prevalence of school refusal has been estimated in general population samples at 28% (Kearney, 2001) and has been particularly linked with anxiety. In a study of 143 chronic school-refusing youth, 43% had a primary anxiety diagnosis, whereas 13% were diagnosed with a primary externalizing disorder and 5% with depression (Kearney & Albano, 2004). Specifically, separation anxiety and social phobia are most commonly associated with subsequent refusal behavior (Bernstein, Warren, Massie, & Thuras, 1999). Kearney and Silverman (1990, 1996) developed a functional classification system to enhance the understanding of school refusal. The identified subtypes include refusal behavior that functions to (1) avoid negative affect in school (anxiety or depression), (2) escape social/evaluative school situations, (3) gain attention, and (4) access reinforcement outside of school. Of these functions, avoidance of negative affect and escape of social or evaluative situations are associated most strongly with an underlying anxiety disorder. Early precursors to school refusal include reluctance to return to school after a break, somatic complaints during the school week, difficulties sleeping the night before school, difficulties eating the morning before school, and increased refusal to complete academic projects and presentations (Evans, 2000). Once an anxiety-related function has been identified, the ensuing treatment plan should include an anxiety-based protocol and a mutual family–school behavior management program to address motivation and expectations about attending school.

Test Anxiety

With the advent of the No Child Left Behind legislation and the propagation of high-stakes testing and accountability programs in schools, test anxiety has become a significant and growing problem for children, parents, and school personnel (Mulvenon, Stegman, & Ritter, 2005). Test anxiety is a unique subtype of performance anxiety that children sometimes experience in an examination setting. Recently investigators have theorized test anxiety to be composed of three primary dimensions: thoughts (e.g., "I think I am going to get a bad grade"), autonomic reactions (e.g., rapid heartbeat, headaches, butterflies in stomach), and off-task behaviors (e.g., looking around the room, checking the time, fidgeting; Wren & Benson, 2004). In addition, the literature has suggested that test anxiety may be associated with low self-esteem, school refusal, poor academic achievement and motivation, high rates of comorbidity with formal anxiety disorders, and overall poor prognosis (Beidel & Turner, 1988; Stober & Pekrun, 2004). Beidel and Turner reported that in a sample of 25 test-anxious children (ages 8–12), 60% met threshold criteria for an anxiety disorder. Specifically, 24% met criteria for social phobia, 8% for separation anxiety disorder, 4% for specific phobia, and 24% for generalized anxiety disorder.

Research has shown that pressure from teachers and parents may exacerbate examination-related fears and associated anxiety in children (Mulvenon et al., 2005; Supon, 2004). Supon suggested that teachers may play the most integral role in managing student test anxiety and proposed the development and implementation of strategies to enhance the instructional process, maximize individual performance, and mitigate examination-based fears. Exposure-based interventions (i.e., systematic desensitization) have demonstrated considerable efficacy in treating test-anxious children in the school setting (Egbochuku & Obodo, 2005).

The Need for School Involvement

Despite the myriad impairments associated with anxiety, many youth go undiagnosed and thus continue to suffer in silence. Because schools emphasize youth social and emotional development and have access to large, diverse populations of students, they have enormous potential as frontline agents for identifying distress in children and adolescents. In addition, schools have an established relationship with students, parents, and community agencies, providing an excellent opportunity for prevention or early intervention that may be acceptable to many families. To initiate a more active role for schools and increase awareness among teachers, counselors, and administrative staff, it is essential that greater psychoeducation in anxiety and mental health issues occur. Accordingly, a number of pragmatic and conceptual considerations must be addressed before implementing CBT programs in the school setting.

Assessing Youth Anxiety in School Settings

Multiple approaches, including professional interviews, paper-and-pencil questionnaires, and behavioral observation tasks have been developed to assess childhood anxiety, primarily in clinical settings. Several considerations are essential when choosing an assessment tool to identify anxiety within school settings. The tool must be sensitive enough to detect clinical as well as subthreshold levels of symptomatology, it must be practical to administer, and the assessment process must protect student privacy and confidentiality. The psychometrics, strengths, and weaknesses of various assessment tools and their potential application in the school sector are discussed next.

Structured Clinical Interviews

Structured clinician-administered interviews are among the most common methods for deriving formal diagnoses in clinical settings. For ex ample, the Anxiety Disorders Interview Schedule for Children (ADIS; C/P; Silverman & Albano, 1997) has demonstrated good interrater and test–retest reliability, concurrent validity, and ability to identify and differentiate anxiety disorders from other comorbid diagnoses (e.g., ADHD, depression, other anxiety disorders) in youth ages 6–18 years (Wood, Piacentini, Bergman, McCracken, & Barrios, 2002; Silverman & Ollendick, 2005). Similarly, the Schedule for Affective Disorders and Schizophrenia for School-Age Children, Present State and Epidemiological Version (Ambrosini & Dixon, 1996) features favorable psychometric properties and sensitivity in diagnosing anxiety, mood disorders, and schizophrenia in the same-age youth.

Although clinical interviews are the assessment of choice in clinical research settings, there are several challenges in transporting their use to schools. First and foremost, effective administration requires extensive reliability training to ensure that interviewers are administering and scoring interviews correctly. This time-consuming and costly process is likely unfeasible for school personnel. Second, administration time for the typical interview is considerable and not conducive to the highly structured school day, where time is limited. Third, clinical interviews tend to cover a broad range of clinical symptoms and diagnostic criteria that may provide more information than needed. Additionally, most interviews focus on clinical symptomatology that may fail to obtain information most relevant to school personnel. Educators may benefit most from a more narrow assessment of anxious behaviors and their impact on attendance, achievement, and social functioning.

Rating Scales

Youth self-report questionnaires may be a more pragmatic option for screening anxiety in the school setting. A variety of youth-report measures historically used with clinical samples have demonstrated moderate to excellent internal consistency and test–retest reliability and are both time and cost efficient (e.g., State–Trait Anxiety Inventory for Children, Spielberger, 1973; Revised Children's Manifest Anxiety Scale, Reynolds & Richmond, 1978; Multidimensional Anxiety Scale for Children [MASC], March, Parker, Sullivan, Stallings, & Conners, 1997; and Revised Child Anxiety and Depression Scales, Chorpita, Yim, Moffitt, Umemoto, & Francis, 2000). The MASC (March et al., 1997) has become one of the standards and has demonstrated good internal consistency, diagnostic sensitivity, and discriminant validity as a screening measure for youth anxiety in school-based intervention trials (Dierker et al., 2001). Traditionally used with children 8–18 years, the MASC comes in a brief format (10 items) and a standard format (39 items), featuring four separate scales of Physical Symptoms (i.e., Somatic Symptoms and Tense Symptoms subscales), Social Anxiety (i.e., Humiliation Fears and Performance Fears subscales), Harm Avoidance (i.e., Perfectionism and Anxious Coping subscales), and Separation/Panic. Despite their potential benefits in the school setting, self-report questionnaires like the MASC do have noteworthy limitations, including a lack of developmental specificity (e.g., younger children may lack the necessary insight and cognitive skills for reliable self-report) and potential bias due to the anxious child's concerns about self-presentation and social evaluation (Kendall & Ronan, 1990).

Third-party reports, such as parent or teacher rating scales, may provide an objective assessment of anxious symptomatology and take advantage of an adult's potentially greater sense of normative childhood behaviors. The Achenbach (1991) behavior checklists are the most widely used multiple-rater system in the clinical literature, employing an empirically derived dimensional classification system to assess psychological functioning across internalizing and externalizing behaviors in children 4–18 years. Although longer than the MASC, the Achenbach system provides a broader coverage of potential problem behaviors and features parent- (Child Behavior Checklist; CBCL) and teacher- (Teacher Report Form; TRF) report forms. The 118-item CBCL features two umbrella groupings of internalizing and externalizing problems, nine syndrome subscales, and one total Problem score. The internalizing rubric includes the Anxious/Depressed, Schizoid, Withdrawn, and Somatic subscales and has been shown to demonstrate good reliability (Ollendick & King, 1994). Similar to the CBCL, the TRF asks the teacher to rate the child's classroom functioning, allowing for direct comparison of the child's anxiety-based impairment across multiple domains (e.g., home, school). Both the CBCL and the TRF have demonstrated good psychometric properties in the literature (Silverman & Ollendick, 2005).

Interestingly, teacher ratings have consistently shown weak concordance with other informant ratings (child, parent) and may be less sensitive to detection of internalizing problems (e.g., anxiety, depression) than externalizing problems (e.g., ADHD, conduct disorder, oppositional defiant disorder; Silverman & Ollendick, 2005). This makes sense given the overt nature of externalizing behaviors that lend themselves to the classroom environment (e.g., calling out, being physically agitated or restless, disrupting teacher or peers) versus the internal nature of most anxiety and mood symptoms (e.g., worry, avoidance, apathy, fatigue). Methodological limitations such as multiple teachers across subjects (e.g., reading, math, etc.) and time of year (e.g., summer, beginning/end of school year) also pose challenges to the reliability and utility of teacher report.

Behavioral Assessment and Self-Monitoring

Behavioral observation is another widely used assessment strategy for youth anxiety seen in the clinical literature. Common behavioral manifestations of anxiety include nail biting, fidgeting, avoiding eye contact, and using soft speech (Kendall, Chu, Pimentel, & Choudhury, 2000). Although direct observation can be a valuable adjunct data source, few standardized procedures have been established for this approach (Silverman & Ollendick, 2005), and behavioral observation may be difficult to apply in the classroom setting (i.e., limited direct contact with peers and teacher). Thus, it may be difficult to collect individual data and compare data across students. Self-monitoring is arguably an efficient substitute for behavioral assessment (Silverman & Ollendick, 2005) and may be an effective approach for school situations (e.g., thought-tracking records, daily diaries). Through a student's self-monitoring of his or her own anxiety cues, cognitions, and behaviors in the classroom, teacher and child alike may learn to identify anxiety-related symptoms and controlling variables and subsequently evaluate behavioral and symptomatic change.

School-Based Assessment

Although the assessment techniques described above each have their strengths and limitations, their application to the school environment is relatively unexplored. Despite this gap in the assessment literature, several rating scales have been popularized in school settings to assess common problems associated with school failure, absenteeism, and dropping out (i.e., test anxiety and school refusal). The Test Anxiety Scale for Children (TASC; Sarason, Davidson, Lighthall, Waite, & Ruebush, 1960) is the measure most often used to assess test anxiety in school-age children. Featuring 30 items with a yes/no response format, the TASC was designed for verbal administration to children in grades 1–6. Despite its continued use, the TASC has been criticized over the past few decades for its outdated and overly complex wording (Wren & Benson, 2004). Additionally, the assessment's verbal administration method is prone to measurement error in this cognitively heterogeneous age range, hence posing challenges to the general validity of scores. Wren and Benson introduced the Children's Test Anxiety Scale (CTAS), a 30-item, Likert-style (*almost never* = 1 to *almost always* = 4) self-report measure featuring three dimensions: thoughts, autonomic reactions, and off-task behaviors. The authors presented initial reliability (CTAS = 0.92; subscale range from 0.76–0.89) and internal construct validity data based on an ethnically diverse sample of third to sixth graders, suggesting the CTAS is a reasonable alternative to the TASC.

Evans (2000) proposed a comprehensive assessment to assess school refusal behavior, consisting of four basic components: (1) a comprehensive history and physical; (2) a school contact to obtain information on absences, classroom behavior, and physical complaints; (3) a formal functional analysis of the child's behavior; and (4) a tentative intervention plan and monitoring process. The School Refusal Assessment Scale (SRAS; Kearney & Silverman, 1993) features both parent and child versions to help clinicians identify the primary and secondary functions of youth school refusal behavior. The SRAS features 16 total questions, 4 per maintaining condition, and uses a Likert format (0 = *never* to 6 = *always*) to calculate the mean item value for each functional condition averaged across parent and child report (Kearney & Silverman, 1993). The highest scoring condition is considered the primary function maintaining the child's behavior. The SRAS features adequate child test–retest (7–14 day; mean of r = .68), parent test–retest (7–14 day; mean of r = .78), and parent interrater (mean of r = .59) reliability, as well as good concurrent and construct validity (Kearney & Silverman, 1993). Additionally, the SRAS has been used successfully to identify cognitive-behavioral interventions that may be most effective for specific functions of school refusal behavior.

Case Conceptualization within a Cognitive-Behavioral Framework

Based on child, parent, teacher, or other report of the child's behavior, a working case conceptualization can be developed. Whereas results from formal assessments can document severity level, complexity, and total impairment of the youth's problems, a case conceptualization is based on the practitioner's integration of assessment material to build a working understanding of the processes maintaining the youth's problems. Such a conceptualization helps the clinician identify key targets of therapy, potentially helpful treatment components, and an estimated timeline and sequence of treatment. As described earlier, the cognitive-behavioral theory highlights the transactional nature of three essential components in the maintenance of anxiety: threat-sensitive cognitive styles, physiological reactivity, and behavioral avoidance. In the presence of a threatening stimulus, each component reacts to the stimulus and interacts with the others to escalate the overall anxious response (Craske & Mystkowski, 2006).

Figure 7.1 illustrates an example of a cognitive-behavioral case conceptualization of a youth demonstrating separation anxiety and school refusal behavior. In the presence of a threatening situation (parent leaving the child at school), the child might report threat-related interpretations of the situation (e.g., "I can't do this without my mother"), catastrophic expectations ("My mother will get into a car accident," "The

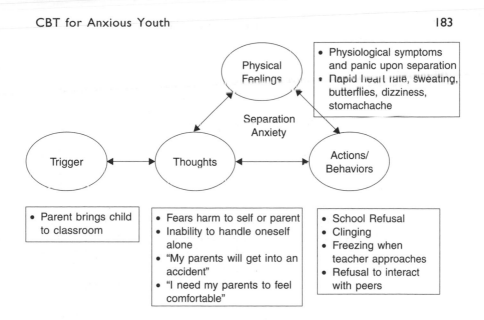

FIGURE 7.1. Cognitive-behavioral conceptualization of child with separation anxiety and school refusal behaviors.

other kids will hate me"), and physiological symptoms similar to those of a panic attack (e.g., increased heart rate, dizziness, stomachache, sweaty palms). The parent or teacher might also observe the child clinging to the parent, pulling away from the classroom, and freezing when the teacher approaches. The observed behaviors and experiences can be divided into one of the three components of the cognitive-behavioral triad (thoughts, feelings, behaviors; see Figure 7.1).

Parsing the anxious experience into these three components helps transform a diffuse experience like anxiety into more concrete and recognizable constructs. The clinician then has readily identifiable and discrete thoughts, behaviors, and somatic symptoms to target in the treatment plan. If the youth is particularly sensitive to his or her physical reactions to separation, therapy might focus on breathing retraining, relaxation, or affective education to target these frightening feelings. If the child emphasizes his or her catastrophic expectations or threat-related cognitions, a treatment plan might target identification of negative thinking, labeling of cognitive distortions, and challenging of anxious thoughts. If behavioral avoidance is primary, treatment might focus on instituting reward programs and behavioral exposures. An integrative cognitive-behavioral intervention is likely to combine therapeutic strategies that address each of these components. Still, a thoughtful case conceptualization helps the practitioner make decisions about sequence and emphasis of treatment elements. We describe common treatment components next.

CBT for Youth Anxiety

CBT is an integrative treatment approach founded on the assumption that both cognitive and behavioral processes maintain a particular problem and that change in these processes (e.g., learning new approach behaviors and problem-solving skills, challenging faulty beliefs) is a necessary precursor to symptomatic change (Brewin, 1996). CBT for youth anxiety focuses on maladaptive cognitions and their effect on the child's subsequent behaviors and emotions (Kendall et al., 2000). Cognitive distortions are considered to play a key role in the etiology, expression, and maintenance of youth anxiety, as they lead to misinterpretations of environmental threats and the child's own coping abilities. CBT also enhances insight into the connection between thoughts, feelings, and behaviors; helps youth cultivate new problem-solving and coping skills; and facilitates new experiences during which children can test both dysfunctional and more adaptive beliefs (Barrett & Shortt, 2003). Techniques such as modeling and direct reinforcement are used to teach new approach behaviors and cognitive strategies associated with information processing, attributional style, and self-talk (Kazdin, 2000). Core CBT techniques include affective education, behavioral relaxation, modeling, role play, cognitive restructuring, imaginal and *in vivo* exposure, reinforcement contingency generation and management, and behavioral parent training (Barrett & Shortt, 2003; Kendall et al., 2000; Ollendick & King, 1998).

Core Components of the CBT Model

Affective Education

Basic education of parents and child about the interrelated physiological, cognitive, and behavioral components of anxiety is an essential ingredient in CBT for anxious youth. Affective education may include role plays, videotapes, and pictures from magazines, books, and so on to help demonstrate different emotions, body postures, and cognitive and physiological correlates.

Behavioral Relaxation

Relaxation training helps anxious children develop awareness and control over their own physiological and muscular responses to anxiety

(Basco, Glickman, Weatherford, & Ryser, 2000). This technique involves the progressive relaxation of major muscle groups through systematic tensing and release. Through this process, children learn to recognize their own bodily tension as a symptom of anxiety; it is a cue to use relaxation.

Modeling

Rooted in the social learning paradigm of Bandura (1986), modeling uses observational or vicarious learning to address children's fears and anxieties. This technique may involve child observation of a live person or video model demonstrating safe and adaptive approach behavior to a feared stimulus. Alternatively, the therapist may serve as a "coping model" whereby he or she models identification of anxious cognitions and generation of coping thoughts.

Role Playing

Role play of cognitive, behavioral, and basic problem-solving strategies is another key component of CBT for anxious children. Practicing skills outloud with the therapist during session is an important step in enhancing the child's confidence, skill proficiency, and perception of his or her own ability to cope with anxiety.

Cognitive Restructuring

Cognitive distortions are thought to be central in the development, expression, and maintenance of youth anxiety. The goal of cognitive restructuring is to help children challenge these maladaptive thought patterns and replace distorted cognitions with more adaptive beliefs. Some basic cognitive strategies include identifying and reducing negative self-talk, generating positive self-statements and verbal self-instruction, stopping thoughts, challenging thoughts (weighing evidence for and against), testing both dysfunctional and adaptive beliefs, and creating a coping plan for feared situations (Basco et al., 2000; Kendall et al., 2000).

Imaginal and In Vivo Exposure

Exposure tasks are a critical component of any CBT program for anxiety. Although the mechanisms through which exposure potentiates change are still unclear (Foa & McNally, 1996), the goals of exposure tasks are to encourage approach behavior by positioning the child in a previously feared or challenging situation. Generally, the child attempts to complete tasks that are listed on a graded "fear hierarchy" such that the child experiences early success before attempting greater challenges. During an individual exposure task, the child may be encouraged to use any number of coping skills depending on the practitioner's particular theory of change. Some may encourage the child to use relaxation to reduce his or her anxiety during the exposure, à la Wolpe's (1961) systematic desensitization. Others might encourage the child to use previously learned coping strategies, such as challenging negative thoughts that arise during an exposure, as is common in Kendall's (1992) Coping Cat. Still others might focus on concrete rewards that the child receives for completing tasks or simply encourage the youth to notice his or her physiological habituation as the exposure proceeds. Whichever particular coping skills are used, the emphasis is on helping the child develop new learning (e.g., ability to complete a task or ability to tolerate distress) in situations where the youth felt previously disabled.

Reinforcement Contingency Generation/Management

Based on the principles of operant conditioning, contingency management aims to alter anxiety-related behaviors by focusing on the consequences of behavior. Maladaptive behaviors can be modified through operant-based procedures such as positive and negative reinforcement, shaping, and extinction (Kendall et al., 2000). Therapists can develop a behavioral contingency plan or reward system where approach behaviors receive tangible, direct rewards (e.g., points, stars, tokens).

Behavioral Parent Training

Modifying parental cognitions and behaviors that are influencing or maintaining child anxiety can significantly attenuate symptoms of youth anxiety disorders. For example, teaching anxiety management skills to anxious parents and imparting basic behavioral parenting strategies (e.g., positive/negative reinforcement, planned ignoring, modeling, the development and maintenance of a behavioral contingency plan) may ensure optimal therapeutic benefit for anxious youth.

Empirical Support for CBT with Anxious Youth in Clinical Settings

In clinical settings, CBT for anxiety has a long history of empirical support using a number of different formats (e.g., individual, family, and group; Barrett, 1998; Barrett, Dadds, & Rapee, 1996; Cobham, Dadds, & Spence, 1998; Flannery-Schroeder & Kendall, 2000; Kendall, 1994;

Kendall et al., 1997; Nauta, Scholing, Emmelkamp, & Minderaa, 2003; Spence, 2003; Spence, Donovan, & Brechman-Toussaint, 2000). Kendall (1994) and Kendall and colleagues (1997) conducted two of the first randomized controlled trials of CBT for anxious youth, testing the efficacy of the Coping Cat manual and workbook (Kendall, 1992; Kendall, 1994; Kendall et al., 1997). The authors reported diagnostic recovery rates of 64% and 71%, respectively, in the treatment conditions compared to only 5% and 6% of the wait-list controls. Follow-up studies revealed the maintenance of treatment gains up to 7.4 years as evidenced on both parent- and child-report ratings (Kendall, Flannery-Schroeder, Safford, & Webb, 2004; Kendall & Southam-Gerow, 1996).

The involvement of family members has been shown to improve outcomes in CBT (Barrett & Shortt, 2003; Roblek & Piacentini, 2005). Family-based CBT views the family environment as the primary vehicle for change in the child's maladaptive cognitions (Barrett & Shortt, 2003). Parents serve as integral role models and catalysts for exposure to new situations and more adaptive processing. Parental reinforcement (e.g., verbal praise, hugs, toys, tokens) of new, more adaptive behaviors and cognitions is also critical to encouraging new behavioral patterns and alleviating anxious symptoms in the long run. Barrett and colleagues (1996) conducted a clinical trial comparing a combined CBT plus family anxiety management training (CBT+FAM) to an abbreviated adaptation of the Coping Cat. In all, 88% of the CBT+FAM group was diagnosis free at posttreatment compared with only 61% of the child-only CBT group and less than 31% of the wait-list condition. The superiority of the combined CBT+FAM group was maintained at 1-year follow-up. Although subsequent investigations of parental involvement in therapy have met with mixed results (Cobham et al., 1998; Nauta et al., 2003), parental involvement is generally encouraged in the treatment of youth anxiety.

Research has also provided initial support for CBT in a group format, which may have relevant implications for the transportation of CBT to school settings. Barrett (1998) randomized 60 children (7–14 years) to either group CBT (GCBT), group CBT plus family management (GCBT+FAM), or a wait-list control group. In all, 71% of children in the GCBT+FAM group and 56% of children in the GCBT group were diagnosis free at posttreatment compared to 25% of the wait-list condition, suggesting that group formats produce similar results as individual treatment. In addition, Flannery-Schroeder and Kendall (2000) compared group CBT, individual CBT, and a wait-list control. At posttreatment, 73% of the individual CBT group no longer met criteria for their primary anxiety disorder compared to 50% of the GCBT group and 8% of the wait-list condition. Although individual treatment seemed to produce greater results, group and individual treatments were not significantly different on most measures, and both treatments produced greater clinical improvements than the wait-list condition. These findings have been replicated in other tests of group treatments (Spence, 2003; Spence et al., 2000).

Empirical Support for School-Based CBT with Anxious Youth

Several research teams have begun examining the effects of cognitive-behavioral interventions in student populations (Fisher, Masia-Warner, & Klein, 2004; Masia, Klein, Storch, & Corda, 2001; Masia-Warner et al., 2005; Mifsud & Rapee, 2005; Shortt, Barrett, & Fox, 2001). Three types of school-based intervention protocols have been discussed in the current literature: universal, selective, and indicated. *Universal* intervention programs provide preventive treatment for all students in the school or classroom regardless of each individual student's level of anxiety or impairment. This proactive and preventive approach is potentially less stigmatizing, more efficient, and more cost effective in the long run than reactive approaches that wait for youth to develop clinical-level disorders. In addition, effective coping tools may be beneficial for all youths, enhancing social–emotional intelligence and diversity of problem-solving skills. Despite these potential advantages, universal treatments may sacrifice individual student attention and require dedication of time and resources, potentially taking some resources away from other academic and extracurricular activities. In contrast, *selective* programs target youth who are already identified at risk (e.g., students with subclinical or prodromal symptoms), whereas *indicated* programs entail early intervention programs that identify and treat youth with current clinical levels of a particular diagnostic or problem area. These targeted interventions focus efforts of specialized treatment on youth with the greatest needs but tend to require more resources and expertise, potentially limiting the number of students served.

There have been a number of attempts to transport CBT programs to schools, providing some indication of their viability and effectiveness in settings other than specialty mental health clinics. Masia and colleagues (2001) developed and tested Skills for Academic and Social Success (Fisher et al., 2004; Masia et al., 2001; Masia-Warner et al., 2005), an indicated school-based intervention targeting social deficits in socially anxious high school adolescents. Treatment included 12 to 14 weekly, 40-minute group sessions that took place during class periods. Each group included six participants and was facilitated by a lead psychologist and an advanced psychology graduate student. Treatment components included psychoeducation, realistic thinking (i.e., cognitive restructuring), social skills training, exposure-based exercises, and relapse prevention. In addition to the group sessions, each participant attended two individualized sessions approximately 15 minutes long, two booster sessions at posttreatment, and four to six weekend social events that included "prosocial peers." These prosocial peers were identified by school personnel as individuals who would provide excellent models for the anxious youth and offer support and acceptance despite potential social difficulties. Finally, the group leaders conducted two teacher psychoeducation/exposure training sessions and two parent psychoeducational meetings. Treatment duration was approximately 3 months.

In the preliminary open trial, 46 youth were identified through teacher nominations and then further assessed via the ADIS-C (Masia et al., 2001). Results indicated that 50% of the students were social anxiety free at posttreatment (Masia et al., 2001). In the follow-up randomized controlled trial, the treatment group demonstrated a 67% rate of remission from their primary social anxiety diagnosis at posttreatment compared to only 6% of the wait-list control group (Masia-Warner et al., 2005). Corroborating these statistically and clinically valuable findings, self-report measures illustrated significant differences between the treatment and control groups, with 94% of the treatment group classified as responders relative to only 11% of the wait-list controls.

In addition to achieving these positive outcome results, the program was determined to be feasible in a school setting. Despite initial concerns about the intervention (e.g., stigma, loss of academic time, pragmatic challenges such as space and scheduling), it was anecdotally labeled acceptable by professionals in the natural school environment, and program administrators received positive responses (e.g., commentaries, notes, requests for the program the following year) from family members and school personnel. Because schools are a prime source for peer contact and real-life exposure tasks, it is encouraging that both parents and school personnel deemed the intervention suitable for implementation during the regular school day.

In addition, The FRIENDS Program for Children (Barrett, Lowry-Webster, & Turner, 2000), a cognitive-behavioral group manual intended for use with a variety of youth anxiety disorders, has demonstrated similar success in both clinical and school-based settings. Adapted from the Coping Koala (Barrett, 1995) and Coping Cat (Kendall, 1992) programs, the FRIENDS program consists of 10 weekly youth group sessions with 4 group parent sessions evenly distributed. The program was first evaluated in a clinical setting, examining its efficacy with and without parental involvement versus a wait-list control group (Shortt et al., 2001). Results indicated that both the CBT and CBT plus parental involvement groups were superior to the wait-list condition.

Lowry-Webster, Barrett, and Dadds (2001) then implemented the FRIENDS protocol as a universal prevention program in the Australian school system, assigning 594 Catholic school students to the treatment group or a wait-list control. The treatment was established as a routine component of the class's curriculum using teacher facilitators, and parents were required to attend three training sessions focusing on cognitive-behavioral techniques and behavioral parent management skills. Results indicated positive change in the treatment group, who reported significantly fewer anxiety symptoms than the nontreatment comparisons. After the treatment, 75% of those identified as at risk at pretest were no longer at risk in the treatment group, whereas 54% of the high-risk individuals in the control group remained in this category. In addition, the highly anxious children in the treatment group demonstrated significant reductions in depressive symptomatology as well. Overall, the program was anecdotally described as effective and feasible (e.g., teachers maintained integrity of the manual) in a school setting.

Of particular importance was the success achieved using teacher facilitators to run the groups, suggesting that similar treatments can be delivered by educators in school settings. Barrett and Turner (2001) compared treatment effects from a teacher-led group, a therapist-led group, and a wait-list control condition, revealing comparable results for both interventions on self-report measures of anxiety (e.g., Spence Children's Anxiety Scale) and greater clinical improvement in the two treatment groups relative to the wait-list controls. Teacher involvement potentially decreases stigma associated with psychological treatment and enhances chances for sustainability once the investigatory team has exited the school system. In addition, teacher facilitation may lead to wider deployment of the program and the increased use of empirically supported techniques in everyday classroom management and general instruction. Considered together, the findings from Lowry-Webster and colleagues (2001) and Masia and colleagues (2001) suggest promise for integrating CBT into the school structure and abiding to routine schedules.

In addition to the Skills for Academic and Social Success and FRIENDS programs, Mifsud and Rapee (2005) tested the effectiveness of the Cool Kids program (Lyneham, Abbott, Wignall, & Rapee, 2003), a selective school-based CBT intervention (i.e., cognitive restructuring, exposure, and skills training) targeting at-risk youth with subclinical levels of anxiety. Nine economically disadvantaged schools were randomly assigned to wait-list or treatment status, and students were recruited from the fourth and fifth grades. The children's families were sent information and consent forms for the study, and those who responded and agreed to participate were included in the assessment. Children (9–10 years) were enrolled in the study if they scored in the top 25% on the

Revised Children's Manifest Anxiety Scale (Reynolds & Richmond, 1978). The program consisted of eight 1-hour group sessions cofacilitated by a licensed school counselor and a mental health professional holding varying degrees and positions within the school. In addition, parents participated in two 2-hour parent training groups to promote the generalization of therapeutic skills to the home environment. Results indicated a significant reduction in anxious symptomatology in the treatment group relative to the wait-list group via child, parent, and teacher reports at posttreatment and 4-month follow-up. Although this study did not directly compare implementation challenges across socioeconomically diverse schools, the findings provide initial evidence that such programs may be feasible and effective in schools with more minimal resources.

Together, the evidence suggests that CBT strategies can successfully treat anxiety disorders and symptoms in school settings. Table 7.1 summarizes the characteristics of six studies testing CBT programs with anxious youth and identifies several similarities. Of the six studies reviewed, most programs employed some combination of teacher referral and youth self-report to identify selected individuals and used structured clinical interviews (ADIS) to confirm clinical diagnoses. All six interventions employed a group or classroom format and were scheduled during the regular school day, suggesting similar programs can be integrated into routine schedules without significant interference with academic subjects. The two universal prevention programs (Barrett & Turner, 2001; Lowry-Webster et al., 2001; detailed above) were routinely implemented as part of the school curriculum. For example the Barrett and Turner intervention was administered during social science class. These sessions took place during normal school hours, as did the other programs, but they were distinguished by a few characteristics (utilizing school personnel, including all children in the classroom regardless of symptoms, and being presented as "just another course" for students). Each of the programs employed adjunctive parent sessions, and many arranged separate meetings with prosocial peers. Teachers were primarily responsible for leading the two prevention programs and cofacilitated in one other study (Mifsud & Rapee, 2005). In general, the evidence shows promise that CBT interventions can be implemented successfully in school settings either as targeted (selected or indicated) group programs or as part of the general curriculum (universal prevention).

Further research evaluating various forms of CBT in school settings is encouraged. Clinical research in schools does require special consideration of consent, confidentiality, and risk (Chu, 2008; Hoagwood, 2003), but many of these issues can be addressed with strong collaboration between the research team, school administration and personnel,

TABLE 7.1. Characteristics of School-Based CBT Programs for Anxious Youth

Study	Participants	Screening used	Therapists	Treatment format	Scheduling	Parent involvement	Teacher involvement	Peer involvement
Masia et al. (2001)	Grades 9–12; 14–17 yo; SOP	Teacher-ref; expert-ADIS	Psychologists; doctoral students	14 groups	During school	2 meetings	Screening	2 wknd ss
Masia-Warner et al. (2005)	13–17 yo; SOP	Self-rated; teacher-ref; expert-ADIS	Psychologists; doctoral students	12 groups, 2 individual	During school	2 psy-ed	2 psy-ed meetings	4 wknd ss
Lowry-Webster et al. (2001)	10–13 yo	Universal prevention	Teacher	10 class sessions	Part of school curriculum	3 (skills training, beh mgmt)	Primary therapists	Classroom setting
Mifsud & Rapee (2005)	9–10; elevated anx	Self-report (RCMAS); teacher-ref	School counselors; mental health workers	8 groups	Unknown	2 psy-ed	Unknown	Unknown
Dadds et al. (1997)	7–14 yo; GAD, SAD, SP, SOP	Self-report (RCMAS); teacher-ref; expert-ADIS	Psychologists; doctoral students	10 class sessions	During school	3 (psy-ed, skills, beh mgmt)	Screening	Unknown
Barrett & Turner (2001)	10–12 yo	Universal prevention	Teachers or psychologists	12 class sessions	Part of school curriculum	4 (psy-ed, beh mgmt)	Primary therapists	Classroom setting

Note. yo, years old; SOP, social phobia; anx, anxiety; teacher-ref, teacher-referred youth; psy-ed, psychoeducational meetings; beh mgmt, behavioral management; wknd ss, weekend sessions; ADIS, Anxiety Disorders Interview Schedule for Children; RCMAS, Revised Children's Manifest Anxiety Scale; GAD, generalized anxiety disorder; SAD, separation anxiety disorder; SP, specific phobia.

and local community. Given the limited legal status of minors, active consent is required from a parent (preferably both) or legal guardian, and informed active consent is preferred over passive consent, particularly in projects where youth are to be identified with a clinical disorder and/or invited into a treatment program. Although it is not legally binding, obtaining youth assent is strongly encouraged (U.S. Department of Health and Human Services, 2005). All documentation should be written in age-appropriate lay language, and the investigator should take special care to ensure that all participants have full understanding of research procedures and can reason through the risks and benefits. It should also be stressed that participation is voluntary and that opting not to participate will not harm the person's relationship with the school or his or her ability to access resources.

Confidentiality requires special attention when research is conducted in non-health-care settings (Chu, 2008; Hoagwood, 2003). A child selected for a study in a school setting could experience immediate and long-term damage to his or her social standing and emotional well-being if the selection criteria for the project were disclosed (Levine, 1981; Roberts, 1998). The investigator should be careful to inform only essential school staff of the study goals and selection criteria. If extra precautions are desired, the investigator can plan a generic description of the program that resembles other neutral programs at the school or even run several "dummy" groups that include non-at-risk youth to blur the nature of the program (e.g., in very small schools). Ultimately, investigators are obligated to ensure that information is private and that the participating family retains control over what is shared and with whom.

Interaction with Special Education

A related question is how preventive and treatment programs might interact or overlap with traditional special education services. According to the U.S. Department of Education's definition of emotional disturbance, which is often referred to as *emotional and behavioral disorders* (EBD), a youth demonstrating a "tendency to develop physical symptoms or fears associated with personal or school problems" could qualify for special education services (Individuals with Disabilities Education Improvement Act, 2006, p. 46756). This definition could apply to youth with generalized anxiety, school refusal, or specific test anxiety that results in long-standing and marked interference. In practice, the EBD designation is more typically assigned to youth with developmental, behavioral, or social skill deficits. It is not clear how anxiety should be treated in this framework. An individualized education plan that emphasizes individualized attention, consultation services, or a behavioral plan could be helpful to an anxious youth remaining in a general education class-room. The necessary research has not yet been completed, but more extensive services, such as resource rooms and self-contained classes, would likely be unnecessary and potentially harmful for the average anxious youth. Receiving a classification of EBD and attending a class comprising primarily externalizing youth would likely be undesirable when supplemental prevention and intervention groups appear to be effective.

Challenges of Implementing CBT in the School Setting

Although a promising and emergent literature supports the efficacy of CBT for anxious youth in school settings, several noteworthy challenges have hindered the wide-scale dissemination of CBT to schools. The following section reviews potential barriers to the successful implementation of school-based treatment programs and offers recommendations for addressing these concerns.

Access to Care

Access to appropriate services remains a major obstacle for children and adolescents with anxiety concerns. Despite its high prevalence in community samples, anxiety may be difficult to identify in the school sector as most symptoms present as internal experiences (e.g., thoughts, feelings, physiological changes), limiting their visibility to teachers and school personnel (Albano, Chorpita, & Barlow, 1996; Silverman & Ollendick, 2005). Additionally, anxious symptomatology may evade clinical or professional attention until associated externalizing behaviors are detected (e.g., truancy, substance abuse, poor academic achievement, physical agitation or restlessness; Albano et al., 1996; Silverman & Ollendick, 2005). Increasing psychoeducation and the presence of effective assessment procedures in schools may help to educate parents and school personnel and enhance diagnostic sensitivity, thereby increasing the likelihood of accurate detection and early intervention.

Stigma

Parents and school staff anecdotally report the risk of identifying and labeling a youth with a psychological disorder. Little research has been conducted on stigma in school settings, although one can speculate that anxious youth might be particularly sensitive to a diagnosis of an anxiety disorder when they may be subject to peer or teacher evaluation.

However, none of the above-cited school-based studies reported any adverse events related to stigma or discrimination. In contrast, most anecdotal evidence illustrated positive experiences for youth, parents, and school personnel alike. Multiple studies have suggested that targeted (i.e., selective and indicated) treatments may be more strongly associated with stigma relative to universal programs in which all students participate (Offord, Kraemer, Kazdin, Jensen, & Harrington, 1998). However, Rapee and colleagues (2006) examined differences in the experience of stigma between youth participating in universal treatment and targeted interventions. Initial findings revealed no significant differences in the experience of stigma across both treatment groups.

Nevertheless, to minimize the risk of inadvertent stigma and discrimination, school-based programs should take measures to ensure the protection of youth privacy and confidentiality. For example, anxiety-specific assessments can be administered as send-home questionnaires or included as part of a more comprehensive evaluation or set of general information forms. Assessments could also be conducted during typical school activities (e.g., meetings with the guidance counselor, common class times such as homeroom, gym, or health class) to obscure the purpose of assessment. Once youth are identified as at risk, school staff might contact parents individually by phone or letter or set up a "routine" meeting with the child's guidance counselor. When forming an intervention group, facilitators can choose to adopt a neutral name (e.g., skill-building or "ACTION") that masks the selection criteria and nature of the program. The school might also normalize the presence of such programs by integrating them into the regular academic curriculum (e.g., health class). Finally, once a group has begun, it is important for leaders and group members to discuss and understand the rules of privacy and confidentiality so participants can feel confident that personal information will remain confidential.

Burden of Implementing Programs

Masia and colleagues (2001; Fisher et al., 2004) proposed several recommendations to help minimize the procedural, administrative, and financial burden required to implement programs in schools. First, school-wide screenings may be costly and cumbersome for schools to implement, and more pragmatic alternatives may include a streamlined process in which teachers nominate at-risk youth to school counselors. Letters to parents might also be a useful approach to inform families of new programs and steps to obtain information or nominate their child. In addition, interventions can be shortened to accommodate the school term (8–12 weeks) or structured around academic courses, and sessions can be reduced to class length (40 minutes). Most of the reviewed treatment programs lasted only 10 weeks and used 40–60 minute sessions. In one trial, 30-minute sessions were used and produced similar results (Dadds, Spence, Holland, Barrett, & Laurens, 1997), suggesting that brief treatments tailored to individual class periods are feasible. Finally, most of the reviewed studies implemented a group format and produced equivalent outcomes to individually focused treatments. Given the current demands on school staff and the large potential need for such interventions, these results encourage the use of group-based programs to most efficiently meet the needs of the large number of anxious youth in school settings. The structured nature of the school day confers a great advantage over traditional clinic settings where groups may be difficult to form due to the challenges inherent in scheduling multiple families at the same time.

Group Leaders: Educators or Specialized Mental Health Staff?

Identification of appropriate facilitators for a school-based CBT program represents a complex challenge. Hiring a specialized mental health expert to remain on staff may be costly and impractical, and many educators, appropriately, view mental health services as outside their area of expertise and responsibility. There may be some compromise that acknowledges these challenges while making mental health programs available in schools. In many ways, educators have already taken the initiative to develop social-emotional skills programs. Programs targeting specific skills areas (e.g., anger management, families with divorce, coping with life stress, assertiveness, communication skills) are becoming more common and receiving public funding across the nation. These programs are often taught by non-mental-health specialists like teachers and school counselors. Although few of these programs have been subjected to formal evaluation, their increasing presence suggests that schools are embracing a larger role in attending to the emotional health of their students.

In addition, studies reviewed in this chapter provide support that teachers may be able to effectively learn and implement targeted CBT programs after receiving specialized training and supervision (Barrett & Turner, 2001; Lowry-Webster et al., 2001). Under routine conditions, this specialized training may be sufficient for successful teacher facilitation of an intervention group. However, we also recommend that the school maintain an affiliation with a mental health specialist or consultant (e.g., social worker, clinical or school psychologist) with expertise in diagnostic assessment and treatment. This advanced training might be necessary to assess severe and complex cases, handle crisis intervention, detect deterioration during treatment, and make appropriate referrals when necessary (e.g., medication consultation). In this capacity, each specialist could be available to consult with multiple schools or districts at the same time. Ultimately, it is incumbent on the school and the mental health professional to discuss and define the roles of each responsible party to ensure that local ethics and legal regulations have been considered and upheld. Further research on teacher facilitation and mental health consultation in schools may help define the conditions under which educators can safely and effectively implement programs and identify the supports and resources required.

Program Participants: Who Should Be Included?

Although individual CBT has demonstrated strong efficacy in the clinical literature, group CBT has demonstrated similar success and may confer additional therapeutic benefits (Barrett, 1998; Flannery-Schroeder & Kendall, 2000). Group treatments maximize peer contact and opportunities for social role plays and *in vivo* exposures. The presence of other youth with similar problems may also encourage mutual support, encouragement, and acceptance, which may be instrumental in the reduction of youth embarrassment and isolation (Glodich & Allen, 1998). Some programs (e.g., Fisher et al., 2004; Masia et al., 2001) include nonanxious or prosocial peers to serve as role models and social skills practice partners throughout the course of therapy. However, in programs targeting anxiety, the facilitator should always aim to make optimal use of the naturalistic school setting. Devising role plays and *in vivo* exposures that involve social interactions in the halls, classrooms, cafeteria, and so on allows for more naturalistic training and skills practice, which subsequently increases the effectiveness, generalization, and maintenance of the skills learned from the intervention. Despite these potential benefits, when exposures involve non-program participants, care should be taken to ensure the group members' privacy and confidentiality.

Inclusion of parents has also been found to improve outcomes in CBT (Barrett et al., 1996; Barrett & Shortt, 2003; Roblek & Piacentini, 2005). The reviewed programs all included group parent meetings to provide psychoeducation and behavioral parent training and solicit help in reinforcing homework compliance. In general, parental involvement appears essential to maximizing therapeutic effectiveness and generalizing treatment gains to the home environment. Compared to most mental health clinics, schools have the advantage of a well-established relationship with parents and geographic proximity within the family's community. Nonetheless, many parents still demonstrate poor school involvement and limited direct contact with teachers and school personnel. One strategy schools might employ to increase the likelihood of parental involvement is pairing mental health meetings with other required or highly attended school functions (e.g., parent–teacher conferences, parent–teacher association meetings, etc.). Ultimately, consistent parent commitment is a universal problem for youth mental health, whether programs are conducted in schools, clinics, or research settings.

Summary

There are a number of appealing aspects to implementing CBT in schools. Schools provide direct access to a large range of youth, have an established relationship with parents and students, and have trained professionals on staff with expertise in child development and education. Schools also address some of the barriers that traditionally inhibit families from seeking clinic-based treatment, such as cost, child care, and transportation. Specific to CBT, implementing programs in school settings maximizes access to same-age peers and enables a broad array of naturalistic exposure tasks. This real-world context may facilitate treatment effectiveness and generalizability of treatment gains. Several issues deserve consideration, including client privacy and confidentiality, CBT program leadership, participant selection, and the logistical and economic costs associated with the program. This chapter provided some initial recommendations for assessment and treatment of anxious youth in school settings and suggestions for how to handle common challenges that arise during school-based intervention. Further research is required to understand the long-term prospects of CBT in schools, but the current literature provides ample support to encourage continued implementation.

References

Achenbach, T. M. (1991). *Child Behavior Checklist*. San Antonio, TX: Psychological Corporation.

Albano, A. M., Chorpita, B. F., & Barlow, D. H. (1996). Childhood anxiety disorders. In E. J. Mash & R. A. Barkley (Eds.), *Child psychopathology* (pp. 196–241). New York: Guilford Press.

Ambrosini, P. J., & Dixon, J. F. (1996). *Schedule for Affective Disorders and Schizophrenia for School Age Children, Present State and Epidemiological Version*. New York: New York State Psychiatric Association.

Angold, A., Costello, J., & Erkanli, E. (1999). Comorbidity. *Journal of Child Psychology and Psychiatry, 40,* 57–87.

Bandura, A. (1986). *Social learning theory*. Englewood Cliffs, NJ: Prentice Hall.

Barlow, D. H., Allen, L. B., & Choate, M. L. (2004). Toward a unified treatment for emotional disorders. *Behavior Therapy, 35*, 205–230.

Barrett, P. M. (1995). *Group Coping koala workbook*. Unpublished manuscript, School of Applied Psychology, Griffith University, Australia.

Barrett, P. M. (1998). Evaluation of cognitive-behavioral group treatments for childhood anxiety disorders. *Journal of Clinical Child Psychology, 27*, 459–468.

Barrett, P. M., Dadds, M. R., & Rapee, R. M. (1996). Family treatment of childhood anxiety: A controlled trial. *Journal of Consulting and Clinical Psychology, 64*, 333–342.

Barrett, P. M., Lowry-Webster, H., & Turner, C. (2000). *FRIENDS program for children: Group leaders manual*. Brisbane: Australian Academic Press.

Barrett, P. M., & Shortt, A. L. (2003). Parental involvement in the treatment of anxious children. In A. E. Kazdin & J. R. Weisz (Eds.), *Evidence-based psychotherapies for children and adolescents* (pp. 101–119). New York: Guilford Press.

Barrett, P., Shortt, A., & Healy, L. (2002). Do parent and child behaviours differentiate families whose children have obsessive–compulsive disorder from other clinic an non-clinic families? *Journal of Child Psychology and Psychiatry, 43*, 597–607.

Barrett, P., & Turner, C. (2001). Prevention of anxiety symptoms in primary school children: Preliminary results from a universal school-based trial. *British Journal of Clinical Psychology, 40*, 399–410.

Basco, M. R., Glickman, M., Weatherford, P., & Ryser, N. (2000). Cognitive-behavioral therapy for anxiety disorders: Why and how it works. *Bulletin of the Menninger Clinic, 64*, A52–A70.

Beidel, D. C., & Turner, S. M. (1988). Comorbidity of test anxiety and other anxiety disorders in children. *Journal of Abnormal Child Psychology, 16*, 275–287.

Bernstein, G. A., Warren, S. L., Massie, E. D., & Thuras, P. D. (1999). Family dimensions in anxious-depressed school refusers. *Journal of Anxiety Disorders, 13*, 513–528.

Brewin, C. R. (1996). Theoretical foundations of cognitive-behavioral therapy for anxiety and depression. *Annual Review of Psychology, 47*, 33–57.

Chorpita, B. F., Yim, L., Moffitt, C., Umemoto, L. A., & Francis, S. E. (2000). Assessment of symptoms of *DSM-IV* anxiety and depression in children: A revised child anxiety and depression scale. *Behaviour Research and Therapy, 38*, 835–855.

Chu, B. C. (2008). Child and adolescent research methods in clinical psychology. In D. McKay (Ed.), *Handbook of research methods in abnormal and clinical psychology*. Thousand Oaks, CA: Sage.

Cobham, V. E., Dadds, M. R., & Spence, S. H. (1998). The role of parental anxiety in the treatment of childhood anxiety. *Journal of Consulting and Clinical Psychology, 66*, 893–905.

Craske, M. G., & Mystkowski, J. L. (2006). Exposure therapy and extinction: Clinical studies. In M. G. Craske, D. Hermans, & D. Vansteenwegen (Eds.), *Fear and learning: From basic processes to clinical implications* (pp. 217–233). Washington, DC: American Psychological Association.

Dadds, M. R., Spence, S. H., Holland, D. E., Barrett, P. M., & Laurens, K. R. (1997). Prevention and early intervention for anxiety disorders: A controlled trial. *Journal of Consulting and Clinical Psychology, 65*, 627–235.

Dierker, L. C., Albano, A. M., Clarke, G. N., Heimberg, R. G., Kendall, P. C., Merikangas, K. R., et al. (2001). Screening for anxiety and depression in early adolescence. *Journal of the American Academy of Child and Adolescent Psychiatry, 40*, 929–936.

Egbochuku, E. O., & Obodo, B. O. (2005). Effects of systematic desensitisation (SD) therapy on the reduction of test anxiety among adolescents in Nigerian schools. *Journal of Instructional Psychology, 32*, 298–304.

Evans, L. D. (2000). Functional school refusal subtypes: Anxiety, avoidance, and malingering. *Psychology in the Schools, 37,* 183–191.

Fisher, P. H., Masia-Warner, C., & Klein, R. G. (2004). Skills for social and academic success: A school-based intervention for social anxiety disorder in adolescents. *Clinical Child and Family Psychology Review, 7,* 241–249.

Flannery-Schroeder, E. C., & Kendall, P. C. (2000). Group and individual cognitive-behavioral treatments for youth with anxiety disorders: A randomized clinical trial. *Cognitive Therapy and Research, 24,* 251–278.

Foa, E. B., & McNally, R. J. (1996). Mechanisms of change in exposure therapy. In M. Rapee (Ed.), *Current controversies in the anxiety disorders* (pp 329–343). New York: Guilford Press.

Glodich, A. M., & Allen, J. G. (1998). Adolescents exposed to violence and abuse: A review of the group therapy literature with an emphasis on preventing trauma reenactment. *Journal of Child and Adolescent Group Therapy, 8,* 135–154.

Hoagwood, K. (2003). Ethical issues in child and adolescent psychosocial treatment research. In A. E. Kazdin & J. R. Weisz (Eds.), *Evidence-based psychotherapies for children and adolescents* (pp. 60–80). New York: Guilford Press.

Hudson, J. L., & Rapee, R. M. (2002). Parent–child interactions in clinically anxious children and their siblings. *Journal of Clinical Child and Adolescent Psychology, 31,* 548–555.

Individuals with Disabilities Education Improvement Act of 2004: Assistance to States for the Education of Children with Disabilities and Preschool Grants for Children with Disabilities, 34 Fed. Reg. 46,756 (Aug. 14, 2006).

Kazdin, A. E. (2000). *Psychotherapy for children and adolescents: Directions for research and practice.* New York: Oxford University Press.

Kearney, C. A. (2001). *School refusal behavior in youth: A functional approach to assessment and treatment.* Washington, DC: American Psychological Association.

Kearney, C. A., & Albano, A. M. (2004). The functional profiles of school refusal behavior. *Behavior Modification, 28,* 147–161.

Kearney, C. A., & Silverman, W. K. (1990). A preliminary analysis of a functional model of assessment and treatment for school refusal behavior. *Behavior Modification, 14,* 340–366.

Kearney, C. A., & Silverman, W. K. (1993). Measuring the function of school refusal behavior: The School Refusal Assessment Scale. *Journal of Clinical Child Psychology, 22,* 85–96.

Kearney, C. A., & Silverman, W. K. (1996). The evolution and reconciliation of taxonomic strategies for school refusal behavior. *Clinical Psychology: Science and Practice, 3,* 339–354.

Kendall, P. C. (1992). *The Coping Cat workbook.* Ardmore, PA: Workbook Publishing.

Kendall, P. C. (1994). Treating anxiety disorders in children: Results of a randomized clinical trial. *Journal of Consulting and Clinical Psychology, 62,* 100–110.

Kendall, P. C. (2000). *Cognitive-behavioral therapy for anxious children: Treatment manual.* Ardmore, PA: Workbook Publishing.

Kendall, P. C., Aschenbrand, S. G., & Hudson, J. L. (2003). Child-focused treatment of anxiety. In A. E. Kazdin & J. R. Weisz (Eds.), *Evidence-based psychotherapies for children and adolescents* (pp. 81–100). New York: Guilford Press.

Kendall, P. C., Chu, B. C., Pimentel, S., & Choudhury, M. (2000). Treating anxiety disorders in youth. In P. C. Kendall (Ed.), *Child and adolescent therapy: Cognitive-behavioral procedures* (2nd ed., pp. 235–290). New York: Guilford Press.

Kendall, P. C., Flannery-Schroeder, E., Panichelli-Mindel, S. M., Southam-Gerow, M., Henin, A., & Warman, M. (1997). Therapy for youths with anxiety disorders: A second randomized clinical trial. *Journal of Consulting and Clinical Psychology, 65,* 366–380.

Kendall, P. C., Flannery-Schroeder, E., Safford, S., & Webb, A. (2004). Child anxiety treatment: Outcomes in adolescence and impact on substance use and depression at 7.4-year follow-up. *Journal of Consulting and Clinical Psychology, 72,* 276–287.

Kendall, P. C., & Ronan, K. R. (1990). Assessment of childhood anxieties, fears, and phobias: Cognitive-behavioral models and methods. In C. R. Reynolds & R. W. Kamphaus (Eds.), *Handbook of psychological and educational assessment of children: Personality, behavior, and context* (pp. 223–244). New York: Guilford Press.

Kendall, P. C., & Southam-Gerow, M. A. (1996). Long-term follow-up of a cognitive-behavioral therapy for anxiety-disordered youth. *Journal of Consulting and Clinical Psychology, 64,* 724–730.

Levine, R. J. (1981). *Ethics and regulation of clinical research.* Baltimore: Urban & Schwartzenberg.

Lonigan, C. J., & Phillips, B. M. (2001). Temperamental influences on the development of anxiety disorders. In M. W. Vasey (Ed.), *The developmental psychopathology of anxiety* (pp. 60–91). New York: Oxford University Press.

Lowry-Webster, H., Barrett, P., & Dadds, M. R. (2001). A universal prevention trial of anxiety and depressive symptomatology in childhood: Preliminary data from an Australian study. *Behaviour Change, 18,* 36–50.

Lyneham, H. J., Abbott, M. J., Wignall, A., & Rapee, R. M. (2003). *The Cool Kids school program: Therapist manual.* Sydney, Australia: Macquarie University, Anxiety Research Unit. Available online at *www.mq.edu/muaru.*

March, J. S., Parker, J. D. A., Sullivan, K., Stallings, P., & Conners, C. K. (1997). The Multidimensional Anxiety Scale for Children (MASC): Factor structure, reliability, and validity. *Journal of the American Academy of Child and Adolescent Psychiatry, 36,* 554–565.

Masia, C. L., Klein, R. G., Storch, E. A., & Corda, B. (2001). School-based behavioral treatment for social anxiety disorder in adolescents: Results of a pilot study. *Journal of the American Academy of Child and Adolescent Psychiatry, 40,* 780–786.

Masia-Warner, C., Klein, R. G., Dent, H. C., Fisher, P. H., Alvir, J., Albano, A. M., et al. (2005). School-based intervention for adolescents with social anxiety disorder: Results of a controlled study. *Journal of Abnormal Child Psychology, 33,* 707–722.

Mifsud, C., & Rapee, R. M. (2005). Early intervention for childhood anxiety in a school setting: Outcomes for an economically disadvantaged population. *Journal of the American Academy of Child and Adolescent Psychiatry, 44,* 996–1004.

Mineka, S., & Zinbarg, R. (2006). A contemporary learning theory perspective on the etiology of anxiety disorders. *American Psychologist, 61,* 10–26.

Mulvenon, S. W., Stegman, C. E., & Ritter, G. (2005). Test anxiety: A multifaceted study on the perceptions of teachers, principals, counselors, students, and parents. *International Journal of Testing, 5,* 37–61.

Nauta, M. H., Scholing, A., Emmelkamp, P. M., & Minderaa, R. B. (2003). Cognitive-behavioral therapy for children with anxiety disorders in a clinical setting: No additional effect of a cognitive parent training. *Journal of the American Academy of Child and Adolescent Psychiatry, 42,* 1270–1278.

Offord, D. R., Kraemer, H. C., Kazdin, A. E., Jensen, P. S., & Harrington, R. (1998). Lowering the burden of suffering from child psychiatric disorder: Trade-offs among clinical, targeted, and universal interventions. *Journal of the American Academy of Child and Adolescent Psychiatry, 37,* 686–694.

Ollendick, T. H., & King, N. J. (1994). Diagnosis, assessment, and treatment of internalizing problems in children: The role of longitudinal data. *Journal of Consulting and Clinical Psychology, 62,* 918–927.

Ollendick, T. H., & King, N. J. (1998). Empirically supported treatments for children with phobic and anxiety disorders: Current status. *Journal of Clinical Child Psychology, 27,* 156–167.

Rapee, R. M. (2002). The development and modification of temperamental risk for anxiety disorders: Prevention of a lifetime of anxiety? *Society of Biological Psychiatry, 52,* 947–957.

Rapee, R. M., Wignall, A., Sheffield, J., Kowalenko, N., Davis, A., McLoone, J., et al. (2006). Adolescents' reactions to universal and indicated prevention programs for depression: Perceived stigma and consumer satisfaction. *Prevention Science, 7,* 167–177.

Reynolds, C. R., & Richmond, O. B. (1978). What I think and feel: A revised measure of children's manifest anxiety. *Journal of Abnormal Child Psychology, 6,* 271–280.

Roberts, L. W. (1998). Ethics of psychiatric research: Conceptual issues and empirical findings. *Comprehensive Psychiatry, 39,* 99–110.

Roblek, T., & Piacentini, J. (2005). Cognitive-behavioral therapy for childhood anxiety disorders. *Child and Adolescent Psychiatric Clinics of North America, 14,* 863–876.

Sarason, S. B., Davidson, K. S., Lighthall, F. F., Waite, R. R., & Ruebush, B. K. (1960). *Anxiety in elementary school children.* New York: Wiley.

Shortt, A. L., Barrett, P. M., & Fox, T. L. (2001). Evaluating the FRIENDS program: A cognitive-behavioral group treatment for anxious children and their parents. *Journal of Clinical Child Psychology, 30,* 525–535.

Silverman, W. K., & Albano, A. M. (1997). *The Anxiety Disorders Interview Schedule for Children* (DSM-IV). San Antonio, TX: Psychological Corporation.

Silverman, W. K., & Ollendick, T. H. (2005). Evidence-based assessment of anxiety and its disorders in children and adolescents. *Journal of Clinical Child and Adolescent Psychology, 34,* 380–411.

Southam-Gerow, M. A., Henin, A., Chu, B., Marrs, A., & Kendall, P. C. (1997). Cognitive-behavioral therapy with children and adolescents. *Child and Adolescent Psychiatric Clinics of North America, 6,* 111–136.

Spence, S. H. (2003). Social skills training with children and young people: Theory, evidence and practice. *Child and Adolescent Mental Health, 8,* 84–96.

Spence, S. H., Donovan, C., & Brechman-Toussaint, M. (2000). The treatment of childhood social phobia: The effectiveness of a social skills training-based, cognitive-behavioural intervention, with and without parental involvement. *Journal of Child Psychology and Psychiatry, 41,* 713–726.

Spielberger, C. (1973). *Preliminary manual for the State–Trait Anxiety Inventory for Children ("How I Feel Questionnaire").* Palo Alto, CA: Consulting Psychologists Press.

Stober, J., & Pekrun, R. (2004). Advances in test anxiety research. *Anxiety, Stress, and Coping, 17,* 205–211.

Supon, V. (2004). Implementing strategies to assist test-anxious students. *Journal of Instructional Psychology, 31,* 292–296.

U.S. Department of Health and Human Services. (2005). *Code of federal regulations: Part 46 Protection of human subjects/Subpart D: Additional protections for children involved as subjects in research.* Retrieved April 14, 2008, from *www.hhs.gov.*

Valles, E., & Oddy, M. (1984). The influence of a return to school on long-term adjustment of school refusers. *Journal of Adolescence, 7,* 35–44.

Van Ameringen, M., Mancini, C., & Farvolden, P. (2003). The impact of anxiety disorders on educational achievement. *Anxiety Disorders, 17,* 561–571.

Wolpe, J. (1961). The systematic desensitization treatment of neuroses. *Journal of Nervous and Mental Disease, 132,* 189–203.

Wood, J. (2006). Effect of anxiety reduction on children's school performance and social adjustment. *Developmental Psychology, 42,* 345–349.

Wood, J. J., McLeod, B. D., Sigman, M., Hwang, W, & Chu, B. C. (2003). Parenting and childhood anxiety: Theory, empirical findings, and future directions. *Journal of Child Psychology and Psychiatry, 44,* 134–151.

Wood, J. J., Piacentini, J. C., Bergman, R. L., McCracken, J., & Barrios, V. (2002). Concurrent validity of the anxiety disorders section of the Anxiety Disorders Interview Schedule for DSM-IV: Child and parent versions. *Journal of Clinical Child and Adolescent Psychology, 31,* 335–342.

Woodward, J. L., & Fergusson, D. M. (2001). Life course outcomes of young people with anxiety disorders in adolescence. *Journal of the American Academy of Child and Adolescent Psychiatry, 40,* 1086–1093.

Wren, D. G., & Benson, J. (2004). Measuring test anxiety in children: Scale development and internal construct validation. *Anxiety, Stress, and Coping, 17,* 227–240.

CHAPTER 8

Cognitive-Behavioral Treatment for Childhood Anxiety Disorders
Exemplary Programs

GRETCHEN SCHOENFIELD
RICHARD J. MORRIS

There has been a rapid proliferation of research investigating the efficacy of cognitive-behavioral methods for treating anxiety disorders in children and adolescents in recent years.[1] Increasingly, research suggests that anxiety disorders affect the daily functioning of children in a variety of ways and can potentially lead to negative outcomes in adulthood (e.g., Liebowitz, Gorman, Fyer, & Klein, 1985; Wittchen, Stein, & Kessler, 1999). In addition, anxiety disorders in children have been found to correlate with depression, substance abuse, and academic and vocational difficulties, as well as impact children's overall social–emotional functioning (e.g., Albano, Marten, Holt, Heimberg, & Barlow,

---

[1]The term *children* or *child* is used throughout this chapter to refer to both children and adolescents. Where it appears appropriate in terms of the research or practice literature, a distinction is made between children and adolescents.

1995; Beidel, Turner, & Morris, 1999; Last, Hanson, & Franco, 1997; McGee & Stanton, 1990). Given the negative potential trajectories associated with childhood anxiety disorders, efforts toward identifying effective treatment and early intervention strategies have increased over the past 10–15 years (see, e.g., Morris, Kratochwill, Schoenfield, & Auster, 2008).

Numerous studies have been published that have evaluated the efficacy of treatment methods for childhood anxiety disorders (Weisz, Hawley, & Doss, 2004). In addition, several authors and groups have proposed various guidelines for evaluating treatment efficacy for not only reducing anxiety disorders in children but also for successfully treating most other types of child and adolescent behavior disorders (e.g., Chambless & Ollendick, 2001; King, Muris, & Ollendick, 2005; Ollendick & King, 1998; see also Lonigan, Elbert, & Johnson, 1998), with each set of guidelines emphasizing the inclusion of only those treatments that are based upon methodologically sound research studies that also include a treatment manual (Chambless & Ollendick, 2001). Several cognitive-behavioral treatment (CBT) methods for reducing anxiety-related symptoms or behaviors in children have been described as being efficacious in this regard. In selecting exemplary programs for this chapter, we adopted those criteria outlined by the American Psychological Association's Division 12 (Clinical Psychology) Task Force on Promotion and Dissemination of Psychological Procedures (Chambless et al., 1998). These criteria are described in Table 8.1.

It should be noted that there are several conditions that fall under the umbrella of "anxiety disorders," as defined by the *Diagnostic and Statistical Manual of Mental Disorders* (4th edition, text revision) (American Psychiatric Association, 2000). Although there is considerable overlap in the etiology and symptomatology of many conditions of anxiety, there are also important distinctions that have implications for treatment. For example, although CBT methods have been found to be "probably efficacious" in treating symptoms of social anxiety disorder, separation anxiety, and generalized anxiety, there is limited empirical support for effective CBT intervention for specific phobias (Morris et al., 2008). Additionally, the effectiveness of CBT interventions has not yet been thoroughly investigated in the treatment of posttraumatic stress disorder or panic disorder.

Examples of Exemplary Interventions

The primary goal of CBT interventions is to help children learn to recognize signs and symptoms of their anxiety and to employ coping strategies

TABLE 8.1. Criteria for Empirically Validated Treatment

Well-established treatments

I. At least two good between-group design experiments demonstrating efficacy in one or more of the following ways:
   A. Superior (statistically significantly so) to pill or psychological placebo or to another treatment.
   B. Equivalent to an already established treatment in experiments with adequate sample sizes.

or

II. A large series of single-case design experiments ($n > 9$) demonstrating efficacy. These experiments must have:
   A. Used good experimental designs and
   B. Compared the intervention to another treatment as in I (A).

Further criteria for both I and II:
III. Experiments must be conducted with treatment manuals.
IV. Characteristics of the client samples must be clearly specified.
V. Effects must be demonstrated by at least two different investigators or investigating teams.

Probably efficacious treatments

I. Two experiments showing the treatment is superior (statistically significantly so) to a wait-list control group.

or

II. One or more experiments meeting the well-established treatment criteria IA or IB, III, and IV, but not V.

or

III. A small series of single-case design experiments ($n > 3$) otherwise meeting well-established treatment.

Note. From Chambless et al. (1998, p. 4). Copyright 1998 by the American Psychological Association. Reprinted by permission.

to reduce or eliminate their symptoms (e.g., Kendall, Hudson, Choudhury, Webb, & Pimentel, 2005). Though it is beyond the scope of this chapter to provide an exhaustive review of all CBT interventions discussed in the literature, we provide an in-depth overview of four specific interventions that show promise for implementation in both school and clinic or community settings. These programs are FRIENDS for Life (FRIENDS; Barrett, 2004, 2005), Cool Kids Child and Adolescent Anxiety Program: School Version (Rapee, Lyneham, et al., 2006), Social Effectiveness Therapy for Children (SET-C; Beidel, Turner, & Morris, 2004), and Skills for Academic and Social Success (SASS; Masia et al., 1999). The FRIENDS program is based on the writings of Phillip Kendall and his colleagues, who developed Coping Cat (Kendall, 2000) and C.A.T.S., and it is designed to ameliorate overanxious disorders, separation anxiety, and avoidant disorders in children and adolescents (Kendall, Choudhury, Hudson, & Webb, 2002). The Cool Kids program (School Version; Rapee, Lyneham, et al., 2006) is adapted from earlier programs (such as Coping Kids, Coping Koala, and originally, Coping Cat), and is a multicomponent program intended for children who meet diagnostic criteria for an anxiety disorder. SET-C was adapted from an adult version of a multicomponent treatment and is intended to alleviate symptoms associated with social phobia (also referred to as *social anxiety disorder*) in children and adolescents (Turner, Beidel, Cooley, Woody, & Messer, 1994). SASS was adapted from SET-C as an intervention transportable to the school environment (Masia et al., 1999).

FRIENDS for Life

The FRIENDS program was developed by Paula Barrett (2004) in Brisbane, Australia, and is a prevention/early intervention and treatment program for anxiety symptoms and disorders in children and adolescents between 7 and 16 years of age. FRIENDS teaches children skills to cope with anxiety, emphasizing techniques such as relaxation, cognitive restructuring, attentional training, assisted exposure, and family and peer support (Barrett & Turner, 2001). FRIENDS is an acronym for the following skills taught within the program:

F = Feelings
R = *Remember to relax*
I = I can do it! I can try my best!
E = Explore solutions and Coping Step Plans
N = *Now reward yourself!*
D = *Don't forget to practice*
S = *Smile, stay calm*

Two versions of the FRIENDS program exist in order to address anxiety symptoms at different developmental levels: FRIENDS for Children 7–11 years and FRIENDS for Youth 12–16 years. Each program comprises 10 weekly sessions and two booster sessions that typically take place 1 and 3 months, respectively, after the final weekly session. The program also includes four sessions for parents intended to provide in-depth information about the program and to discuss strategies for parenting and use of reinforcement procedures. Table 8.2 provides a summary of each session.

FRIENDS is designed to be implemented within a school or clinic setting. Implementation within a clinic setting can follow either an indi-

TABLE 8.2. FRIENDS Treatment Components and Procedures

Session 1. *Purpose:* Introduce group members; overview of program
  • Understanding feelings of anxiety
  • Coping strategies: helping others in group recognize the signs of anxiety; remembering happy events, people, and/or situations, feeling confident and brave
  • Home activities: setting personal goals and identifying happy, comforting thoughts
  • Negotiating rewards

Session 2. *Purpose:* Discuss "feelings" and "thoughts" and how they determine behavior
  • Identify feelings and recognize facial expressions and body language
  • Learn to control behaviors and thoughts by choosing alternative ways to think and feel
  • Make lists of people, activities, events, objects, and/or situations that evoke both feelings of anxiety and comfort

Session 3. *Purpose:* Introduce F (Feelings) and R (Remember to Relax and Feel Good)
  • Recognize physiological signs of worry and identify anxiety-provoking situations
  • Deep breathing and muscle relaxation techniques
  • Homework activities: practice deep breathing and muscle relaxation

Session 4. *Purpose:* Introduce I (I can do it! I can try my best!)
  • Introduce self-talk and discuss how thoughts can influence coping
  • Strategies: transform negative thoughts into positive thoughts; consider different ways to react to feared situations
  • Homework activities: identify negative thoughts in a workbook scenario and practice replacing these thoughts with positive self-talk; monitor and record thoughts during the upcoming week

Session 5. *Purpose:* Introduce E (Explore Solutions and Coping Step Plans)
  • Discuss how attention to details can affect feelings and thoughts
  • Introduce the Coping Step Plans: breaking down anxiety-provoking situations into smaller, manageable steps
  • Homework activities: think of an anxiety-provoking situation and create Coping Step Plans; identify helpful thoughts that will assist in moving through each of the steps in the plans

Session 6. *Purpose:* Reintroduce E (Explore Solutions and Coping Step Plans) and additional problem-solving strategies
  • Discuss the importance of social support, identifying role models, and forming a social support team
  • Introduce 6-Block Problem-Solving Plan: identify a problem, how to resolve it, potential outcomes, choose the best solution, put the solution into action, and evaluate the outcome
  • Homework activities: solve a problem using the 6-Block Problem-Solving Plan with family or friends; discuss role models with family members; and practice the first step in the Coping Step Plans; practice relaxation and positive self-talk

(*continued*)

TABLE 8.2. (*continued*)

Session 7. *Purpose:* Introduce N (Now reward yourself! You've done your best!)
- Learn positive reinforcement strategies
- Homework activities: identify positive aspects of difficult situations; move through additional steps in the Coping Step Plans

Session 8. *Purpose:* Reintroduce N (Now reward yourself!); introduce D (Don't forget to practice); and S (Smile! Stay calm), a reminder to remain calm in fearful situations. Using the FRIENDS plan to cope with difficult situations.

Session 9. *Purpose:* consider ways that coping skills can be generalized
- Practice all of the steps within Coping Step Plans
- Homework activities: practice Coping Step Plans; reward for effort; evaluate plan implementation

Session 10. *Purpose:* Maintaining coping skills
- Overcoming setbacks, preparing for future challenges
- Review of program components

Booster sessions. *Purpose:* Review of program components
- Homework activities: review steps in forming support teams; generalize skills to new situations; practice

Note. Adapted from Barrett (2004). Copyright 2004 by Australian Academic Press Pty Ltd. Adapted by permission.

vidual or group format. In both cases, however, family involvement is a necessary part of the program in order to encourage client compliance with and practice of acquired skills and provide support to the child. Within a school setting, FRIENDS is intended to be implemented by teachers and other trained school personnel during the school day as a part of a universal prevention program (Barrett, 2004). FRIENDS can also be conducted as a classroom-wide program or implemented within small groups of selected students.

The philosophy underlying the FRIENDS program is based on a peer learning model and experiential learning. FRIENDS is intended to be implemented in safe, familiar, and naturalistic environments with a peer group. Additionally, FRIENDS emphasizes the value of those experiences and skills that each individual can lend to the group. This approach also encourages individuals to actively participate in all stages of the process and, therefore, provides an opportunity for participants to take initiative and build self-confidence.

Theoretical Principles

FRIENDS is designed for the prevention of and early intervention in anxiety and targets cognitive, physiological, and learning processes that are considered to be factors in the development and subjective experience of anxiety. The cognitive component addressed within the FRIENDS framework examines the thoughts that children have about themselves, others, and situations related to feelings of anxiety. Approaches to modifying cognitions and related feelings contributing to anxiety include the use of positive self-talk and self-reward. Children experiencing anxiety are believed to engage in *negative self-talk*, which refers to negative self-evaluations and thoughts about future events, as well as dissatisfaction with performance, fears of failure, and concerns regarding others' negative evaluations (Barrett, Dadds, & Rapee, 1996; Kendall et al., 2005). FRIENDS seeks to teach participants to cope with anxiety-provoking situations by replacing negative thoughts with more positive, constructive thoughts or "positive self-talk" (Barrett, 2004). To help mediate unrealistic standards of perfection, FRIENDS encourages children to reward themselves for attaining realistic goals.

The physiological component addressed within the FRIENDS program refers to the physical reactions that often accompany feeling anxious, worried, or fearful. FRIENDS teaches participants to recognize physiological indicators of worry that are associated with anxiety-provoking situations. The program then teaches participants deep breathing and muscle relaxation techniques, which they are encouraged to employ when they experience the physical symptoms of anxiety.

The learning component focuses on the acquisition of coping and anxiety management skills, such as problem-solving, exposure, and reward systems. Problem-solving skills are addressed within a six-stage segment that targets a child's belief that he or she is unable to cope with difficult situations. FRIENDS also incorporates an exposure component, referred to as the *Coping Step Plan*, which involves gradually exposing an individual to anxiety-provoking events or situations (Sheslow, Bondy, & Nelson, 1983). Children are instructed to break down these situations into smaller, manageable steps, which ideally reduces the potential for avoiding them altogether. The reward systems component teaches children to reward themselves for successfully attempting each step outlined in the Coping Step Plan, thus encouraging them to positively reinforce practice of newly acquired skills.

Overview of Supportive Research

FRIENDS has demonstrated effectiveness in anxiety prevention and treatment for up to 6 years following children's initial participation in the program (Barrett, Duffy, Dadds, & Rapee, 2001). The program has been evaluated in several clinical trials and has been implemented in schools and clinics in Australia, New Zealand, Europe, and North America (Barrett, 2004). Additionally, FRIENDS is one of few universal prevention programs that has specifically examined anxiety symptoms as an outcome measure (Hudson, Flannery-Schroeder, & Kendall, 2004) using structured clinical interviews such as the *Anxiety Disorders Interview Schedule for Children* (Silverman & Albano, 1996), self-report instruments including the Spence Children's Anxiety Scale (Spence, 1998) and the Revised Children's Manifest Anxiety Scale (Reynolds & Richmond, 1985), and parent-report instruments like the Child Behavior Checklist (Achenbach & Edelbrock, 1991).

Research supporting the effectiveness of FRIENDS has been conducted in Australia, Canada, Germany, Netherlands, New Zealand, the United Kingdom, and the United States (Barrett, Webster, & Turner, 2003; Bernstein, Layne, Egan, & Tennison, 2005; Conradt & Essau, 2003; Muris & Mayer, 2000). The program has also been adapted to accommodate Australian children from non-English-speaking backgrounds as well as in Australian Indigenous populations (Barrett, Moore, & Sonderegger, 2000; Barrett, Sonderegger, & Sonderegger, 2001; Barrett, Sonderegger, & Xenos, 2003).

With regard to implementing FRIENDS in a school setting, research suggests that the program is effective in addressing anxiety symptoms when implemented by teachers, school nurses, or trained clinicians (Lowry-Webster, Barrett, & Dadds, 2001; Lowry-Webster, Barrett, & Lock, 2003; Stallard, Simpson, Anderson, Hibbert, & Osborn, 2007). Additionally, children participating in the study who initially presented with high levels of anxiety and depression were found at posttest to have fewer symptoms of depression after having participated in the FRIENDS program (Lowry-Webster et al., 2001, 2003). However, there is little support for amelioration of depressive symptoms when depression, as the primary diagnostic category, is the target of treatment.

Cool Kids Child and Adolescent Anxiety

The Cool Kids Child and Adolescent Anxiety program is a group cognitive-behavioral intervention designed to address symptoms of anxiety within a variety of settings. The program is based upon earlier anxiety management programs such as Coping Koala (Barrett et al., 1996) and Coping Cat (Kendall, 1994) and has been adapted to school and community clinic settings, as well as for CD-ROM and bibliotherapy-based interventions (Cunningham, Rapee, & Lyneham, 2006; Lyneham & Rapee, 2006; Mifsud & Rapee, 2005; Rapee, 2000; Rapee, Abbott, & Lyneham, 2006; Rapee, Cunningham, & Lyneham, 2005). Treatment components include cognitive restructuring, gradual exposure, assertiveness, relapse prevention, and parent training.

Cool Kids: School Version (Rapee, Lyneham, et al., 2006) is an extension of the community-based intervention and is designed to meet the demands of the school environment. The program is intended for children between 6 and 12 years of age or in grades 1 though 6. An adolescent version of the intervention, called the Chilled program, is also available for students between 13 and 18 years of age or in grades 7 through 12. The Cool Kids program is designed to be conducted over 10 in-school sessions (typically over a 10-week period) either within an individual student or small-group format. Groups generally consist of four to eight students who are of similar ages. Cool Kids also comprises parent training and consultation sessions, as well as booster sessions for students who have successfully completed the program. Table 8.3 provides a summary of each session.

Program Components

The Cool Kids program is based on the view that the cycle of anxiety can be reduced by teaching a child to reverse his or her tendency to avoid feared situations. Cool Kids addresses this tendency through cognitive restructuring and exposure exercises, in combination with teaching parents to more effectively control anxious behavior and model effective coping styles. Additional strategies are introduced, such as social skills and assertiveness training.

Linking Thoughts to Feelings. The first stage of the Cool Kids program involves teaching children to recognize feelings, symptoms, and thoughts associated with anxiety. With regard to feelings, children learn to evaluate and quantify the intensity of their anxiety, as well as recognize that feelings vary depending on the situation. Within the Cool Kids program, symptoms of anxiety refer to various physical feelings that the child may experience when confronted with threatening situations. Children participate in activities that help them learn to identify the physical manifestations of fear and worry. These exercises include drawing self-portraits and marking different areas on the portraits that are affected by anxiety (for adolescents, brainstorming activities may be preferable).

Children are encouraged to discuss their thoughts and are taught about the relationship between fearful situations, thoughts, and feelings. Children are also asked to imagine certain situations and predict the thoughts and feelings that they will have. The program also emphasizes that children can have different thoughts about situations, and that these thoughts can change feelings. These exercises set the stage for cognitive restructuring, which is an integral component of the Cool Kids program.

TABLE 8.3. Overview of Sessions in the Cool Kids Child and Adolescent Anxiety Program

Session number	Session title	Content area
Session 1	What, Why, and How? An Overview of the Program	• Link between thoughts and feelings • Nature and causes of anxiety • Setting goals
Session 2	Learning to Think Realistically	• Cognitive restructuring
Session 3	Rewards	• Introduce self-reward • Monitor realistic thinking
Session 4	Fighting Fear by Facing Fear	• Introduce principles of exposure • Develop fear hierarchies
Session 5	Creative Exposure	• Discuss and design "stepladders"
Session 6	Problem Solving	• Begin in-session exposure tasks
Session 7	Assertiveness	• Introduce problem-solving skills
Session 8	Dealing with Teasing	• Being assertive in the face of bullying and being teased
Session 9	Reviewing Progress	• Review progress • Final push toward stepladder goals
Session 10	Maintaining Gains and Dealing with Setbacks	• Celebrate Cool Kids "graduation" • Discuss future plans and relapse management
Parent Information Session 1		• Provide information on the nature and causes of anxiety • Explain "detective thinking"—the first anxiety management skill
Parent Information Session 2		• Dealing with anxious behavior • Overview of using the stepladder to manage anxiety • Highlight other skills emphasized in the program
Individual Parent Consultations		• Parents provide specific information about their child's fears and worries • Troubleshoot implementation of skills at home
Booster Sessions		• Review the continued use of anxiety management skills • Problem solve any current or anticipated challenges

Note. Adapted from Rapee, Lyneham, et al. (2006). Copyright 2006 by the Centre for Emotional Health and Macquarie University. Adapted by permission.

Realistic Thinking. The technique of cognitive restructuring is introduced using the terms *worried thinking* and *calm thinking* with younger children and *realistic thinking* with adolescents. The goal of cognitive restructuring is to modify feelings that are out of proportion to the demands of a given situation by replacing irrational thoughts with more realistic patterns of thinking (Rapee, Wignall, Hudson, & Schniering, 2000). Through a process called *detective thinking,* children are taught to do the following:

1. Identify the situation that is causing them to feel fearful or worried.
2. Identify the thoughts that are leading to these feelings.
3. Look for realistic evidence.
4. Brainstorm outcomes to the feared situation.
5. Identify realistic thoughts about the feared situation. (Rapee, Lyneham, et al., 2006)

The goal of detective thinking is to reduce fears and worries associated with unrealistic concerns by investigating the evidence for a given thought, and to arrive at a conclusion regarding whether the thought is realistic. Children are also taught to consider the consequences of confronting a threatening situation. In considering these consequences, the program emphasizes that even the worst case scenario is not usually as bad as they might imagine and that there are always effective ways to manage these threatening scenarios.

Stepladders. Cool Kids teaches children to face their fears through gradual exposure exercises, during which they first confront their least intense fears, then face increasingly more intense fears over time. Children create graduated fear hierarchies, called *stepladders,* which consist of several steps that will ultimately lead them to face a specific fear (e.g., playing with other children during recess, speaking aloud in class, etc.). Children are taught to remain in the feared situation defined within each step for a period of time and to repeat that step several times until they no longer feel frightened. Children are given an agreed-upon reward promptly after the successful completion of each step. If a child does not successfully complete the step, he or she is given a "backup reward" to acknowledge his or her effort. The goal of the stepladder approach is for the child to build confidence, which will ultimately reduce feelings of helplessness.

Worry Surfing. The Cool Kids program teaches children to increase tolerance of fears and worries by continuing to function in everyday life despite feeling anxious. This process, referred to as *worry surfing,* consists of the following steps:

1. Becoming aware of the concern, and choosing to address it.
2. Identifying tasks or activities that the child should be doing.
3. Concentrating on the task or activity, or "riding the worry wave," rather than spending time focusing on concerns.
4. Rewarding successful attempts at moving past the fears. (Rapee, Lyneham, et al., 2006)

Assertiveness and Dealing with Teasing. The Cool Kids program emphasizes the importance of confidence and assertive behavior in dealing with fears and worries about social situations. Disadvantages associated with not being assertive are discussed, such as difficulties with friendships and vulnerability to teasing and bullying. Three different types of behavior are presented: assertive, passive, and aggressive. Children brainstorm how a person might respond or appear when behaving in each of these ways, focusing on characteristics such as a person's posture, voice quality, or what his or her eyes might be doing. Children then role-play each of these behavior types with the goal of eventually adopting all identified characteristics associated with assertiveness.

Children learn to cope with being teased and bullied by being introduced to ways in which they can outsmart a student who is engaging in bullying behavior. Skills emphasized include identifying sources of support and talking through feelings of being hurt, staying close to groups when a bully approaches, seeking ways to circumvent teasing, and identifying clever comebacks.

Parent Training. Working with parents or caregivers typically occurs over four sessions that include two parent information sessions and two individual parent consultations. Parent information sessions are intended to introduce parents to the Cool Kids program, provide information about the nature and treatment of anxiety, and facilitate discussion of the anxiety management skills emphasized within the program. Parents are taught to play the role of a coach by providing encouragement, reinforcement, and opportunities for their child to practice new skills. Parents learn to manage their child's anxious behaviors more effectively by considering the following factors:

1. The role of attention in the development and maintenance of avoidance behaviors.
2. The role of praise in increasingly the likelihood of courageous behaviors.

3. Use of rewards and positive reinforcement.
4. Modeling effective coping strategies.
5. Encouraging a child's independence and reducing overly protective behaviors. (Rapee, Lyneham, et al., 2006)

Individual parent consultations are intended to provide parents with the opportunity to convey specific information regarding their child's anxiety, as well as to discuss potential problems with implementing skills within the home environment.

Relapse Prevention. The Cool Kids program addresses relapse prevention in a variety of ways. First, the final session of the program is primarily devoted to maintaining treatment gains and coping with obstacles. Children are urged to consider challenging situations that they may encounter in the future and to discuss plans for managing potential fears or worries. Additionally, the program emphasizes the importance of being prepared to expect anxiety from time to time, and that continued practice of skills and reliance on social support can assist in dealing with setbacks. Second, parental training and consultation teaches parents to anticipate and respond effectively to obstacles. Ongoing involvement familiarizes parents with program steps so that they can review and practice skills with their child. Additionally, parents are trained to identify signs of fear and worry in their child so that they can help address anxiety when it first arises. Finally, booster sessions provide an opportunity for continued review of anxiety management skills and also help children overcome unanticipated challenges or setbacks.

Participant Considerations

The Cool Kids program is designed for children who meet criteria for a primary diagnosis of an anxiety disorder based upon assessment via a clinical interview and structured questionnaires (Rapee, Lyneham, et al., 2006). A child who is at risk for anxiety (i.e., does not meet the diagnostic criteria for an anxiety disorder) may benefit from an abbreviated version of the program. In such cases, Rapee and colleagues (2000) recommend shortening the skill implementation phase. Rapee, Lyneham, et al. (2006) stated that the Cool Kids program should be deferred for children who are experiencing more severe emotional or behavior disorders until those problems are resolved. For example, in the case of a child who is also experiencing depression, Rapee and colleagues (Rapee, Lyneham, et al., 2006), suggest that the presence of this diagnosis or related behaviors may interfere with a child's progress within the Cool Kids program, because the child may not have the motivation or confidence to take the initiative in progressing through the program. Similarly, a child with oppositional behaviors may not progress through the program due to resistance to cooperating with parents when encouraged to practice skills between sessions.

Overview of Supportive Research

The Cool Kids program has been evaluated in several clinical trials and has been shown to be effective in treating anxiety symptoms in a variety of settings (e.g., Lyneham & Rapee, 2006; Mifsud & Rapee, 2005; Rapee, 2000). For example, one study investigated the program's effectiveness within a sample of economically disadvantaged schoolchildren and found significant reductions in anxiety symptoms based upon child, parent, and teacher reports (Mifsud & Rapee, 2005). Significant treatment gains have also been demonstrated with CD-ROM and bibliotherapy-based versions of the program, as well as within clinic settings (Cunningham et al., 2006; Lyneham & Rapee, 2006; Rapee, 2000; Rapee, Abbott, et al., 2006). A variety of instruments have been used to measure program effectiveness, including structured clinical interviews such as the Anxiety Disorders Interview Schedule for Children (Silverman & Albano, 1996) and the Development and Well-Being Assessment (Goodman, Ford, Richards, Gatward, & Meltzer, 2000); and anxiety screening questionnaires such as the Spence Children's Anxiety Scale (Spence, 1998), the School Anxiety Scale–Teacher Report (Lyneham, Street, Abbott, & Rapee, 2008), the Children's Automatic Thoughts Scale (Schniering & Rapee, 2002), and the Strengths and Difficulties Questionnaire (Goodman, 1999).

Social Effectiveness Therapy for Children (SET-C)

SET-C was developed by Deborah Beidel and her colleagues (e.g., Beidel et al., 2004; Beidel & Roberson-Nay, 2005; Beidel, Turner, Young, & Paulson, 2005; Beidel, Turner, & Young, 2006) at the University of Maryland at College Park. SET-C is a brief, intensive CBT treatment for children with social phobia. SET-C was originally developed for children between 8 and 12 years of age, but has also been adapted more recently for adolescents between 13 and 17 years of age. The program involves 24 therapy sessions during a 12-week period, which includes weekly group training as well as weekly exposure sessions conducted on an individual basis.

SET-C also includes peer generalization sessions that are intended to provide opportunities to apply skills to real-life situations. Additionally, the program includes homework assignments and a parent–child education component. In this regard, parents play an integral role in the treatment through the education component and through assisting with homework activities. SET-C is designed to be implemented in a clinic or community setting and conducted by a trained clinician.

Theoretical Principles

SET-C is a multidimensional treatment intervention intended to enhance social skills and self-esteem and to reduce social anxiety and avoidance. The program is designed primarily to improve social competence by targeting a variety of behaviors. An important aspect of SET-C is exposure, which is a key component within each session. Exposure occurs in individual and group sessions as well as in peer generalization sessions.

Unlike the FRIENDS and the Cool Kids programs, SET-C does not include a direct cognitive component; it has similar goals as those programs but has more of an emphasis on directly observable anxiety-related behaviors than on cognitions. The SET-C program is based on the premise that avoiding fearful stimuli prevents an individual from developing appropriate social skills (Beidel et al., 1999). Thus, SET-C focuses exclusively on individual exposure, peer generalization experiences, and social skills training. In this regard, SET-C shares several therapeutic ingredients with CBT interventions like the FRIENDS and the Cool Kids programs, such as the emphasis on exposure, performance feedback, modeling, and generalization of skills, as well as the emphasis on like CBT objective measures for evaluating treatment effectiveness.

Treatment Components and Procedures

The initial session of SET-C is conducted in a group format and includes participants and their parents. During this session, the clinician provides an overview of the program's goals and components, discusses the nature and etiology of social phobia, and also addresses individual differences in the subjective experience and presentation of social phobia and related anxieties. The clinician also provides participants and their parents with an opportunity to ask questions.

Social Skills Training. The second component of SET-C involves social skills training. Due to the social isolation that is often associated with social phobia and related anxieties, youth may not have opportunities to gain social skills through everyday social interactions. Social skills training, therefore, addresses some potential gaps by teaching appropriate social skills that can be generalized to a variety of situations. Group sessions provide opportunities for social interaction among group members, which allows participants to practice their newly acquired skills. SET-C sessions are cumulative, with a new skill being introduced each week. A structured peer generalization program is also an essential component of the social skills training program. In this regard, participants are encouraged to partake in a variety of activities, such as sports or roller skating, with a group of peers who are not experiencing social phobia or related anxieties. These practice sessions are considered to be critical to the generalization of acquired skills because they provide socially anxious children with an opportunity to practice social skills in natural settings, as well as to capitalize on the positive effects of peer role models. The practice sessions occur weekly following the group intervention session.

Social skills training groups are generally composed of four to six similar-age peer participants. The group training sessions are typically 60 minutes in length and are conducted by one or two clinicians. Each of the 12 social skills training sessions consists of two components, with each focusing on a given set of common problems. These components are "social environment awareness" and "interpersonal skills enhancement." The former emphasizes the "where, when, and why" to initiate and terminate social interactions. The latter focuses on the "verbal and nonverbal" aspects of appropriate social interaction, with special emphasis placed on those situations that are challenging for individuals with social phobia (e.g., initiating social interactions, being assertive, and participating in activities with peers). The SET-C social skills training approach draws upon principles of modeling, instruction, behavior rehearsal, corrective feedback, and positive reinforcement. Behavioral rehearsal is particularly emphasized during the group sessions, where participants role-play with one another and with the clinician until each one has successfully demonstrated the targeted social skill. The procedures for the acquisition of each skill are outlined in the following training model: (1) instructing in the target skill, (2) modeling appropriate behaviors, (3) rehearsing behaviors until all participants have demonstrated them successfully, and (4) providing feedback and positive reinforcement. Content areas and their respective sessions included in the SET-C skills training model are listed in Table 8.4.

Peer Generalization. SET-C peer generalization sessions follow each social skills training session. As mentioned previously, these sessions provide participants with the opportunity to practice learned social skills in a natural environment with peers. The sessions are 90 minutes in length and occur in a variety of settings, such as a museum, roller skating rink, or a sporting event. Participants are encouraged to greet five new people during each session. Same-age peers help participants ac-

TABLE 8.4. Content Areas Covered in the Social Effectiveness Therapy for Children Program

Session number	Content area
Session 1	Recognition of social cues
Session 2	Initiating conversations and appropriate conversation topics
Session 3	Maintaining appropriate conversations and topic transitions
Session 4	Attending and remembering
Session 5	Skills for joining groups
Session 6	Establishing and maintaining friendships
Session 7	Giving and receiving compliments
Session 8	Refusing unreasonable requests
Session 9	Asking for a change in behavior
Session 10	Assertion with authority figures
Session 11	Telephone skills
Session 12	Review and wrap-up

Note. From Beidel and Roberson-Nay (2005). Copyright 2005 by the American Psychological Association. Reprinted by permission.

complish this activity, either by being one of the five individuals that the participant must greet or by first modeling an appropriate greeting.

Exposure. SET-C draws upon graduated *in vivo* exposure techniques (i.e., graduated exposure to anxiety-provoking stimuli in a natural setting) in order to promote learning and the application of skills when approaching fearful or anxiety-provoking situations. Exposure sessions occur weekly and are typically 60–90 minutes in length, depending on the time required for participants to habituate. With several opportunities to successfully practice skills in natural settings, participants will ideally habituate during each session, as well as to natural settings between sessions. The goal of the exposure exercises is that the experience of anxiety associated with various social settings gradually decreases.

As part of the *in vivo* exposure technique, each participant is also encouraged to create his or her own fear hierarchy, which consists of several steps associated with approaching the feared or anxiety-provoking social situation, with each step increasingly more anxiety provoking. Participants practice each step until they have attained habituation.

Homework Activities. Homework is assigned following each skills training and exposure session. Homework activities typically provide an opportunity for participants to practice newly learned skills in a variety of settings. For example, a homework assignment for an exposure session that addresses eating in front of others may involve practicing eating at a lunch table at school throughout the week. Reinforcement is provided in order to ensure compliance.

Participant Considerations

SET-C is intended for children between 8 and 12 years of age and adolescents between 13 and 17 years of age who have social phobia and related anxieties. Though the program is designed to ameliorate symptoms associated with social phobia, preliminary empirical evidence suggests that children with certain comorbid disorders may also benefit from the program, provided the primary diagnosis is social phobia (Beidel & Roberson-Nay, 2005). For example, SET-C has been implemented with children having selective mutism; however, Beidel and Roberson-Nay recommend individual therapy for those children who are unable to participate in social interactions, role-play, or answer the clinician's questions. Children with a primary diagnosis of major depression and a secondary diagnosis of social phobia may also benefit from social skills training. Beidel and Roberson-Nay indicated that symptoms associated with depression should be addressed first using evidence-based treatment procedures for depression.

SET-C is not recommended for children having a primary or secondary diagnosis of attention-deficit/hyperactivity disorder, conduct disorder, oppositional defiant disorder, psychosis, mental retardation, or pervasive developmental disorder. Though these children may benefit from social skills training, SET-C either may not adequately address their specific skill deficits or may not be appropriate for their cognitive and/or developmental levels.

Overview of Supportive Research

Effectiveness of the SET-C program in reducing symptoms associated with social phobia and related anxieties has been evaluated in clinical trials using structured diagnostic interviews (e.g., Silverman & Albano, 1996), self-report measures such as the Social Phobia and Anxiety Inventory for Children (Beidel, Turner, & Morris, 1995) and the State–Trait Anxiety Inventory for Children (Spielberger, 1973), and parent and teacher ratings such as the Child Behavior Checklist (Achenbach & Edelbrock, 1991). In addition, a behavioral avoidance test (see, e.g., Morris & Kratochwill, 1983) and daily diaries (Beidel & Roberson-Nay, 2005) have also been used to assess anxiety symptoms.

Several clinical trials in Brazil, Canada, Spain, and the United States have supported the effectiveness of the SET-C in reducing social anxiety symptoms (e.g., Beidel, Turner, & Morris, 2000; Olivares, Beidel, Albano, & Hidalgo, 2002; Beidel et al., 2005, 2006). Long-term treatment gains have also been reported in the literature. For example, researchers have found that participants reported significantly fewer anxiety symptoms at 3- and 5-year follow-up (Beidel et al., 2005, 2006).

Skills for Academic and Social Success (SASS)

SASS (Masia et al., 1999) is a program that is designed to address social skills deficits in children with symptoms of social anxiety. SASS is essentially an adaptation of the SET-C program (Beidel et al., 2004), with an added emphasis on the relationship between thoughts, feelings, and behaviors that is based upon the work of Ronald Rapee (1998). The program is intended for implementation in a high school setting (Fisher, Masia-Warner, & Klein, 2004). Masia et al. (1999) modified the SET-C program when developing SASS to adapt it to an adolescent population within a school environment. First, sessions were shortened to approximate the time of a typical class period (estimated at 42 minutes). Second, sessions were implemented in a manner that avoids the interruption of the class. Third, exposure exercises took place within the school environment. Fourth, teachers were recruited to provide support in classroom-based exposures. Peer assistants were enlisted in order to provide referred adolescents with the opportunities for practicing social interaction. The program also involved teaching parents techniques to discourage avoidance behaviors in their children as well as to enhance generalization of skills.

The SASS program is administered over a period of 3 months and can be adapted to accommodate a school's calendar. SASS comprises 12 weekly group sessions that are approximately 40 minutes in length, two booster sessions that are intended to address residual difficulties or relapse, as well as two 15-minute individual meetings. The program also includes four social events that occur on weekends that serve to provide real-world exposure and generalization of skills. Parents also participate in psychoeducational sessions in order to learn about symptoms of social anxiety and anxiety reduction techniques. Additionally, teachers participate in two psychoeducational sessions that last approximately 30 minutes each. Teachers learn to identify signs of anxiety in students as well as strategies for facilitating classroom-based exposure.

Each student meets with the group leader on an individual basis twice during the course of the program. These sessions are intended for discussing individual goals, specific setbacks, as well as any issues that may interfere with successful implementation of newly learned skills. These sessions also provide an opportunity for group leaders to individualize skills training to each student when needed as well as to establish rapport.

Social events are an integral part of the program. These events include a variety of different activities, all providing opportunities for social interaction. In this regard, high school classmates are recruited to assist in helping group members practice newly learned social skills within several commonly feared social situations. School personnel identify students who are potential peer assistants. They are selected on the basis of their ability to serve as adequate models for appropriate social situations, as well as for their academic performance, friendship, maturity, and interest in and commitment to participating in the program. The peer assistants help facilitate smooth interaction within the four planned weekend social events and provide assistance as needed with exposure practice activity during the week.

The first parent meeting occurs at the beginning of the program and is devoted to providing information about social anxiety. Sessions are intended to help parents understand the nature of their child's avoidance behaviors as well as understand their child's experience of anxiety. Parents are also provided with training in how to encourage effective coping, how to provide positive reinforcement and support to their child, as well as how to appropriately model responses to anxiety-provoking situations. At this meeting, parents are encouraged to constructively discourage their child's avoidance of social situations.

Meetings with teachers are intended as part education about social anxiety and part description of the goals of the anxiety reduction program. At the first meeting, teachers are asked to identify specific difficulties that they observe in students experiencing anxiety and provide suggestions for classroom-based exposure exercises. The second meeting is designed to discuss students' progress as well as to plan for additional exposure exercises as needed.

SASS treatment components include *psychoeducation* for the targeted student, as well as his or her parents and teachers; *realistic thinking* about the feared social situations; *social skills training*; real-life *exposure*; and *relapse prevention*. Group sessions are typically led by a psychologist and an assistant (often a school counselor or graduate student) and consist of no more than six students per group. The first session presents the psychoeducation component. Group leaders discuss cognitive, physical, and behavioral manifestations of social anxiety. Students are encouraged to reflect upon their own symptoms of social anxiety and to consider the ways in which social anxiety is maintained by a combination of negative thoughts, physical symptoms, and avoidance behaviors. Situations that commonly evoke anxiety responses are also discussed.

Realistic thinking is the focus of the second session. Based upon the work of Ronald Rapee (1998), this component includes a discussion of the relationship between thoughts, feelings, and behavior. The tendency to exaggerate the probability of negative outcomes, as well as to exaggerate the consequences of anxiety-provoking situations, is discussed. Students are encouraged to reflect upon negative expectations, such as poor performance or appearing foolish speaking in class, and are encouraged to examine the degree to which these thoughts are realistic.

The next component, a social skills training module called Social Skills for Success, includes four sessions devoted to the following: (1) initiating conversation, (2) maintaining conversations and establishing friendships, (3) listening and remembering, and (4) assertiveness training. During each session, group leaders introduce each skill and its rationale as well as encourage group discussion. Each skill is demonstrated through role playing and simulating common situations and experiences. Students participate in at least two role-playing sessions and receive feedback from group leaders and other students participating in the group. Positive feedback is encouraged, as are constructive suggestions for improvement in the performance of the social skill. Students are urged to practice each skill outside of the group environment.

The exposure component begins with a discussion of the procedure as well as its rationale. Group leaders discuss how avoidance perpetuates anxiety and how anxiety can only be reduced with increased exposure to feared stimuli. Each group member develops a fear hierarchy, which consists of 10 situations that commonly evoke anxiety, rank-ordered from least to most fearful situation. Group leaders and members also identify characteristics of a given context that make a situation less fear provoking or more comfortable.

During exposure sessions, group leaders select items on the fear hierarchy that address each student's fears in a series of graduated steps. Exposure includes working with school personnel or peer assistants. Students rate their level anxiety using subjective units of distress ratings from 1 to 100, where 1 is the most calm and 100 represents feeling terrified. After each in-session exposure, students discuss their experiences and group members provide feedback. Students are asked to practice skills at home between exposure sessions.

The final session is devoted to relapse prevention. Group leaders discuss signs of relapse and discuss potential setbacks. Strategies for addressing relapse are also given. Booster sessions occur monthly over a period of 2 months after program termination. The purpose of these sessions is to monitor progress, discuss setbacks, and problem solve new ways to initiate social interactions. Additional exposures may be included in booster sessions as well.

Overview of Supportive Research

The SASS program has been shown to be effective in reducing symptoms of social anxiety within a school environment (Masia, Klein, Storch, & Corda, 2001; Masia-Warner, Fisher, Shrout, Rathor, & Klein, 2007; Masia-Warner et al., 2005). Effectiveness of the SASS program has been evaluated in randomized wait-list control trials consisting of 35 adolescents (Masia-Warner et al., 2005). Participants in the treatment group demonstrated significant reductions in symptoms of social anxiety at posttreatment and at a 9-month follow-up using independent evaluator ratings, self-report ratings, and parent ratings. Additionally, participants in the intervention group reported an improvement in overall affective functioning. A more recent study evaluated the effectiveness of the SASS program against an attention control group (Masia-Warner et al., 2007). A significant reduction in symptoms of social anxiety was found in the treatment group based upon independent evaluation and self-report. Specifically, in comparison to the attention control group, participants in the treatment group had significantly fewer members meet the diagnostic criteria for social anxiety at the completion of the program, and these treatment differences were maintained at the 6-month follow-up period.

Core CBT Components

Though there are variations in how various CBT-based interventions are implemented, the underlying treatment components are largely the same. Specifically, the components of CBT often include (1) psychoeducation (2) relaxation training, (3) modeling, (4) role playing, (5) cognitive restructuring, (6) exposure, (7) positive reinforcement and performance feedback, and (8) parent training.

The psychoeducation component is used by each of the four programs presented above and teaches parents and children about the three primary pathways through which anxiety is manifested: physiological, cognitive, and behavioral (Lawyer & Smitherman, 2004). The relaxation training component is used by FRIENDS and teaches children progressive relaxation techniques through the systematic tensing and releasing of muscles (see Morris & Kratochwill, 1983; Morris et al., 2008). Children also learn how to monitor their own bodies for physiological symptoms of anxiety.

The modeling component is used by all four programs and involves having a child observe an individual—either live or through video/ DVD—safely approach a fearful stimulus (Davis & Ollendick, 2005). Modeling can include demonstrating adaptive coping strategies when faced with negative or maladaptive thoughts. Role playing is also used by each of the four programs and provides an opportunity for the child to practice coping strategies, which ultimately boosts the child's confidence in his or her ability to effectively deal with anxiety.

In the CBT tradition, cognitive distortions are held as being primarily responsible for the development and perpetuation of anxiety (Kendall, Chu, Pimentel, & Choudhury, 2000). Cognitive restructuring, used by FRIENDS, Cool Kids, and SASS, involves having the child evaluate his or her own negative cognitions and replace them with more positive, adaptive thought patterns (Rapee et al., 2000).

Graduated and controlled exposure to situations that evoke anxiety is used by all four programs. Exposure provides the child with an opportunity to employ newly learned coping strategies in a series of graduated steps, such that he or she may experience success with each approximation. Positive reinforcement and positive performance feedback techniques, used by each of the four programs, can include play or some other type of reward system, where successive approximations are promptly rewarded. The child also learns to provide his or her own positive reinforcement.

The parent training component is used by all four programs and involves teaching parents to modify their own cognitions and behaviors that may be contributing to the maintenance of their child's anxiety (Kendall et al., 2005). Techniques emphasized include modeling effective coping strategies as well as developing and implementing contingency management plans. Moreover, involving parents provides an additional avenue through which the child can practice and generalize newly learned coping strategies.

Conclusions and Directions for Future Research

In this chapter, we have reviewed four exemplary programs designed to prevent and reduce anxiety-related symptoms in children and adolescents. These approaches have demonstrated long-term success in treating several types of anxiety-related disorders, such as separation anxiety, overanxious disorder, avoidant disorder, and social phobia. These approaches have also been found in many cases to successfully treat children from different countries as well as those who do not necessarily speak English. However, it should be noted that these programs have only shown effectiveness in clinical trials when, in most cases, they were compared to control conditions that either received no treatment, were placed in an attention placebo condition, or received treatment that had little empirical support. These programs have not yet been compared to one another or to other evidence-based procedures. More research is therefore needed comparing efficacious treatments in order to determine their relative effectiveness as well as the conditions under which such effectiveness is found.

In addition, although the FRIENDS and SASS programs have been found to be effective in clinic, community, and school settings, little outcome research has been conducted in school settings using the SET-C program. Though the Cool Kids program has demonstrated treatment gains in a variety of settings, further investigation is needed to determine effectiveness within a broader population of children in a school setting. Additionally, some writers, including Barrett and Turner (2001), Hudson et al. (2004), and Morris et al. (2008), have suggested that developing programs designed to intervene prior to the onset of children's clinical symptoms may ultimately prove to be the most effective form of

TABLE 8.5. Resources for Further Information on FRIENDS for Life, Cool Kids, Skills for Academic and Social Success, and Social Effectiveness Therapy

Friends for Life
Australian Academic Press
32 Jeays Street
Bowen Hills, QLD 4006, Australia
www.friendsinfo.net

Cool Kids: Child and Adolescent Anxiety Program
Macquarie University Anxiety Research Unit (MUARU)
c/o Department of Psychology
Macquarie University
Sydney, NSW 2109, Australia
www.psy.mq.edu.au/MUARU/

Social Effectiveness Therapy
Multi-Health Systems, Inc.
P.O. Box 950
North Tonawanda, NY 14120-0950
www.mhs.com

Skills for Academic and Social Success
Carrie Masia-Warner, PhD
New York University School of Medicine
Child Study Center
215 Lexington Avenue, 13th Floor
New York, NY 10016
www.aboutourkids.org

intervention. In this regard, more research is needed to investigate the relative effectiveness of each of these programs in working with children who are at high risk for developing anxiety disorders.

The four exemplary programs that are described in this chapter nevertheless represent a tremendous advancement over the past 10–15 years in the availability of evidence-based treatment programs for successfully reducing children's anxiety-related disorders. Please see Table 8.5 for more information regarding the programs discussed in this chapter.

Acknowledgment

Preparation of this chapter was supported in part by the Jacqueline Anne Morris Memorial Foundation's Arizona Children's Policy and Research Project at the University of Arizona.

References

Achenbach, T. M., & Edelbrock, C. (1991). *Manual for the Teacher's Report Form and teacher version of the child behavior profile.* Burlington: University of Vermont, Department of Psychiatry.

Albano, A. M., Marten, P. A., Holt, C. S., Heimberg, R. G., & Barlow, D. H. (1995). Cognitive-behavioral group treatment for social phobia in adolescents: A preliminary study. *Journal of Nervous and Mental Disease, 183,* 649–656.

American Psychiatric Association. (2000). *Diagnostic and statistical manual of mental disorders* (4th ed., text rev.). Washington, DC: Author.

Barrett, P. M. (2004). *FRIENDS for Life group leaders' manual for children.* Bowen Hills, Queensland: Australian Academic Press.

Barrett, P. M. (2005). *FRIENDS for Life group leaders' manual for youth.* Bowen Hills, Queensland: Australian Academic Press.

Barrett, P. M., Dadds, M. R., & Rapee, R. M. (1996). Family treatment of childhood anxiety: A controlled trial. *Journal of Consulting and Clinical Psychology, 64,* 333–342.

Barrett, P. M., Duffy, A. L., Dadds, M. R., & Rapee, R. M. (2001). Cognitive-behavioral treatment of anxiety disorders in children: Long-term (6-year) follow-up. *Journal of Consulting and Clinical Psychology, 69,* 135–141.

Barrett, P. M., Moore, A. F., & Sonderegger, R. (2000). The FRIENDS program for young former-Yugoslavian refugees in Australia: A pilot study. *Behaviour Change, 17,* 124–133.

Barrett, P. M., Sonderegger, R., & Sonderegger, N. L. (2001). Evaluation of an anxiety-prevention and positive-coping program (FRIENDS) for children and adolescents of non-English speaking background. *Behaviour Change, 18,* 78–91.

Barrett, P. M., Sonderegger, R., & Xenos, S. (2003). Using FRIENDS to combat anxiety and adjustment problems among young migrants to Australia: A national trial. *Clinical Child Psychology and Psychiatry, 8,* 241–260.

Barrett, P. M., & Turner, C. (2001). Prevention of anxiety symptoms in primary school children: Preliminary results from a universal school-based trial. *British Journal of Clinical Psychology, 40,* 399–410.

Barrett, P. M., Webster, H., & Turner, C. (2003). *Introduction to FRIENDS: A program for enhancing life skills promoting psychological resilience.* Bowen Hills, Queensland: Australian Academic Press.

Beidel, D. C., & Roberson-Nay, R. (2005). Treating childhood social phobia: Social effectiveness therapy for children. In E. D. Hibbs & P. S. Jensen (Eds.), *Psychosocial treatments for child and adolescent disorders: Empirically based strategies for clinical practice* (2nd ed., pp. 75–96). Washington, DC: American Psychological Association.

Beidel, D. C., Turner, S. M., & Morris, T. L. (1995). A new instrument to assess childhood social anxiety and phobia: The Social Phobia and Anxiety Inventory for Children. *Psychological Assessment, 1,* 73–79.

Beidel, D. C., Turner, S. M., & Morris, T. L. (1999). Psychopathology of childhood social phobia. *Journal of the American Academy of Child and Adolescent Psychiatry, 38,* 643–650.

Beidel, D. C., Turner, S. M., & Morris, T. L. (2000). Behavioral treatment of childhood social phobia. *Journal of Consulting and Clinical Psychology, 68,* 1072–1080.

Beidel, D. C., Turner, S. M., & Morris, T. L. (2004). *Social effectiveness therapy for children: A treatment manual.* Toronto, Canada: Multi-Health Systems.

Beidel, D. C., Turner, S. M., & Young, B. J. (2006). Social effectiveness therapy for children: Five years later. *Behavior Therapy, 37,* 416–425.

Beidel, D. C., Turner, S. M., Young, B. J., & Paulson, A. (2005). Social effectiveness therapy for children: Three-year follow-up. *Journal of Consulting and Clinical Psychology, 27,* 721–725.

Bernstein, G. A., Layne, A. E., Egan, E. A., & Tennison, D. M. (2005). School-based interventions for anxious children. *Journal of American Academy of Child and Adolescent Psychiatry, 44,* 1118–1127.

Chambless, D. L., Baker, M. J., Baucom, D. H., Beutler, L. E., Calhoun, K. S., Crits-Christoph, P., et al. (1998, Winter). Update on empirically validated therapies: II. *The Clinical Psychologist, 51,* 3–16.

Chambless, D. L., & Ollendick, T. H. (2001). Empirically supported psychological interventions: Controversies and evidence. *Annual Review of Psychology, 52,* 685–716.

Conradt, J., & Essau, C. A. (2003, July). *Feasibility and efficacy of the FRIENDS program for the prevention of anxiety in children.* Paper presented at the 24th International Conference of the Stress and Anxiety Research Society, Lisbon, Portugal.

Cunningham, M., Rapee, R., & Lyneham, H. (2006). The Cool Teens CD-ROM: A multimedia self-help program for adolescents with anxiety. *Youth Studies Australia, 25,* 50–56.

Davis, T. E., & Ollendick, T. H. (2005). Empirically supported treatments for specific phobia in children: Do efficacious treatments address the components of phobic response? *Clinical Psychology, 12,* 144–160.

Fisher, P. H., Masia-Warner, C., & Klein, R. (2004). Skills for social and academic success: A school-based intervention for social anxiety disorder in adolescents. *Clinical Child and Family Psychology Review, 7,* 241–249.

Goodman, R. (1999). The extended version of the Strengths and Difficulties Questionnaire as a guide to child psychiatric caseness and consequent burden. *Journal of Child Psychology and Psychiatry and Allied Disciplines, 40,* 791–799.

Goodman, R., Ford, T., Richards, H., Gatward, R., & Meltzer, H. (2000). The Development and Well-Being Assessment: Description and initial validation of an integrated assessment of child and adolescent psychopathology. *Journal of Child Psychology and Psychiatry, 41,* 645–655.

Hudson, J. L., Flannery-Schroeder, E., & Kendall, P. C. (2004). Primary prevention of anxiety disorders. In J. A. Dozois & K. S. Dobson (Eds.), *The prevention of anxiety and depression: Theory, research, and practice* (pp. 101–130). Washington, DC: American Psychological Association.

Kendall, P. C. (1994). Treating anxiety disorders in children: Results of a randomized clinical trial. *Journal of Consulting and Clinical Psychology, 62,* 100–110.

Kendall, P. C. (2000). *Cognitive-behavioral therapy for anxious children: Treatment manual* (2nd ed.). Ardmore, PA: Workbook Publishing.

Kendall, P. C., Choudhury, M., Hudson, J., & Webb, A. (2002). *The C.A.T. project manual for the cognitive behavioral treatment of anxious adolescents.* Ardmore, PA: Workbook Publishing.

Kendall, P. C., Chu, B. C., Pimentel, S. S., & Choudhury, M. (2000). Treating anxiety disorders in youth. In P. C. Kendall (Ed.), *Child and adolescent therapy: Cognitive-behavioral procedures* (pp. 235–287). New York: Guilford Press.

Kendall, P. C., Hudson, J. L., Choudhury, M., Webb, A., & Pimentel, S. (2005). Cognitive behavioral treatment for childhood anxiety disorders, In E. D. Hibbs & P. S. Jensen (Eds.), *Psychosocial treatments for child and adolescent disorders: Empirically based strategies for clinical practice* (2nd ed., pp. 47–73). Washington, DC: American Psychological Association.

King, N. J., Muris, P., & Ollendick, T. H. (2005). Childhood fears and phobias: Assessment and treatment. *Child and Adolescent Mental Health, 10,* 50–56.

Last, C. G., Hanson, C., & Franco, N. (1997). Anxious children in adulthood: A prospective study of adjustment. *Journal of the American Academy of Child and Adolescent Psychiatry, 36,* 645–652.

Lawyer, S. A., & Smitherman, T. A. (2004). Trends in anxiety assessment. *Journal of Psychopathology and Behavioral Assessment, 26,* 101–106.

Liebowitz, M. R., Gorman, J. M., Fyer, A. J., & Klein, D. F. (1985). Social phobia: Review of a neglected disorder. *Archives of General Psychiatry, 42,* 729–736.

Lonigan, C. J., Elbert, J. C., & Johnson, S. B. (1998). Empirically supported psychosocial interventions for children [Special issue]. *Journal of Clinical Child Psychology, 27,* 138–145.

Lowry-Webster, H. M., Barrett, P. M., & Dadds, M. R. (2001). A universal prevention trial of anxiety and depressive symptomatology in childhood: Preliminary data from an Australian study. *Behaviour Change, 18,* 36–50.

Lowry-Webster, H., Barrett, P., & Lock, S. (2003). A universal prevention trial of anxiety symptomatology during childhood: Results at one-year follow-up. *Behaviour Change, 20,* 25–43.

Lyneham, H. J., & Rapee, R. M. (2006). Evaluation of therapist-supported parent-implemented CBT for anxiety disorders in rural children. *Behavior Research and Therapy, 44,* 1287–1300.

Lyneham, H. J., Street, A. K., Abbott, M. J., & Rapee, R. M. (2008). Psychometric properties of the School Anxiety Scale—Teacher Report (SAS-TR). *Journal of Anxiety Disorders, 22,* 292–300.

Masia, C. L., Beidel, D. C., Albano, A. M., Rapee, R. M., Turner, S. M., Morris, T. L., et al. (1999). *Skills for academic and social success.* Available from Carrie Masia-Warner, PhD, Child Study Center, New York University School of Medicine, 215 Lexington Avenue, 13th Floor, New York, NY 10016.

Masia, C. L., Klein, R. G., Storch, E. A., & Corda, B. (2001). School-based behavioral treatment for social anxiety disorder in adolescents: Results of a pilot study. *Journal of the American Academy of Child and Adolescent Psychiatry, 40,* 780–786.

Masia-Warner, C., Fisher, P. H., Shrout, P. E., Rathor, S., Klein, R. G. (2007). Treating adolescents with social anxiety disorder in school: An attention control trial. *Journal of Child Psychology and Psychiatry, 48,* 676–686.

Masia-Warner, C., Klein, R., Dent, H., Fisher, P., Alvir, J., Albano, A., et al. (2005). School-based intervention for adolescents with social anxiety disorder: Results of a controlled study. *Journal of Abnormal Child Psychology, 33,* 707–722.

McGee, R., & Stanton, W. R. (1990). Parent reports of disability among 13-year-olds with DSM-III disorders. *Journal of Child Psychology and Psychiatry and Allied Disciplines, 31*, 793–801.

Mitsud, C., & Rapee, R. M. (2005). Early intervention for childhood anxiety in a school setting: Outcomes for an economically disadvantaged population. *Journal of the American Academy of Child and Adolescent Psychiatry, 44*, 996–1004.

Morris, R. J., & Kratochwill, T. R. (1983). *Treating children's fears and phobias: A behavioral approach.* Elmsford, NY: Pergamon Press.

Morris, R. J., Kratochwill, T. R., Schoenfield, G., & Auster, E. R. (2008). Fears, phobias and related anxieties. In R. J. Morris & T. R. Kratochwill (Eds.), *The practice of child therapy* (4th ed., pp. 93–142). Mahwah, NJ: Erlbaum.

Muris, P., & Mayer, B. (2000). Early treatment of anxiety disorders in children. *Gedrag und Gezondheid: Tijdschrift voor Psychologie und Gezondheid, 28*, 235–242.

Olivares, J., Beidel, D. C., Albano, A. M., & Hidalgo, M. D. (2002). Results at long-term among three psychological treatments for adolescents with generalized social phobia: Statistical significance. *Psicologia Conductual, 10*, 147–164.

Ollendick, T. H., & King, N. J. (1998). Empirically supported treatments for children with phobic and anxious disorders: Current status. *Journal of Clinical Child Psychology, 27*, 156–167.

Rapee, R. M. (1998). *Overcoming shyness and social phobia: A step-by-step guide.* North Bergen, NJ: Book-mart Press.

Rapee, R. M. (2000). Group treatment of children with anxiety disorders: Outcome and predictors of treatment response. *Australian Journal of Psychology, 52*, 125–129.

Rapee, R. M., Abbott, M. J., & Lyneham, H. J. (2006). Bibliotherapy for children with anxiety disorders using written materials for parents: A randomized controlled trial. *Journal of Consulting and Clinical Psychology, 74*, 436–444.

Rapee, R. M., Cunningham, M. J., & Lyneham, H. J. (2005). *The Cool Teens CD-ROM.* Sydney: Macquarie University Anxiety Research Unit.

Rapee, R. M., Lyneham, H. J., Schniering, C. A., Wuthrich, V., Abbott, M. A., Hudson J. L., et al. (2006). *The Cool Kids Child and Adolescent Anxiety Program therapist manual (school version).* Sydney: Centre for Emotional Health, Macquarie University.

Rapee, R. M., Wignall, A., Hudson, J. L., & Schniering, C. A. (2000). *Treating anxious children and adolescents—An evidence-based approach.* Oakland, CA: New Harbinger.

Reynolds, C. R., & Richmond, B. O. (1985). *Revised Children's Manifest Anxiety Scale (RCMAS): Manual.* Los Angeles: Western Psychological Services.

Schniering, C. A., & Rapee, R. M. (2002). Development and validation of a measure of children's automatic thoughts: The Children's Automatic Thoughts Scale. *Behaviour Research and Therapy, 40*, 1091–1109.

Sheslow, D. V., Bondy, A. S., & Nelson, R. O. (1983). A comparison of graduated exposure, verbal coping skills and their combination in the treatment of children's fear of the dark. *Child and Family Behavior Therapy, 4*, 33–45.

Silverman, W. K., & Albano, A. M. (1996). *The Anxiety Disorders Interview Schedule for DSM-IV, child and parent versions.* San Antonio, TX: Psychological Corporation.

Spence, S. H. (1998). A measure of anxiety symptoms among children. *Behavior Research and Therapy, 36*, 545–566.

Spielberger, C. (1973). *Manual for the State–Trait Anxiety Inventory for Children.* Palo Alto, CA: Consulting Psychologists Press.

Stallard, P., Simpson, N., Anderson, S., Hibbert, S., & Osborn, C. (2007). The FRIENDS emotional health programme: Initial findings from a school-based project. *Child and Adolescent Mental Health, 12*, 32–37.

Turner, S. M., Beidel, D. C., Cooley, M. R., Woody, S. R., & Messer, S. C. (1994). A multicomponent behavioral treatment of social phobia: Social effectiveness therapy. *Behaviour Research and Therapy, 32,* 381–390.

Weisz, J. R., Hawley, A. J., & Doss, K. M. (2004). Empirically tested psychotherapies for youth internalizing and externalizing problems and disorders. *Child and Adolescent Psychiatric Clinics of North America, 13,* 729–815.

Wittchen, H. U., Stein, M. B., & Kessler, R. C. (1999). Social fears and social phobia in a community sample of adolescents and young adults: Prevalence, risk factors and comorbidity. *Psychological Medicine, 29,* 309–323.

PART IV

COGNITIVE-BEHAVIORAL INTERVENTIONS FOR DEPRESSION

CHAPTER 9

Cognitive-Behavioral Interventions for Depression in Children and Adolescents

Meta-Analysis, Promising Programs, and Implications for School Personnel

JOHN W. MAAG
SUSAN M. SWEARER
MICHAEL D. TOLAND

Depression is a mood (affective) disorder that affects approximately 2% of children and adolescents in the general population (Kashani et al., 1983; Kashani & Simonds, 1979). Once considered exclusively the domain of psychiatry, depressive disorders can and should be considered by school personnel in identification, assessment, and treatment (Reynolds & Stark, 1987). Students with emotional and behavioral disorders (EBD) and learning disabilities (LD) may be particularly at risk for developing depression. For example, Maag and Behrens (1989a) found that about 21% of these students experienced significant depressive symptomatology. However, an important distinction should be made between depressive symptomatology and the clinical disorder:

As a symptom, depression refers to sad affect and as such is a common experience of everyday life. As a syndrome or disorder, depression refers to a group of symptoms that go together. Sadness may be part of a larger set of problems that include the loss of interest in activities, feelings of worthlessness, sleep disturbances, changes in appetite and others. (Kazdin, 1990, p. 121)

These distinctions may explain part of the discrepancies and debate over the actual prevalence of depression among students with EBD and LD. For example, Maag and Reid (1994) found that 10% of students with LD experienced significant depressive symptomatology. However, only 2% of students with LD obtained Beck Depression Inventory scores that corresponded to levels of clinical depression (> 29). This prevalence estimate is the same as exists in the general population of youngsters. In their meta-analytic review, Maag and Reid (2006) concluded that although students with LD had statistically greater depressive symptomatology than their nondisabled peers, the magnitude was most likely not great enough to place them in the clinical range for a depressive disorder.

Regardless of the exact prevalence of depressive disorders among students with EBD and LD—which would prove difficult to accurately determine in the absence of using clinical interviews—the potential increased risk for students with EBD and LD to experience depression has direct implications for educators. First, school personnel should play an important role identifying (but not diagnosing) students who may be depressed. Youths spend more time in school than in most structured environments outside the home and have their most consistent and extensive contact with trained professionals in the school setting. Furthermore, students' behaviors, interpersonal relationships, and academic performance—all important indicators of mood and the ability to cope—are subject to ongoing scrutiny in the classroom. Accordingly, school personnel may be the first professionals to notice a burgeoning depressive disorder (Powers, 1979; Stark, 1990). Second, students with EBD and LD who are depressed may be best served with counseling as a related service (Maag & Katsiyannis, 1996; Yell, 1998). There are several school-based programs to treat depression in youths (e.g., Clarke, De-Bar, & Lewinsohn, 2003; Reynolds & Stark, 1987; Stark, Kendall, et al., 1996). Third, many of the intervention techniques used to treat depression, such as social skills training, self-management training, and various cognitive-behavioral approaches, have all been used by special educators to address a variety of problematic behaviors (Maag, 1993).

More than 15 years ago, Reynolds and Stark (1987) began describing school-based intervention strategies to treat depression in children and adolescents and pointed to implementation challenges. First, depression is a serious mental disorder that may have life-threatening consequences that must be addressed by well-trained personnel using evidence-based methods in a systematic manner. Second, clinically trained individuals, such as school psychologists, counselors, and social workers, should work collaboratively with teachers to provide consultation in the development and implementation of interventions. Third, prevention may be the best approach for treating depression in schools. However, preventive approaches would require that teachers receive training in cognitive and behavioral techniques used for treating depression—something that relatively few typically receive.

There are a variety of theories on depression including, but not limited to, behavioral, attachment, learned helplessness, self-control, biochemical, and cognitive ones. Theories form the basis for explaining the etiology and characteristics of depression, assessment and diagnostic approaches, and—most important—approaches to treating depression. These interventions range from those relying heavily on traditional psychodynamic theory to behavioral techniques (e.g., Anthony, 1970; Frame, Matson, Sonis, Fialkov, & Kazdin, 1982). However, it was Beck's (1976) cognitive theory that revolutionized the understanding of depressive disorders. According to Beck, depression results from the activation of three major cognitive patterns: (1) intepreting experiences in a negative way, (2) viewing oneself in a negative way, and (3) viewing the future in a negative way. Individuals with these cognitive patterns tend to experience depressed mood and paralysis of will, engage in avoidance tactics and suicidal ideation, and be prone to increased dependency.

Beck's cognitive therapy for depression (Beck, Rush, Shaw, & Emery, 1979) is perhaps the most widely used treatment approach—either as a main therapy or adjunctive therapy to pharmacological approaches (American Psychiatric Association, 2000; Reinemann & Swearer, 2005). Clients are taught to identify dysfunctional thoughts and maladaptive assumptions—either through recall or imagined situations—that may be contributing to feelings of depression. Several techniques, such as "reality checking" or "hypothesis testing," are then used to counteract the debilitating thought or dysfunctional assumption contributing to depression. After clients have identified the debilitating belief or thought and learned to distinguish it as a hypothesis rather than as a reality, they test it experimentally. For example, if a boy believes that everyone at school who smiles is teasing him, then he might be helped to devise a system for reading context and judging peers' facial expressions and body language so that he can determine objectively if the thoughts behind his problem are indeed accurate.

Virtually all effective cognitive therapies with youngsters include be-

havioral components (Braswell & Kendall, 1988). This approach en-
compasses techniques for promoting emotional and behavioral change
by teaching children to change thoughts and cognitive processing in an
overt, active, and problem-oriented way (Reinecke, Ryan, & DuBois,
1998). In a recent review of the literature, Maag and Swearer (2005) found
that the most common cognitive components of cognitive-behavioral interventions (CBIs) involved aspects of Beck's therapy for depression,
problem-solving training, and self-control training (e.g., self-monitoring,
self-evaluation, self-reinforcement). The behavioral techniques most commonly used included activity scheduling, reinforcement, modeling, rehearsal, and role playing. Behavioral components are often a necessary
prerequisite for cognitive techniques to be effective (Kaslow & Rehm,
1991; Maag & Forness, 1991; Stark, Swearer, Kurowski, Sommer, &
Bowen, 1996). This temporal sequence helps youngsters elevate their
mood before they can engage in, and benefit from, cognitive restructuring.

CBIs have been considered to offer the greatest nonpharmaceutical
promise for treating childhood and adolescent depression (Clarizio,
1985). Results of recent research point to the combination of medication
(i.e., fluoxetine) and cognitive-behavioral therapy as the "gold standard" for treating adolescent depression (Treatment for Adolescents
with Depression Study [TADS] Team, 2004).

Reviews of CBIs to treat childhood and adolescent depression began
appearing in the literature around a decade ago (Marcotte, 1997) and
have continued into the present (Maag & Swearer, 2005; Weisz, McCarty,
& Valeri, 2006). Seven of the reviews were narrative (Curry, 2001; Finn,
2000; Harrington, Whittaker, & Shoebridge, 1998; Maag & Swearer,
2005; Marcotte, 1997; Sherrill & Kovacs, 2002; Southam-Gerow, Henin,
Chu, Marrs, & Kendall, 1997), whereas two were meta-analytic (Lewinsohn & Clarke, 1999; Reinecke et al., 1998). The number of studies reviewed ranged from 6 (Reinecke et al., 1998) to 22 (Maag & Swearer,
2005). There were differences in the variables coded for the meta-analytic
studies, making it difficult to draw unequivocal conclusions. Although
there was overlap in the studies and variables addressed in each review,
no comprehensive review exists that has examined the extant literature
over a full range of variables using meta-analytic methodology.

The purpose of this chapter is threefold. First, a meta-analysis of all
published studies in refereed journals is presented. This restriction was
imposed to eliminate doctoral dissertations and data appearing in book
chapters that may not have been subjected to the rigor of blind peer review in order to determine whether CBI was statistically significant for
ameliorating depression in children and adolescents. Second, the most
promising CBI programs for treating childhood and adolescent depres-

sion are described. Third, implications for school personnel using CBIs are discussed within a collaborative framework involving school psychologists, counselors, and special educators.

Meta-Analytic Review of CBI Studies

Quantitative research syntheses offer a means of providing a more generalized picture about the efficacy of CBIs for depressed youngsters than that obtained from a traditional narrative review of the literature. Meta-analysis is the main quantitative method, and its procedures have been well described previously. It is considered an accepted means for statistically summarizing a body of research (e.g., Glass, McGaw, & Smith, 1981; Rosenberg, Adams, & Gurevitch, 2000; Rosenthal, 1984; Wolf, 1986).

Meta-analytic reviews of CBIs for depression began appearing in the late 1990s. It has been difficult to draw definitive conclusions because of the irregularity of variables coded in these reviews. For example, Lewinsohn and Clarke (1999) coded the general treatment approach (e.g., cognitive, behavioral, family, affective education and management) but not the specific CBI components such as problem-solving training, self-instruction training, or self-control training. Reinecke et al. (1998) coded together both general (i.e., CBI) and specific (e.g., problem-solving training, relaxation training) treatment variables but did not isolate those that were most effective. Neither review coded whether treatment followed a manual or specific protocol. CBIs have also been used in a preventive framework. Two recent meta-analytic reviews exist on the efficacy of CBIs to prevent childhood and adolescent depression (Horowitz & Garber, 2006).

The most recent meta-analysis was conducted by Weisz et al. (2006). It is the most comprehensive meta-analysis because it includes data-based book chapters and doctoral dissertations in additional to journal articles. The primary treatment approach in the studies was CBI, although other treatments analyzed included social skills training, behavior therapy, and a variety of family therapy approaches. The authors obtained an overall effect size (*ES*) of 0.34, which was of much lower magnitude than the average *ES* of 0.99 obtained in other reviews. One of the reasons for the modest *ES* may be that the study included dissertations and book chapters, which have not gone through the rigors of anonymous peer review. The purpose of the present meta-analysis was to update findings from previous studies of this nature and determine whether the average *ES* of 0.99 was accurate or more of an anomaly based on studies obtained only from peer-reviewed journals and the accompanying file-drawer problem.

Method

Meta-analysis can employ different methods and degrees of complexity (Hedges & Olkin, 1985). Meta-analyses range from simple reporting of *ES* to sophisticated approaches such as fixed effects models or random effects models that consider the statistical contribution of moderator variables (e.g., gender, ethnicity, study quality). This approach is used when multiple variables are being assessed over a large number of studies. Regardless of the approach, several elements need to be addressed when conducting any type of meta-analysis (Cooper & Hedges, 1994; Kavale, 1984).

Problem Formulation

In order to achieve a broad scope, the problem should be formulated using comprehensive questions. For the present analysis, the question of interest was the following: Are children and adolescents more likely to experience quantifiably lower levels of depression after receiving CBI than their counterparts receiving a different treatment, placebo, or no treatment?

Sample

Meta-analysis should be representative and inclusive. To this end, articles for analysis were obtained using the following parameters: (1) published in peer-reviewed journals, (2) used standardized depression measures or clinical interviews, (3) reported disaggregated data (i.e., children and adolescents were not combined with adults), (4) included at least one cognitive and behavioral technique described in the extant literature, (5) used random assignment to designate participants to a control/wait-list condition, placebo group, or active cognitive-behavioral treatment condition, and (6) used children of high school age or younger. It is important to note that by our choosing to use only published peer-reviewed journals for our meta-analysis, there is the possibility of a file-drawer problem (Rosenthal, 1979) or what may be known as *source bias* (i.e., findings differing between published and unpublished papers). However, we chose to use only peer-reviewed papers because of the work presented by Glass et al. (1981) and Rosenthal (1984), which found that there was virtually no difference on the average or median *ES* between published and unpublished papers. Furthermore, Hunter and Schmidt (1990) discussed how meta-analytic research in their field of employment testing has supported the conclusions by Glass et al. and Rosenthal (1984).

Studies were located using three procedures. First, searches of the PsychLit and Education Resources Information Center First Search databases were conducted using the descriptors *cognitive behavioral interventions, depression,* and *children/adolescents.* These databases searched articles beginning in 1970 and continuing to February 2007. The year 1970 was selected because it was the oldest year used in previous reviews (Reinecke et al., 1998) and was the first year that controlled research on CBIs with youngsters began to appear. Results of this search were then examined for studies that met the inclusion criteria. Second, an ancestor search was conducted of all articles that met inclusion criteria. Third, references were examined from the 10 extant review articles on CBIs to treat depression in children and adolescents (Curry, 2001; Finn, 2000; Haby, Tonge, Littlefield, Carter, & Vos, 2004; Harrington, Whittaker, & Shoebridge, 1998; Lewinsohn & Clarke, 1999; Maag & Swearer, 2005; Marcotte, 1997; Reinecke et al., 1998; Sherrill & Kovacs, 2002; Southam-Gerow et al., 1997). A total of 20 studies appearing in Table 9.1 were used in the meta-analysis.

Classification

A coding form was developed that included basic participant and demographic data (e.g., gender, average age, IQ, sample size), mean performance of treated and untreated participants, standard deviation of control/wait-list participants, and study variables (e.g., internal validity, duration of training, hours of training per week, respondents assessing outcomes, types of outcomes measured). Content validity of the coding form was assessed by two researchers with expertise in CBIs for depression who judged the appropriateness of the form. The 20 studies were then coded by a graduate assistant and the two primary authors to judge coding accuracy. When discrepancies were identified in coding, the graduate student and two primary authors reviewed and discussed the results until all three reached consensus.

Data Analysis

The primary statistic in meta-analysis is the *ES.* It permits quantification and standardization of individual study findings (Kavale, 1984). One *ES* value was computed per study for postintervention. The following standardized *ES* statistic was used in this analysis to examine the impact of CBI on measures of depression:

$$ES = (\overline{X}_{\text{treatment}} - \overline{X}_{\text{control}}) / SD_{\text{pooled}}$$

where

$$SD_{\text{pooled}} =$$

$$\sqrt{([n_{\text{treatment}} - 1]SD^2_{\text{treatment}} + [n_{\text{control}} - 1]SD^2_{\text{control}})/(n_{\text{treatment}} + n_{\text{control}} - 2)}$$

Hedges and Olkin's (1985) correction formula was used to adjust all *ES* values for any bias created by small sample sizes:

$$ES_{\text{adjusted}} = ES(1-3)/[4(n_{\text{treatment}} + n_{\text{control}}) - 9])$$

ES values were calculated so that negative scores indicated that the treatment group improved more than the control group. *ES* values can be interpreted as the degree, in standard deviation units, that the average study participant receiving CBIs was different from the average control/wait-list or placebo group participant.

When computing *ES* one study did not include the necessary information about the standard deviations for either the control or treatment groups (Butler, Miezitis, Friedman, & Cole, 1980). To compute the *ES* for this study we found another study, consisting of normative data for the same depression measure and comparable sample characteristics, and used the standard deviation reported in the normative study as the standard deviations for both groups in the study not reporting standard deviations.

To maintain independence of *ES* values we computed only one *ES* value per study. Six studies included two or more CBI conditions in their comparisons (Clarke, Rohde, Lewinsohn, Hops, & Seeley, 1999; Lewinsohn, Clarke, Hops, & Andrews, 1990; Rohde, Lewinsohn, & Seeley, 1994; Rohde, Clarke, Lewinsohn, Seeley, & Kaufman, 2001; Sheffield et al., 2006; Hains, 1992). In these cases, study information was pooled/collapsed to represent one CBI treatment condition for each study. For example, information was combined by using the weighted mean, pooled standard deviation, and summed sample size for studies containing two CBI treatment groups. In addition, one study had two independent samples: The second sample showed the replicability of the first sample (Rohde et al., 1994). In this case, the two groups were pooled together to represent one study in the meta-analysis. Another study did not report unadjusted means (Rohde et al., 2001). Consequently, the adjusted means reported from an analysis of covariance were used for computing the *ES* value. Finally, one study did not report the sample size per group

(Asarnow, Scott, & Mintz, 2002); we assumed the sample size was the same for both control and CBI conditions to compute the *ES* value.

All analyses were conducting using the weighted least squares approach so that each *ES* was weighted by its inverse variance component (Hedges & Olkin, 1985). Each *ES* value was adjusted for heterogeneity of variance. In addition, a homogeneity analysis was conducted to test whether all *ES* values could be treated as an estimate of the same population mean, and to justify the use of a random effects analysis appearing subsequently. All analyses were conducted using Wilson's (2005) SPSS for Windows Meta-Analysis Macros. Maximum likelihood (ML) estimation was used with the random effects models weighted by the inverse of the variance estimate.

Results

A summary of all *ES* values is presented in Table 9.1, with negative *ES* values indicating lower depression levels for the treatment group relative to the control/wait-list group. A homogeneity analysis was conducted to test whether it was reasonable to assume that all the *ES* values were estimating the same population mean (Hedges & Olkin, 1985). Results from this analysis were significant, $Q(19) = 67.12$, $p < .001$, indicating that the variability across *ES* values exceeded what would be expected based on sampling error. A random effects model was used because homogeneity was not supported. The random effects weighted mean *ES* value for depression measures at postintervention was $-.50$ (REVC [random effects variance component] $= .09$), which was significantly different from zero ($z = -5.37$, $p < .01$).

Four possible variables were considered to help explain the heterogeneity in *ES* values: (1) percent female, (2) average age, (3) site of intervention, and (4) length of intervention in weeks. Weighted regression analyses with random effects were performed to test these quantitatively important sources of variability. Separate models were conducted for the variables percent female (pfemale; $n = 19$), average age (avgage; $n = 20$), site of intervention (site; $n = 20$), and length of intervention (lngthint; $n = 16$). For the first three models results indicated insignificant effects: $Q_{\text{pfemale}}(1) = 0.04$, $p = .85$, $R^2 = .00$, $b = .00$, $SE = .01$, $B = .04$, $\text{REVC}_{\text{ML}} = .15$; $Q_{\text{avgage}}(1) = 3.46$, $p = .88$, $R^2 = .14$, $b = -.08$, $SE = .04$, $B = -.37$, $\text{REVC}_{\text{ML}} = .10$; $Q_{\text{site}}(1) = .17$, $p = .68$, $R^2 = .01$, $b = -.09$, $SE = .21$, $B = -.09$, $\text{REVC}_{\text{ML}} = .13$. However, a significant effect was found for the variable length of intervention in weeks, $Q_{\text{lngthint}}(1) = 7.58$, $p = .006$, $R^2 = .28$, $b = .07$, $SE = .03$, $B = .53$, $\text{REVC}_{\text{ML}} = .03$. It is important to note that the random effect weighted regression model for length of intervention in weeks had

TABLE 9.1. Cognitive-Behavioral Interventions for Depressive Disorders in Children and Adolescents

Study	CBI components	N	Length of intervention (weeks)	% female	Age	Setting	Dependent measures	ES	Results
Asarnow et al. (2002)	Problem solving, taking emotional temperature, setting personal goals, relaxation, stopping negative thoughts, saying positive things, planning fun activities	23[i]	5	65.22	$M = 10^a$; grades 4–6	Clinic	CDI	−0.30	Intervention group showed improvements in depressive symptoms, reductions in negative automatic thoughts, and less internalizing coping.
Butler et al. (1980)[b]	Recognize irrational automatic thoughts, adopt logical thinking, enhance listening skills, recognize relation between thoughts and feelings	27	10	42.86	$M = 11.5$; grades 5–6	Public school	SES, CDI, MMSAQ, NSLCSC	−0.09	Statistically significant improvement in CDI and NSLCSC, but role-play condition was more effective; no follow-up.
Clarke et al. (1995)	Identify and challenge irrational beliefs, role playing, group discussions	120	5	70	$M = 15.3$	High school	CES-D, HDRS, GAF	−0.34	Significantly fewer cases of depression; results maintained at 12-month follow-up.
Clarke et al. (1999)[c]	Mood monitoring, improving social skills, activity scheduling, communication training, conflict resolution training	96	8	70.8	$M = 16.2$	Outpatient clinic	BDI, HDRS, K-SADS-E, GAF, CBCL	−0.53	Positive results on all measures; 100% recovery at 12 months, 35.7% recovery at 24 months.

244

Study	Intervention	N	Sessions	%	Age	Setting	Measures	ES	Outcome
Clarke et al. (2002)	Relaxation skills training, cognitive restructuring, pleasant activities, communication and conflict reduction	88	8	68.91[d]	$M = 15.25$[l]	Clinic	CES-D, CBCL-D, K-SADS, HAM-D	-0.20	No significant advantage of cognitive-behavioral program over usual care, either for depression diagnoses, continuous depression measures, nonaffective measures, or functioning outcomes.
Hains (1992)[c]	Self-monitoring, identify and monitor self-defeating thoughts	25		0	$M = 15.5$[j]	Parochial high school	CSE, RADS, STAXI, STAI, ASSQ	-1.21	Treatment groups showed significant reductions in levels of state and trait anxiety, state anger, anger expression, and depression.
Jaycox et al. (1994)	Social problem solving, coping strategies	121	12[k]	48.25	$M = 11.4$	Outpatient clinic	CP-CN, CN, CP	-0.27	Depressive symptoms were significantly reduced and classroom behavior was significantly improved in the treatment group.
Kahn et al. (1990)	Constructive thinking, self-monitoring, self-reinforcement, pleasant events scheduling, role playing, problem solving, social skills training	34	7	52.94	$M = 13.0$[a]	Middle school	RADS, BID, CDI	-1.64	Positive changes in all dependent measures; improvements maintained at 1- and 6-month follow-up.

(continued)

TABLE 9.1. (*continued*)

Study	CBI components	N	Length of intervention (weeks)	% female	Age	Setting	Dependent measures	ES	Results
Kerfoot et al. (2004)	Assessment and goal setting, emotional recognition, self-monitoring, activity scheduling	46		46.33	M = 13.88	Clinic	K-SADS	0.06	No significant difference between the groups on post outcomes or at follow-up.
Lewinsohn et al. (1990)[c]	Increasing pleasant activities, relaxation, controlling depressive thoughts, improving social interaction, conflict resolution	59	7	61.00	M = 16.23	Outpatient clinic	K-SADS-E, BDI, CES-D	−1.29	Improvements in all measures; gains maintained at 2-year follow-up
Liddle & Spence (1990)	Problem solving, Beck's (1976) cognitive therapy, instructions, discussion, modeling, role playing, feedback, reinforcement	21	8	47.62[f]	M = 9.2[e]	Catholic primary schools	CDI, CDRS, MESSY, LSSP	−0.35	Decline in depression scores; decreases maintained at 2-month follow-up.
Reynolds & Coats (1986)	Emphasized training of self-control skills including self-monitoring, self-evaluation, self-reinforcement	16	5	63.33[f]	M = 15.65[e]	High school	RADS, BDI, BID, RSES, ASCS-HS, STAI	−1.40	Improvements on all measures; gains maintained at 5-week follow-up

Study	Intervention	N		%	Age	Setting	Measures	ES	Results
Roberts et al. (2003)	Social skills, less internalizing and externalizing problems	179	12[m]	49.74	M = 11.89	Middle school	CDI, RCMAS, CASQ, CBCL	0.05	Intervention group children reported less anxiety than the control group after the program and at 6-month follow-up.
Rohde et al. (1994)[g]	Increasing pleasant activities, relaxation, controlling depressive thoughts, improving social interaction, conflict resolution training	58		71.29	M = 16.3	Outpatient clinic	K-SADS-E, BDI, HDRS, GAF	-1.12	Improvements on all measures; no follow-up.
Rohde et al. (2001)[b]	Mood-monitoring, social skills, pleasant activities, anxiety, depressogenic cognitions, improving communication, conflict resolution, relapse prevention plan	151	NA	67.5	M = 16.2	Clinic	BDI, GAF	-1.04	Comorbid anxiety disorders were associated with higher depression measure scores at intake and greater decrease in depression scores by posttreatment.
Rossello & Bernal (1999)	Identify how thoughts, daily activities, and interactions with others influence mood	39	12		M = 14.7	Outpatient clinic	CDI, PHCSCS, SASCA, FEICS, CBCL	-0.34	Significant reduction in CDI scores; gains maintained at 3-month follow-up.

(continued)

247

TABLE 9.1. (*continued*)

Study	CBI components	N	Length of intervention (weeks)	% female	Age	Setting	Dependent measures	ES	Results
Sheffield et al. (2006)	Evaluate impact of universal, indicated, and combined universal plus indicated cognitive-behavioral approaches to prevention of depression	468	13.33	69.0	$M = 14.34$	School	CDI, CES-D, BHS, CATS, NPS, SCAS, YSR-Ext	−0.12	Significant decline in depressive symptoms and improvement in emotional well-being in high-symptom students.
Spence et al. (2005)	Life problem-solving skills, positive problem-solving orientation, and optimistic thinking styles	1,266	8	51.57[d]	$M = 12.9$	Middle school	BDI, CASQ-R, CASAFS	−0.27	Adolescents who completed the teacher-administered cognitive-behavioral intervention did not differ significantly from adolescents in the monitoring control condition.
Stark et al. (1987)	Self-monitoring, self-evaluation, attributing cause of good and bad outcomes, self-consequating	18	5	44.44	$M = 11.26$	Elementary school	CDI, CDS, CDRS-R, CBCL, CSEI, RCMAS	−1.01	Significant improvements on all measures; results maintained at 8-week follow-up.

| Weisz et al. (1997) | Skill building, identify depressogenic thoughts | 48 | 8 | 45.83 | $M = 9.6$ | Elementary school | CDI, CDRS-R | -0.52 | The treatment group showed greater reductions than the control group in depressive symptomatology on the CDI and the CDRS-R. |

[a]Average was taken as average age for grade levels.

[b]SD for treatment and control from normative data presented in Kovacs (1992).

[c]Two cognitive-behavioral treatment groups.

[d]Used weighted average for percent female.

[e]Assumed mean age taken from total study.

[f]Percent female taken from total study.

[g]Average of Sample 1 and Sample 2 data.

[h]Used adjusted means from analysis of covariance.

[i]Sample size per group not given; assumed 12 for control and 11 for treatment based on $N = 23$.

[j]Age is average of age range.

[k]Length of intervention was estimated as time elapsing since preassessment.

[l]Used weighted average for average age.

[m]Estimated length of intervention from Jaycox et al. (1994).

$Q_{residual}(14) = 19.67$, $p = 0.14$, whereas the fixed effects model for this same variable had $Q_{residual}(14) = 29.87$, $p = .01$, and $Q_{total}(15) = 39.37$, $p < .001$. This value indicates that studies including lengthier treatment interventions had smaller ES values closer to zero, whereas those with shorter treatment interventions had larger, negative ES values.

We split the data into two groups in order to explore the diminishing returns that lengthier treatment interventions had on post treatment depression scores: (1) CBI studies conducted for 10 or more weeks ($n = 5$) and (2) CBI studies conducted for 8 or fewer weeks. The groups were based on a natural gap in the length of intervention between 8 and 10 weeks. Results from the random effects analysis of variance showed a significant effect for the grouping variable, $Q_{group}(1) = 6.43$, $p = .01$, $REVC_{ML} = 0.04$. Specifically, those CBI studies involving 10 or more weeks of intervention had weaker effects (mean $ES = -0.13$, $SE = 0.13$) than those studies involving 8 or fewer weeks of intervention (mean $ES = -0.54$, $SE = 0.10$).

Descriptive statistics were computed for the two CBI groups formed: 10 or more weeks ($n = 5$) and 8 or fewer weeks ($n = 11$). Both groups had similar demographics in terms of mean age ($M = 12.8$ and $M = 13.1$) and mean percent female (52.5% and 58.3%), respectively. Both groups also had similar types of samples—only one study in the 10 or more weeks group consisted of adolescents with major depressive disorder, whereas three studies in the 8 or fewer weeks group consisted of adolescents with major depressive disorder. Both groups consisted of roughly the same number of studies conducted in schools or in clinical settings (see Table 9.1). The general treatment design for studies in either group was a treatment versus wait-list control group. Moreover, two studies in the 10 or more weeks group and four studies in the 8 or fewer weeks group were treatment versus no-treatment control. All studies consisted of random assignment. Also, all five studies in the 10 or more weeks group had one treatment per week, whereas three studies in the 8 or fewer weeks group had one treatment per week and eight studies had two or more treatments per week. In general, studies with fewer treatment weeks tended to give two or more treatments per week, whereas most studies lasting more than 8 weeks tended to have only one treatment per week.

Implications

A significant source of heterogeneity in the meta analysis was due to length of CBIs: Larger effects were found for shorter term interventions than longer term interventions. Consequently, future research should focus on determining the point in time at which the effects of CBIs diminish. The meta-analytic results indicated that the diminishing point was approximately 8 weeks. However, this extrapolation should be considered tentative, because this analysis was post hoc in nature rather than driven by theory. It is possible that the current results may be an artifact of the study lengths examined. It is also important to point out that results may have favored shorter treatment programs because they tended to have two or more treatment sessions per week, whereas longer treatment programs (i.e., 10 or more weeks) only had treatment sessions once per week. So, this may mean that having more frequent treatment sessions per week for a shorter period of time is more beneficial than only one treatment session per week for a longer period of time. However, it is unclear from this meta-analysis if treatment program duration and frequency of treatment sessions work in tandem, because there is not a sufficient amount of information available from the studies examined (i.e., no studies more than 10 weeks long had more than one session per week). Future studies would be advised to examine whether there is a treatment duration by frequency interaction.

Another area for future research would involve examining the effects of a specific CBI technique (e.g., self-instruction training, problem-solving training) on a particular measure of depression under various conditions (e.g., schools, outpatient clinics, hospitals) using more ethnically diverse samples. The important point is that CBIs for children and adolescents who are depressed are often effective—especially under shorter intervention periods.

The ES value obtained here was larger than that found in Weisz et al. (2006). However, this discrepancy may be due to the method of computation. If the current ES value had been computed using the SD of the mean instead of the pooled SD, values of –0.41 or |0.41| would have been obtained that would have been similar to the ES reported by Weisz et al. (ES = 0.34 or |0.34|). In addition, the current ES may differ from Weisz et al. because only studies obtained from peer-reviewed journals were examined here. Weisz et al. analyzed data from book chapters and dissertations. In addition, the studies Weisz et al. obtained from journals differed slightly from the ones analyzed here.

The current meta-analysis provides some important directions for future research on depression among school-age youth. It is clear that researchers need to report more detailed methodology such as length of intervention in weeks, number of therapy sessions, length of each session, treatment provider information, demographic variable means, SDs, ranges, and frequencies.

Overview of Promising CBI Programs

CBIs underscore the complex relations among cognitive factors (cognitive content, products, structures), affect, overt behaviors, and the environment in contributing to various mental illnesses (Braswell & Kendall, 1988; Kendall, 2000). Although many studies have used CBIs to treat childhood and adolescent depression, few comprehensive, manual-driven CBI programs exist. The three notable exceptions are Mufson's Interpersonal Psychotherapy for Depressed Adolescents (IPT-A) treatment (Mufson, Moreau, Weissman, & Klerman, 1993), Lewinsohn and Clarke's Adolescents Coping with Depression (CWD-A) course (Lewinsohn, Clarke, Rohde, Hops, & Seeley, 1996), and Stark's ACTION program (Stark, Boswell, et al., 2006).

In this section the IPT-A and CWD-A programs are briefly described. A more detailed description of the ACTION program is warranted because of its potential impact for treating depression in school settings. It is designed for girls between the ages of 9 and 13 years who are depressed. One of the reasons for focusing on girls is because, following puberty, they are twice as likely to experience depression as boys (e.g., Birmaher et al., 1996; Rushton, Forcier, & Schectman, 2002). Furthermore, women who became depressed during adolescence are more at risk for being hospitalized, abusing tranquilizers, dropping out of school, and experiencing marital discord (Kandel & Davies, 1986).

IPT-A and CWD-A Programs

The IPT-A treatment has three phases, consisting of four sessions each, to help adolescents decrease symptoms of depression and increase their interpersonal functioning (Mufson et al., 1993). During Phase I one or two problem areas (e.g., grief, interpersonal deficits are identified by the adolescent and therapist), a rationale for treatment is provided, a therapeutic contract is developed and signed, and the adolescent's role in therapy is defined. In Phase II, the identified problems are clarified, specific intervention strategies are selected, and a treatment plan is developed and implemented. During both phases, the therapist and adolescent work as a team. The primary purpose of Phase II is to prepare the adolescent for termination and establish a sense of empowerment for dealing with future problems.

The CWD-A course includes eight components that are delivered over sixteen 2-hour sessions during an 8-week period for up to 10 adolescents (Lewinsohn et al., 1996). Adolescents receive a workbook of short readings, take quizzes, carry out structured learning tasks, and perform homework assignments for each session. At the outset, adolescents are taught to monitor their moods. The remaining sessions focus on teaching assorted skills such as social skills, increasing pleasant activities, decreasing anxiety and depression related cognitions, resolving conflicts, and engaging in maintenance activities. Participants' parents are involved in a similar course designed to help them accelerate the learning of the adolescents' new skills and reinforce their occurrence. Booster sessions are provided after the course ends at 4-month intervals over 2 years.

Aspects of the ACTION Treatment

The ACTION treatment is a group program that is developmentally sensitive and follows a structured therapist's manual and workbook for both the girls and their parents (Stark, Simpson, et al., 2004; Stark, Simpson, Yancy, & Molnar, in press; Stark, Schnoebelen, et al., 2004). A unique aspect of this program is that it is conducted in the schools in groups of two to five girls. There are several reasons for this approach. First, children spend more time in school than any environment outside the home, and in schools their behavior, interpersonal relationships, and mood can be observed on an continuing basis. Second, Maag and Swearer (2005) found that most recent CBI studies have been conducted in psychiatric hospitals or mental health clinics on an outpatient basis. Third, they also found the most recent school-based CBI study was conducted in 1995—more than a decade ago. Consequently, the ACTION program represents a recent emerging evidence-based and comprehensive program for school-based delivery.

Stark, Boswell, et al. (2006) described the ACTION treatment being based on a self-control model in which the girls are taught coping skills using a variety of CBI techniques during 20 meetings plus two individual meetings over 11 weeks. A consistent sequence is followed to provide the girls with a sense of security and knowledge of how each session is structured. Specifically, each meeting begins with a rapport-building activity, then the therapist asks the girls whether they had made progress toward their goals, the effectiveness of using coping skills is demonstrated, and praise is delivered. In addition to the routine areas covered during the meetings, the ACTION treatment also includes seven specific key aspects that are described shortly. ACTION kits and homework are used to help the girls remember central therapeutic concepts and apply newly acquired skills.

Parent training is designed to teach parents how to support their child's efforts to learn coping skills, indirectly teach parents the same skills as the girls, teach parents behavior management and communication skills, and help them reduce conflict and assist the girls to identify and change their negative thoughts (Stark, Boswell, et al., 2006). In addition to parent training, the girls' teachers receive consultation with the therapist to collaboratively develop plans to help the girls apply learned skills to the classroom. Teachers are taught to use a variety of student-specific interventions including, but not limited to, self-monitoring positive peer interactions, negative predictions, successful experiences, coping skills, and problem solving. These and other techniques are used to help teachers facilitate girls' using skills acquired in the seven specific key aspects of the ACTION treatment: (1) affective education, (2) goal setting, (3) recognizing progress toward goals, (4) coping skills training, (5) problem-solving training, (6) cognitive restructuring, (7) building a positive sense of self.

Stark and his colleagues are currently in the fourth year of a 5 year investigation funded by the National Institute of Mental Health. Preliminary results of this investigation indicated that 70% of participating girls no longer experience any depressive symptoms due to their participation in the ACTION treatment (Stark, Boswell, et al., 2006).

Implications for School Personnel

There is enough definitive research to demonstrate that CBIs are an evidence-based approach for treating depressive disorders in children and adolescents—at least in clinical settings. The question remains as to whether CBIs are a viable approach for school personnel. Preliminary results from the ACTION treatment are encouraging. Furthermore, in the majority of CBI studies conducted in school settings, school psychologists and counselors have been shown to be effective treatment providers, with special educators serving as ancillary agents (e.g., Clarke et al., 1995; Kahn, Kehle, Jenson, & Clarke, 1990; Reynolds & Coats, 1986). Therefore, CBIs appear to have the potential for school personnel to use for treating depressive symptomatology in students with EBD and LD as well as those who are at risk.

Primary Role of School Psychologists and Counselors

School psychological and counseling services have evolved to the point of considerable compatibility (Murphy, DeEsch, & Strein, 1998). Training accreditation standards for both professions include skill development in the areas of assessment, consultation, and counseling and in facilitating the delivery of comprehensive services within a multidisciplinary team concept (Council for Accreditation of Counseling and Related Educational Programs, 1994; National Association of School Psychologists,

1994). In addition, both school psychologists and counselors obtain licenses in their respective areas that permit them to conduct psychotherapy and receive third-party reimbursement. They also have unique training and expertise that complement each other—especially when it comes to addressing the needs of students who display depressive symptomatology. Specifically, school counselors have skills in small-group counseling, large-group developmental interventions, and vocational and career development. School psychologists possess expertise in applied behavior analysis, cognitive and personality assessment, individual therapy, and organizational consultation. Although there are some administrative, professional, and personal barriers, the partnership between both professionals can greatly enhance outcomes for students with depression.

The ensuing discussion of the roles of school psychologists and counselors is couched within the clinically accepted framework of prevention, treatment, and maintenance (Institute of Medicine [IOM], 1994). The traditional classification system of primary, secondary, and tertiary prevention was based on the implied link between the cause and occurrence of a disease. It tended to be linear and case based and had considerable overlap between prevention and intervention phases. Conversely, the IOM framework is more risk/population based, makes specific distinctions between prevention and treatment, and pays attention to multiple layers of risk and protective factors and their mutual effects.

Roles for School Psychologists

Although many school psychologists serve primarily as assessment specialists, many schools and school districts utilize their expertise in counseling and consultation. The school psychologist can play a vital role assessing students who may experience a depressive disorder and working with these youngsters and their families to obtain appropriate services. These services may be delivered or supervised by the school psychologist, or the school psychologist may refer the youngster and his or her family for professional care in the community.

Nastasi, Varjas, Bernstein, and Pluymert (1997) described four levels of services across which school psychologists can be involved either directly or indirectly in developing mental health programs in schools:

1. *Prevention:* helping a school choose a program for students to manage their feelings.
2. *Risk reduction:* helping counselors target students whose parents suffer from depressive disorders and work with these students in a support group.

3. *Early intervention:* helping preschool and elementary teachers recognize the signs and symptoms of depressive disorders.
4. *Treatment:* delivering direct treatment to students experiencing a depressive disorder.

Universal preventive measures may consist of the school psychologist implementing Reynold's (1986) three-stage screening to identify youngsters who are at risk for experiencing depression in school settings: (1) conducting large-group screening with self-report depression measures; (2) retesting students 3 to 6 weeks later who, on the basis of the large-group screening in Stage 1, meet cutoff score criteria for depression; and (3) conducting individual clinical interviews with students who manifest clinical levels of depression at both Stage 1 and Stage 2 evaluations. A selective preventive measure might include the school psychologist identifying students whose parents have a depressive disorder and then working with those students to educate them about the nature of depression and ways to cope with depressed mood. The third and fourth steps of early intervention and treatment includes case identification and standard treatment for known disorders. Educating teachers and school personnel in the identification of depressive symptomatology would be a vital component for referral. School psychologists can provide inservice training for teachers regarding the signs and symptoms of depression.

Nastasi and colleagues' (1997) delineation of the school psychologist's role in effective mental health services in the schools did not include the IOM (1994) maintenance component. However, school psychologists are well equipped to aid in treatment maintenance by developing follow-up plans with depressed youth and their parents. Additionally, school psychologists can help coordinate after-care plans with community providers. School psychologists are often the link to community mental health agencies and can help facilitate home–school–community communication (Cowan & Swearer, 2004).

Roles for School Counselors

One of the roles of school counselors for the past 20 years—at least at the elementary level—has been to conduct individual and group counseling (Hargens & Gysbers, 1984). More recently, they have been assuming an increased role as mental health counselors (Lockhart & Keys, 1998). Nowhere is this role as important as it is in providing services for students who are depressed or experiencing depressive symptomatology. J. R. Evans, Van Velsor, and Schumacher (2002) described the role of school counselors using CBIs as that of active collaboration with the student. They ask questions, summarize, get feedback, and promote alternative responses. This active approach fits well into the culture of schools and helps avoid awkward silences that make many students ill at ease (M. Evans & Murphy, 1997; Platts & Williamson, 2000). J. R. Evans et al. also described three classic levels of prevention using CBIs that school counselors can undertake: primary, secondary, and tertiary.

Applying the IOM (1994) model, the recommendations of J. R. Evans et al. (2002) may be modified and elaborated on in the following ways. Primary prevention would be the responsibility of the school psychologist implementing Reynold's (1986) three-stage screening program described previously. J. R. Evans et al. also recommend the use of problem-solving and social skills training during this phase because the goal of these approaches is enhancing coping mechanisms and interpersonal abilities of students at risk for developing depression. Problem-solving techniques can help students confront issues they face in normal growth and development. Social skills training can promote positive socialization, thereby giving students greater access to reinforcement, which is important to prevent depression. However, these two techniques more typically have been associated with the IOM treatment phase. Problem-solving training and social skills training have been used individually to treat depression and also have been incorporated into some CBI approaches (Maag & Forness, 1991; Stark, Swearer, et al., 1996). J. R. Evans et al. recommended school counselors' role in maintenance be to maintain open communication with community mental health care providers in order to monitor compliance with long-term goals and reduce the risk of relapse when after-care services are provided.

Ancillary Role of Special Educators

Special educators are not trained, nor do they hold licenses, to provide counseling services to students with disabilities. That is not to say, however, that they cannot play an important ancillary role. There is some evidence to suggest that students with EBD, LD, and mental retardation experience depressive symptomatology at higher levels than their nondisabled peers (e.g., Maag & Behrens, 1989b; Reynolds & Miller, 1985). In addition, special educators have received training in some of the techniques typically incorporated into CBIs.

Self-monitoring has been used to improve students' academic achievement and decrease inappropriate social behaviors such as aggression and noncompliance (Reid, 1996; Webber, Scheuermann, McCall, & Coleman, 1993). In a review of research on self-monitoring, Reid concluded that it is an intervention repeatedly proved to be effective by any objective standard and easily incorporated into existing classroom structures and activities. It has been successfully used by special educators to increase appropriate verbalizations and decrease inappropriate verbalizations in students with EBD (DiGangi & Maag, 1992). It would be a simple matter to design self-monitoring sheets for students who are depressed to record the number and type of positive interactions they have with others and daily accomplishments.

Special education teachers have also successfully used a variety of CBI strategies for improving students' decoding and reading comprehension, vocabulary, spelling, writing, and mathematics skills (e.g., Pressley et al., 1990). However, there is an important distinction between CBI strategies used to teach academics and those used to treat depression. Specifically, cognitive strategies for remediating academics assume the problem is a cognitive deficit; that is to say, a student is lacking a specific strategy to perform a given task. For example, a student may be competent at adding, subtracting, and multiplying numbers and yet not understand how to divide. What is lacking is a strategy to combine those prerequisite skills into competent performance. Conversely, cognitive distortions exist when an individual interprets information irrationally and in an erroneous fashion. In this case, CBI strategies would focus on teaching the individual to identify his or her maladaptive thoughts, dispute those thoughts, and replace them with more adaptive ones. There is some research to suggest that the cognitive functioning of children and adolescents who are depressed is characterized more by negative self-evaluations than a lack of active information processing (Kendall, Stark, & Adam, 1990). Therefore, special educators' role may be to help a student follow through on personal experiments designed by the school psychologist or counselor to refute negative self-statements.

Teachers have been using social problem-solving curricula for many years. One of the earliest programs was developed by Shure and Spivack (1974) for use with preschoolers. Since then, other programs have been developed for use with elementary and high school students both for prevention and intervention (Gesten, Weissberg, Amish, & Smith, 1987). Classroom teachers have successfully served as trainers in many problem-solving training studies (Pellegrini & Urbain, 1985). Most published curricula contain easy-to-follow scripted lessons. Therefore, it would be logical to envision special educators carrying out problem-solving training lessons that were modified by the school psychologist or counselor for specific use with students who are depressed.

Conclusion

Depression is one of the most commonly diagnosed psychiatric disorders among school-age youths. As such, school personnel should play an important role in its identification, assessment, and treatment with regard to school-related problems. School-based treatment of depression is especially relevant for special educators who work with students with EBD and LD, because these students may be at a higher risk than their nondisabled peers for developing depression. Three major areas were addressed in this chapter: (1) meta-analysis of the extant literature, (2) description of the ACTION program, and (3) implications for school personnel.

A meta-analysic review of the literature was undertaken to determine the efficacy of CBIs for treating depression in youths. The *ES* value was significant and commensurate with *ES* values obtained by other researchers (e.g., Weisz, Thurber, Sweeney, Proffitt, & LeGagnoux, 1997). There was considerable heterogeneity that was primarily due to the length of the CBI treatments: Larger effects were found for shorter durations than for longer durations. Maximum length of CBI treatments should be the focus of future research.

Three school-based programs for treating depression were described. The ACTION program developed by Stark, Yancy, et al. (in press) was viewed as a particularly promising evidence-based approach for use in schools. Treatment is based on a self-control model in which girls are taught coping skills using a variety of CBI techniques during 20 small-group meetings plus two individual meetings over 11 weeks. A consistent sequence is followed to provide the students with a sense of security and knowledge of how each session is structured. The ACTION program includes seven specific key aspects, which were described.

School personnel—specifically school psychologists, counselors, and special educators—may play important collaborative roles in the treatment of students who are depressed. School psychologists can be involved in assessing students who may be depressed and working to obtain appropriate services, which may either be delivered or supervised by them; likewise, they may refer the student and family to community mental health providers. School psychologists may also provide consultation to general and special education teachers. School counselors can provide direct individual and group counseling services to students who are depressed. Their role is especially important when students have a disability and require counseling as a related service. Special educators can play an important ancillary role for students with disabilities who are experiencing depression. Special educators have been trained in the use of many of the CBI techniques, including self-instruction training, problem-solving training, and self-monitoring. The school psychologist or counselor could modify these approaches for the special educator to deliver, under the former's supervision, to students who are depressed.

This type of collaborative relationship requires that additional CBI research be conducted in schools. One the one hand, clinic-based treatment may provide greater control over extraneous variables. However, school-based treatment may allow children—especially younger ones—to receive mental health services where they may not have access to them because of lack of either insurance or transportation. Regardless of the particular service delivery model, early CBI treatment may be the key to preventing or at least mitigating the negative impact depression has on children's functioning.

Acknowledgments

We gratefully acknowledge Nicole Willmes and Rhonda Turner for their hard work and diligence coding and entering data for the meta-analysis.

References

American Psychiatric Association. (2000). Practice guidelines for the treatment of patients with major depressive disorder (revision). *American Journal of Psychiatry, 157*(Suppl. 4), 1–45.

Anthony, E. J. (1970). Two contrasting types of adolescent depression and their treatment. *Journal of the American Psychoanalytic Association, 18,* 841–859.

Asarnow, J. R., Scott, C. V., & Mintz, J. (2002). A combined cognitive-behavioral family education intervention for depression in children: A treatment development study. *Cognitive Therapy and Research, 26,* 221–229.

Beck, A. T. (1976). *Cognitive therapy and the emotional disorders.* New York: International Universities Press.

Beck, A. T., Rush, A. J., Shaw, B. F., & Emery, G. (1979). *Cognitive therapy of depression.* New York: Guilford Press.

Birmaher, B., Ryan, N. D., Williamson, D. E., Brent, D. A., Kaufman, J., Dahl, R. E., et al. (1996). Childhood and adolescent depression: A review of the past 10 years, Part II. *Journal of the American Academy of Child and Adolescent Psychiatry, 35,* 1575–1583.

Braswell, L., & Kendall, P. C. (1988). Cognitive-behavioral methods with children. In K. S. Dobson (Ed.), *Handbook of cognitive-behavioral therapies* (pp. 167–213). New York: Guilford Press.

Butler, L., Miezitis, S., Friedman, R., & Cole, E. (1980). The effect of two school-based intervention programs on depressive symptoms in preadolescents. *American Education Research Journal, 17,* 111–119.

Clarizio, H. F. (1985). Cognitive-behavioral treatment of childhood depression. *Psychology in the Schools, 22,* 308–322.

Clarke, G. N., DeBar, L. L., & Lewinsohn, P. M. (2003). Cognitive-behavioral group treatment for adolescent depression. In A. E. Kazdin & J. R. Weisz (Eds.), *Evidence-based psychotherapies for children and adolescents* (pp. 120–134). New York: Guilford Press.

Clarke, G. N., Hawkins, W., Murphy, M., Sheeber, L. B., Lewinsohn, P. M., & Seeley, J. R. (1995). Targeted prevention of unipolar depressive disorder in an at-risk sample of high school adolescents: A randomized trial of a group cognitive intervention. *Journal of the American Academy of Child and Adolescent Psychiatry, 34,* 312–332.

Clarke, G. N., Hornbrook, M., Lynch, F., Polen, M., Gale, J., O'Connor, E., et al. (2002). Group cognitive behavioral treatment for depressed adolescent offspring of depressed parents in a health maintenance organization. *Journal of the American Academy of Child and Adolescent Psychiatry, 41,* 305–313.

Clarke, G. N., Rohde, P., Lewinsohn, P. M., Hops, H., & Seeley, J. R. (1999). Cognitive-behavioral treatment of adolescent depression: Efficacy of acute group treatment and booster sessions. *Journal of the American Academy of Child and Adolescent Psychiatry, 38,* 272–279.

Cooper, H., & Hedges, L. V. (Eds.). (1994). *Handbook of research synthesis.* New York: Russell Sage.

Council for Accreditation of Counseling and Related Educational Programs. (1994). *Accreditation procedures manual and application.* Alexandria, VA: Author.

Cowan, R. J., & Swearer, S. M. (2004). School-community partnerships. In C. Spielberger (Ed.), *Encyclopedia of applied psychology* (pp. 309–318). Oxford, UK: Elsevier.

Curry, J. F. (2001). Specific psychotherapies for childhood and adolescent depression. *Biological Psychiatry, 49,* 1091–1100.

DiGangi, S. A., & Maag, J. W. (1992). A component analysis of self-management training with behaviorally disordered youth. *Behavioral Disorders, 17,* 281–290.

Evans, J. R., Van Velsor, P., & Schumacher, J. E. (2002). Addressing adolescent depression: A role for school counselors. *Professional School Counseling, 5,* 211–219.

Evans, M., & Murphy, A. (1997). CBT for depression in children and adolescents. In K. N. Dwivedi & V. P. Varma (Eds.), *Depression in children and adolescents* (pp. 75–93). London: Whurr.

Finn, C. A. (2000). Treating adolescent depression: A review of intervention approaches. *International Journal of Adolescence & Youth, 8,* 253–269.

Frame, C., Matson, J. L., Sonis, W. A., Fialkov, M. J., & Kazdin, A. E. (1982). Behavioral treatment of depression in a prepubertal child. *Journal of Behavior Therapy and Experimental Psychiatry, 13,* 239–243.

Gesten, E. L., Weissberg, R. P., Amish, P. L., & Smith, J. K. (1987). Social problem-solving training: A skills-based approach to prevention and treatment. In C. A. Maher & J. E. Zins (Eds.), *Psychoeducational interventions in the schools* (pp. 26–45). New York: Pergamon Press.

Glass, G. V., McGaw, B., & Smith, M. L. (1981). *Meta-analysis in social research.* Beverly Hills, CA: Sage.

Haby, M. M., Tonge, B., Littlefield, L., Carter, R., & Vos, T. (2004). Cost-effectiveness of cognitive behavioural therapy and selective serotonin reuptake inhibitors for major depression in children and adolescents. *Australian and New Zealand Journal of Psychiatry, 38,* 579–591.

Hains, A. A. (1992). Comparison of cognitive-behavioral stress management techniques with adolescent boys. *Journal of Counseling & Development, 70,* 600–605.

Hargens, M., & Gysbers, N. C. (1984). How to remodel a guidance problem while living in it: A case study. *School Counselor, 32,* 119–125.

Harrington, R. C., Kerfoot, M., Dyer, E., McNiven, F., Gill, J., Harrington, V., et al. (1998). Randomized trial of a home-based family intervention for children who have deliberately poisoned themselves. *Journal of the American Academy of Child and Adolescent Psychiatry, 37,* 512–518.

Harrington, R., Whittaker, J., & Shoebridge, P. (1998). Psychological treatment of depression in children and adolescents: A review of treatment research. *British Journal of Psychiatry, 173,* 291–298.

Hedges, L., & Olkin, I. (1985). *Statistical methods for meta-analysis*. New York: Academic Press.

Horowitz, J. L., & Garber, J. (2006). The prevention of depressive symptoms in children and adolescents: A meta-analytic review. *Journal of Consulting and Clinical Psychology, 74*, 401–415.

Hunter, J. E., & Schmidt, F. L. (1990). *Methods of meta-analysis: Correcting error and bias in research findings*. Newbury Park, CA: Sage.

Institute of Medicine. (1994). *Reducing risks for mental disorders: Frontiers for preventive intervention research*. Washington, DC: National Academy Press.

Jaycox, L. H., Reivich, K. J., Gillham, J., & Seligman, M. E. P. (1994). Prevention of depressive symptoms in school children. *Behavior Research and Therapy, 32*, 801–816.

Kahn, J. S., Kehle, T. J., Jenson, W. R., & Clarke, E. (1990). Comparison of cognitive-behavioral, relaxation, and self-modeling interventions for depression among middle-school students. *School Psychology Review, 19*, 195–210.

Kandel, D. B., & Davies, M. (1986). Adult sequelae of adolescent depressive symptoms. *Archives of General Psychiatry, 43*, 255–262.

Kashani, J. H., McGee, R. O., Clarkson, S. E., Anderson, J. C., Walton, L. A., Williams, S., et al. (1983). Depression in a sample of 9-year-old children. *Archives of General Psychiatry, 40*, 1217–1233.

Kashani, J. H., & Simonds, J. F. (1979). The incidence of depression in children. *American Journal of Psychiatry, 136*, 1203–1205.

Kaslow, N. J., & Rehm, L. P. (1991). Childhood depression. In R. J. Morris & T. R. Kratochwill (Eds.), *The practice of child therapy* (2nd ed., pp. 27–51). New York: Pergamon Press.

Kavale, K. A. (1984). Potential advantages of the meta-analysis technique for special education. *Journal of Special Education, 18*, 61–72.

Kazdin, A. E. (1990). Childhood depression. *Journal of Child Psychology and Psychiatry, 31*, 121–160.

Kendall, P. C. (2000). Guiding theory for therapy with children and adolescents. In P. C. Kendall (Ed.), *Child and adolescent therapy* (pp. 3–27). New York: Guilford Press.

Kendall, P. C., Stark, K. D., & Adam, T. (1990). Cognitive deficit or cognitive distortion in childhood depression. *Journal of Abnormal Child Psychology, 18*, 255–270.

Kerfoot, M., Harrington, R., Harrington, V., Rogers, J., & Verduyn, D. (2004). A step too far? Randomized trial of cognitive-behaviour therapy delivered by social workers to depressed adolescents. *European Child & Adolescent Psychiatry, 13*, 92–99.

Kovacs, M. (1992). *Children's depression inventory manual*. North Tonawanda, NY: Multi-Health Systems.

Lewinsohn, P. M., & Clarke, G. N. (1999). Psychosocial treatments for adolescent depression. *Clinical Psychology Review, 19*, 329–342.

Lewinsohn, P. M., Clarke, G. N., Hops, H., & Andrews, J. A. (1990). Cognitive-behavioral treatment for depressed adolescents. *Behavior Therapy, 21*, 385–401.

Lewinsohn, P. M., Clarke, G. N., Rohde, K. P., Hops, H., & Seeley, J. R. (1996). A course in coping: A cognitive-behavioral approach to the treatment of adolescent depression. In E. Hibbs & P. S. Jensen (Eds.), *Psychosocial treatments for child and adolescent disorders: Empirically based strategies for clinical practice* (pp. 109–135). Washington, DC: American Psychological Association.

Liddle, B., & Spence, S. H. (1990). Cognitive-behavior therapy with depressed primary school children: A cautionary note. *Behavioral Psychotherapy, 18*, 85–102.

Lockhart, E. J., & Keys, S. G. (1998). The mental health counseling role of school counselors. *Professional School Counseling, 1*, 3–6.

Maag, J. W. (1993). Cognitive-behavioral strategies for depressed students. *Journal of Emotional and Behavioral Problems, 2*(2), 48–53.

Maag, J. W., & Behrens, J. T. (1989a). Depression and cognitive self-statements of learning disabled and seriously emotionally disturbed adolescents. *Journal of Special Education, 23,* 17–27.

Maag, J. W., & Behrens, J. T. (1989b). Epidemiologic data on SED and LD adolescents reporting extreme depressive symptomatology. *Behavioral Disorders, 15,* 21–27.

Maag, J. W., & Forness, S. R. (1991). Depression in children and adolescents: Identification, assessment, and treatment. *Focus on Exceptional Children, 24*(1), 1–19.

Maag, J. W., & Katsiyannis, A. (1996). Counseling as a related service for students with emotional or behavioral disorders: Issues and recommendations. *Behavioral Disorders, 21,* 293–305.

Maag, J. W., & Reid, R. (1994). The phenomenology of depression among students with and without learning disabilities: More similar than different. *Learning Disabilities Research & Practice, 9,* 91–103.

Maag, J. W., & Reid, R. (2006). Depression among students with learning disabilities: Assessing the risk. *Journal of Learning Disabilities, 39,* 3–10.

Maag, J. W., & Swearer, S. M. (2005). Cognitive-behavioral interventions for depression: Review and implications for school personnel. *Behavioral Disorders, 30,* 259–276.

Marcotte, D. (1997). Treating depression in adolescence: A review of the effectiveness of cognitive-behavioral treatments. *Journal of Youth & Adolescence, 26,* 273–283.

Mufson, L., Moreau, D., Weissmann, M. M., & Klerman, G. L. (1993). *Interpersonal psychotherapy for depressed adolescents.* New York: Guilford Press.

Murphy, J. P., DeEsch, J. B., & Strein, W. O. (1998). School counselors and school psychologists: Partners in student services. *Professional School Counseling, 2,* 85–87.

Nastasi, B. K., Varjas, K., Bernstein, R., & Pluymert, K. (1997). *Exemplary mental health programs: School psychologists as mental health service providers.* Bethesda, MD: National Association of School Psychologists.

National Association of School Psychologists. (1994). *Standards for training and credentialing in school psychology.* Washington, DC: Author.

Pellegrini, D. S., & Urbain, E. S. (1985). An evaluation of interpersonal cognitive problem solving training with children. *Journal of Child Psychology and Psychiatry, 26,* 17–41.

Platts, J., & Williamson, Y. (2000). The use of cognitive-behavioural therapy for counseling in schools. In N. Barwick (Ed.), *Clinical counseling in schools* (pp. 96–107). Philadelphia: Taylor & Francis.

Powers, D. (1979). The teacher and the adolescent suicide threat. *Journal of School Health, 49,* 561–563.

Pressley, M., Burkell, J., Cariglia-Bull, T., Lysynchuk, L., McGoldrick, J. A., Schneider, B., et al. (1990). *Cognitive strategy instruction.* Cambridge, MA: Brookline.

Reid, R. (1996). Research in self-monitoring with students with learning disabilities: The present, the prospects, the pitfalls. *Journal of Learning Disabilities, 29,* 317–331.

Reinecke, M. A., Ryan, N. E., & DuBois, D. L. (1998). Cognitive-behavioral therapy of depression and depressive symptoms during adolescence: A review and meta-analysis. *Journal of the American Academy of Child and Adolescent Psychiatry, 37,* 26–34.

Reinemann, D. H. S., & Swearer, S. M. (2005). Depressive disorders. In S. Goldstein & C. R. Reynolds (Eds.), *Handbook of neurodevelopmental and genetic disorders in adults* (pp. 195–224). New York: Guilford Press.

Reynolds, W. M. (1986). A model for the screening and identification of depressed children and adolescents in school settings. *Professional School Psychology, 1,* 117–129.

Reynolds, W. M., & Coats, K. I. (1986). A comparison of cognitive-behavioral therapy and relaxation training for the treatment of depression in adolescents. *Journal of Consulting and Clinical Psychology, 54,* 653–660.

Reynolds, W. M., & Miller, K. L. (1985). Depression and learned helplessness in mentally retarded and nonretarded adolescents: An initial investigation. *Applied Research in Mental Retardation, 6,* 295–307.

Reynolds, W. M., & Stark, K. D. (1987). School-based intervention strategies for the treatment of depression in children and adolescents. In S. G. Forman (Ed.), *School-based affective and social interventions* (pp. 69–88). New York: Haworth Press.

Roberts, C., Robert, K., Thomson, H., Bishop, B., & Hart, B. (2003). The prevention of depressive symptoms in rural school children: A randomized controlled trial. *Journal of Consulting and Clinical Psychology, 71,* 622–628.

Rohde, P., Clarke, G. N., Lewinsohn, P. M., Seeley, J. R., & Kaufman, N. K. (2001). Impact of comorbidity on a cognitive-behavioral group treatment for adolescent depression. *Journal of the American Academy of Child and Adolescent Psychiatry, 40,* 795–802.

Rohde, P., Lewinsohn, P. M., & Seeley, J. R. (1994). Response of depressed adolescents to cognitive-behavioral treatment: Do differences in initial severity clarify the comparison of treatments? *Journal of Consulting and Clinical Psychology, 62,* 851–854.

Rosenberg, M. S., Adams, D. C., & Gurevitch, J. (2000). *Metawin.* Sunderland, MA: Sinauer.

Rosenthal, R. (1979). The "file drawer problem" and tolerance for null results. *Psychological Bulletin, 86,* 638–641.

Rosenthal, R. (1984). *Meta-analytic procedures for social research.* Beverly Hills, CA: Sage.

Rossello, J., & Bernal, G. (1999). The efficacy of cognitive-behavioral and interpersonal treatments for depression in Puerto Rican adolescents. *Journal of Consulting and Clinical Psychology, 6,* 734–745.

Rushton, J. L., Forcier, M., & Schectman, R. M. (2002). Epidemiology of depressive symptoms in the national longitudinal study of adolescent health. *Journal of the American Academy of Child and Adolescent Psychiatry, 41,* 199–205.

Sheffield, J. K., Spence, S. H., Rapee, R. M., Kowalenko, N., Wignall, A., Davis, A., et al. (2006). Evaluation of universal, indicated, and combined cognitive-behavioral approaches to the prevention of depression among adolescents. *Journal of Consulting and Clinical Psychology, 74,* 66–79.

Sherrill, J. T., & Kovacs, M. (2002). Nonsomatic treatment of depression. *Child and Adolescent Psychiatric Clinics of North America, 11,* 579–593.

Shure, M. B., & Spivack, G. (1974). *Interpersonal cognitive problem-solving (ICPS): A mental health program for kindergarten and first-grade children: Training script.* Philadelphia: Hahnemann University, Department of Mental Health Sciences.

Southam-Gerow, M. A., Henin, A., Chu, B., Marrs, A., & Kendall, P. C. (1997). Cognitive-behavioral therapy with children and adolescents. *Child and Adolescent Psychiatric Clinics of North America, 6,* 111–136.

Spence, S. H., Sheffield, J. K., & Donovan, C. L. (2005). Long-term outcome of a school-based, universal approach to prevention of depression in adolescents. *Journal of Consulting and Clinical Psychology, 73,* 160–167.

Stark, K. D. (1990). *Childhood depression: School-based intervention.* New York: Guilford Press.

Stark, K. D., Boswell, S. J., Hargrave, J., Schnoebelen, S., Simpson, J., & Molnar, J. (2006). Treatment of depression in children and adolescence: Cognitive-behavioral procedures for the individual and family. In P. C. Kendell (Ed.), *Cognitive behavioral therapy with children and adolescents* (pp. 169–216). New York: Guilford Press.

Stark, K. D., Kendall, P. C., McCarthy, M., Staford, M., Barron, R., & Thomeer, M. (1996). *ACTION: A workbook for overcoming depression.* Ardmore, PA: Workbook Publishing.

Stark, K. D., Reynolds, W. M., & Kaslow, N. J. (1987). A comparison of the relative efficacy of self-control and behavior therapy for the reduction of depression in children. *Journal of Abnormal Child Psychology, 15,* 91–113.

Stark, K. D., Sander, J., Hauser, M., Simpson, J., Schnoebelen, J., Glenn, R., et al. (2006). Mood disorders. In E. Mash & R. A. Barkley (Eds.), *Treatment of childhood disorders* (3rd ed.). New York; Guilford Press.

Stark, K. D., Schnoebelen, S., Simpson, J., Hargrave, J., Glenn, R., & Molnar, J. (2004). *Children's workbook for ACTION.* Ardmore, PA: Workbook Publishing.

Stark, K. D., Simpson, J., Schnoebelen, S., Hargrave, J., Glenn, R., & Molnar, J. (2004). *Therapist's manual for ACTION.* Ardmore, PA: Workbook Publishing.

Stark, K. D., Simpson, J., Yancy, M., & Molnar, J. (2007). *Parents workbook for ACTION.* Ardmore, PA: Workbook Publishing.

Stark, K. D., Swearer, S., Kurowski, D., Sommer, D., & Bowen, B. (1996). Targeting the child and the family: A holistic approach to treating child and adolescent depressive disorders. In E. D. Hibbs & P. S. Jensen (Eds.), *Psychosocial treatments for child and adolescent disorders: Empirically based strategies for clinical practice* (pp. 207–238). Washington, DC: American Psychological Association.

Stark, K. D., Yancy, M., Simpson, J., & Molnar, J. (2007). *Treating depressed children: Therapist manual for parent component of "ACTION."* Ardmore, PA: Workbook Publishing.

Treatment for Adolescents with Depression Study (TADS) Team. (2004). Fluoxetine, cognitive-behavioral therapy, and their combination for adolescents with depression: Treatment for adolescents with depression study (TADS) randomized controlled trial. *Journal of the American Medical Association, 292,* 807–820.

Webber, J., Scheuermann, B., McCall, C., & Coleman, M. (1993). Research on self-monitoring as a behavior management technique in special education classrooms: A descriptive review. *Remedial and Special Education, 14,* 38–56.

Weisz, J. R., McCarty, C. A., & Valeri, S. M. (2006). Effects of psychotherapy for depression in children and adolescents: A meta-analysis. *Psychological Bulletin, 132,* 132–149.

Weisz, J., Thurber, C. A., Sweeney, L., Proffitt, V. D., & LeGagnoux, G. L. (1997). Brief treatment of mild to moderate child depression using primary and secondary control enhancement training. *Journal of Consulting and Clinical Psychology, 65,* 703–707.

Wilson, D. B. (2005). *SPSS for Windows meta-analysis macros.* Retrieved January 10, 2007, from *mason.gmu.edu/~dwilsonb/ma.html.*

Wolf, F. M. (1986). *Meta-analysis: Quantitative methods for research synthesis.* Beverly Hills, CA: Sage.

Yell, M. L. (1998). *The law and special education.* Columbus, OH: Merrill.

CHAPTER 10

Cognitive-Behavioral Interventions for Depression during Childhood

Exemplary Programs

KEVIN D. STARK
JENNY HERREN
MELISSA FISHER

Three treatment programs for depressed youth are described in this chapter: the ACT and ADAPT program (Connor-Smith, Polo, Jensen Doss, & Weisz, 2004), interpersonal psychotherapy for adolescents (IPT-A; e.g., Mufson, Moreau, Weissman, & Klerman, 1993), and ACTION (e.g., Stark, Simpson, et al., 2006). The latter program is described in greater detail since we developed it and evaluated its efficacy over the past 5 years. The ACT and ADAPT and the ACTION programs represent cognitive-behavioral therapies (CBTs) for depressed youth. IPT-A is derived from interpersonal theory and therapy. Despite their differences in theoretical underpinnings, the three interventions share many of the same treatment components and they have more similarities than differences. In fact, Mufson, Moreau, Dorta, and Weissman (2004) has stated that IPT-A and CBT are very similar. A review of the IPT-A treatment manual reveals that the primary treatment strategy is interpersonal problem solving, which is a cognitive-behavioral strategy.

ACT and ADAPT

Overview

ACT and ADAPT is designed to treat and prevent depression in children and adolescents ages 10 to 14 and follows a structured leader's manual (Connor-Smith et al., 2004) and workbook (Polo, Connor-Smith, Jensen Doss, & Weisz, 2004). The program is school based and consists of 10 sessions, an introductory session, and two review sessions. The meetings are designed to last approximately 90 minutes. The program teaches participants to gain control over their mood by using learned skills to solve problems they can change and to adapt to problems they cannot change. Each structured session introduces coping techniques, and participants then learn how to apply the skills through discussion, role plays, worksheets, and individualized assignments. Practice assignments facilitate personalization of the skills.

The program is designed to target specific skill deficits and negative thinking that are thought to increase risk for depression and maintain current depressive symptoms. ACT and ADAPT was developed using the primary and secondary control models of coping. Primary control reflects efforts to cope by changing problematic situations; secondary control reflects efforts to cope by adapting to situations that cannot be changed. Primary control strategies presented in the manual include problem solving, engaging in fun activities, relaxation, and positive self-presentation skills. Secondary control strategies include positive thinking, distraction, and seeking support from others. The program presents a toolbox approach to treatment in which participants are encouraged to identify particular skills that they find to be the most useful.

ACT and ADAPT includes a video guide that presents important information about the primary and secondary control skills. The video consists of a series of vignettes that follow the lives of three adolescents as they cope with everyday life and stressors. The video explains the basic points, and group discussion and activities are used to develop an understanding of these skills. Thus, the video serves as a jumping-off point for discussions, and the actors model for the adolescents the application of the skills being taught.

The skills are taught through group activities that are incorporated into each session, and the skills are applied outside of the sessions through homework assignments. An incentive system is used to encourage desirable group behaviors such as attending the session, bringing materials, and completing therapeutic homework assignments. At the end of each meeting participants answer a short feedback questionnaire about what they learned during the meeting so that the leaders can assess participants' level of engagement and retention of information.

ACT and ADAPT Sessions

In addition to the 10 skill-building sessions, there are 3 meetings that do not include any training in new skills. Instead, these meetings are designed to build a group environment that is conducive to skill building and to consolidate skill acquisition. The first of these sessions is the first group meeting. The overall objectives of this session are to introduce the participants, begin to build a therapeutic environment, establish the purpose of the group, and establish group rules. An incentive program is introduced, and the rules and rewards are discussed. The connection between life events and mood is established, a mood meter is introduced, and the group completes an activity that illustrates how mood can be changed by thoughts and behaviors. The second of these sessions occurs between the fourth and fifth skill-building sessions, and the primary objective of this meeting is to review the ACT skills learned through Session 4 by completing a charades review game. Participants also take an ACT skills quiz and complete some *in vivo* skills practice. The third meeting occurs between the seventh and eighth skill-building sessions. Termination is introduced and discussed, and the ADAPT or secondary control skills presented in previous sessions are reviewed.

Session 1 of ADAPT introduces a systematic problem-solving strategy that helps participants better develop their problem-solving skills. The acronym STEPS is used to help participants learn and remember the problem-solving steps. S is for "Say what the problem is." T is for "Think of solutions." E is for "Examine solutions." P is for "Pick One." S is for "See if it worked." Participants identify a current problem and apply the STEPS to it.

The main point of Session 2 is that behaviors affect feelings. The relationship between behavior and emotion is highlighted, and participants discuss times when they had a bad day and what they could have done to improve it. The idea that doing something fun produces an improvement in mood is introduced. Participants then identify activities that make them feel good and things that they can do to stay busy or help others. Participants then pick one of their fun activities and spend some group time doing it.

The purpose of the Session 3 is to help participants learn that they are able to exert some control over their physical and emotional responses to stress. Group members are helped to recognize that everyday events can lead to stress that produces unpleasant emotions. Participants identify their own stressors and reactions to them. Group members then participate in a progressive muscle relaxation exercise. Quick calming, an imagery activity in which participants imagine being in a different situation, is presented as a technique to deal with stress when a need exists to relax in a hurry.

Session 4 focuses on helping group members develop a positive self-presentation. This process begins by presenting examples of how depressed and irritable emotions can negatively impact other people. Group members identify specific negative behaviors they exhibit when irritated or sad. Positive self-presentation is presented as an active, conscious choice, and group members identify ways that they can act positively. Participants practice role playing putting their worst and best foot forward.

The goal of the Session 5 is to help participants learn to identify their negative thoughts. Group members are taught that multiple perspectives can occur in any situation. Participants are presented with the acronym BLUE to help them recognize cognitive errors. **B** is for "Blaming myself." **L** is for "Looking for the bad news." **U** is for "Unhappy guessing." **E** is for "Exaggerating." Participants are provided with vignettes and video clips in which they label the cognitive errors of the characters. Then they identify examples of their own negative thoughts and work on changing them to more realistic thoughts.

Session 6 is an extension of the previous meeting and focuses on continuing to help the participants learn how to identify negative thoughts and then change them. Vignettes, worksheets, role plays, and video segments are used to help the participants learn how to recognize negative thoughts. An enjoyable activity is used to help lift the group's mood, as the session can be emotionally difficult.

Additional skills that are particularly helpful for uncontrollable situations are introduced during Session 7, including obtaining social support, identifying the positive aspects of the situation, and distracting oneself. Group activities are used to help the participants personalize the three skills.

Often the first coping or problem-solving plan that a participant tries does not work. Thus, it is important for the child to persist and try multiple plans. In addition, some problems require the participant to use multiple strategies to reduce stress and improve mood. It is very difficult for many depressed children and adolescents to persist and try multiple strategies, as their helplessness causes them to give up prematurely. Session 8 emphasizes perseverance and the importance of trying different plans and integrating skills learned in the program either by acting on or adapting to a problem. Participants also learn to focus on solving one problem at a time to avoid becoming overwhelmed. The last part of the session focuses on role playing and identifying skills that are going to be most helpful.

Strategies that are used to try to control situations are not going to be effective with situations that are uncontrollable. Attempting to use these strategies in uncontrollable situations is going to lead to failure and frustration that could be devastating for a depressed participant. Thus, it is important to try to teach the participants how to match the strategies to the situations. Aspects of a situation that can and cannot be changed and matching responsibility to one's ability to control the situation are discussed. Role plays are used to teach the children how to apply appropriate skills to address problems and improve mood.

The purpose of the final session is to review the skills and provide participants with an opportunity to say goodbye. A game is used as a method for reviewing both the ACT and ADAPT skills. Participants also make a video interview that provides them with an opportunity to review and share the knowledge they have gained. The last part of the meeting is a celebration in which group members say goodbye, receive their diplomas, and take a group photo.

Evidence Base for ACT and ADAPT

The evidence base for the ACT and ADAPT program is being evaluated at this time. Thus, the program does not yet have an evidence base independent from that for other CBT interventions in general. For a review of the efficacy of CBT, see Stark, Hargrave, Schnoebelen, Simpson, and Molnar (2005). Based on the existing research, including the more recent findings reported for the Treatment of Adolescent Depression Study (e.g., Curry, 2006), it is clear that CBT is an effective intervention for depression and, although it does not produce improvements as quickly as Prozac, over time it is as effective as Prozac and has a lower relapse rate.

Summary and Conclusions

The ACT and ADAPT program is a brief intervention in which participants learn strategies for changing stressful situations and for managing their emotional upset. The program emphasizes behavioral activation strategies and problem solving, and it has a minimal cognitive restructuring component. The intervention is manual driven rather than guided by a case conceptualization. Consequently, the intervention requires less staff training to be able to implement. Skills are taught within the sessions, and participants apply the skills to everyday life through structured homework assignments. Therapists take more of a psychoeducational approach to the intervention in which the participants are taught specific skills that they personalize on their own. Thus, the intervention can be delivered by individuals who do not have training in applied psychology, such as classroom teachers and school counselors. Of the three programs described in this chapter, the ACT and ADAPT program requires the least training to deliver effectively and requires the least sophisticated therapy background. The ACT and ADAPT program could be used as a prevention program. It also would fit nicely into a life skills curriculum that would be completed by children within general education, or it could be used as part of the life skills curriculum in a special education classroom or pull-out program. Unlike the other two treatments discussed in this chapter, the intervention does not target parenting behaviors or family interactions. In fact, parents are not included in any of the meetings.

IPT-A

In the early 90s Laura Mufson and colleagues adapted interpersonal psychotherapy (IPT) to create a brief, evidence-based intervention designed to meet the needs of depressed adolescents (IPT-A; Mufson et al., 1993). The primary goals of IPT-A are to reduce depressive symptoms and to improve interpersonal functioning through enhancement of communication and other interpersonal skills. To accomplish these goals, the adolescent and therapist identify one or two problem areas that may be contributing to or exacerbating depression. The problem areas may be one or more of the following: grief, interpersonal role disputes, role transitions, interpersonal deficits, or single-parent families. Thus, although the targets are interpersonal in nature, the treatment strategies applied to these targets are primarily cognitive behavioral in nature.

Treatment is divided into three phases, and each phase consists of four sessions. During the initial phase, problem areas are identified, a rationale for treatment is provided, a formal therapeutic contract is negotiated and signed, and the adolescent's role in therapy is defined. The adolescent and the adolescent's parents are educated about depression to facilitate an understanding of the disorder and its implications. Additionally, the therapist works with the adolescent and his or her parents to ensure that the adolescent is socially engaged in the family, in school, and with friends. Parents are asked to encourage their child to engage in as many regular activities as possible. Thus, psychoeducation and behavioral activation are used as primary treatment strategies during the first phase of treatment.

During the middle phase of treatment, Sessions 5–8, the nature of each previously identified problem is clarified, effective strategies for attacking the problems are determined, and relevant plans are developed and implemented. When developing plans, an overarching goal is the desire to improve interpersonal functioning. Adolescents are also taught to monitor the experience of depressive symptoms, and their emotional experiences more generally. Thus, self-monitoring and interpersonal problem solving are the primary treatment strategies used during the middle phase of treatment.

To achieve these therapeutic objectives, the therapist utilizes exploratory questioning, encouragement of affect, linking affect with events, clarification of conflicts, communication analysis, and behavior change techniques such as role playing. Throughout these sessions, the therapist provides the adolescent with feedback about symptom change in an attempt to enhance the adolescent's self-esteem. The therapist and adolescent work together as a team as they assess the accuracy of the initial formulation of problem areas and evaluate the impact of ongoing events occurring outside of the sessions for their impact on depressive symptoms. The therapist evaluates the adolescent's interpersonal style through observing within-session interactions, and, with the adolescent's informed permission, the family is encouraged to support treatment goals.

The final phase of treatment, Sessions 9–12, composes the termination phase. The foremost objectives of this phase are to prepare the adolescent for termination and to establish a sense of personal competence for managing future problems. The adolescent's feelings about termination are discussed, and feelings of competence are engendered. Thus, the child's sense of self-efficacy is enhanced at the same time that his or her sense of helplessness is diminished, thus achieving a change in core beliefs.

Evidence Base for IPT-A

Research has established the efficacy of IPT for the treatment of depression in adults, and the results of outcome studies on adolescents treated with IPT-A suggest it is an efficacious and effective treatment modality for adolescent depression (Mufson, Dorta, & Olfson, 2004; Mufson, Weissman, Moreau, & Garfinkel, 1999; Rossello & Bernal, 1999). Using an open clinical trial methodology, Mufson, Moreau, and Weissman (1994) investigated the effects of 12 weeks of IPT-A on 14 depressed adolescents. Results indicated a significant decrease in the participants' depressive symptomatology and symptoms of psychological and physical distress, and a significant improvement in functioning, over the course of treatment. In another investigation, Mufson and Fairbanks (1996) found that 10 adolescents with depression who were treated with IPT-A for 3 months reported a significant improvement in depressive symptoms and maintained improvements in their social functioning 1-year posttreatment.

A study conducted by Mufson, Dorta, and Olfson (2004) examined the effectiveness of IPT-A in school-based mental health clinics to determine whether IPT-A could be successfully implemented in community settings and delivered by community-based clinicians. Results demonstrated that adolescents treated with IPT-A showed greater symptom reduction and improvement than adolescents in the treatment-as-usual condition. Because the majority of youth will be treated in community settings (Weisz, Donenberg, Han, & Weiss, 1995), it is important to close the gap between treatment delivered in a tightly controlled laboratory and treatment delivered in clinical practice.

Summary and Conclusions

Although IPT-A is developed from a different theoretical base, it shares much in common with the ACT and ADAPT and ACTION programs. In fact, other than the difference in the theoretical model about what produces change, IPT-A and the CBT interventions are similar with respect to therapeutic strategies and the therapeutic process employed within the sessions. IPT-A consists of 12 sessions that are organized around three phases of treatment. The primary objective of the first phase is behavioral activation through engaging in pleasant activities and encouraging the adolescent's parents to help their child to increase engagement in social activities in the family, home, and school. The second phase emphasizes problem identification and problem solving as strategies for dealing with five possible interpersonal difficulties. Role playing is used to help the participants learn how to overcome their interpersonal problems, and their affect is linked to events in their lives. Interpersonal conflicts are identified, and plans are developed to solve these conflicts. Attempts are made to enhance self-efficacy through demonstrating how the adolescents' attempts to change produce an improvement in depressive symptoms. The therapeutic alliance is established during this phase as the adolescent and therapist develop a common conceptualization of the interpersonal problems and plans for resolving them. The primary objective of the final phase of treatment is enhancement of the adolescent's sense of personal competence for resolving his or her interpersonal problems.

Given the interpersonal nature of many of the problems faced by adolescents during the school day and outside of school with their families, IPT-A would be a useful form of treatment in the schools as mental health professionals could help the students deal with their interpersonal problems as they come up. IPT-A is more of a traditional form of therapy; thus, it requires that the therapist have more therapy training. IPT-A could not be delivered by teachers, and because school counselors and psychologists are not likely to have had training in this therapy model, they are likely to require additional training and supervision to be able to effectively implement the intervention. The intervention has not been modified for use as a prevention program. However, the content would fit nicely into a life skills curriculum or a social skills curriculum. Thus, it may be possible to modify the manual so that it could be delivered by a mental health professional in the classroom as a prevention program.

ACTION

Overview

Most of the existing treatment manuals for depressed youth provide a minimal to modest cognitive restructuring component. Typically this involves teaching the participants that negative thoughts contribute to their depression and that they should catch the negative thoughts and change them to positive thoughts. The ACTION program represents a purposeful attempt to create a cognitive-behavioral intervention that is true to cognitive therapy for depression and thus includes a significant (in terms of time and strategies employed), developmentally sensitive cognitive restructuring component. In addition, because children develop critical beliefs and self-regulatory strategies from their interactions with significant others, the ACTION program includes a parent training component. This component was designed to create a more positive family environment that will lead to the development of adaptive core beliefs, and effective coping and problem-solving skills.

The child component consists of 20 group and 2 individual meetings (see Table 10.1 for a session-by-session outline). Each meeting lasts approximately 60 minutes, and meetings are conducted twice a week for 11 weeks. The parent training component consists of eight group meetings and two individual family meetings (see Table 10.2 for a session-by-session outline) completed over the same 11 weeks. An attempt is made to help the children and their caregivers experience the benefits of the treatment strategies within the meetings as a means of increasing the likelihood that they will apply the skills to their everyday lives. The skills are then applied to their depressive symptoms, interpersonal difficulties, and other stressors through therapeutic homework. Completion of therapeutic homework is encouraged through an in-session reward system.

In order to manage depression, children learn three core strategies: (1) If the undesirable situation cannot be changed, use a coping strategy; (2) If the undesirable situation can be changed, use problem solving to improve it; and (3) Catch negative thoughts, evaluate them, and change them to more realistic and positive thoughts. Four primary treatment

TABLE 10.1. Session-by-Session Outline of ACTION Primary Child
Treatment Components

1. Introductions and discussion of pragmatics
2. Affective education and introduction to coping
3. Affective education, coping skills, and introduction to Catch the Positive Diaries

Individual meeting: Review therapeutic concepts and establish treatment goals.

4. Extend group cohesion, review participant goals, application of coping skills
5. Extend coping skills, introduction to problem solving
6. Cognition and emotion, introduction to cognitive restructuring
7. Apply problem solving
8. Apply problem solving
9. Apply problem solving

Individual meeting: Review therapeutic concepts, identify common negative thoughts, individualize Catch the Positive Diaries, and introduce cognitive restructuring.

10. Prepare for cognitive restructuring and introduction to cognitive restructuring
11. Cognitive restructuring
12. Cognitive restructuring and self-maps
13. Cognitive restructuring and self-maps
14. Cognitive restructuring and self-maps
15. Cognitive restructuring and self-maps
16. Cognitive restructuring and self-maps
17. Cognitive restructuring and self-maps
18. Cognitive restructuring and self-maps
19. Cognitive restructuring and self-maps
20. Bring it all together and termination activity

procedures are used to help participants apply the three core strategies: (1) affective education, (2) coping skills, (3) problem solving, and (4) cognitive restructuring. The first of these procedures, affective education, involves educating the participants about the nature of depression, the cognitive-behavioral model of depression, and their own experiences of depression. In addition to having didactic discussions about depression and the cognitive-behavioral model of depression, participants complete activities within the meetings and as homework to help them become more aware of their personal experiences and the links between their thoughts, behaviors, and emotions.

The second treatment procedure is coping skills training. A change in mood is used as a cue to evaluate the degree of controllability of the situation. When the situation cannot be changed, the children take action to improve their mood and other depressive symptoms through coping skills that are taught and applied during the first nine meetings. Participants experience the benefits of using coping skills within the session,

TABLE 10.2. Session-by-Session Outline of ACTION Parent Training Sessions

1. Positive behavior management
2. Self-esteem enhancement
3. Family recreation
4. Empathic listening
5. Effective communication
6. Family problem solving
7. Conflict resolution
8. Changing negative parental messages

and they are encouraged to use these skills outside of meetings through self-monitoring and recording their use.

The third treatment procedure is problem-solving training, and the children are taught to use it when they are experiencing undesirable situations that can be changed or managed and that are within the children's control. They are taught a five-step problem-solving procedure to change undesirable situations and thus to reduce distress and the accompanying emotional upset. Over time, the therapist helps the children apply problem solving to promote desirable changes in their lives.

By the middle of treatment, participants typically are proficient at using coping and problem-solving skills, and this enables them to focus on cognitive restructuring, the fourth treatment procedure. A variety of within-session activities and therapeutic homework exercises are used to teach participants to be "thought judges" who evaluate the validity of their negative thoughts using two questions: (1) What is another way of looking at it? (2) What is the evidence? If the negative thought is realistic and reflects a situation that can be changed, then the participant is encouraged to use problem solving to develop and follow a plan that produces improvement. If the situation is real but cannot be changed, then a coping strategy is used to manage the participant's reaction to the situation.

The parent training component has two broad objectives:

1. Create a positive family environment that encourages adaptive behavior and the development of emotion regulation, problem-solving skills, and healthy core beliefs.
2. Help the parents to acquire and use the same skills that the children are learning.

To create the positive family environment parents are taught (1) the use of positive behavior management strategies and reduction of punitive strategies, (2) family problem solving, (3) communication skills, (4) conflict resolution skills, and (5) how their behavior impacts their child's thinking and belief system. Children are present during half of the meetings.

Case Conceptualization

Implementation of the ACTION treatment program is driven by a cognitive-behavioral case conceptualization. Case conceptualization is an ongoing hypothesis-generating and -testing process that begins prior to treatment, during the initial assessment, and continues throughout treatment. Assessment data, historical information, thoughts verbalized during treatment, and patterns in the child's behavior are used to develop and test hypotheses about core beliefs. To determine which core belief(s) are operating for each child, the therapist listens to the child's self-references and the meanings that he or she draws from daily experiences. The beliefs are reflected in the themes and consistencies found in each child's thoughts. The meanings of events can be deduced from the discussions and by following the "downward arrow" technique (Beck, 1995). Once the core beliefs have been identified, the therapist continually and very actively looks for ways to change them. The next step in the case conceptualization process is identification of the environmental events that are maintaining the beliefs.

Core Therapeutic Components

Affective Education

Affective education is threaded throughout the program and is the focus of the first few meetings. It is the treatment component in which the participants are taught a simplified CBT model of depression, how this model applies to them, and how they are going to overcome depression. The children are provided with experiences that facilitate greater self-awareness, particularly of their depressive thoughts, unpleasant emotions, and other depressive symptoms. These experiences are used as cues to engage coping skills, problem solving, and cognitive restructuring strategies.

Participants identify their emotions by acting like "emotion detectives" who investigate their own experience of the "3 Bs": Body, Brain, and Behavior. Participants are taught greater awareness of their emotional experiences by tuning into how their body is reacting, what they are thinking, and how they are behaving. The participants also complete therapeutic homework assignments in which they identify their emotional experiences and independently assess their experience of the 3 Bs.

To recognize that a problem exists, the children are taught to look for a shift to unpleasant affect, the occurrence or potential occurrence of an undesirable outcome, and a feeling of anxiety or worry about something. A number of strategies and activities are used to help the children learn about the distorted nature of depressive cognition, and they learn how to identify negative thoughts. The methods for accomplishing this are described in the section on cognitive restructuring.

Goal Setting

CBT is a collaborative approach to therapy in which the child is fully informed of the treatment objectives and the methods that are going to be employed to achieve these objectives. Central to this collaborative process is helping the participant to identify personal goals for therapy. In the case of treating children, this may also involve helping the parents to identify their goals for their child's treatment and for changing their family and/or parenting practices.

In the ACTION program, the therapist translates the conceptualization into treatment goals, which are positively worded statements about desired outcomes. Between the third and fourth group meetings, the therapist merges his or her goals with the child's goals and concerns to develop a set of three or four collaboratively generated treatment goals. In addition, the therapist describes treatment procedures that will be used to help the child achieve these goals. Before the end of the goals meeting, the therapist asks the child if he or she would be willing to share his or her goals with the group. At the beginning of every other subsequent meeting, there is a "goals check-in" time to report progress toward goal attainment and to celebrate progress. As goals are achieved, the therapist helps the participants identify new goals.

Coping Skills Training

A central objective of CBT for depression is to behaviorally activate the depressed participant. In the ACTION program, coping skills are used to achieve this therapeutic objective. Emotion-focused coping is taught both as a general strategy for enhancing mood and more specifically for managing distress when the child is experiencing an undesirable or stressful situation that cannot be changed. Coping skills are taught and practiced during Meetings 2–9. Coping skills training is emphasized at the beginning of treatment, because these skills help the children produce an immediate improvement in mood. This improvement makes it easier for the participants to learn and benefit from problem solving and cognitive restructuring that are taught later.

The children learn how to use five broad categories of coping skills to help themselves feel better: (1) Do something fun and distracting, (2) Do something soothing and relaxing, (3) Seek social support, (4) Do something that expends lots of energy, and (5) Change your thinking. The participants experience the benefits of using the coping skills within the treatment sessions. The therapist chooses the coping skills to be taught and applied during each meeting based on what he or she believes to be most needed by the group.

Talking about coping skills and how they work is inadequate, as it becomes nothing more than an intellectual exercise for children. Children have to experience the benefits of coping skills in group before they will try to use them outside of group. When a coping strategy is taught, the therapist asks the participants to rate their mood at that moment and then to participate in an activity in which they use one of the coping skills. After completing the activity, they rerate their moods. Inevitably, their moods dramatically improve. The therapist processes the experience with them. Then the group generates a list of examples of things they can do from the general category of coping strategies. In addition to teaching coping strategies, the therapist helps the children to identify situations when it is most advantageous to use specific coping skills.

Although it is apparent that the participants can learn and benefit from using coping skills, therapeutic improvement is dependent on applying the skills outside of meetings. To facilitate this, therapeutic homework is assigned. This homework progresses from identifying changes in emotion and the accompanying thoughts to noting a change in emotions, the context of the emotional change, and the coping skill used to improve mood. In general, participants have a relatively easy time learning coping skills and applying them to their depressive symptoms.

Catch the Positive Diary (CPD): A Tool to Promote Activation and Coping

CPD is designed to help participants attend to positive events by self-monitoring and recording occurrences of therapeutically important events. CPD is used to (1) activate the child through engagement in fun activities, (2) redirect the child's attention from negative to positive events, (3) increase the child's completion of therapeutically relevant activities, and (4) help the child find evidence that supports new more adaptive beliefs and counters negative beliefs. CPD directs a change in the child's attention from negative to positive information, helping to restructure his or her maladaptive thoughts and beliefs.

An overarching goal of the treatment program and of CPD is to improve mood by increasing the frequency and types of coping skills used.

As other categories of coping skills are taught and their benefits are experienced in session, the participants' favorite examples of these coping skills are added to the list. Thus, the list expands from fun activities to include soothing and relaxing activities, activities that vigorously expend energy, social activities, and coping thoughts.

Participants may be asked to include other commonly occurring positive events on the list as a means of redirecting attention and restructuring maladaptive beliefs. Based on each child's case conceptualization and negative thoughts verbalized during meetings, he or she is instructed to add specific events to the list that will lead to changes in core beliefs. Thus, self-monitoring of these events restructures core beliefs and the negative thoughts that arise from them. CPD is a very flexible tool that can be used for many therapeutic purposes.

Problem-Solving Training

As participants acquire a better understanding of their emotions, accurately identify them, recognize their impact on behavior and thinking, and understand that they can take action to moderate the intensity and impact of their emotions, participants are taught that some of the undesirable situations can be changed. Problem solving is the strategy used to develop a plan for changing undesirable situations. The five-step problem-solving sequence is formally introduced during the fifth meeting. During this meeting, the group also creates a comprehensive list of the problems that children their age typically face. Then the group goes through the list and determines whether each problem can be changed or whether it is a problem that they cannot change. If they cannot change the problem, then the therapist queries them about which coping skill they would use to moderate the impact of the event.

The problem-solving procedure used is a modification of the one described by Kendall (e.g., Kendall & Braswell, 1993). Children are taught to break problem solving down into five component steps through education, modeling, coaching, rehearsal, and feedback. To simplify the process and to help the children remember the steps, the therapist refers to the steps as the "5 Ps." Steps include (1) problem definition (Problem), (2) goal definition (Purpose), (3) solution generation (Plans), (4) consequential thinking (Predict and Pick), and (5) self-evaluation (Pat on the back). Steps are defined in a developmentally sensitive manner, and activities are used to illustrate the meaning and purpose of each step.

The negativity of depressed youth can interfere with implementation of problem solving; however, steps can be taken to minimize its impact. Once the participants have learned problem solving and the therapist and other group members have helped them generate a plan that has a high probability of success, the children have to actually implement the plan. Children are more likely to try it if they believe the plan will work and if they believe that they possess the ability to successfully implement it. Thus, it is important to address both of these issues as plans are developed and the participants are assigned homework to implement them. It may be useful to ask the child if he or she can foresee anything that would get in the way of trying the plan. A problem-solving homework form can be completed during the meeting as the therapist and other group members help the child work through the steps and develop a plan. The child can then refer to this form as he or she tries to implement it. It is helpful to begin applying the problem solving to less complex problems with solutions that are more likely to be successful. Thus, a history of success with problem solving is established, which increases the probability that the children will use the strategy in the future.

Negative thinking can derail problem solving. To a depressed child, the existence of a problem means that there is something wrong with him or her, or the problem represents an impending loss or an insurmountable problem. In addition, depressed children with a helpless core belief think that they cannot solve existing problems, and that even if they could, more would appear. Thus, their sense of hopelessness has to be combated through concrete evidence in their life experiences that demonstrates that they can overcome problems. It often takes the participants a number of weeks to build enough of a new learning history to begin to believe that they can use problem solving to produce significant changes in their lives. Thus, cognitive restructuring strategies have to be used to get them over the cognitive roadblocks that prevent them from using problem solving outside of the meetings. The first step in this process is to teach the children to combine coping skills with problem solving. They are taught to use the coping skills to elevate mood or to overcome pessimism, and then they engage in problem solving when they have more emotional distance and can think more realistically. Subsequently, they use the cognitive restructuring strategies to further reduce the cognitive blocks to using problem solving.

Cognitive Restructuring

Establishing the Rationale for Cognitive Restructuring. In order to effectively restructure a child's distorted thoughts and beliefs, it is necessary to first establish a relationship between negative thoughts and unpleasant mood. A number of procedures are used to establish this relationship. The therapist is alert for opportunities to educate the children about the relationship between their negative thoughts and depressive mood. Whenever a child states how he or she feels, the therapist links it to the thoughts the child had. This procedure of using the child's own experiences to illustrate the link between thoughts and feelings is the most desirable way to build the child's understanding of this relationship. It is necessary to repeatedly do this throughout treatment. Over time, the children begin to create this link for themselves. They notice a change in mood and then begin to monitor their own thinking in an attempt to identify the thoughts that underlie the shift in mood.

Within-session activities are used to supplement the linking of the participants' thoughts to their emotions, and these activities extend the children's understanding of the nature of cognition and its relationship to depression. The activities are designed to be experiential in nature. In other words, they are designed to teach the children through their own within-session experiences. It is important for the children to understand that they construct their thoughts, that their thoughts may not be true, and that they can change them. By the time the participants are beginning to focus on their own negative thoughts and are learning how to evaluate and restructure them so that they are more realistic, they understand that their thoughts affect their emotions. They also understand that their thoughts are constructed, that they may not be true, and that it is desirable to think more positively and realistically because it will help them feel better.

Identifying Negative Thoughts. In order to independently restructure negative thoughts and the beliefs that underlie them, the participants must become aware of their own thoughts. It is easier to recognize when someone else expresses negative thoughts; therefore, we begin by asking the children to do this as a bridge to recognizing and identifying their own. To accomplish this, the therapist and participants discuss how to recognize negative thoughts and then they make a game of catching one another's. Subsequently, they are asked to catch and record their own negative thoughts on homework forms.

Cognitive Restructuring Strategies. A primary objective of the ACTION treatment for depressed children is to change their negatively distorted thinking to more positive and realistic thinking. To accomplish this objective, the therapist must identify the core beliefs that underlie the participant's depressive thoughts and then develop a plan for providing each child with corrective learning experiences to help the child evaluate and change these dysfunctional beliefs. These corrective learning experiences can be completed through verbal discussions or by using a more powerful strategy of giving the children behavioral experiments that help them to have new experiences that contradict the negative belief while supporting new more realistic and positive beliefs.

Negative thoughts are restructured by the therapist throughout treatment as they are identified. Children are introduced to the cognitive restructuring procedure during Meeting 6 so that they can better understand what the therapist is helping them do during the early meetings. During the first nine meetings, the therapist identifies negative thoughts and asks the questions that lead to cognitive restructuring. Consequently, the participants are not required to do a lot of self-reflection outside of the meetings. Cognitive restructuring becomes the focus of later treatment (Meetings 10–20) because it requires the participants to become more self-focused and to focus on negative thoughts that can exacerbate depressive symptoms. Armed with coping and problem-solving skills earlier in treatment, the children can manage the upset that comes with increased self-focus. In addition, the cognitive restructuring that the therapist completes helps to start the shift in thinking, and it serves as a model for how to do it. It also appears as though the improvement in mood and symptoms that results from other treatment components and the therapist-led cognitive restructuring provide the participants with some distance from their depressive thoughts and beliefs that opens them to restructuring their thoughts.

Once a negative thought has been identified, the child asks one of the two "thought detective questions" as a means of evaluating the thought's validity and developing adaptive thoughts to replace the negative one. The two thought detective questions are (1) What's another way to think about it? and (2) What's the evidence? The children learn the question that is best suited for different negative thoughts. "What's another way to think about it?" is used to generate alternative, plausible, and positive thoughts for a distressing situation. So this is a good question to use when the children draw a negative conclusion from a situation from which many other viable conclusions could be drawn. "What's the evidence?" is used when the objective facts do not support the child's negative thought.

Due to developmental differences, the standard cognitive restructuring procedure used with adults and older adolescents is difficult to teach children. A powerful restructuring tool is what the girls in our research groups refer to as "talking back to the muck monster." When the participants are having difficulty changing, or letting go of, negative thinking, the therapist refers to this as being "stuck in the negative muck." When they are stuck in the negative muck, it is the "muck monster" that is filling them with negative thoughts and holding them back from extricating themselves. Blaming depressive thoughts on the muck monster externalizes negative thinking, creates emotional distance between the child and depressive thinking, and creates a concrete opponent to defeat. Talking back to the muck monster is completed as many times as needed between the 10th meeting and termination.

To help the children learn how to independently apply cognitive restructuring, they are asked to talk back to the muck monster using the two thought detective questions. To accomplish this, an extra chair is brought to the group meetings. The chair is for the muck monster. The therapist moves to the empty chair and holds the child's picture of the muck monster while he or she states one of the child's negative thoughts. The child forcefully uses the two thought detective questions to guide talking back to the muck monster. Group members help the child to do this by providing additional evidence or alternative interpretations. The children may be encouraged to very forcefully talk back to the muck monster by yelling at it. Other group members assist and cheer as the child forcefully evaluates negative thoughts and then replaces them with more realistic positive ones. Sometimes it is helpful to have the child play the role of the muck monster and have him or her hold the drawing of the muck monster while verbalizing negative thoughts while the therapist forcefully talks back to the muck monster by using the two thought detective questions. To provide the children with additional help applying cognitive restructuring outside of the meetings, the workbook has forms that guide the process of catching, evaluating, and replacing negative thoughts.

Restructuring negative thoughts is also completed indirectly through guided learning experiences incorporated into treatment. These learning experiences are chosen based on the case conceptualization. Thus, the therapist is watching for opportunities to use the children's own experiences to help them process evidence that contradicts their negative beliefs and supports new, more adaptive beliefs. The therapist also gives the children specific homework assignments that provide them with learning experiences that contradict existing negative beliefs and build new, more adaptive beliefs.

Building a Positive Sense of Self

The primary objective of cognitive restructuring is to help the children build positive core beliefs about the self. During the last eight meetings, additional activities are used to support this positive sense of self. One of the tools used is the "self-map" (see Figure 10.1). Each circle within the figure represents an area of the child's life and an aspect of self-definition. Overall, the self-map helps the children broaden their self-definition and recognize more strengths than they previously acknowledged. Participants are asked to fill in each bubble with relevant strengths. In addi-

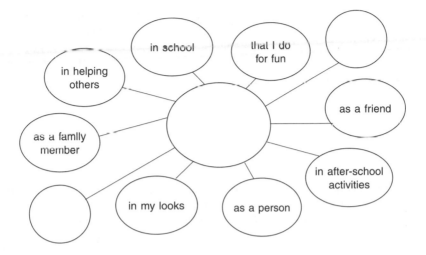

FIGURE 10.1. Example of the self-map.

tion, parents and teachers are interviewed by the therapist to identify their perceptions of the child's strengths in each of the domains. This information is provided to the participants by the therapist. We have found that this information can be very powerful. Group members provide one another with positive feedback for each circle. Once again, receiving this information from peers appears to be very powerful and believable.

CPD is used as children are asked to self-monitor evidence that supports the positive self-description outlined on the self-map. For example, a child may base much of his or her self-worth on musical talent. The child would be instructed to self-monitor personal successes during class, individual instruction, practice, and concerts. In addition, emphasis would be placed on efforts toward becoming a better musician rather than on comparing oneself to others. Furthermore, the personal pleasure derived from playing an instrument would be monitored.

In some instances, the children's negative self-evaluations are accurate and the children can benefit from change. In such instances, the goal of treatment is to help the participants to translate personal standards into realistic goals and then to develop and carry out plans for attaining their goals. Following the translation process, children prioritize the areas where they are working toward self-improvement. Initially, a plan is formulated for producing improvement in an area where success is probable. The long-term goal is broken down into subgoals, and problem solving is used to develop plans that will lead to subgoal and eventually goal attainment. Prior to enacting plans, children try to identify possible impediments to carrying out the plans. Once again, problem solving is used to develop contingency plans for overcoming the impediments. Once the plans, including contingency plans, have been developed, children self-monitor their progress toward change. Alterations to plans are made along the way.

Parent Training

Overview

Parent training (Stark, Simpson, Yancy, & Molnar, 2006a, 2006b, 2007a) is designed to support the child treatment component by teaching parents how to (1) reinforce their child's efforts to apply therapeutic skills and (2) apply the same skills to themselves. Parents are taught a number of skills that are designed to remediate possible disturbances in family functioning. The parent training meetings are completed in groups at their child's school after school hours. Meetings are conducted by the child's therapist, and they last approximately 90 minutes. There are eight group parent meetings and two individual family meetings completed over the 11 weeks that their children are participating in treatment. The individual family meetings occur between the third and fourth group meetings and again between the seventh and eighth group meetings. The children also participate in half of the parent meetings and both individual family meetings. The meetings are structured similarly to the child meetings. However, prior to reviewing the main points from the previous parent meeting, the children provide the parents with a description of the skills they have learned and try to teach the parents how to use them.

Skills Taught to the Parents

Parents are provided with information about depression in children and young adolescents, our model of depressive disorders, and how to successfully treat depression. To create a more positive environment, parents are taught to manage their children's behavior through the use of reinforcement for desirable behavior. At the same time, they are instructed to decrease their use of punitive and coercive strategies. Teaching parents this more positive approach to managing their children's behavior creates a home environment that has a positive affective valence, and it sends the children a positive message about themselves ("I am a good person") and about their parents ("They pay attention to me"). Parents learn about how to effectively use positive reinforcement and learn about the impact of positive reinforcement on their children during the first two meetings, and they apply this technique during meetings when their children are present. They are instructed to monitor their use of reinforcement at home. During the second meeting, the children help their parents develop a reward menu and identify areas where they think they could benefit from some more parental encouragement. In addition, during this meeting, parents experience the power of doing fun things with their children as they play a game together. Parents are encouraged to help their children do more fun things as a coping strategy, and they are encouraged to do more recreational things as a family. During the third meeting, the parents are taught the deleterious effects of excessive use of punishment. They are helped to identify all of the forms of punishment that they use, and they are encouraged to decrease the use of punishment and to replace it with positive reinforcement.

During the same week that the children set their goals for treatment and collaboratively work with the therapist to identify plans for obtaining their goals, the therapist conducts individual family meetings and collaborates with the parents to identify the parents' goals for their children and their families. In addition, with the child's permission, the therapist and child go over his or her goals for treatment and the plans for obtaining the goals. Parents are encouraged to support these goals. Actions that parents can take to help their children achieve goals are discussed.

Parents are taught a variety of communication skills. Initially they are taught empathic listening. This skill is important because it sends the message that the child is being listened to and understood, which leads to a sense of being loved and worthy. In addition, it is a cornerstone of good communication. The children are taught to ask their parents if it is a good time to talk when they are feeling upset or experiencing a problem. Likewise, the parents are taught to initiate a conversation with their children when they sense the children are upset. Once the conversation is initiated, the parent clears his or her mind of distractions and then listens to the child without providing any quick comforts or solutions. The parent listens for the emotion or message that underlies the child's statements. This is very difficult for parents, as they have a hard time just listening and an even harder time identifying the underlying emotions or broader meaning. It takes a good deal of role playing and coaching for the parents to be able to listen empathically. In some cases, it seems like the best that can be done is to teach the parent to become an active listener. Parents are taught the following additional communication skills: (1) Keep it brief, (2) Don't blame, (3) Be specific, (4) Make feeling statements, and (5) Give options if possible. These skills are modeled by the therapists, role-played by the therapists and parents, and practiced during sessions by the parents and their children. The training begins with discussions about easy topics and then progresses to more emotionally laden topics.

Parents are taught the same five-step problem-solving procedure that the children learn. Parents are taught to view misbehavior and problems the family faces as merely problems to be solved. The children teach their parents the steps, and then they play a game with their parents as a procedure for demonstrating the meaning of each step as well as how to apply each step to a simple situation—the game. Once parents have been exposed to the steps and understand the process, the therapist breaks the parents and children into family units and provides them with a hypothetical problem to be solved.

Elevated levels of conflict are commonly reported in families with depressed children (Stark, Humphrey, Crook, & Lewis, 1990) and are related to the duration of time that it takes for a depressive episode to naturally remit. Thus, parents are taught conflict resolution skills. More specifically, they are taught how to structure and use family meetings as a tool for reducing conflict. The families role-play the meeting process with coaching from the therapists. Emphasis is placed on catching the conflict early before the upset gets so bad that it cannot be constructively managed. Over the course of the next few meetings, the therapist works with the parents to eliminate barriers, such as parent beliefs, to resolving conflict.

Parents can play a significant role in helping their children to catch, evaluate, and restructure negative thoughts and beliefs. During the second individual family meeting and during the seventh and eighth group parent meetings, parents learn about the impact of negative thinking on their children's emotional well-being. During the group meetings, parents learn about the impact of negative thoughts and beliefs on their children's emotional functioning, and they are taught to look at the messages that they inadvertently send to their children through their own actions and through the things that they say. During the individual family meeting and while the families are broken up into their own constellations within the larger group meeting, the children describe the impact that their specific negative thoughts have on their emotions, and then the parents help them talk back to the thoughts. Parents are encouraged to identify their own negative thoughts and to restructure them using the same procedures as their children use.

Evidence Base for ACTION

The efficacy of the ACTION treatment program with and without a parent training (PT) component relative to a minimal contact control condition has been evaluated over the preceding 5 years in a study sponsored by the National Institute of Mental Health. Preliminary results with 137 girls indicate that 84% of the girls in the CBT condition and 81% of the girls in the CBT + PT condition compared to 47% in a minimal-contact control condition were no longer experiencing a depressive disorder at posttreatment. These very promising results were achieved with a sample that is similar in severity and rate of comorbidity to that reported in the Treatment for Adolescents with Depression Study (March, 2004). The data for the NIMH study are being entered at this time. Experience suggests that the slightly lower remission rate for the girls in the CBT + PT condition is primarily due to a lower efficacy rate among the girls whose parents did not attend the parent training meetings. The parents' failure to attend the meetings often sent a very negative message—either "You are not important enough for me to attend these meetings" or "I don't love you enough to attend these meetings." Although it also is possible that the parents who did not attend the meetings were more psychologically impaired or the families were more disorganized, due to random assignment across treatment conditions it is not very likely that this could account for the differences. Results also indicate that comorbid anxiety disorders also improved as a result of participating in the active treatments. The long-term maintenance of the treatment has not been determined at this writing. The participants received three booster meetings each semester following treatment to help them to continue to apply the skills to their lives as they develop and face new stressors.

Summary and Conclusions

The ACTION treatment program has proven to be a very effective intervention for depressive disorders among 9- to 14-year-old girls. The primary treatment components include affective education, goal setting, coping skills training, problem-solving training, and cognitive restructuring. The treatment is implemented in 20 group sessions and 2 individual sessions completed over 11 weeks. The parents of the girls also participate in eight group parent training meetings and two individual family meetings conducted over the same 11-week period. Parents lean positive behavior management strategies, family problem-solving skills, conflict resolution skills, communication skills (including empathic listening), and ways to change their behaviors to support their child's core beliefs.

The ACTION child treatment program was delivered in the schools during school hours, and the parent training was completed after school hours in the schools. Although the school was an ideal setting as it eliminated transportation issues and the necessity for parental involvement (at least in the CBT-only condition) and increased attendance, the intervention could not be effectively delivered by typical school personnel. The therapists for the study received extensive training, including a year of general coursework and practicum experiences in CBT, a half of a year in training in the ACTION manual, a half of a year of observing a senior therapist deliver the intervention, a half of a year of co-leading a group with a senior therapist, and finally time leading their own group while receiving intense supervision. Based on listening to supervision tapes, we conclude that the therapists truly became skilled after independently leading their second group. Thus, the level of training may make the intervention difficult to disseminate to the schools, especially to therapists who do not have a background of training experience in CBT. Clearly, it could not be delivered by paraprofessionals. The treatment is being translated into a prevention program that can be used in the classroom and be delivered by school psychologists, school counselors, and teachers.

Discussion

A number of interventions have proven to be efficacious for treating depressed youth. Two cognitive-behavioral interventions including the ACT and ADAPT program and the ACTION program were described here along with IPT-A, a form of interpersonal psychotherapy. It is an exciting point in the development of treatments for depressed youth, as a growing body of research indicates that a number of psychosocial and pharmacological interventions can be used alone and together to effectively treat depression (for a review of the literature, see Stark, Schnoebelen, et al., 2006). The fact that both psychosocial and pharmacological interventions are effective expands the number of youth who are likely to respond to one or the other mode of treatment, and the combination should enable experts to reach even more depressed youngsters. Results of the Treatment for Adolescents with Depression Study indicate that CBT is as effective as Prozac, but the improvements take longer to appear. However, the relapse rate is lower for adolescents who receive CBT (J. F. Curry, personal communication, March 20, 2006).

Although there is room for optimism, a need exists for developing more powerful psychosocial interventions that work in a shorter period of time. It is not clear how this may be accomplished. Perhaps it is possible to increase potency by increasing the number of meetings held each week, by targeting the school and family for change, by developing gender-specific treatments, and by using highly structured and yet flexibly focused interventions. The inclusion of a case conceptualization component that directs treatment also may be helpful. Based on our own experience with the ACTION treatment, it is clear that the training of the therapists is a critical part of the process. Even though a highly structured therapist's manual has been constructed, it may take a good deal of training in basic CBT concepts and the treatment manual itself along with three opportunities to lead a group with a great deal of supervision before therapists are skilled at conducting the intervention. Thus, more effective models for teaching therapists how to implement evidence-based interventions are necessary. The idea that therapists can pick-up a manual and successfully implement it is not valid. Similarly, attending a workshop for a day or two is not going to be adequate training for effectively implementing a manualized treatment. Furthermore, the structure of the manual may be a determining factor in the efficacy of a manualized intervention. If there is too much structure, the intervention becomes psychoeducation instead of psychotherapy. In contrast, too little structure could lead to a great deal of variability in the implementation of the treatment and possibly to a sloppy, invalid implementation. Future research and clinical efforts may identify the necessary and sufficient ingredients for producing an improvement in depression. This could lead to more streamlined and focused treatment programs that are less complicated to administer.

References

Beck, J. (1995). *Cognitive therapy: Basics and beyond.* New York: Guilford Press.

Connor-Smith, J., Polo, A., Jensen Doss, A., & Weisz, J. (2004). *Leader's manual: ACT and ADAPT video-guided PASCET program for prevention and treatment of youth depression.* Los Angeles: University of California.

Kendall, P. C., & Braswell, L. (1993). *Cognitive-behavioral therapy for impulsive children (2nd ed.).* New York: Guilford Press.

March, J. (2004). The Treatment for Adolescents with Depression Study (TADS): Short-term effectiveness and safety outcomes. *Journal of the American Medical Association, 292,* 807–820.

Mufson, L., Dorta, K. P., & Olfson, M. (2004). Effectiveness research: Transporting interpersonal psychotherapy for depressed adolescents (IPT-A) from the lab to school-based health clinics. *Clinical Child and Family Psychology Review, 7,* 251–261.

Mufson, L., Dorta, K. P., Wickramaratne, P., Nomura, Y., Olfson, M., & Weissman, M. M. (2004). A randomized effectiveness trial of interpersonal psychotherapy for depressed adolescents. *Archives of General Psychiatry, 61,* 577–584.

Mufson, L., & Fairbanks, J. (1996). Interpersonal psychotherapy for depressed adolescents: A one-year naturalistic follow-up study. *Journal of the American Academy of Child and Adolescent Psychiatry, 35,* 1145–1155.

Mufson, L., Moreau, D., Dorta, K. P., & Weissman, M. M. (2004). *Interpersonal psychotherapy for depressed adolescents (2nd ed.).* New York: Guilford Press.

Mufson, L., Moreau, D., & Weissman, M. M. (1994). Modification of interpersonal psycho therapy with depressed adolescents (IPT-A): Phase I and II studies. *Journal of the American Academy of Child and Adolescent Psychiatry, 33,* 695–705.

Mufson, L., Moreau, D., Weissman, M. M., & Klerman, G. L. (1993). *Interpersonal psychotherapy for depressed adolescents.* New York: Guilford Press.

Mufson, L., Weissman, M. M., Moreau, D., & Garfinkel, R. (1999). Efficacy of interpersonal psychotherapy for depressed adolescents. *Archives of General Psychiatry, 56,* 573–579.

Polo, A., Connor-Smith, J., Jensen Doss, A., & Weisz, J. (2004). *Youth workbook: ACT and ADAPT video-guided PASCET program for prevention and treatment of youth depression.* Los Angeles: University of California.

Rossello, J., & Bernal, G. (1999). The efficacy of cognitive-behavioral and interpersonal treatments for depression in Puerto Rican adolescents. *Journal of Consulting and Clinical Psychology, 67,* 734–745.

Stark, K. D., Hargrave, J. L., Sander, J., Custer, G., Schnoebelen, S., Simpson, J. P., et al. (2005). Treatment of childhood depression. In P. C. Kendall (Ed.), *Child and adolescent therapy: Cognitive behavioral procedures* (3rd ed., pp. 169–216). New York: Guilford Press.

Stark, K. D., Humphrey, L. L., Crook, K., & Lewis, K. (1990). Perceived family environments of depressed and anxious children: Child's and maternal figure's perspectives. *Journal of Abnormal Child Psychology, 18,* 527–547.

Stark, K. D., Schnoebelen, S., Simpson, J., Hargrave, J., Glenn, R., & Molnar, J. (2007). *Children's Workbook for ACTION.* Broadmore, PA: Workbook Publishing.

Stark, K. D., Simpson, J., Schnoebelen, S., Hargrave, J., Glenn, R., & Molnar, J. (2007). *Therapist's Manual for ACTION.* Broadmore, PA: Workbook Publishing.

Stark, K. D., Simpson, J., Yancy, M., & Molnar, J. (2007a). *Parent training manual for ACTION.* Broadmore, PA: Workbook Publishing.

Stark, K. D., Simpson, J., Yancy, M., & Molnar, J. (2007b). *Workbook for ACTION parent training manual.* Broadmore, PA: Workbook Publishing.

Weisz, J. R., Donenberg, G. R., Han, S. S., & Weiss, B. (1995). Bridging the gap between laboratory and clinic in child and adolescent psychotherapy. *Journal of Consulting and Clinical Psychology, 63,* 688–701.

PART V

COGNITIVE-BEHAVIORAL INTERVENTIONS ADDRESSING OTHER NEEDS

CHAPTER 11

Cognitive-Behavioral Interventions for Attention-Deficit/ Hyperactivity Disorder

GEORGE J. DuPAUL
LAUREN A. ARBOLINO
GENERY D. BOOSTER

Attention-deficit/hyperactivity disorder (ADHD) is a disruptive behavior disorder characterized by developmentally inappropriate levels of inattention and/or hyperactivity–impulsivity that are associated with significant impairment in social, academic, or occupational functioning (American Psychiatric Association, 2000). ADHD typically begins in early childhood and can continue across the life span for many individuals (Barkley, 2006). The disorder affects between 3 and 10% of school-age children in the United States, with a significantly higher prevalence rate in boys (American Psychiatric Association, 2000; Barkley, 2006). Given these prevalence figures, it is likely that there is at least one child with ADHD in every classroom.

The behavioral symptoms of ADHD include nine inattention (e.g., failing to give close attention to details, difficulty sustaining attention to task or play activities) and nine hyperactivity–impulsivity (e.g., fidgeting with hands or feet, blurting out answers before questions have been completed) symptoms (American Psychiatric Association, 2000). In order

295

for the diagnosis of ADHD to be made, at least six inattention and/or hyperactivity–impulsivity symptoms need to be present at a significantly higher frequency than in others of the same age and sex. Furthermore, symptoms must be chronic (i.e., occur for at least 6 months), begin before the age of 7 years old, and be associated with social and/or academic impairment across at least two settings (American Psychiatric Association, 2000). Thus, this diagnosis is specific to those students who are extremely inattentive and/or hyperactive–impulsive and, as a result, are experiencing significant difficulties in one or more major life activities.

Because ADHD is identified based on high levels of inattention and/or hyperactivity–impulsivity, students with this disorder typically experience difficulties with behavior control in classroom settings. Specifically, students with ADHD exhibit significantly higher rates of off-task behavior relative to their non-ADHD classmates (e.g., Abikoff et al., 2002; Vile Junod, DuPaul, Jitendra, Volpe, & Cleary, 2006). Hyperactive–impulsive symptoms are associated with disruptive behaviors in the classroom and other school environments, including talking without permission, leaving the assigned area, bothering other students, and interrupting teacher instruction. Rates of on-task behavior are particularly low when passive classroom activities (e.g., listening to teacher instruction and reading silently) are required (Vile Junod et al., 2006). Furthermore, between 45 and 84% of children with ADHD are diagnosed with oppositional defiant disorder (ODD), and students with ODD may frequently disobey teacher commands and overtly defy school rules (Barkley, 2006). The combination of ADHD and disruptive behavior often interferes with learning and classroom activities for students with ADHD and their classmates.

Not surprisingly, ADHD frequently is associated with deficits in academic skills and/or performance. In fact, students with ADHD score between 10 and 30 points lower than their classmates on norm-referenced, standardized achievement tests (e.g., Barkley, DuPaul, & McMurray, 1990; Brock & Knapp, 1996; Fischer, Barkley, Fletcher, & Smallish, 1990). Academic skills difficulties are particularly severe for the 20 to 30% of students with ADHD who also have a specific learning disability in reading, math, or writing (DuPaul & Stoner, 2003; Semrud-Clikeman et al., 1992). Core ADHD symptoms have been found to be significant predictors of concurrent and future academic difficulties (e.g., performance on achievement tests, report card grades, and teacher ratings of educational functioning). The relationship between ADHD symptoms and achievement outcomes is evident for both referred (DuPaul et al., 2004) and nonreferred (Fergusson & Horwood, 1995) samples. As a result, students with ADHD are at higher risk for grade retention, placement in special education classrooms, and dropping out of high school (e.g., Fischer et al., 1990). Fewer students with ADHD go on to postsecondary education relative to similarly achieving non-ADHD classmates (Mannuzza, Gittelman-Klein, Bessler, Malloy, & LaPadula, 1993).

Although most students with ADHD are placed in general education classrooms, they are at higher than average risk of being identified for special education services (Barkley, 2006). Of those children with ADHD receiving special education services, most are identified with specific learning disabilities (41%) and speech/language impairments (15%; U.S. Department of Education, 2005). In addition, students with ADHD make up a significant percentage of children identified with a variety of educational disabilities, including other health impairment (65.8%), emotional disturbance (57.9%), mental retardation (20.6%), learning disabilities (20.2%), and speech/language impairment (4.5%; Schnoes, Reid, Wagner, & Marder, 2006). Thus, ADHD may be associated with one or more educational difficulties that further compromise school functioning and may require specialized intervention services.

Given the myriad difficulties that students with ADHD are likely to experience in classroom settings, the implementation of evidence-based interventions is imperative. The purpose of this chapter is to review research examining the effectiveness of school-based, cognitive-behavioral interventions (CBIs) for children and adolescents with ADHD. First, a brief overview of a recent theoretical conceptualization of ADHD is provided. Understanding the core impairment underlying ADHD symptoms is critical for establishing a theoretical basis for effective treatment design. Second, a brief overview of major treatment strategies for this disorder (i.e., psychotropic medication and behavior modification) is provided. Next, two primary approaches to CBIs are described, including cognitive-behavior modification (CBM) and self-regulation. The results of empirical studies assessing the efficacy of these two approaches are summarized. Finally, recommendations are provided regarding the use of CBIs for treating ADHD as are directions for future research in this area.

ADHD as a Disorder of Impaired Delayed Responding

The crucial role that the interaction of within-child, biological factors and environmental events play in determining the severity of ADHD symptoms has led to recent changes in the conceptualization of the deficits underlying this disorder. Specifically, the core feature of ADHD may be an impairment in delayed responding to the environment (i.e., behavioral inhibition) rather than a deficit in attention per se (Barkley, 1997a, 1997b, 2006). Many important settings (e.g., classroom) and abilities (e.g., internalization of speech) require the capacity to delay responding to the environment. Thus, deficits in delayed responding lead to the exhibition of ADHD symptoms in multiple settings and deleteriously affect the development of rule-governed behavior.

Barkley (1997a, 1997b, 2006) has articulated a theoretical model of ADHD as a disorder of behavioral inhibition. Children's inability to inhibit and delay their responses to the environment compromises the development of four critical executive functions. The latter include working memory, self-regulation of affect, motivation, and arousal, internalization of speech, and behavioral analysis/synthesis. Impairments in the development of these executive functions consequently lead to numerous difficulties in cognitive, academic, and social functioning. This theoretical model makes intuitive sense and is consistent with the extant literature on this disorder (for a review, see Barkley, 1997a, 1997b, 2006). Nevertheless, investigations using this theoretical model a priori to formulate hypotheses are just beginning to emerge in the literature. Thus, the full value of this theory for explaining ADHD and formulating intervention strategies awaits further empirical scrutiny.

Despite the need for more research, the implications of this conceptualization of ADHD are clear. Interventions for this disorder must include changes in within-child variables (e.g., temporary change in brain functioning through stimulant medication) and/or changes in antecedent and consequent stimuli to increase the probability of delayed responding, thereby leading to attentive, productive behavior (Barkley, 1997a, 1997b). Unfortunately, most classrooms are structured in a manner that provides delayed, infrequent reinforcement under the assumption that students become "internally motivated" to comply with rules and complete academic tasks. These are precisely the conditions most likely to lead to inattentive, disruptive behaviors (i.e., impaired response inhibition) in children with ADHD. Thus, the challenge to education professionals is to incorporate environmental stimuli known to enhance student success into all classrooms where impulsive, inattentive students are being taught. Stated differently, treatment must be applied at "the point of performance" to directly influence impaired delayed responding (Barkley, 2006; Ingersoll & Goldstein, 1993). CBIs, especially those that provide environmental stimuli that elicit and maintain self-regulation, may be consistent with this theoretical formulation.

Treatment of ADHD

The two most effective treatments for children and adolescents with ADHD include psychotropic medication, especially stimulants, and behavior modification strategies implemented in home and school settings (Barkley, 2006; DuPaul & Stoner, 2003). Dozens of research studies conducted over the past several decades have documented the efficacy of these two treatment modalities in reducing ADHD symptoms (for a review, see Barkley, 2006). Psychostimulants and behavior modification also appear to enhance academic and social functioning, although these effects are not as strong as those found for reduction of core symptoms. Data from several large studies indicate that the combination of these two treatments is superior to either approach in isolation, particularly for students with comorbid disorders and especially when effects on functional impairments are considered (Conners et al., 2001; Jensen et al., 2001).

The single most effective treatment for the *reduction of ADHD symptoms* is carefully titrated, stimulant medication (MTA Cooperative Group, 1999, 2004). This class of medication includes methylphenidate (i.e., Ritalin, Concerta, and Metadate), dextroamphetamine (Dexedrine), and mixed amphetamine compounds (Adderall). Stimulants reduce inattentive and impulsive behavior as well as enhance task engagement and rule compliance in the majority of children and adolescents with ADHD receiving this treatment (for a review, see Connor, 2006a). Other medications, such as atomoxetine (Strattera) or clonidine (Catapres), may be used for those children who do not respond to stimulants or experience significant adverse side effects (e.g., insomnia and appetite reduction; Connor, 2006b).

Behavior modification strategies are effective in reducing ADHD symptoms and enhancing academic and social functioning of children with ADHD (Pelham et al., 2005). Behavioral approaches for this population have included the manipulation of antecedent and/or consequent events in order to increase adaptive behaviors or reduce inappropriate actions (DuPaul & Stoner, 2003). Antecedent-based approaches, such as providing task-related choices (e.g., Dunlap et al., 1994), are proactive and focused on reducing the probability of disruptive, off-task behavior before it occurs. Consequent-based approaches, such as response cost (e.g., Rapport, Murphy, & Bailey, 1982), are reactive and involve the addition or removal of reinforcing events following a specific target behavior. A balanced behavioral treatment plan that includes both proactive and reactive procedures has been advocated for use in both home (Barkley, 1997c) and school (DuPaul & Stoner, 2003) settings. Furthermore, behavioral interventions can directly address the putative core deficit underlying ADHD (i.e., impaired delayed responding) at the point of performance.

Given the academic and social difficulties experienced by most students with ADHD, interventions that directly address each functioning area also have been investigated. Academic interventions (e.g., peer tutoring, direct instruction, and computer-assisted instruction) may improve both achievement and on-task behavior in children with ADHD (DuPaul & Eckert, 1997; DuPaul et al., 2006). In similar fashion, social relationship interventions have been implemented in school settings to enhance the peer interactions and friendship-building skills of students with this disorder (e.g., Sheridan, Dee, Morgan, McCormick, & Walker, 1996). Ultimately, some combination of psychotropic medication, behavior modification, academic intervention, and social relationship training will be necessary to address the needs of most children with ADHD. Furthermore, given that ADHD typically is chronic, treatment strategies must be implemented over a long time period (i.e., across school years) to optimize long-term outcome.

Overview of CBIs

ADHD is essentially a disorder of self-control in that the core deficit appears to be impaired delayed responding to the environment (Barkley, 1997a, 1997b). Specifically, as a consequence of deficits in behavioral inhibition, individuals with this disorder are theorized to experience difficulties with four critical executive functions including nonverbal working memory; verbal working memory; self-regulation of affect, motivation, and arousal; and behavioral analysis/synthesis (Barkley, 1997a, 1997b). Given these putative underlying deficits, it is not surprising that various CBIs have been proposed as ideal strategies to enhance self-control, either in lieu of existing treatments (e.g., stimulants) or as an adjunctive treatment approach.

CBIs that have been investigated in the treatment of ADHD can be divided into two distinct approaches. Early research in this area emphasized the use of cognitively based CBM strategies. Specifically, this approach involves training students to engage in various cognitive strategies (e.g., "Stop, look, and listen"), particularly in task situations. Alternatively, more recent studies have examined the use of self-regulation strategies. In this approach, students are taught to monitor, evaluate, and/or reinforce their own behavior. External contingencies often are used to elicit and maintain self-regulated behaviors. The results of studies examining the outcomes of both CBI approaches are summarized in the next two sections.

CBM

In general, CBM approaches to mitigating symptoms of children with ADHD involve integration of cognitive problem-solving strategies with reinforcement. These interventions may include, but are not limited to, interpersonal skills training; counseling; modeling; manipulation of reinforcement schedules and types; and student, teacher, or parent training in behavioral modification. From a behavioral perspective, these interventions include both antecedent-based (i.e., proactive) and consequent-based (i.e., reactive) components. Typically, strategies focus on disruptive behavior alone; however, academic functioning may also be targeted. Often, interventions are used together and a multicomponent program will be created. Many of the studies examining CBM for students with ADHD used a combination of strategies to address desired target outcomes.

Two meta-analyses have been conducted to examine school-based interventions for students with behavior problems. These meta-analyses demonstrate the effectiveness of specific types of interventions for behaviors symptomatic of children diagnosed with ADHD. Stage and Quiroz (1997) examined 99 studies that utilized interventions in an effort to decrease disruptive behavior in the classroom. Interventions included in these studies were group contingencies, time out, differential reinforcement, anger control programs, problem solving, counseling, and parent training. Results indicated that behavioral interventions were more effective than CBM strategies. Disruptive behavior was reduced for 78% of the participants on average, compared with control groups. Additionally, students in more restrictive environments (i.e., self-contained classes) showed a greater decrease in disruptive behaviors.

Another applicable meta-analysis examined the effects of school-based interventions for students with ADHD (DuPaul & Eckert, 1997). The authors analyzed 63 studies that examined the effects of contingency management and CBIs; only a few studies included control groups or random assignment of participants to treatment groups. Effect sizes were larger in studies involving academic and contingency management interventions compared with CBIs. Also, students receiving special education services demonstrated greater behavioral effects than those in general education.

These meta-analyses reveal the effectiveness of behavioral and academic interventions alone as well as the success of combined interventions. When examined in isolation, it is clear that studies have demonstrated some success with CBM for students with ADHD or hyperactive behavior. In order to examine CBM effects more closely, a comprehensive literature search was conducted to identify treatment outcome studies conducted between 1971 and 2006 that were published in peer-reviewed journals. A total of 10 studies were found (see Table 11.1). The results of these investigations are summarized below.

Evans, Axelrod, and Langberg (2004) investigated the effects of

TABLE 11.1. Studies Examining Cognitive-Behavior Modification for Students with Attention-Deficit/Hyperactivity Disorder (ADHD)

Authors (Year)	Design	Dependent variable	Intervention	No. and age of participants	Control group	Outcome
Evans et al. (2004)	Small N; pilot data	• Change in ADHD symptoms (ADHD Rating Scale) • Functioning (Children's Impairment Scale) • Academic performance (grades)	• Challenging Horizons Program (behavioral and educational school-based treatment research program) • At least 3 months in study • 2 hours 3 times per week • Individual meeting with counselor, group therapy (interpersonal skills training), recreation activities, education, family intervention	7 middle school students (grades 6–8) diagnosed with ADHD	No	• Effect sizes for ADHD symptoms, social functioning, and grades were moderate to high. • Effect of the program was greatest on disruptive behavior and academic performance. • One-third of score moved from impaired range to healthy range on ADHD Rating Scale.
Cameron & Robinson (1980)	Small N; multiple baseline across children	• Improve math accuracy • Improve on-task behavior • Self-correction in reading	• Self-instructional skills • Visual–perceptual tasks into academic activities	3 boys, ages 7–8	No	• Significant improvements for math were found across all subjects. • Two thirds demonstrated improvements in off-task behavior. • Improvements were seen on math, reading, and on-task behavior. • Generalization behaviors also noted.

Study	Design	Measures	Intervention	Sample		Results
Woltersdorf (1992)	Small N; multiple baseline across children	• Fidgeting (no. of intervals) • Distractibility (no. of intervals) • Vocalizations (no. of intervals) • Math performance (no. of accurate) • Teacher rating scale IOWA, Conners • WRAT	• Videotape self-modeling • During baseline, child filmed on fifth day • Three phases follow baseline: intervention (daily treatment), maintenance (weekly treatment), and follow-up (no treatment)	4 boys, ages 9–10, diagnosed with ADHD		• Videotape self-modeling effective for reducing behavioral symptoms and increasing math productivity.
Brown et al. (1986)	Group	• WISC • MFFT • CT • WRAT • Parent and Teacher Conners	• Cognitive-behavioral self-control training • Attention control training • Methylphenidate therapy	28 boys and 5 girls, ages 5–13	Yes	• No significant differences pre- to post- on any of the domains: academic, behavioral at home or school. • Slight improvement on impulsivity, but this was not persistent over time.
Meichenbaum & Goodman (1971)	Group	• Porteus Maze test • Kagan's MFF impulsivity test • WISC	• Cognitive training (four half-hour treatments over 2 weeks)	15 children, ages 7–9	Yes	• Impulsive behavior mitigated. • Errors on academic performance lessened but not significantly. • Children seemed to approach cognitive tasks differently.

(continued)

TABLE 11.1. Studies Examining Cognitive-Behavior Modification for Students with Attention-Deficit/Hyperactivity Disorder (ADHD)

Authors (Year)	Design	Dependent variable	Intervention	No. and age of participants	Control group	Outcome
Bloomquist et al. (1991)	Group multicomponent and teacher only	• Structured behavioral observations • Conners Teacher Rating scale • Self-Control Rating Scale • Piers–Harris Self-Concept scale • Teacher Report, Walker–McConnell Scale of Social Competence and School Adjustment	• Child, teacher, and parent cognitive-behavioral therapy • Child groups met for two 1-hour sessions each week for 10 weeks • Teacher groups met for one 2-hour in-service and six consultation sessions over 10 weeks • Parent groups met for seven 90-minute sessions	36 boys and 16 girls in elementary school	Yes (wait-list control)	• No differences among all three groups on any of the areas. • Multicomponent group had greater reduction in off-task/disruptive behavior, but no difference among groups at follow-up.
Miranda et al. (2002)	Group	• Neuropsychological tasks • Behavioral rating scales for parents and teachers • Direct observation in class • Academic records	• 29 teachers (of the 50 students) trained in behavior modification techniques, cognitive-behavioral strategies, and instructional management strategies	50 students with ADHD	Yes (N = 21)	• Rating scales indicated improvements in inattention, disorganization, and hyperactivity. • Rating scales indicated improvement in behavioral difficulties: antisocial behavior, psychopathological disorders, and anxiety. • Increased academic scores. • Improved teacher knowledge.
Hinshaw et al. (1984)	Group	• Amount of appropriate and inappropriate social interactions • Ability to utilize anger management strategies	• Match Game • Modeling and reinforcement • Anger management strategies	24 boys, ages 8–13	No	• Increased appropriate social interactions. • Decreased amount of inappropriate social interactions.

Study	Design	Dependent measures	Intervention	Participants	Control	Results
Hinshaw & Melnick (1992)	Case study	• Observation of effective anger management strategy	• Training in anger management strategy through Match Game	1, age 9, African American boy with ADHD; 1, age 10, Caucasian boy with ADHD	No	• Both cases showed effective and consistent use of the self-control strategies and calming down. • Both were able to become angry and noncompliant if the setting/provocation was specific; both used self-management strategies in new settings.
Paniagua (1987)	Small N; multiple baseline across subjects	• Off-task behaviors • Overactivity/hyperactivity • Verbal behavior	• Correspondence training • Reinforcement contingent on reports of hyperactivity prior to activity occurring	3 children, ages 7, 9, and 10, all with ADHD; also 1 CD, 1 anxiety disorder, 1 PTSD	No	• Efforts were maintained at follow-up. • Generalized to other settings. • Teacher ratings reduced (not statistically analyzed).
Stage & Quiroz (1997)	Meta-analysis	• Variety including CBA, rating scales, achievement tests, observation	• Variety including contingencies, time out, anger management, DRO, counseling, parent training	Variety including elementary and middle school; ranging from small n to group	Control, wait-list control, and none	• Variety including no improvement, little improvement, or improvement in specific or isolated areas
DuPaul & Eckert (1997)	Meta-analysis	• Variety including CBA, rating scales, achievement tests, observation	• Variety including contingencies, time out, anger management, DRO, counseling, parent training	Variety including elementary and middle school; ranging from small n to group	Control, wait-list control, and none	• Variety including no improvement, little improvement, or improvement in specific or isolated areas.

Note. CBA, curriculum-based assessment; CCT, children's checking task; CD, conduct disorder; Conners, Conners Rating Scale; DRO, differential reinforcement of other behavior; IOWA, Iowa Conners Rating Scale; MFF, Matching Familiar Figures Test; PTSD, posttraumatic stress disorder; WISC, Wechsler Intelligence Scale for Children; WRAT, Wide Range Achievement Test.

combined antecedent-based interventions for 7 middle school students with a medical diagnosis of ADHD. Intervention was for 2 hours, 3 days a week. First, participants were assigned to and met with counselors. The counselor and student were responsible for identifying and prioritizing goals (e.g., accurate completion of homework assignments, answering questions appropriately), monitoring those goals, and modifying when necessary. Following the meeting with the counselors, interpersonal skills training was conducted to increase knowledge and use of appropriate social interactions. Recreational time was a component used to allow students to practice skills learned. Educational intervention comprised time to practice recording assignments, developing written language skills, and creating effective systems for organizing school materials. Finally, family involvement included group parent training (e.g., homework management, supporting positive peer relations) and individual family counseling. Dependent measures included school grades as well as adult ratings of ADHD symptoms and related behaviors. The greatest improvement for the students was demonstrated in academic functioning and disruptive behavior. Additionally, some of the participants moved into the normal range for ADHD symptom ratings. It should be noted that this study did not employ a control group and used a small sample size. Additionally, the intervention utilized was described as labor intensive. For these effects, a labor-intensive intervention on a small sample needs to be replicated on a larger group. Finally, the specific effects of CBM components in this comprehensive treatment package are impossible to determine.

Modeling has also been examined as an antecedent-based strategy and has been used in a variety of ways in an effort to address students' aggressive, hyperactive, and off-task behaviors. Hinshaw, Henker, and Whalen (1984) were interested in analyzing the possible reduction of negative social interactions by training students to engage in positive behaviors through modeling and reinforcement. Hinshaw and colleagues examined 24 hyperactive boys between the ages of 8 and 13. Boys were separated into two groups (older and younger) and trained daily in cognitive-behavioral self-control skills. The Match Game was utilized for training. The procedure dictated that trainers model appropriate behavior (e.g., paying attention) and then have the student engage in the same behavior. Additionally, the student would rate his own ability to engage in the behavior and then compare (i.e., "match") the score with the trainer's score. The student was then provided with reinforcement contingent on successful modeling and matching. Finally, students were placed in peer provocation situations to test their ability to utilize the anger control strategies that they had learned. Results showed improvements in reducing negative social interactions and increasing appropriate interactions for both age groups. Because this intervention included both CBM and reinforcement components, it is difficult to discern the specific effects of each treatment. Furthermore, the generalizability of these results is limited. The program took place during one summer, and the 24 participants returned to 23 different schools. Long-term maintenance was not demonstrated.

In a later study, Hinshaw and Melnick (1992) examined the case studies of two elementary-age hyperactive boys. Both participants engaged in the Match Game and received training in anger management, as in the earlier study. Both boys demonstrated success utilizing skills learned by tempering their anger and displaying control in intentionally provocative situations. Although both Hinshaw studies examined social interaction, the extent to which these interventions impacted achievement or behavior at home or in the class is questionable. Additionally, results from the case studies suggest that further research with a control group is needed to generalize any findings.

Several studies have examined benefits to directly teaching cognitive strategies to teachers or students. Miranda, Presentacion, and Soriano (2002) examined a multistrategy intervention carried out by teachers. Neuropsychological tasks, behavior rating scales, academic records, and direct observation data were used to determine efficacy of the treatment. A sample of 50 children who met research criteria for ADHD and 29 teachers participated. Teachers were trained in the use of behavior modification techniques, CBM, and instructional management strategies. As compared with the control group, the participants demonstrated improvements in ADHD primary symptoms (i.e., inattention, disorganization, hyperactivity, and impulsivity) and in behavioral difficulties (e.g., antisocial behavior, anxiety). Additionally, academic scores increased and behavioral observations improved. As the case for other studies in this area, the specific effects of the CBM components of the treatment package are unclear. Furthermore, participants were not clinically referred, and so the extent to which the same results would be found with a clinically diagnosed ADHD population is unclear. Additionally, effects on participants were not demonstrated over time.

Paniagua (1987) examined providing students with correspondence training. *Correspondence* is generally explained as the relationship between what people say they will do and what they do, or between what they do and then what they say they have done. Essentially, it is the relationship between nonverbal and verbal behavior. Correspondence training attempts to teach children truthful behavior related to this relationship. In this study, three boys between the ages of 7 and 10 with a medical diagnosis of ADHD received correspondence training that decreased hyperactivity as compared with baseline. Despite some of the effects noted, this study used a small number of participants in a highly controlled setting. These effects cannot be generalized to other settings. Also, the effects of the treatment were examined for a brief period of time. The extent to which any results would maintain is unclear. Finally, a comparison of correspondence training with medication and behavioral techniques is needed to comprehensively examine the effectiveness of these approaches.

Two additional studies examined training students in CBM strategies. Cameron and Robinson (1980) and Woltersdorf (1992) both demonstrated behavior and academic gains in their participants. Cameron et al. examined three elementary-age hyperactive boys in an effort to improve classroom behavior and math skills. Participants were taught to problem solve and to reinforce themselves when engaging in an appropriate task or providing a correct answer. An experimenter worked individually with each student to teach these skills, reinforce skills learned, and provide prompts when needed. Two of the three subjects demonstrated improvements in off-task behavior. Math improvement was found for all three subjects. Although the training focused on math skills, generalization of these behaviors was found for reading performance.

Woltersdorf (1992) used videotapes for training student participants to decrease disruptive behavior and increase math productivity. Four 9- to 10-year-old boys who met research criteria for ADHD were identified by teachers as engaging in disruptive behavior. Experimenters videotaped the participants and then edited out disruptive behaviors (fidgeting, vocalizations, and distractibility). After viewing their own videos, students were sent back to class. This procedure was repeated. Over 5 months time, students' disruptive behavior decreased and math productivity increased. This study did not control for therapist attention or nonspecific effects of this intervention.

Three other studies over the past 3 decades specifically examined cognitive-behavioral therapy training. In the seminal study in this area, Meichenbaum and Goodman (1971) looked at the efficacy of a self-instructional cognitive training in reducing impulsivity in schoolchildren. Fifteen second-grade students were divided among three groups. The cognitive training groups received four 30-minute treatment sessions over a 2-week period. The cognitive training procedure consisted of the experimenter performing a task and talking aloud while the student observed. The student then performed the task as instructed by the experimenter; the student then performed the task alone while talking aloud; then the student performed the task while whispering. Finally, the student performed the task alone with no speaking or whispering. Amount of error in performance was an outcome examined in this study.

Laboratory tests of planning, impulse control, and cognitive ability were utilized. Results indicated that the cognitive self-guidance training possibly encouraged students to approach tasks more deliberately and with fewer errors. However, the reduction of performance errors was not statistically significant. Furthermore, generalization of these results to actual performance on school tasks was not demonstrated.

Brown and colleagues (1986) also examined the effects of a cognitive training therapy with or without stimulant medication. The students were divided among four groups: (1) methylphenidate/attention control, (2) cognitive therapy/placebo, (3) methylphenidate/cognitive therapy and (4) attention control/placebo. A total of 28 boys and 5 girls ranging in age from 5 to 13 who met research criteria for ADHD were included in the study. Participants were assessed prior to treatment, 1 week following treatment, and 3 months following termination of treatment. Outcome measures included laboratory tests of impulse control and behavior ratings completed by parents and teachers. Cognitive-behavioral self-control training was individual and included 1 hour sessions twice a week for 22 weeks over 3 months. The goals of the training were to teach children to cope more effectively and independently with cognitive problems and to develop a systematic approach to problem solving. Attention control training was similar to the cognitive-behavioral therapy but excluded the problem-solving strategies. No significant academic or behavioral improvements occurred over the 22-week treatment. There were slight improvements on impulse control for the treatment group receiving cognitive-behavioral therapy; however, these effects did not maintain over time. There were also no differences prepost for either of the methylphenidate groups. Findings suggest that there is minimal support for this type of training in reducing impulsivity or in improving attention, achievement, or behavior.

Bloomquist, August, and Ostrander (1991) found similar results to Brown et al. (1986) in their cognitive-behavior training study of 52 students who met research criteria for ADHD. Students were divided among three groups: (1) mutlicomponent, (2) teacher only, and (3) wait-list control. The child, teacher, and parent each had a training component. The child training included two 1-hour sessions each week for 10 weeks. The participants were trained to identify a problem, generate possible solutions, think of consequences for those solutions, anticipate obstacles, and then choose specific behaviors to solve the problem. Behavioral principles were utilized and homework was given for the purposes of practicing skills. Teacher training consisted of one 2-hour inservice and six 45- to 60-minute consultations over a 10-week period. No distinction was made between the teacher-only group and the teacher component of the multicomponent group. Teachers were trained in cognitive restructuring strategies and problem-solving exercises to use in an effort to teach their students. The parent component included seven 90-minute sessions. Parents received information on ADHD and cognitive-behavioral strategies. Outcome measures included structured behavioral observations as well as behavior ratings of ADHD symptoms and social behavior. No differences were found among groups on any of the measures at follow-up. The only significant result was a decrease in observed off-task/disruptive behavior for the multicomponent group; however, this finding was not confirmed by teacher ratings.

Some of the studies reviewed for CBM demonstrated slight results in specific areas. However, these studies have not been replicated and did not all show strong methodological design. Additionally, some of the studies with control groups and multiple intervention groups across a variety of outcomes were not able to show specific effects for cognitive training in reducing attention problems or improving academic and behavioral concerns. The lack of effects is not surprising, because traditional CBM approaches do not involve modifying environments at the point of performance as is indicated by viewing ADHD as a disorder of impaired delayed responding (Barkley, 2006).

Self-Regulation Interventions

Self-regulation interventions teach students to monitor, evaluate, and/or reinforce their own behavior and can include a number of different procedures. Self-monitoring, for example, requires students to observe and self-record a particular dimension of their own behavior, such as the occurrence or nonoccurrence of attention to task. Similarly, self-evaluation or self-management requires students to observe their own behaviors but includes a component in which they must rate their behavior according to a predetermined criterion. External contingencies often are used in conjunction with self-regulation procedures to elicit and maintain self-regulated behaviors. In addition to external reinforcement, the students themselves can self-administer reinforcers when they determine they have reached the predetermined criterion.

A recent meta-analysis conducted by Reid, Trout, and Schartz (2005) examined the effectiveness of self-monitoring, self-monitoring plus reinforcement, self-reinforcement, and self-management for the problematic behaviors of students who met research criteria for ADHD. Overall, the 16 included studies showed strong results, with effect sizes ranging from 1.76 to 1.88 for inappropriate/disruptive behaviors and from 1.26 to 2.96 for on-task behavior. Although the small number of participants in the studies limits generalization, this meta-analysis provides preliminary evidence that self-regulation interventions can be used effectively to reduce inappropriate or disruptive behaviors and to increase the on task behaviors of children with symptoms of ADHD.

A comprehensive literature search was undertaken to identify self-regulation outcome studies (1) including students who either met research criteria for ADHD or had a medical diagnosis of ADHD and (2) that were published between 1980 and 2006 in peer-reviewed journals. A total of 14 investigations are included in this review (see Table 11.2).

Several studies have demonstrated the effectiveness of self-monitoring for the problem behaviors of students with ADHD. An early study by Christie, Hiss, and Lozanoff (1984), for example, used self-monitoring procedures to reduce inattentive and inappropriate behaviors and increase attention to task for two fourth-grade and one third-grade boys within a general education classroom. All students had exhibited attention problems since the first grade and received teacher ratings of ADHD-related behaviors that were at least 1.96 standard deviations above the norm. No students, however, were taking medication. The students were taught a complex observational code assessing inattention, out-of-seat behavior, off-task behaviors, aggression, emotional outbursts, disruptive noises, attention soliciting, talking, and on-task behaviors during six 1-hour training sessions. Students were given a verbal or nonverbal signal to self-record their behaviors on a sheet that was left on their desks for teacher checking. Results revealed reductions in inattentive and inappropriate behaviors as well as increases in on-task behavior.

The naturalistic setting and high levels of interobserver agreement lend credence to the assertion that self-monitoring can be an effective intervention for students who meet research criteria for ADHD within a classroom setting. The complex coding system and intensive training required, however, may not be feasible for all students, especially without external supports. In addition, a reversal design was used with only one subject, and therefore a functional relationship between the independent and dependent variables was not completely demonstrated. Furthermore, the intervention was not faded over time, and generalization was not established.

In contrast to the complex system employed by Christie and colleagues (1984), Mathes and Bender (1997) employed a simple intervention in which three 8- to 11-year-old boys with a medical diagnosis of ADHD self-monitored their on-task behaviors by checking "yes" or "no" when a tone was played. Training required a single 15-minute session on the first day of intervention, which was conducted within a special education resource classroom. In addition, a fading procedure in which students were told to self-monitor "whenever they thought about it" was implemented after 10 days of intervention. Results showed that, for all students, levels of on-task behaviors increased from baseline to intervention, decreased during a return to baseline, and then returned to high levels when the intervention was reintroduced. Importantly, the increases in on-task behaviors were maintained during fading periods.

Mathes and Bender's (1997) use of a multiple-baseline reversal design provides clear evidence of a functional relationship between self-monitoring and an increase in on-task behavior. In addition, the authors provided evidence for social validity, as all three subjects reported that they felt the intervention was helpful. The first author (Mathes), however, served as the primary observer, which could have biased outcomes. In addition, the study was conducted in a restrictive setting and therefore the results may not generalize to a general education setting.

In addition to student behaviors, self-monitoring has been used to address academic performance. Shimabukuro, Prater, Jenkins, and Edelen-Smith (1999), for example, taught three sixth- and seventh-grade boys with a medical diagnosis of ADHD to self-monitor their academic productivity and accuracy using a multiple-baseline design across math, reading, and writing activities. The intervention required students to self-correct their own assignments, compute their accuracy, and record the results on a graph. In addition, students monitored their productivity by comparing the number of items completed with the number of items assigned. Although all students showed improvement during the intervention, gains in productivity were greater than those for accuracy. In addition, all students showed improvement in levels of on-task behavior. In general, students showed the most improvement in math, whereas the least improvement was found in writing. Importantly, the teacher indicated that she liked the intervention and felt that it was useful.

The results from Shimabukuro et al. (1999) provide further evidence that self-monitoring procedures can be used effectively in schools; however, the study was conducted in a self-contained classroom and thus results may not generalize to general education settings. In addition, the intervention was implemented by the same individual who served as the observer of on-task behavior, which could have led to bias and experimenter effects. Similarly, data regarding academic productivity and accuracy were collected by the students themselves with undocumented levels of accuracy.

Although the studies discussed thus far indicate that self-monitoring may improve on-task behaviors as well as academic productivity and accuracy, it is unclear which intervention is the most beneficial. This question was partially addressed by Harris, Friedlander, Saddler, Frizzelle, and Graham (2005), who compared the effectiveness of self-monitoring of attention (SMA) to self-monitoring of academic performance (SMP) in addressing the off-task behaviors and academic accuracy of six third- to

TABLE 11.2. Studies Examining Self-Regulation Interventions for Students with Attention-Deficit/Hyperactivity Disorder (ADHD)

Authors (Year)	Design	Setting	Dependent variable	Intervention	No. and age of participants	Outcome
Ajibola & Clement (1995)	Single subject: modified Latin square design, baseline followed by six counterbalanced treatments	Laboratory-based tutoring class	Inattention, impulsivity, hyperactivity, academic accuracy, and productivity	Self-reinforcement vs. high and low dosages of a psychostimulant	3 African American, 1 Hispanic, and 2 white boys, ages 9–12	In general, stimulants plus self-reinforcement had a greater effect on academic performance than either of the treatments alone, however medication had no effect on inattention or academic productivity.
Bowers et al. (1985)	Single subject: counterbalanced reversal design	Resource classroom	Attention to task and reading comprehension accuracy	Teacher-administered reinforcement vs. self-administered reinforcement plus self-monitoring of attention (SMR)	6 8- to 11-year-old boys diagnosed with a specific learning disability (including attention deficits)	Amount of sustained attention and comprehension accuracy increased for both interventions, slightly higher for SMR.
Chase & Clement (1985)	Single subject: operant and inverted design; baseline followed by seven counterbalanced treatments	30-minute tutoring class before school	Academic accuracy and productivity	Self-monitoring of work completion and accuracy plus self-reinforcement (SMR) vs. Ritalin	6 white boys, ages 9–12	SMR was superior to Ritalin alone, but Ritalin plus SMR was superior to both SMR alone and Ritalin alone.

(continued)

TABLE 11.2. (*continued*)

Authors (Year)	Design	Setting	Dependent variable	Intervention	No. and age of participants	Outcome
Christie et al. (1984)	Single subject: AB for two subjects, ABAB for one	General education classroom	Percentage inattentive behavior, on-task behavior, inappropriate behavior	Self-monitoring of target behaviors	2 fourth-grade boys, 1 third-grade boy	Two out of three showed reductions in inattention (the other did not display the behavior at all throughout the study). All subjects showed increases in on-task behavior and decreases in inappropriate behaviors.
Davies & Witte (2000)	Single subject: ABAB	Third-grade general education classroom	Frequency of inappropriate verbalizations	Classwide self-monitoring plus token system	30 third-grade students. Target students: 2 boys and 2 girls with ADHD	The number of inappropriate verbalizations reduced during the intervention.
Edwards et al. (1995)	Single subject: ABABC	General education classroom	On-task behavior, percentage of reading comprehension questions answered correctly	Self-monitoring of on-task behavior plus token system	3 boys diagnosed with ADHD, ages 8–9	Intervention led to increases in on-task behavior and academic accuracy. Gains were maintained at 1- and 2-month follow-ups.
Ervin et al. (1998)	Single subject: ABAB	Boys' Town School: math class	On-task behavior	Self-evaluation of behavior plus token reinforcement	14-year-old Hispanic boy diagnosed with ADHD and oppositional defiant disorder	Intervention resulted in increases in on-task behavior.

314

Citation	Design	Setting	Dependent variable	Intervention	Participants	Results
Gureasko-Moore et al. (2006)	Single subject: multiple baseline across subjects	General education classroom: math and language arts	Percentage of classroom preparation skills demonstrated	Self-monitoring of organizational behavior with checklist. Self-evaluation regarding classroom preparation in log	3 seventh-grade boys diagnosed with ADHD	All students were at 100% preparedness by the end of the intervention. Improvements were generally maintained during fading and maintenance phases.
Harris et al. (2005)	Single subject: counterbalanced multiple baseline across students	General education classroom	On-task behavior and academic performance (total no. of words correct)	Self-monitoring of attention (SMA) vs. self-monitoring of performance (SMP)	5 boys and 1 girl with ADHD, grades 3–5	Both SMA and SMP increased students' on-task behavior and performance, but SMA resulted in greater improvements in performance. Students reported that they preferred SMP.
Hoff & DuPaul (1998)	Single subject: multiple baseline across subjects	General education classroom	Amount of disruptive behavior	Self-management	2 boys and 1 girl, age 9, with ADHD-type behaviors	Level of disruptive behavior decreased in classroom and at recess. Results were maintained in the absence of teacher feedback.
Mathes & Bender (1997)	Single subject: multiple-baseline across subjects	Resource room	On-task behavior	Self-monitoring of on-task behavior	3 boys, ages 8–11	All subjects showed increases in on-task behavior, which were maintained when the intervention was faded over time.

(continued)

TABLE 11.2. (*continued*)

Authors (Year)	Design	Setting	Dependent variable	Intervention	No. and age of participants	Outcome
Shapiro et al. (1998)	Single subject: case study, ABC	Self-contained classroom for students with learning disabilities and a general education classroom	Teacher-rated ADHD symptoms, on-task behavior	Teacher management followed by contingency-based self-management of target behaviors	2 12-year-old boys diagnosed with ADHD and identified as learning disabled	Improvements in on-task behaviors and decreases in teacher ratings of ADHD resulted after teacher management intervention and were maintained during the self-management intervention.
Shimabukuro et al. (1999)	Single subject: multiple baseline across academic area	Self-contained, mixed-grade classroom in a private school for students with learning disabilities	Academic accuracy, productivity and, on-task behavior	Self-monitoring of academic accuracy and productivity	3 boys, grades 6 and 7	All subjects showed increases in academic accuracy, productivity, and on-task behavior, but gains in productivity were greater than gains in accuracy.
Stewart & McLaughlin (1992)	Single subject: ABAB	General education English classroom	Off-task behavior	Self-recording of off-task behavior; point system and teacher praise	15-year-old boy	Intervention led to decreases in off-task behavior.

fifth-grade students who met research criteria for ADHD. During the SMA condition, students used a procedure very similar to that used by Mathes and Bender (1997). When students self-monitored their performance, they were required to count and graph the number of times they spelled a word correctly. Results showed that both procedures improved students' academic performance and the amount of time they spent on task, but SMA resulted in more correct spelling practices for each child. Importantly, the authors' counterbalanced design revealed that SMA maintained its advantage regardless of whether it occurred before or after the SMP intervention. Although the counterbalanced multiple-baseline design and high interobserver agreement lend support to the positive findings, the reliance on high-support external cues and short-term duration may limit the generalization of the intervention effects. The inclusion of a fading and maintenance period would have strengthened the intervention's applicability to a general education classroom.

Self-monitoring has also been examined in combination with reinforcement. Stewart and McLaughlin (1992), for example, investigated the effectiveness of self-monitoring and reinforcement to reduce the off-task behaviors of a 15-year-old boy with a medical diagnosis of ADHD. In addition to self-monitoring, the student earned a "good behavior mark" and received teacher praise for each interval he remained on task. A similar study by Edwards, Salant, Brougher, and McLaughlin (1995) paired self-monitoring with a token system in which three 8- to 9-year-old boys who met research criteria for ADHD received 5 points for on-task behavior at or above 60% and lost 2 points if they were on task for less than 40% of the intervals. In addition, the students were able to earn a larger reward at the end of the week if their behavior averaged at least 70%. Both studies found that the interventions increased on-task behavior, and Edwards et al. also found improvements in reading comprehension accuracy. Importantly, Edwards and colleagues demonstrated that gains were maintained at 1- and 2-month follow-ups. All students did not improve equally, however, as one showed a downward trend during fading of the intervention. Although the latter student's on-task behavior remained above baseline levels, Edwards et al. suggested that some students may require longer periods of intervention before fading is introduced.

Despite these promising findings, both studies had limitations. For example, in Stewart and McLaughlin's (1992) study, the classroom teacher implemented the intervention, and in the Edwards et al. (1995) study, the classroom teacher conducted the observations. As a result, both studies could have been affected by experimenter bias. This use of natural classroom resources, however, provides evidence that these interventions can be implemented with minimal external support. Finally, because the studies implemented both the self-monitoring and token systems simultaneously, it is difficult to tell whether the results were due to the self-monitoring procedure, the token system, or the combination of interventions.

This latter question was partially addressed through a study by Bowers, Clement, Fantuzzo, and Sorensen (1985) in which the authors compared the effects of teacher-administered reinforcers (TR) to self-monitoring and self-reinforcement (SMR) using a counterbalanced reversal design. Participants were six 8- to 11-year-old boys in a learning resource classroom who were diagnosed with a specific learning disability, which included but was not limited to attentional deficits. During the TR condition, students received a point, which could be exchanged for 5 cents, each time they were paying attention when the teacher looked at them. In the SMR condition, students were required to self-monitor their attentive behaviors using a vibrating device and self-administer a point each time they were self-observed to be on task. Results indicated that both conditions increased attention to task and academic accuracy, but the greatest amount of improvement occurred during the SMR intervention. Differences were small, however, and conclusions must be tempered by the large number of overlapping data points. In addition, it is unclear which students, if any, had a medical diagnosis of ADHD.

In addition to self-monitoring of on-task behaviors, researchers have investigated the effects of self-evaluation, in which students monitor and rate the appropriateness of their behaviors. A study by Shapiro, DuPaul, and Bradley-Klug (1998), for example, examined the effectiveness of a contingency-based self-management procedure with two 12-year-olds with a medical diagnosis of ADHD and identified as learning disabled. Based on the procedure developed by Rhode, Morgan, and Young (1983), the authors implemented a token reinforcement program aimed at increasing behaviors such as time on task, work completion, and compliance. Once the student achieved desirable levels of behavior, a self-management procedure was introduced in which the students were required to rate their own behavior in conjunction with the teacher. Points were then awarded if the students' ratings were within 1 point of the teacher's rating. Results showed that the students' behaviors improved during the teacher-implemented token system and were maintained at or above this level during the matching condition. A reversal design was not used, however, which limits the conclusions that can be drawn.

A similar study by Ervin, DuPaul, Kern, and Friman (1998) used a functional analysis to develop an individualized self-management intervention for a 14-year-old Hispanic boy who met research criteria for ADHD and ODD. The intervention was implemented during math class at a private school and involved having the student rate his own behavior on a scale from 0 (*unacceptable*) to 5 (*excellent*) at the end of each class period. The teacher rated the student's behavior as well, and the student received points if his ratings were within 1 point of the teacher's ratings. Results revealed that the percentage of intervals in which the student was observed to be on task increased during the self-management intervention. High treatment integrity, adequate interobserver agreement, a reversal design, and few overlapping data points lend strength to the study's conclusions, but the use of a single subject limits generalization. Furthermore, this and the intervention described in the study by Shapiro and colleagues (1998) required a significant effort from the teacher and thus may not be suitable for long-term implementation in general education settings.

In contrast, Hoff and DuPaul (1998) expanded the procedures used by Rhode et al. (1983) to include a fading and generalization phase. They examined the effectiveness of this procedure within a general education classroom for three 9-year-old students with a medical diagnosis of ADHD or ODD and demonstrated ADHD-type behaviors. This intervention mirrored those by Shapiro and colleagues (1998) but also included a fading and generalization procedure. During the fading procedure, matching was determined by having the student blindly select a piece of paper from a container containing one red and three black papers. If the student selected the red paper, matching would occur. Teacher matching was gradually reduced from 75% to no matching. In addition to the classroom intervention, a shortened matching procedure was conducted in the playground setting. Results showed that all students decreased their levels of disruptive behavior both in the classroom and at recess. Importantly, these improvements were maintained in the absence of teacher feedback. Although this study provides substantial support for self-management, it is important to note that order effects may have played a role in the findings. As a result, the conclusions must be interpreted in terms of the package of intervention provided (including teacher feedback) and cannot be attributed to self-monitoring alone.

Although the studies discussed thus far involved individualized intervention, there is some evidence that self-monitoring can be applied within a classwide system. A study by Davies and Witte (2000) employed a classwide self-monitoring intervention to reduce the inappropriate vocalization of four third graders who met research criteria for ADHD. The class was divided into groups of five and provided with a chart that was divided so that it was 50% green, 25% red, and 25% blue. Equal numbers of dots were placed in the green space, and the child was required to move one dot into the blue section each time he or she exhibited the target behavior. If the child failed to do so after 10 seconds, the teacher moved the dot into the red space. Group rewards were then given depending on the number of dots left in the green space at the end of each period. Results showed that the number of inappropriate verbalizations exhibited by the target children reduced dramatically during the intervention. Importantly, the reversal period revealed a functional relationship between the intervention and child behavior, as behavior levels rose when the intervention was removed. The intervention was fairly intrusive, however, requiring a restructuring of classroom procedures; this may not be feasible in all situations.

In addition to inattentive and disruptive behaviors, there is evidence that self-monitoring can be used for other problems presented by students with ADHD. Gureasko-Moore, DuPaul, and White (2006), for example, utilized a self-monitoring and self-evaluation procedure to improve the classroom preparation of three seventh-grade students who met research criteria for ADHD. These students were taught to self-monitor their classroom preparation using a checklist of preparation behaviors. They were also required to keep logs in which they wrote down weekly goals for classroom preparation, identified their current problems with preparation, and quantified their performance by calculating the number of items from the checklist they had completed. Finally, students had to write down what they did to accomplish their goals, what kept them from meeting their goals, and what they could do to be more effective; and they had to evaluate their satisfaction with their performance on a scale from 0 to 5. During the monitoring phase, students had daily meetings with the consultant to discuss compliance and strategies. After students exhibited 100% of the classroom preparation behaviors at least four out of five consecutive days, meetings were faded to once a week and students were given the option to stop the log portion of the intervention.

By the end of the monitoring phase, all students exhibited 100% of the classroom preparation behaviors, and although there was a delay in effect for one student, preparation levels were maintained during the maintenance phase. Gureasko-Moore et al. (2006) did not, however, examine academic productivity or accuracy, and it is therefore impossible to determine whether the increase in classroom preparation had an effect on academic performance. In addition, it is important to note that the intervention was implemented by an external consultant who continued to meet with the students throughout the intervention. Additional follow-up and continued fading of consultant meetings would have provided better data regarding generalization.

Although the results discussed thus far provide promising support for self-regulation as an effective treatment for the behavior problems associated with ADHD, there is some question how these interventions compare to use of psychostimulant medications such as methylphenidate. In an attempt to address this question, Chase and Clement (1985) compared the individual and combined effects of self-monitoring and stimulant medication with six 9- to 12-year-old boys with a medical diagnosis of ADHD. The study was conducted during a 30-minute tutoring session before school, and students were paid 80 cents a day. After a baseline period, the authors counterbalanced three interventions: methylphenidate plus noncontingent reinforcers, SMR plus a drug placebo, and methylphenidate plus SMR (see Figure 11.1). During the SMR interventions, students were required to record the completion of reading questions on a wrist counter. If the student met the goal determined at the beginning of the session, he or she would self-administer points that could be exchanged for backup reinforcers. Results revealed that although SMR was superior to methylphenidate alone, the combination of SMR and methylphenidate resulted in the greatest improvement in amount and accuracy of academic performance.

A similar study by Ajibola and Clement (1995) examined the effects of SMR compared to and in combination with both high and low dosages of stimulant medication. Six boys ages 9 to 12 participated in a "tutoring class" that met every day for 30 minutes, during which the students were required to work silently on reading and word recognition tasks. The baseline period was followed by six counterbalanced conditions: (1) drug placebo plus noncontingent reinforcers, (2) low-dose stimulant medication plus noncontingent reinforcers, (3) high-dose stimulant medication plus noncontingent reinforcers, (4) low-dose stimulant medication plus SMR, (5) high-dose stimulant medication plus SMR, and (6) drug placebo plus SMR. During SMR conditions, students self-administered 1 point each time they answered a reading question. These points could then be exchanged for a preselected backup reinforcer at the end of a 2-week period. In general, the combination of stimulant medication and SMR resulted in greater improvements in academic performance than either treatment given alone. Interestingly, both high and low dosages of methylphenidate resulted in levels of academic accuracy that were lower than baseline. In addition, methylphenidate had no effect on attention levels. Low dosages did, however, reduce impulsivity. The counterbalanced design and high interobserver agreement in both studies lend credence to the findings, but the artificial settings limit generalization. Furthermore, treatment was not faded, and no follow-up assessment was conducted. The results suggest, however, that self-monitoring may contribute to improvements in behavior and academic performance above and beyond stimulant medication treatment.

In sum, the self-regulation literature suggests that interventions such as self-monitoring, self-management, and self-reinforcement can be used effectively to reduce the problem behaviors of students with ADHD. The studies discussed above provide evidence that these procedures can be employed to address a number of behaviors such as attention to task, disruptive behaviors, and poor organizational skills. Importantly, preliminary evidence suggests that these interventions can be implemented within the general education setting utilizing natural classroom resources. Furthermore, because self-regulation strategies require, at least initially, environmental changes at the point of performance, these interventions appear consistent with the theoretical view of ADHD representing a disorder of impaired delayed responding.

Conclusions and Future Research

The effects of CBIs on the school functioning of students with ADHD are mixed. Findings from studies investigating more traditional CBM approaches are equivocal. Investigations that included multicomponent treatment packages (e.g., contingency management and/or stimulant medication in addition to CBM) have shown improvements in on-task behavior and academic performance. Alternatively, studies examining CBM strategies in isolation have not consistently found positive effects. Thus, it is unclear how much CBM has contributed to improved outcomes over and above effects of other treatment strategies (e.g., contingency management). Results of investigations examining self-regulation interventions for this population have been more positive. Specifically, techniques such as self-monitoring, self-evaluation, and self-reinforcement are associated with improvements in task-related attention, social interactions, and academic performance. Most self-regulation studies have included very small samples and have not examined maintenance of effects over time or generalization across settings and/or behaviors.

Given the potential contribution of self-regulation approaches in the treatment of ADHD, further research in this area should attend to several key factors. First, investigations of self-regulation strategies need to be conducted with larger samples in order to demonstrate the broader effects of this treatment for the population of students with ADHD. In particular, researchers need to know what factors (e.g., symptom severity, grade level, and ADHD subtype) might account for differential outcomes of this treatment. Second, studies should be designed so that the effects of specific treatment components (e.g., self-monitoring) can be isolated from other strategies in the context of a multicomponent intervention protocol. This would help delineate which self-regulation strategy may be optimal under specific conditions. Third, most investigations of CBIs have been conducted over relatively short time periods (e.g., a few months). Given that ADHD is a chronic disorder, it is imperative

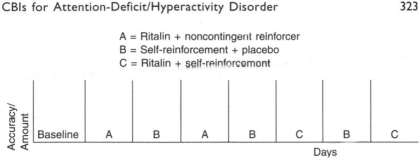

FIGURE 11.1. Research design of Chase and Clement (1985). Chase and Clement employed an alternating-treatments design in which conditions were counterbalanced across all six participants.

that putative treatment effects are examined using longer term follow-up assessment. Similarly, the generalization of obtained effects across settings, behaviors, and academic subjects should be investigated more rigorously. In particular, it would be important to replicate findings obtained under controlled laboratory school conditions in more naturalistic settings, such as general education classrooms. Fourth, most treatment outcome studies have included samples that are predominantly white, male, and middle class. In light of the changing demographics of the U.S. school population, it is critical for investigations to include samples that are diverse with respect to gender, ethnicity, and socioeconomic status. Finally, the clinical significance and/or social validity of self-regulation effects are rarely investigated. It is important to know whether this treatment modality leads to "normalization" of performance and whether statistically significant improvements make a real difference in children's lives.

Empirical findings, to date, indicate that stimulant medication and behavioral interventions are the primary treatments for ADHD. Traditional approaches to CBM are limited; however, self-regulation strategies are promising and deserve further investigation. Given that the primary treatments for this disorder rarely are sufficient in addressing all functional deficits associated with ADHD, school and mental health professionals should consider adjunctive strategies such as self-regulation interventions as part of a comprehensive treatment plan.

Acknowledgments

Preparation of this chapter was supported in part by National Institute of Mental Health Grant Nos. R01-MH62941 and R01-61563.

References

Abikoff, H. B., Jensen, P. S., Arnold, L. E., Hoza, B., Hechtman, L., Pollack, S., et al. (2002). Observed classroom behavior of children with ADHD: Relationship to gender and comorbidity. *Journal of Abnormal Child Psychopathology, 30*, 349–360.

Ajibola, O., & Clement, P. W. (1995). Differential effects of methylphenidate and self-reinforcement on attention-deficit hyperactivity disorder. *Behavior Modification, 19*, 211–233.

American Psychiatric Association. (2000). *Diagnostic and statistical manual of mental disorders* (4th ed., text rev.). Washington, DC: Author.

Barkley, R. A. (1997a). *ADHD and the nature of self-control*. New York: Guilford Press.

Barkley, R. A. (1997b). Behavioral inhibition, sustained attention, and executive functions: Constructing a unifying theory of ADHD. *Psychological Bulletin, 121*, 65–94.

Barkley, R. A. (1997c). *Defiant children: A clinician's manual for assessment and parent training* (2nd ed.). New York: Guilford Press.

Barkley, R. A. (2006). *Attention-deficit hyperactivity disorder: A handbook for diagnosis and treatment* (3rd ed.). New York: Guilford Press.

Barkley, R. A., DuPaul, G. J., & McMurray, M. B. (1990). Comprehensive evaluation of attention deficit disorder with and without hyperactivity as defined by research criteria. *Journal of Consulting and Clinical Psychology, 58*, 775–789.

Bloomquist, M. L., August, G. J., & Ostrander, R. (1991). Effects of a school-based cognitive-behavioral intervention for ADHD children. *Journal of Abnormal Child Psychology, 19*, 591–605.

Bowers, D. S., Clement, P. W., Fantuzzo, J. W., & Sorensen, D. A. (1985). Effects of teacher-administered and self-administered reinforcers on learning disabled children. *Behavior Therapy, 16*, 357–369.

Brock, S. W., & Knapp, P. K. (1996). Reading comprehension abilities of children with attention-deficit/hyperactivity disorder. *Journal of Attention Disorders, 1*, 173–186.

Brown, R. T., Wynne, M. E., Borden, K. A., Clingerman, S. R., Geniesse, R., & Spunt, A. L. (1986). Methylphenidate and cognitive therapy in children with attention deficit disorder: A double-blind trial. *Developmental and Behavioral Pediatrics, 7*(3), 163–170.

Cameron, M. I., & Robinson, V. M. J. (1980). Effects of cognitive training on academic and on-task behavior of hyperactive children. *Journal of Abnormal Chil Psychology, 8*, 405–419.

Chase, S. N., & Clement, P. W. (1985). Effects of self-reinforcement and stimulants on academic performance in children with attention deficit disorder. *Journal of Clinical Child Psychology, 14*, 323–333.

Christie, D. J., Hiss, M., & Lozanoff, B. (1984). Modification of inattentive classroom behavior: Hyperactive children's use of self-recording with teacher guidance. *Behavior Modification, 8*, 391–406.

Conners, C. K., Epstein, J. N., March, J. S., Angold, A., Wells, K. C., Klaric, J., et al. (2001). Multimodal treatment of ADHD in the MTA: An alternative outcome analysis. *Journal of the American Academy of Child and Adolescent Psychiatry, 40*, 159–167.

Connor, D. F. (2006a). Stimulants. In R. A. Barkley (Ed.), *Attention-deficit/hyperactivity disorder: A handbook for diagnosis and treatment* (3rd ed., pp. 608–647). New York: Guilford Press.

Connor, D. F. (2006b). Other medications. In R. A. Barkley (Ed.), *Attention-deficit/hyperactivity disorder: A handbook for diagnosis and treatment* (3rd ed., pp. 658–677). New York: Guilford Press.

Davies, S., & Witte, R. (2000). Self-management and peer-monitoring within a group contingency to decrease uncontrolled verbalizations of children with attention-deficit/hyperactivity disorder. *Psychology in the Schools, 37,* 135–147.

Dunlap, G., DePerczel, M., Clarke, S., Wilson, D., Wright, S., White, R., et al. (1994). Choice making to promote adaptive behavior for students with emotional and behavioral challenges. *Journal of Applied Behavioral Analysis, 27,* 505–518.

DuPaul, G. J., & Eckert, T. L. (1997). The effects of school-based intervention for attention deficit hyperactivity disorder: A meta-analysis. *School Psychology Review, 26,* 23–28.

DuPaul, G. J., Jitendra, A. K., Volpe, R. J., Tresco, K. E., Lutz, G., Vile Junod, R., et al. (2006). Consultation-based academic interventions for children with ADHD: Effects on reading and mathematics achievement. *Journal of Abnormal Child Psychology, 34,* 633–646.

DuPaul, G. J., & Stoner, G. (2003). *ADHD in the schools: Assessment and intervention strategies* (2nd ed.). New York: Guilford Press.

DuPaul, G. J., Volpe, R. J., Jitendra, A. K., Lutz, J. G., Lorah, K. S., & Gruber, R. (2004). Elementary school students with AD/HD: Predictors of academic achievement. *Journal of School Psychology, 42,* 285–301.

Edwards, L., Salant, V., Howard, V. F., Brougher, J., & McLaughlin, T. F. (1995). Effectiveness of self-management on attentional behavior and reading comprehension for children with attention deficit disorder. *Child and Family Behavior Therapy, 17,* 1–17.

Ervin, R. A., DuPaul, G. J., Kern, L., & Friman, P. C. (1998). Classroom-based functional and adjunctive assessments: Proactive approaches to intervention selection for adolescents with attention deficit hyperactivity disorder. *Journal of Applied Behavior Analysis, 31,* 65–78.

Evans, S. W., Axelrod, J., & Langberg, J. M. (2004). Efficacy of a school-based treatment program for middle school youth with ADHD. *Behavior Modification, 28,* 528–547.

Fergusson, D. M., & Horwood, L. J. (1995). Predictive validity of categorically and dimensionally scored measures of disruptive childhood behaviors. *Journal of the American Academy of Child and Adolescent Psychiatry, 34,* 477–485.

Fischer, M., Barkley, R., Fletcher, K., & Smallish, L. (1990). The adolescent outcome of hyperactive children diagnosed by research criteria: II. Academic, attentional, and neuropsychological status. *Journal of Consulting and Clinical Psychology, 58,* 580–588.

Gureasko-Moore, S., DuPaul, G. J., & White, G. P. (2006). The effects of self-management in general education classrooms on the organizational skills of adolescents with ADHD. *Behavior Modification, 30,* 159–183.

Harris, K. R., Friedlander, B. D., Saddler, B., Frizzelle, R., & Graham, S. (2005). Self-monitoring of attention versus self-monitoring of academic performance: Effects among students with ADHD in the general education classroom. *Journal of Special Education, 39,* 145–156.

Hinshaw, S. P., Henker, B., & Whalen, C. K. (1984). Cognitive-behavioral and pharmacological interventions for hyperactive boys: Comparative and combined effects. *Journal of Consulting and Clinical Psychology, 52,* 739–749.

Hinshaw, S. P., & Melnick, S. (1992). Self-management therapies and attention-deficit/hyperactivity disorder. *Behavior Modification, 12,* 253–273.

Hoff, K. E., & DuPaul, G. J. (1998). Reducing disruptive behavior in general education classrooms: The use of self-management strategies. *School Psychology Review, 27,* 290–303.

Ingersoll, B., & Goldstein, S. (1993). *Attention deficit disorder and learning disabilities: Realities, myths, and controversial treatments.* New York: Doubleday.

Jensen, P. S., Hinshaw, S. P., Kraemer, H. C., Lenora, N., Newcorn, J. H., Abikoff, H. B., et al. (2001). ADHD comorbidity findings from the MTA study: Comparing comorbid subgroups. *Journal of the American Academy of Child and Adolescent Psychiatry, 40,* 147–158.

Mannuzza, S., Gittelman-Klein, R., Bessler, A., Malloy, P., & La Padula, M. (1993). Adult outcome of hyperactive boys: Educational achievement, occupational rank, and psychiatric status. *Archives of General Psychiatry, 50,* 565–576.

Mathes, M. Y., & Bender, W. N. (1997). The effects of self-monitoring on children with attention-deficit/hyperactivity disorder who are receiving pharmacological interventions. *Remedial and Special Education, 18,* 121–128.

Meichenbaum, D. H., & Goodman, J. (1971). Training impulsive children to talk to themselves: A means of developing self-control. *Journal of Abnormal Psychology, 77,* 115–126.

Miranda, A., Presentacion, M. J., & Soriano, M. (2002). Effectiveness of a school-based multicomponent program for the treatment of children with ADHD. *Journal of Learning Disabilities, 35,* 547–563.

MTA Cooperative Group. (1999). A 14-month randomized clinical trial of treatment strategies for attention-deficit/hyperactivity disorder. *Archives of General Psychiatry, 56,* 1073–1086.

MTA Cooperative Group. (2004). National Institute of Mental Health multimodal treatment study of ADHD follow-up: 24-month outcomes of treatment strategies for attention-deficit/hyperactivity disorder. *Pediatrics, 113,* 754–761.

Paniagua, F. A. (1987). Management of hyperactive children through correspondence training procedures: A preliminary study. *Behavioral Residential Treatment, 2,* 1–23.

Pelham, W. E., Fabiano, G. A., Gnagy, E. M., Greiner, A. R., Hoza, B., Manos, M., & Janakovic, F. (2005). Comprehensive psychosocial treatment for ADHD. In E. Hibbs & P. Jensen (Eds.), *Psychosocial treatments for child and adolescent disorders: Empirically based strategies for clinical practice* (2nd ed., pp. 377–410). New York: American Psychological Association Press.

Rapport, M. D., Murphy, H. A., & Bailey, J. S. (1982). Ritalin vs. response cost in the control of hyperactive children: A within-subject comparison. *Journal of Applied Behavior Analysis, 15,* 205–216.

Reid, R., Trout, A. L., & Schartz, M. (2005). Self-regulation interventions for children with attention-deficit/hyperactivity disorder. *Exceptional Children, 71,* 361–377.

Rhode, G., Morgan, D. P., & Young, K. R. (1983). Generalization and maintenance of treatment gains of behaviorally handicapped students from resource rooms to regular classrooms using self-evaluation procedures. *Journal of Applied Behavior Analysis, 16,* 171–188.

Schnoes, C., Reid, R., Wagner, M., & Marder, C. (2006). ADHD among students receiving special education services: A national survey. *Exceptional Children, 72,* 483–496.

Semrud-Clikeman, M., Biederman, J., Sprich-Buckminster, S., Lehman, B. K., Faraone, S. V., & Norman, D. (1992). Comorbidity between ADHD and learning disability: A review and report in a clinically referred sample. *Journal of the American Academy of Child and Adolescent Psychiatry, 31,* 439–448.

Shapiro, E. S., DuPaul, G. J., & Bradley-Klug, K. (1998). Self-management as a strategy to improve the classroom behavior of adolescents with ADHD. *Journal of Learning Disabilities, 31,* 545–555.

Sheridan, S. M., Dee, C. C., Morgan, J. C., McCormick, M. E., & Walker, D. (1996). A multimethod intervention for social skills deficits in children with ADHD and their parents. *School Psychology Review, 25,* 57–76.

Shimabukuro, S. M., Prater, M. A., Jenkins, A., & Edelen-Smith, P. (1999). The effects of self-monitoring of academic performance on students with learning disabilities and ADD/ADHD. *Education and Treatment of Children, 22,* 397–414.

Stage, S. A., & Quiroz, D. R. (1997). A meta-analysis of interventions to decrease disruptive classroom behavior in public education settings. *School Psychology Review, 26,* 333–368.

Stewart, K. G., & McLaughlin, T. F. (1992). Self-recording: Effects on reducing off-task behavior with a high school student with an attention deficit hyperactivity disorder. *Child and Family Behavior Therapy, 14,* 53–58.

U.S. Department of Education. (2005). *25th annual report to Congress on the implementation of the Individuals with Disabilities Education Act.* Washington, DC: Author.

Vile Junod, R. E., DuPaul, G. J., Jitendra, A. K., Volpe, R. J., & Cleary, K. S. (2006). Classroom observations of students with and without ADHD: Differences across types of engagement. *Journal of School Psychology, 44,* 87–104.

Woltersdorf, M. A. (1992). Videotape self-modeling in the treatment of attention-deficit hyperactivity disorder. *Child & Family Behavior Therapy, 12*(2), 53–73.

CHAPTER 12

Cognitive-Behavioral Interventions for Students with Autism Spectrum Disorders

LAURA GROFER KLINGER
AMIE WILLIAMS

> He seemed as though he were living "within a world of his own imagining," within a fog of autism so dense that nothing existed beyond the fog. He was a solitary boy, curious only about things he already knew, but wanted to hear repeated. Order and calm lived only within sameness; odd rules came to govern his daily interactions. It was a horrible, frightening, out of control world. . . . Every social misstep was a blow to his fragile self-esteem; every misunderstanding a testament that something was inherently wrong with him, that he was "bad." (Grandin & Barron, 2005, pp. xiv–xv)

This description of Sean Barron's childhood experiences with autism not only highlights the difficulties of living with this disorder, it also describes some of the social difficulties, anxiety, and depressive symptoms of high-functioning autism and Asperger syndrome that might be amenable to cognitive-behavioral interventions (CBIs). Indeed, children and adolescents with high-functioning autism report more loneliness than their peers (Bauminger, Shulman, & Agam, 2003). The social difficulties are lifelong, with only 8% of adolescents and adults with autism and Asperger syndrome reporting having reciprocal friendships (Orsmond, Krauss, & Seltzer, 2004). Furthermore, approximately 44% of children and adolescents with autism and Asperger syndrome experience specific phobias (Leyfer et al., 2006), and approximately 17–27% of children with autism and Asperger syndrome experience various depressive symptoms (Kim, Szatmari, Bryson, Streiner, & Wilson, 2000; Leyfer et al., 2006). Although there are limited empirical data regarding the effectiveness of using CBIs to treat these symptoms in individuals with autism and Asperger syndrome, these techniques are growing in popularity among clinicians (see Attwood, 2003; Beebe & Risi, 2003, for previous reviews). An important caveat to readers of this chapter is the fact that the empirical literature has not evaluated the majority of the interventions discussed in this chapter, and much of the discussion is based on the clinical experiences of us and others in the field. When available, empirical evidence is provided. With this caveat in mind, it does make intuitive sense that CBIs should be effective in treating some of the symptoms displayed by children and adolescents with high-functioning autism and Asperger syndrome. Specifically, the impaired social skills, symptoms of anxiety, and symptoms of depression that are experienced by individuals with autism and Asperger syndrome have been treated effectively using CBIs in other populations. Before discussing specific CBIs, we begin by providing a brief overview of these disorders and the cognitive difficulties that are associated with them.

Autism spectrum disorders (ASD) are pervasive developmental disorders defined by the presence of a triad of impairments including qualitative impairments in reciprocal social interaction, communication (both verbal and nonverbal), and the presence of repetitive behaviors and obsessive interests (*Diagnostic and Statistical Manual of Mental Disorders*, 4th ed.; American Psychiatric Association, 1994). The term *pervasive developmental disorder* represents a category of diagnoses including autistic disorder, Asperger's disorder, and pervasive developmental disorder not otherwise specified. More recently, researchers have used the term *autism spectrum disorders* to denote the fact that these disorders fall along a spectrum of severity and are not reliably differentiated using most current diagnostic instruments. The term *ASD* is used throughout the current chapter.

Historically, CBIs have not been used in the treatment of ASD. Previous conceptualizations of ASD have focused on more impaired individuals with significant cognitive delays that have not been amenable to cognitive-behavioral techniques. However, the rates of both ASD diagnoses and the number of individuals with ASD who have intact intellectual ability have increased greatly in the past few years. Recent epidemiological estimates indicate that 1 in every 150 individuals has an ASD

(Centers for Disease Control and Prevention, 2007). Average intelligence is seen in 29–60% of individuals diagnosed with autistic disorder (Fombonne, 2005). Within the diagnoses of pervasive developmental disorder not otherwise specified and Asperger syndrome, the rates of average intelligence are even higher, ranging from 51 to 94% (see Fombonne, 2005, for a review). Regardless of whether these increased rates of individuals with ASD are due to a broadening of the ASD diagnostic criteria to include diagnoses such as Asperger syndrome and/or whether there is truly an increased rate of these diagnoses, there are more individuals being diagnosed with high-functioning ASD.

Individuals with high-functioning ASD have been characterized as having impairments in reciprocal social interaction, circumscribed interests, imposition of their own interests or routines onto other people, difficulty with reciprocal conversations despite language development occurring within normal limits, difficulties with nonverbal communication (e.g., facial expressions and gestures), and motor clumsiness (American Psychiatric Association, 1994). This unique profile of difficulties coupled with intact intellectual and academic skills presents a specific challenge in the school setting (Greig & MacKay, 2005). Because of their test scores, it is easy to believe that students with high-functioning ASD have subtle impairments that are unlikely to influence school performance. However, in our clinical practice, it is evident that although they are intellectually prepared for the mainstream education setting, children and adolescents with high-functioning ASD are often ill prepared for the organizational and social demands of the regular education classroom. As a result, these children are at high risk for social, emotional, and behavioral problems within the school setting. With the increase in diagnosis of individuals with high-functioning ASD and the increased emphasis on education in an inclusive setting, there is a growing need for treatment approaches that address these social, emotional, and behavioral problems in the school setting (Greig & MacKay, 2005). Cognitive-behavioral approaches seem particularly applicable to both the symptoms that need to be addressed and the need for short-term, manualized interventions that can be implemented in a school setting. In our experience, special education professionals within the school setting (e.g., school psychologist, speech therapist, special education teacher) have the most training in developing an individualized education program that includes CBIs. However, once developed, these programs can be implemented in a variety of settings including the regular and special education environments and in individual or group settings.

CBIs used for students with high-functioning ASD are similar to the techniques used with other clinical populations. However, the specific characteristics of ASD necessitate that CBIs be adapted to fit the developmental and cognitive difficulties that characterize this disorder. The specific cognitive processing styles that characterize children and adolescents with ASD may lead to the comorbid anxiety and depressive symptoms in individuals with this disorder (Farrugia & Hudson, 2006). Thus, a main goal of CBIs with children and adolescents with ASD is to understand the children's unique cognitive processing style so that appropriate interventions can be developed (Beebe & Risi, 2003).

Cognitive Impairments in Persons with ASD

Cognitive impairments in persons with ASD are thought to develop early in life and persist throughout the life span (Klinger, Klinger, & Pohlig, 2007). These cognitive impairments significantly impact the way in which individuals with ASD function in their everyday lives, particularly in their social interactions. There are several theories regarding early-developing cognitive impairments in perception, attention, and learning. Specifically, researchers have proposed that ASD are characterized by atypical perceptual processing (Happe & Frith, 2006; Mottron, Dawson, Soulieres, Hubert, & Burack, 2006), attention control (Courchesne et al., 1994; Renner, Klinger, & Klinger, 2006), implicit or intuitive learning (Klinger et al., 2007), flexible thinking (Ozonoff & Jensen, 1999), and reasoning about other people's perspectives (Baron-Cohen, 2001). Although each theory addresses a separate cognitive impairment, it is likely that these impairments are intricately linked, such that a problem in one area of cognition has cascading effects on other areas. Thus, rather than reviewing each cognitive impairment in isolation, it seems most appropriate to discuss the resulting difficulties in everyday life in thinking about how to develop appropriate CBI strategies.

Failure to See the Big Picture

Several researchers have argued that persons with ASD fail to "see the big picture" in everyday life and instead tend to focus on the minute details in their environment. Happe and Frith argued that this "weak central coherence" results in individuals with ASD failing to abstract the "gist" from a situation and instead focusing on specific details that may or may not be relevant to the situation (see Happe & Frith, 2006, for a review). It is unclear whether this tendency to focus on details (e.g., a "local bias") is due to impaired perceptual or attentional processes. Mottron and colleagues (Mottron & Burack, 2001; Mottron et al., 2006) suggested that this preference for details results from enhanced visual and auditory perception that allows for superior performance on tasks that require attention to perceptual details (e.g., drawing) but that leads to impaired performance on tasks requiring integration across perceptual details. The attention literature suggests that individuals with ASD are not impaired in their ability to focus and sustain their attention (Garretson, Fein, & Waterhouse, 1990; Pascualvaca, Fantie, Papageorgiou, & Mirsky, 1998; Casey, Gordon, Mannheim, & Rumsey, 1993). However, individuals with ASD have difficulties disengaging and shifting their attention (Casey et al., 1993; Courchesne et al., 1994; Renner et al., 2006; Townsend, Courchesne, & Egaas, 1996). That is, they tend to get "stuck" on a particular object or topic and have difficulty refocusing their attention. Both the perceptual and attention theories of ASD suggest that persons with ASD are able to consider the "big picture" when explicitly told where to focus their attention. Thus, ASD are characterized by a preference for detail-oriented processing rather than an inability to focus on the larger situation. Both theories have implications for understanding the social difficulties in persons with ASD. Certainly, a focus on details during social interaction may not produce an understanding of the larger social situation. For example, focusing on a person's mouth during social interaction (see Klin, Jones, Schultz, Volkmar, & Cohen, 2002) rather than the entire face may cause a person with ASD to miss the overall emotional tone of the situation expressed by eye contact, facial expressions, and hand gestures. Thus, any CBI program designed for individuals with ASD needs to include instruction on focusing attention beyond the minute details of the situation to notice the larger context.

Rule-Based, Inflexible Thinking

Persons with ASD tend to have a rule-based, inflexible thinking style evident in a preference for sameness and routine and difficulty generalizing information from one setting to another. Klinger and colleagues (Klinger & Dawson, 2001; Klinger et al., 2007) proposed that rule-based thinking in persons with ASD is a result of impairments in more flexible, intuitive thinking abilities. Typically, a great deal of learning is implicit and takes place independent of conscious thought (Reber, 1993). For example, young children learn to speak in grammatically correct sentences long before they learn the specific grammatical rules of their language. Similarly, young children understand their parents' and teachers' facial expressions without ever having to be taught what the different expressions mean. For example, a kindergarten-age child quickly understands that when his or her teacher sighs and frowns at the same time, that the teacher is unhappy with the child's behavior. This learning is intuitive in the sense that the teacher does not have to teach children in the class how to interpret her sighs and facial expressions. Klinger et al. (2007) proposed that some of the social and communication difficulties in persons with ASD result from impairments in this type of intuitive learning. Furthermore, they argued that persons with ASD compensate for this impairment by using more rote, rule-based thinking. That is, they try to explicitly learn the rules for each specific situation. This desire to learn the rules for situations that individuals with typical development understand intuitively is often expressed in writings of individuals with ASD. For example, Donna Williams, an adult with ASD, reported that she does not understand all of the "rules" that people use for each situation that they encounter. She wrote: "My behavior puzzled others, but theirs puzzled me, too. It was not so much that I had no regard for their rules as that I couldn't keep up with many rules for each specific situation" (D. Williams, 1992, p. 69). She doesn't appear to automatically generalize information from one situation to the next and instead appears to be explicitly learning rules for each specific situation that she encounters.

A rigid thinking style can also result from impairment in flexible thinking during problem solving (i.e., impaired executive function; Ozonoff & Jensen, 1999; Ozonoff & McEvoy, 1994). Executive functions are cognitive skills thought to involve the ability to maintain an appropriate problem-solving set in order to attain a future goal. These frontal-lobe-mediated functions include planning, impulse control, inhibition of irrelevant responses, and working memory. Ozonoff and Jensen documented specific impairments on executive functioning tasks requiring flexibility and planning. Executive function impairments are often exhibited in school when a child with ASD persists in using an inappropriate problem-solving strategy despite continued feedback from the teacher that a new approach is needed. These types of difficulties are present even in high-functioning individuals with ASD and are likely lifelong (Ozonoff & Jensen, 1999).

Both the implicit learning and executive function theories can explain some of the rule-based thinking and the irrational thinking that are present in students with ASD. In order to be successful, CBI programs designed for individuals with ASD need to provide explicit rules for why a particular behavior or thought is inappropriate and irrational and what alternate behavior or thought might be more appropriate.

Difficulty Understanding Other People's Perspectives

Persons with ASD also have trouble understanding that other people do not share their same beliefs, desires, and intentions. This impairment in understanding that others can have a different perspective from one's own perspective is called an *impaired theory of mind*. Theory of mind impairments are pervasive across a number of different situations that require taking another's perspective, including understanding humor and deception, being able to distinguish appearance from reality, and knowing that thoughts can be inferred by the direction of eye gaze (see Baron-Cohen, 2001, for a review). This impairment in metarepresentation could explain some of the difficulties that children with ASD have in social understanding and communication. For example, a child with ASD may not understand that other children do not share his fascination in particular topics (i.e., electrical cords, clocks, maps, etc.) or experience the same anxiety about particular situations (i.e., being in Wal-Mart). Theory of mind abilities are not completely absent in high-functioning persons with ASD, although delays appear to be lifelong (Happe, 1995; Ozonoff & McEvoy, 1994). Theory of mind impairments are particularly striking in high-functioning adolescents with ASD who have age-appropriate intellectual and academic skills yet have the social understanding skills of a preschooler. In the school setting, this often results in socially inappropriate behaviors that are rarely seen in a regular education classroom environment (e.g., a high school student who screams when others are laughing because he can't tell whether they are laughing at him or whether they are laughing at something else in the room). Thus, any CBI program designed for individuals with ASD needs to include instruction on how to interpret other people's behaviors or how to apologize when a misinterpretation occurs (Attwood, 2005).

Linking Cognitive Impairments to Intervention

Although we describe a tendency to focus on details; rule-based, rigid thinking; and difficulty understanding another's perspective as resulting from specific cognitive impairments, they are clearly linked. For example, an overly narrow focus of attention can certainly be linked to impairments in theory of mind. Individuals with difficulty disengaging and shifting attention may tend to focus on only one aspect of a social situation (e.g., the brand name of a person's watch) and miss the social intent of the social situation (e.g., the social partner is looking at his or her watch to indicate a desire to leave the interaction). Indeed, integrating across these cognitive theories, there is a developing picture of the cognitive impairments in ASD as resulting from a narrow focus of attention that prevents individuals from considering the larger picture, including another person's perspective, which leads to a rigid, rule-based learning style. For an intervention to be effective in treating symptoms of ASD, it must consider these underlying cognitive impairments. The cognitive-behavioral approaches to treating social skill impairments, anxiety symptoms, and depressive symptoms that are described in this chapter are adapted to consider the specific cognitive impairments of students with ASD.

Social Skills Impairments in ASD

ASD are characterized by difficulties initiating and sustaining reciprocal social interactions. One of the main goals of inclusive education for students with high-functioning ASD is to provide an opportunity for increased successful social interaction. Indeed, children with ASD are more socially involved with peers when placed in a regular education classroom setting (Robertson, Chamberlain, & Kasari, 2003). However, their social skills difficulties often prevent students with high-functioning ASD from developing truly reciprocal friendships. In a study of 35 children and adolescents with high-functioning ASD, Bauminger et al. (2003) reported that participants initiated and responded to their peers about half as often as age- and IQ-matched children and adolescents with typical development. Furthermore, children and adolescents with ASD reported higher levels of loneliness than peers with typical development. Bauminger and colleagues concluded that individuals with ASD appear to be interested in interacting with peers but do not have the knowledge about how to interact appropriately. These social difficulties are lifelong. Orsmond et al. (2004) examined peer relationships in 235 adolescents and adults with ASD. They found that only 8% of adolescents and adults with ASD reported having a reciprocal friendship that involved activities outside of prearranged contexts, and almost half (46%) of the sample reported no peer interactions at all.

These social impairments often result from the narrowed focus of attention and the inability to integrate social cues across experiences described above. For example, a student with ASD may not attend to the entire constellation of social cues present in each social interaction (e.g., facial expressions, tone of voice, emotional expressions, and gestures) and as a result will not recognize when his or her behavior is upsetting teachers or peers. Furthermore, social impairments often occur when persons with ASD are not able to understand the subtle differences in social behavior across contexts (e.g., it is appropriate to use slang with peers, but not the teacher). Social impairments may also be related to theory of mind difficulties that lead to awkward initiations (e.g., how and when to join a group) and responses to social bids (e.g., interpreting the thoughts and emotions of another during a conversation) with peers.

Individuals with high-functioning ASD who experience repeated failures during interactions with their peers as a result of social impairments may cope by withdrawing from or avoiding social situations. The combination of difficulties attending to and interpreting social cues, understanding other people's perspectives, and repeatedly failing in social interactions often leads to decreased motivation to engage in social interactions and may also lead to social isolation or rejection for many individuals with ASD.

Assessment of Social Skills

Few social skills rating scales specifically target the social skills difficulties experienced by students with ASD. As a result, more general social skills rating scales are often used in the school setting. For example, the Social Skills Rating System (Gresham & Elliott, 1990) and the Behavior Assessment System for Children (Reynolds & Kamphaus, 2004) are often used to assess social skill impairments in students with ASD. Both instruments have caregiver and teacher versions, which makes them particularly helpful in comparing behavior in home and school environments. However, because these instruments were not designed to measure autism-specific symptoms, they often fail to show improvements in social skills as a result of interventions that target autism-specific symptoms (Barry et al., 2003; Ozonoff & Miller, 1995). Most intervention studies have developed their own instruments to measure the specific skills that were taught by that intervention. Constantino, Davis, and Todd (2003) recently developed the Social Reciprocity Scale to measure social difficulties in ASD, with both parent and teacher versions available. This may prove to be a useful measure of treatment outcome, although the instrument is not specific to social skills and assesses other behaviors that are typical of ASD (e.g., repetitive behaviors).

Furthermore, Attwood (2003) suggested the importance of assessing the developmental stage of each student with ASD in understanding friendships. In children with typical development, friendships progress from engaging in parallel play with a peer, to playing cooperative games with a peer, to developing mutually supportive relationships with a peer. The choice of social skills intervention for a student with ASD might depend on the student's current understanding of friendships. That is, if a fifth grader with ASD has never learned to play cooperative games (e.g., board games or sports activities), this might be a better first goal than developing a friendship that involves mutual sharing. Again, there is no formal tool for this type of assessment, and Attwood recommended questioning children with ASD about their idea of friendships to gain a better understanding of their developmental level.

Interventions for Social Skills

There are relatively few empirically supported CBIs to treat ASD. However, a variety of strategies are being used by clinicians (see Krasny, Williams, Provencal, & Ozonoff, 2003; Rogers, 2000; S. K. Williams, Johnson, & Sukhodolsky, 2005, for reviews). The majority of these strategies use a "compensation" philosophy that explicitly teaches students with ASD how to recognize social cues and engage in appropriate behavior in social settings. These approaches do not treat the autism per se but provide students with ASD the coping skills needed for more successful social interactions. Although this compensation approach is not a traditional CBI method in the sense that it does not teach individuals with ASD to recognize and change cognitions, it is cognitive-behavioral in the sense that it teaches children with ASD how to examine a social setting and implement an appropriate, practiced behavior to increase social performance. In this review, we discuss social interventions related to three social skills impairments: initiating and sustaining social interactions, interpreting social cues, and understanding social norms (see Table 12.1). Although the types of techniques used to address each of these social skills impairments are similar, it is important to target the underlying reason for a student's difficulties before intervening. For example, a student with ASD may be perceived as being rude (e.g., talking about a peer's acne or his own acne) due to a lack of knowledge about how to initiate appropriate conversation or a lack of understanding that personal issues are often discussed at home rather than school (e.g., he can discuss acne with his mother but not his peers). Although either interpretation leads to an understanding that the student's behavior is not intentionally rude, one interpretation suggests that the student needs to be taught more appropriate greeting skills, and the other interpretation suggests that the student needs to be taught about social norms.

Initiating and Sustaining Social Interactions

Children and adolescents with ASD often struggle with initiating and then sustaining reciprocal conversations. For example, a student with ASD may respond appropriately when others approach him or her or converse with him or her at lunch but may eat alone everyday as a result of lacking the social skills necessary to approach a group of children and ask to join them for lunch. Students with ASD may often have difficulties conversing about topics that require spontaneous conversation and instead prefer to turn the conversation toward safe, familiar topics that are often related to their interests (e.g., state capitals, anime, and military figures). The above struggles may lead to children and adolescents

TABLE 12.1. Social Skills Interventions for Students with Autism Spectrum
Disorders (ASD)

Techniques for teaching specific skills	
Social scripts	Teach specific nonverbal and verbal behaviors expected in specific situations
Social stories	Short stories that describe expected behavior of self and others in specific situations
Social norms	Teach hierarchy of social rules or norms, including rules that can and cannot be broken
Role plays	Opportunities to practice appropriate social behavior
Self-monitoring	Use of checklists or videotapes for students with ASD to monitor their own social skills
Emotion thermometer	Use a thermometer to understand intensity of emotions felt by self and others
Incidental teaching	Teachers use naturally occurring events to teach social skills
Peer-mediated activities	
Peer education	Educate peers about the social difficulties experienced by students with ASD
Peer buddy	Assign a peer to include student with ASD during unstructured activities (e.g., physical education class)
Lunch bunch	Structured lunch groups with a teacher facilitating a discussion
Incidental teaching	Peers use naturally occurring events to teach social skills

with ASD feeling uncomfortable in social situations or avoiding them altogether and may cause social rejection or isolation from peers.

A variety of social skills interventions have been developed to teach students with ASD how to initiate and maintain social interactions. The goals of most of these interventions are to teach and rehearse specific social skills that individuals can use in everyday situations (see Barry et al., 2003, for a review). Various skills such as greeting others, giving and receiving compliments, and asking others appropriate questions may be taught as step-by-step routines through the use of explicit social rules or scripts. For example, a child may be taught a script for introducing himself to another person:

1. Turn your body toward the person.
2. Look at the person's eyes.
3. Smile.
4. Say "Hello, I'm Sam. What's your name?"
5. Wait for the person to say his or her name.
6. Say "It's nice to meet you."

Although this type of scripting may appear unnatural in the beginning, it is more appropriate than atypical repetitive initiations that are often based on the idiosyncratic interest of the student with ASD (e.g., walking up to a new peer and asking how many light bulbs are in his or her house). Barry et al. found that scripts are effective at treating the specific social behavior that is targeted (e.g., greetings) but do not generalize to new social behaviors (e.g., asking to join a game). Thus, children with ASD often need to learn a variety of scripts that can be applied to different social settings. The goal is that, with practice, these scripts will gradually become more elaborate and more natural in social settings. Because of difficulties generalizing across settings, it is often helpful to provide specific rules about when and where to use a particular script. For instance, it may be useful to create specific rules about using physical contact when greeting someone (e.g., it is OK to hug Grandma when greeting her, but it is not OK to hug the cafeteria worker at school when greeting her).

Using social stories is another method of providing students with ASD specific guidelines for behavior in a variety of social situations. Gray (1998, 2000) described *social stories* as short stories that explain social situations to students with ASD. Social stories have become a widely used teaching tool to clarify the complex and puzzling aspects of social situations and provide practical, tangible social information for students with ASD. For example, whereas most children learn to engage in the common social ritual of shaking hands without being explicitly taught the components of the interaction, individuals with ASD may need explicit direction about how to engage in the interaction. An example of a social story that could explain this specific social interaction (i.e., shaking hands) comes from Gray (2000):

> When I meet new people, they sometimes hold out their hand. People do this as a way to say "hello." I can put my right hand toward theirs and tightly squeeze their hand. I will try to look at the person and smile. Sometimes they will smile back. After holding hands for a short time, each person may let go. I can learn to feel comfortable with this new way to say "hello." (p. 14)

This social story explains the expected behavior of the student with ASD but also explains the likely behavior of other individuals in the environment. Like scripts, social stories are specific to each given situation, and a variety of social stories are needed to address the individual social skills impairments of each student with ASD.

Self-monitoring is another common tool for teaching students with ASD how to initiate and sustain social interactions. For example, students with ASD can be taught that they should ask relevant questions or make comments about what their conversational partner is discussing. Students with ASD can monitor their behavior by using a checklist that targets appropriate conversation components: (1) comment, (2) listen, (3) ask a question, (4) listen, (5) comment, (6) listen, (7) ask a question or say goodbye. Oftentimes, adolescents with ASD can then monitor the frequency with which they ask questions or comment during conversations with others so that they can become increasingly proficient in increasing reciprocity during social interactions. Group role plays are particularly helpful, as students with ASD can both practice monitoring their own social behavior and observe and monitor the social behavior of others in the group. In our clinic, adolescents with ASD enjoy making videotapes of these role plays and then observing and critiquing their own and others' videotapes.

Incidental teaching methods within the classroom can also be used to discuss social problems as they arise (McGee, Morrier, & Daly, 2001). For example, a teacher can point out when a child with ASD has changed the topic of conversation to something only he or she is highly interested in and prompt him or her to instead comment or ask a question about the previous topic of conversation. A teacher can also discuss topics of conversation that would be more appropriate, such as video or computer games, television shows, the weather, current events, and so on. In this way, the student with ASD would have several relevant and appropriate topics of conversation at his or her disposal that he or she could use to initiate and sustain conversation with peers.

In addition to teaching children with ASD specific rules for social interactions, in our clinical experiences we have found that it is also helpful to teach them how to play the same games as their peers. Because playground games often involve a social component, children with ASD often fail to learn the rules of the games. Thus, school personnel can determine which games other children of the same age participate in frequently (e.g., kickball, four square, board games, card games, etc.) and then teach the student with ASD the rules of these games. This is likely to help a student with ASD feel more competent when approaching other children to play the game at school or in other settings.

In addition to teaching specific skills to the students with ASD, a variety of social skills techniques include teaching typical peers how to provide social support to students with ASD. When a child with a sensory impairment (e.g., deafness) is included in a regular education classroom, often a peer education program is provided to help the other students in the classroom understand what to expect and how they can help their new classmate be successful (e.g., they may learn a few words in sign language). However, in our clinical experiences, this type of peer education is rarely provided when a child with ASD enters a regular education classroom. As a result, high-functioning children with ASD are often viewed as being "odd," "standoffish," and a "behavior problem" by their peers. A particularly helpful education program for peers in an elementary school setting is Gray's (2002) Sixth Sense curriculum. This curriculum teachers peers with typical development about ASD by describing ASD as an impairment in the sixth or "social sense." Whereas some children have sensory impairments in hearing or vision, children with ASD are described as having difficulties in understanding other people. Peers with typical development are encouraged, then, to help students with ASD understand how to interact socially. Once children understand more about their classmate with ASD, interactions between students with ASD and their peers may be more successful, and peers may be able to participate in "peer buddy" or "lunch bunch" activities (Wagner, 1999, 2001). A peer buddy can assist the student with ASD in navigating the social aspects of school by helping the student with ASD join social groups at lunch, recess, or other less structured activities. A peer buddy can also be taught to use some of the incidental teaching strategies described above. In addition to peer buddies, a lunch bunch program can be implemented such that children with ASD eat lunch with typical peers while a teacher facilitates discussions on various topics and gives feedback on social behaviors and interactions with others.

Attending to and Interpreting Social Cues

Most social situations involve a variety of complex and subtle cues that must be recognized, interpreted, and then applied in an effective manner. Whereas social cues such as body posture, facial expressions, personal space, and tone of voice are usually obvious and automatically interpreted by many individuals with typical development, children and adolescents with ASD often have difficulty automatically attending to and interpreting these cues. As a result of difficulties attending to the "big picture," students with ASD often focus on one aspect of a social situation while ignoring other very relevant cues. For example, Temple Grandin, an adult with ASD, reported that she never realized that other people communicated emotional information with their eyes until she read a book about the difficulties that persons with ASD have in understanding social cues (Grandin & Barron, 2005). Interventions designed to teach children with ASD to attend to a broader range of social cues are more difficult to design and evaluate than interventions that teach specific social behavior. Social cues are often subtle and change from one setting to the next. Thus, interventions that target social cues often focus on explicitly teaching students with ASD to attend to specific social cues rather than telling them how to behave in specific settings. For example, students with ASD may be taught to pay attention to another person's gestures and then practice attending to these skills during role plays. Peer buddies and teachers can also use naturally occurring incidents to point out the importance of attending to a variety of social cues. A teacher can point out when a student with ASD has misinterpreted a peer's sarcastic comments as indicating that the peer is angry because the student with ASD did not attend to the fact that the peer was smiling.

Difficulties with social cues are also related to impairments in theory of mind. Subtle changes in facial expression, tone of voice, posture, and gesture are critical components that allow one to understand the behaviors, thoughts, and emotions of others. Children with ASD may struggle with determining which behaviors are indicative of teasing by a peer and which are indicative of the peer joking around with them in a friendly manner. A child with ASD may also believe that whenever his or her peers laugh or swear in his presence, they are laughing or swearing at him or her.

A variety of methods can be utilized to increase a child's ability to understand and interpret the perspectives of others. A peer buddy can help the child with ASD learn to take another child's perspective by pointing out when a comment might be interpreted as being rude or hurtful to another peer. Incidental or naturally occurring opportunities can be utilized to instruct the child with ASD about the perspectives of others. Teachers are encouraged to take advantage of every opportunity to point out when people may have different perspectives. This can be done during a wide variety of school situations (e.g., physical education, lunch, academic group work). For example, at lunch, different food preferences can be discussed. During physical education class, differing feelings between the losing and winning teams can be discussed. During reading activities, feelings experienced by different characters can be discussed.

Oftentimes, students with ASD have difficulty understanding their own emotions. Thus, it is often helpful to teach students with ASD to identify and describe their own emotions as a first step in being able to sympathize with other people's emotions. A thermometer picture can be used to teach students to identify the intensity of their feelings (Beebe & Risi, 2003). Buron and Curtis (2003) have used a 5-point rating scale to teach children and adolescents with ASD how to modulate their emotions and behaviors in social settings. For example, a rating of 1 might indicate that a student is feeling calm, a rating of 3 might indicate that a student is beginning to get angry at peers as evidenced by jaw clenching and pacing around the classroom, and a rating of 5 might indicate that the student has lost control (e.g., is swearing and throwing things at peers). Ideally, the student can learn to control his or her emotions before a rating of 5 occurs. A thermometer or rating scale can also be used to compare how others might feel in a particular situation. For example, children could rate how angry they would feel if someone tattled on them for accidentally breaking a toy, or a teacher could rate his or her anger when something has made him or her upset in the classroom. Thus, the child could gain a better understanding of how others feel in similar situations and also how his or her behavior affects others.

In addition to learning how to attend to and interpret another person's social cues, students with ASD need to recognize the impact of their own social behavior on other people. Students with ASD often fail to provide social cues during social interactions. As a result, peers may have difficulty reading the social intent of the students with ASD. For example, if a student with ASD often takes a long time to respond to questions or statements, peers may feel that the student with ASD is ignoring them. Thus, it is often helpful to teach students with ASD to provide specific social cues to others. For example, the student who takes a long time to respond could be taught to put his finger up, rub his chin, or say "Hmm" to indicate he needs a moment to think and gather his thoughts. Once students with ASD have learned to recognize social cues, self-monitoring may be an effective intervention approach. Checklists, role plays, or videotapes can be used by students with ASD to monitor whether they are using social cues regularly.

Understanding Social Norms and Rules

Individuals with ASD often have difficulties understanding social norms and how they should be applied to particular situations (Attwood, 2005; Grandin & Barron, 2005; Myles, Trautman, & Schelvan, 2004). For example, a student with ASD may not understand that tattling to a teacher on another child for not being in line or for chewing gum may lead to rejection and bullying by his or her peers. The child may simply believe that he or she is doing the right thing by following the rules, but instead he or she is ignoring a social norm of not tattling on one's peers. Children with ASD may also violate social norms in various situations by making inappropriate comments to others. For example, a student with ASD may approach a teacher and comment on the teacher's weight or physical appearance and have little understanding that this is inappropriate or that it may affect the teacher. Social norms and rules may be particularly perplexing for students with ASD because they are often never directly taught.

One way to increase understanding of social norms is to explicitly teach social rules that could be applied in social situations. With regard to social rules and norms and how to teach them, Temple Grandin wrote:

> When I was in high school, figuring out the "social rules" was a major challenge. . . . Over time, I observed that some rules could be broken with minor consequences and other rules, when broken, had serious consequences. It perplexed me that other kids seemed to know which rules they could bend and break and which rules could never be broken. . . . However, I knew I had to learn these social rules if I wanted to function in social situations. If I had to learn them, they somehow had to be meaningful to me, to make sense to me within my own way of thinking and viewing the world. (Grandin & Barron, 2005, p. 129)

Grandin went on to discuss that she explicitly categorized the social rules of life into four main categories: (1) really bad things, (2) courtesy rules, (3) illegal but not bad, (4) sins of the system. Thus, for example, stealing falls under really bad things, cutting in line falls under courtesy rules, speeding falls under illegal but not bad, and socially complex situations such as dating one's best friend's boyfriend fall under sins of the system. She was able to place various social rules and norms into these categories based on the severity of the offense, punishment of the offense, how the offense affected other people, and her own personal thoughts about and experiences with various offenses. Although Grandin's system may not be helpful for all individuals, it is an example of how to create explicit rules to help govern behavior in social situations. Her system could be applied to instruct a child on when the breaking of a rule warrants tattling to a teacher and what comments are appropriate and inappropriate.

Another resource that may be helpful when trying to instruct children with ASD about the various rules and norms that govern social situations is *The Hidden Curriculum* (Myles et al., 2004), which gives concrete rules for certain situations. For example, the authors discuss basic rules about eating meals; eating at a friend's house; and eating at a restaurant, buffet, or fast food restaurant. A rule for eating at a friend's house is "Eat what you are served if there are no choices. If you do not like what is being served, say, 'Just a little bit, please; I'm not very hungry' instead of 'I don't want anything—I don't like it' " (Myles et al., 2004, p. 48). A rule for eating at a restaurant is "Refrain from talking about other people sitting next to you—do not comment on what they are eating or drinking, or what they look like" (Myles et al., 2004, p. 48). Discussing these rules with students with ASD will help make social expectations in various situations much more clear, which will then allow them to have more successful social experiences.

Social Skills Intervention Studies Incorporating Cognitive-Behavioral Techniques

There are few empirical studies examining the effectiveness of social skills intervention programs for individuals with ASD (e.g., Barry et al., 2003; Bauminger, 2002; Lopata, Thomeer, Volker, & Nida, 2006; Ozonoff & Miller, 1995). The studies that have been published were based on small sample sizes and did not include comparison groups. Studies have addressed a combination of the social skills difficulties described above, including difficulty initiating and sustaining social interactions, interpreting social cues, and understanding social norms and rules. Additionally, studies have used a variety of approaches, including an outpatient clinic social skills group, school-based individual therapy, and a summer day treatment program.

Barry et al. (2003) used an eight-session social skills group intervention program for four elementary-age children with ASD. Using a multiple baseline across behaviors approach, researchers taught children social scripts targeting initiating and responding to greetings, engaging in reciprocal conversations, and joining a peer in play. Skills were taught through explicit instruction and role plays. Practice with typical peers occurred at the end of each session. Results were promising and demonstrated increased use of greeting and peer initiation behaviors. Less clear changes were observed in reciprocal conversation, presumably because it is difficult to specifically script a conversation when the partner's response cannot be predicted ahead of time. Individuals with ASD rated themselves as having increased feelings of social support from their classmates at school, although less generalization from the clinic setting was evident in parent ratings.

Bauminger (2002) evaluated the effectiveness of a school-based intervention program for 7- to 17-year-old children and adolescents with ASD. Each participant's individualized education plan included 3 hours per week of intervention targeting understanding of social relationships (e.g., definition of friendship), affective education (e.g., teaching emotion identification in self and others), and social-interpersonal problem solving (e.g., appropriate ways to initiate a conversation or share experiences with a friend). Fifteen participants received individualized instruction, practiced with the teacher by using social vignettes, and received twice weekly practice with a peer. Across a 7-month intervention, participants demonstrated improvements in all three areas of intervention. Participants showed an increased ability to produce relevant solutions to social problems, increased their understanding of complex emotions, and showed an increased desire to share interests with a peer and increased eye contact during peer interactions.

Lopata et al. (2006) studied 21 elementary-school age children with Asperger syndrome who participated in a 6-week day treatment program that included a combination of social skills groups and naturalistic opportunities to practice social skills. Treatment targeted explicit social skills instruction, affect recognition, and expansion of interests to include more age-appropriate topics. Improvements in parent ratings of social skills and adaptability to new situations were reported. Additionally, parents reported decreased rates of atypical behavior.

Although promising, the lack of control groups and relatively small sample sizes make it difficult to interpret whether these are true intervention effects or whether these results are naturally occurring changes in social behavior across time. Furthermore, the issue of generalization from the therapy setting to more naturalistic social interactions and the issue of long-term maintenance of effects need to be addressed in future research.

Summary

Students with ASD often engage in inappropriate social behaviors that interfere with peer relationships. Rather than view these inappropriate behaviors as "behavior problems," it is helpful to consider the underlying difficulty in social understanding that may have produced the behavior. Possible social skills difficulties include difficulty initiating and sustaining social interactions, interpreting social cues, and understanding social norms and rules. Once the underlying difficulty has been identified, a variety of strategies can be used to explicitly teach appropriate social skills to students with ASD. More research is needed to identify the specific intervention or combination of CBI-supported social skills interventions that is most effective with students who have high-functioning ASD, and whether these improvements are maintained across time and setting.

Anxiety Symptoms in Individuals with ASD

There is a growing consensus that individuals with ASD experience significant levels of anxiety symptoms that are greater than the anxiety symptoms experienced by children and adolescents in the general population and that are equivalent to symptoms experienced by children and adolescents with diagnosed anxiety disorders (Farrugia & Hudson, 2006; Green, Gilchrist, Burton, & Cox, 2000; Kim et al., 2000; Leyfer et al., 2006). The most common anxiety symptoms in children and adolescents with ASD are compulsive/ritualistic behavior and irrational fears and beliefs. Leyfer et al. reported that 44% of the children and adolescents with ASD in their study experienced specific phobias (e.g., fears of needles/shots, crowds, loud noises) and 37% experienced symptoms consistent with obsessive–compulsive disorder (e.g., compulsive insistence on following verbal and behavioral routines, asking repetitive questions). In contrast to the popular belief that individuals with ASD are not bothered by their anxiety symptoms, 60% of adults with high-functioning ASD reported being distressed by their obsession and 56% reported moderate levels of anxiety if prevented from performing compulsive rituals (Russell, Mataix-Cols, Anson, & Murphy, 2005). At present, it is unclear whether these anxiety symptoms are part of having an ASD diagnosis or whether a secondary diagnosis is warranted. Regardless, specific interventions designed to ameliorate anxiety symptoms in children and adolescents with ASD are needed.

Assessment of Anxiety Symptoms

A variety of assessment instruments have been used to measure comorbid symptoms of anxiety in children and adolescents with ASD. However, these instruments have not been tested to examine whether they are reliable and valid measures with this special population (Leyfer et al., 2006) and must be used with caution. The recently developed Autism Comorbidity Interview—Present and Lifetime Version (Leyfer et al., 2006) is the first instrument specifically developed to assess comorbid psychiatric disorders in children and adolescents with ASD. Although this instrument holds promise in helping clinicians to understand the overlap between ASD and psychiatric disorders, it is a lengthy parent interview that is unlikely to be feasible for use within a school setting.

Thus, at present, instruments designed to measure anxiety in children and adolescents in the general population are the most appropriate for school-based assessment of students with ASD. An important caveat, however, is that these measures must be interpreted with an understanding of the symptoms that characterize ASD. Because children and adolescents with ASD have difficulty understanding their own thoughts and feelings, self-report measures have not been widely used. However, Farrugia and Hudson (2006) found that self-reports of adolescents with Asperger syndrome were remarkably consistent with parent ratings of anxious behaviors and thoughts. Thus, for adolescents with high-functioning ASD, self-reports such as the Spence Children's Anxiety Scale (Spence, 1998) and the Children's Automatic Thoughts Scale (Schniering & Rapee, 2002) may be appropriate. At present, parent and teacher ratings (e.g., Behavior Assessment Scale for Children; Reynolds & Kamphaus, 2004) and observations are the most appropriate assessments for elementary-age students with ASD.

Interventions for Anxiety Symptoms

Several different anxiety symptoms are likely to interfere with school functioning. Students with high-functioning ASD are often anxious when routines are changed, have obsessive interests, develop irrational beliefs and fears, and are nervous and self-conscious about their performance in social settings. Anxiety symptoms are varied and can range from behavioral outbursts (yelling, aggression), to repetitive behaviors (asking repetitive questions, reciting quotes from movies, pacing in circles), to withdrawal and refusal to engage in certain activities. There is limited research in using CBIs to support the treatment of these different types of anxiety symptoms among students with ASD. However, clinicians have adapted techniques from the CBI literature for students with ASD. In this review, we discuss interventions related to anxiety symptoms, including rituals and routines, obsessive and repetitive thoughts and behaviors, irrational thoughts and fears, and social anxiety (see Table 12.2).

Rituals and Routines

Because of difficulties with flexible thinking, students with ASD may prefer routines and become anxious when routines are altered (Klinger et al., 2007). Students with ASD may become anxious when an assembly is scheduled during the time typically dedicated to reading. Similarly, a student with ASD may have difficulty deviating from the typical order for completing assignments (e.g., when a teacher asks students to complete

TABLE 12.2. Anxiety and Depression Interventions for Students with Autism Spectrum Disorders

Daily schedules	Use daily schedules and task schedules to decrease anxiety about unexpected changes
Limit obsessions	Use rules to limit obsessive behavior and questions
Chill outs	Use progressive muscle relaxation and visual images to calm down
Graded exposure	Student gradually participates in anxiety-provoking events until fear is reduced
Emotion toolbox	Create a box that includes objects or pictures that symbolize calming activities
Identifying irrational beliefs	Teach students to identify irrational thoughts and use a coping statement
Emotion thermometers	Use a thermometer to understand intensity of emotions
Emotion journals or diaries	Use a diary or journal that describes emotions and events that produce them

even-numbered math problems when he or she usually assigns odd-numbered math problems). In unstructured settings, students with ASD may develop their own idiosyncratic routines or rituals. For example, a student with ASD may develop a routine at recess that consists of running three laps around the playground, swinging for 5 minutes, and then reciting a favorite movie. Typically, a preventive approach is the most effective at reducing anxiety around changes in routine. Students with ASD often benefit from a schedule that lists the activities planned for each day. For students with ASD who can read, a simple written list of planned activities is appropriate. Eventually, students with ASD are encouraged to create their own schedules, similar to the way that professionals learn to use a day planner. Rather than causing students to be more inflexible, a daily schedule provides an opportunity to indicate when a change is planned to reduce anxiety (see Kunce & Mesibov, 1998). Similarly, when teaching a new skill, it is often helpful to create a mini-schedule that lists the components involved in learning the new skills (e.g., a written list of steps involved in checking books out of the school library).

Obsessive and Repetitive Thoughts and Behaviors

The presence of restricted and repetitive behaviors and interests is one of the hallmark symptoms of ASD (American Psychiatric Association, 1994). Obsessive interests are often idiosyncratic, typically involving memorization of specific nonsocial facts. Obsessive interests vary widely (e.g., insects, train schedules, maps, light bulbs, presidential funerals, Beanie Baby stuffed animals, and Pokemon). At times, these obsessive interests are all consuming and prevent students with ASD from thinking and talking about other activities. Furthermore, students with ASD often ask repetitive questions about their interests even when they already know the answers. When these repetitive behaviors interfere with social and academic performance, it is appropriate to set limits on, for example, the time of day or the number of minutes a topic can be discussed or the number of times that a question can be asked (Beebe & Risi, 2003). The goal is to teach students with ASD to self-monitor their own behavior so that they gradually decrease the amount of time they spend focused on obsessive interests. If the obsessive interests do not interfere with academic and social functioning, teachers can use them to motivate students with ASD to persist with difficult academic tasks (e.g., a student obsessed with presidents who is struggling with reading can be given books about presidents) or to reward appropriate behavior in the classroom.

At times, these repetitive behaviors serve an anxiety reduction function. If students with ASD increase their repetitive behaviors and language when anxious, it may be helpful to teach alternative anxiety reduction approaches. For example, it is often helpful for students with ASD to briefly remove themselves from anxiety-provoking settings. Because of their preference for routine, we have found that students with ASD often benefit from a specific "calm down routine" to use while they are taking a break from the anxiety-provoking setting. In our clinic, we adapted a progressive muscle relaxation program for children to teach students with ASD to take a "chill out" when they are upset. They have a specific place in the classroom (e.g., the reading area) or the school (e.g., the counselor's office) that they can go to to implement their calm down routine. It is often helpful to use visual cues to help students remember the steps involved in progressive muscle relaxation (e.g., students might imagine squeezing a lemon when tightening and relaxing their fists). Students may benefit from a cue card that lists the different steps involved in muscle relaxation. When upset, students with ASD often have even greater difficulty processing social information. Thus, trying to reason with students about their behavior when they are upset is not typically effective. Instead, this discussion can occur after the relaxation routine has been followed. The logic behind this sequential approach mirrors that of commonly used CBI procedures addressing anger and other difficulties, where students are taught to first initiate a relaxation procedure prior to following a problem-solving script that requires focused social information processing.

Attwood and colleagues (Attwood, 2003; Sofronoff, Attwood, & Hinton, 2005) developed a group-based intervention program that teaches students with ASD to develop an emotional "tool box" filled with different "tools" or techniques that could be used to decrease anxiety. Students learned to identify their different emotional, physical, and behavioral symptoms of anxiety and then chose the appropriate tool to reduce their anxiety. For some students, physical activity such as running laps may be relaxing, whereas another student may find it helpful to listen to classical music. For example, in our clinic, a teenage boy experiences anxiety when in inclusion classrooms because of the increased noise in the classroom. He has learned to wear a baseball cap when he goes into the regular education classroom as a way to decrease the noise level. Sofronoff et al. examined the effectiveness of Attwood's anxiety reduction treatment using a six-session group-based program for 10- to 12-year-old children with high-functioning ASD. Compared to a waitlist control group, children in the intervention group showed significant improvements on parent report measures of anxiety. Anxiety symptoms were most improved when parents were involved in the treatment. Furthermore, anxiety symptoms continued to improve across a 6-week followup period. These results suggest that children with ASD are capable of utilizing cognitive-behavioral strategies to reduce their anxiety symptoms.

Irrational Thoughts and Fears

Due to difficulties with flexible thinking and considering another's perspective, students with ASD often fail to realize that the same statement can be interpreted in several different ways. As a result, they are often rigid and literal in their interpretation of information. For example, we recently saw an 8-year-old girl with ASD who interpreted her therapist's comment that it was "raining cats and dogs" literally. This girl was quite anxious at the thought that animals could truly come out of the clouds. Had we not explained the therapist's figure of speech, this girl could understandably have developed an irrational belief and fear about storms. It is often helpful to teach students with ASD that they might misunderstand another person's intentions because of their difficulty "reading" people. Students with ASD should learn to ask for clarification about what other people intended (Attwood, 2003). For example, the 8-year-old girl who thought that the therapist literally meant that it was raining cats and dogs could learn to say that she is confused by what someone says to her or ask whether the other person is joking.

Irrational beliefs are often linked to a child's obsessive interests. Although obsessive interests typically serve an anxiety reduction purpose, we have observed several instances in which an anxiety-provoking event is linked to a child's obsessive interests. For example, a teenager in our clinic who was obsessed with weather facts linked this obsession with his anxiety over school failure. He became convinced that if he failed a test at school, his house would be damaged by a tornado. As a result, he developed extreme test anxiety. Although few empirical articles exist, therapists are beginning to use traditional CBI techniques to help students with ASD recognize and challenge their irrational beliefs. In our clinic, we have adapted the *SOS Help for Emotions: Managing Anxiety, Anger, and Depression* (Clark, 2002) program to use with children and adolescents with high-functioning ASD. Using a typical rational emotive behavior therapy approach, the program teaches that irrational beliefs lead to negative outcomes. The comic strip illustrations are appealing and also provide a concrete, visual image of the behavior that needs to be changed. Because the book was designed for adults, we often draw our own illustrations and simplify the terminology. For example, we describe irrational thoughts as being "crooked thinking" rather than "straight thinking" and use the visual images of crooked and straight roads to reach a destination. Children are taught the ABC's of crooked thinking. They are taught to identify the Activating event (i.e., the unpleasant situation or wrongful behavior of others), the irrational Belief or crooked thinking, and the resulting Consequence (i.e., unpleasant emotion and maladaptive behavior). Then they are taught to provide a more rational or straight-thinking statement about the situation. For example, the student who believed that his failed exams would produce bad weather was taught to identify the activating event (the failed test), the irrational belief (that bad weather would occur), and the consequence (he was afraid to take a test). Next he was taught to use coping statements such as "Tornadoes are caused by nature, not because I didn't get an A on my spelling test." He was taught to use these self-statements along with progressive muscle relaxation whenever he became anxious about taking tests.

Reaven and Hepburn (2003) described a case study using cognitive-behavioral techniques to treat excessive fears and worries in an 8-year-old girl with Asperger syndrome. They identified her irrational fears (e.g., contamination worries that she would catch a disease that she heard someone talk about, fears that her body was changing and she would become someone else) and compulsive behaviors (e.g., handwashing, insistence on reading every word on a sign) as being similar to obsessive–compulsive disorder. In this intervention, the girl learned to identify the situations or objects that made her nervous, develop a hierarchy of events ranging from little to extreme anxiety, and then gradually expose herself to these events. She used a "stress-o-meter" to rate the level of anxiety felt at each stage of the hierarchy. At the conclusion of the 14-week intervention, a 65% decrease in symptoms was reported on the Children's Yale–Brown Obsessive Compulsive Scale (a self- and parent-report interview). Reaven et al. (2007) are conducting an ongoing larger scale study examining the effects of a 12-week program based on this original case study. In addition to using the hierarchy and exposure techniques described above, children work with partners to create "face your fears" videotapes where they act out a scene in which an anxiety-provoking situation is encountered and appropriate relaxation techniques and coping statements are used to reduce anxiety. Although no intervention data are available yet, this approach seems particularly appealing as a treatment for irrational fears that prevent children with ASD from participating in everyday activities. For example, an elementary-age child with an irrational fear of blacktop that prevents him from leaving the school for recess might benefit from this type of graded exposure intervention.

Social Anxiety

Social anxiety is an intense fear of social situations or performance situations where embarrassment may occur (Bellini, 2006). Research suggests that children and adolescents with high-functioning ASD do experience social anxiety, with estimates ranging from 11 to 49% (Bellini, 2004; Leyfer et al., 2006). Bellini (2006) proposed that social skills deficits and physiological arousal combine to produce social anxiety symptoms in adolescents with ASD. From this perspective, social anxiety results from an awareness of social skills difficulties and fear of continued failure in social situations. This model predicts that social skills interventions should lead to more positive social interactions and decreased social anxiety. Furthermore, this theory suggests that school-based programs that focus on social skills training with opportunities for successful peer interaction (e.g., peer buddies, lunch bunch) may be effective in treating social anxiety.

Cardaciotto and Herbert (2004) reported a case study utilizing cognitive-behavioral therapy to treat social anxiety disorder in a young adult with Asperger syndrome. The young man reported fearing and avoiding situations involving other people, particularly familiar people (e.g., fear of speaking in front of a group, fear of initiating a conversation). The intervention included a combination of social skills training along with the use of cognitive restructuring exercises immediately before and following social interactions. Results showed a decrease in self-reported symptoms of social anxiety and depression, along with increased social interaction. These results suggest that a combination of cognitive restructuring and social skills interventions may be an effective treatment for social anxiety in ASD, although more research is clearly needed.

Summary and Case Study

Although interventions for various anxiety symptoms were discussed separately, and to some extent have been studied separately in the intervention research described above, students with ASD frequently experience multiple symptoms. A case study provides an example of how these interventions can be integrated. We conducted a school consultation for Connor, a 12-year-old boy with Asperger syndrome who was having social skills difficulties and behavioral outbursts at school. He had an IQ of 112 and was in all regular education classes. Connor became quite anxious when rules were broken at school, and, as a result, he tattled obsessively when he saw peers breaking a rule (e.g., when peers talked to one another when the teacher was out of the room). His peers were becomingly increasingly frustrated by his behavior and had begun to physically attack him on the playground. His teachers were frustrated because they felt compelled to address minor rule infractions that they would typically ignore. Furthermore, Connor started to have academic difficulties in math, and he developed an irrational belief that he could not pass math assignments without his lucky Pokemon ruler. He was obsessed with Pokemon and would talk about little else. As a result of his peer and academic difficulties, Connor began to develop a school phobia and refused to attend school. We conceptualized Connor's difficulties as being primarily a result of anxiety symptoms that were negatively influencing his social interactions. Connor's anxiety was manifested as rigid, rule-based behavior, obsessive interests and repetitive conversations about those interests, and irrational thoughts and fears. We recommended and implemented the following school-based treatment plan that included a mix of social skills interventions and anxiety reduction interventions:

1. Begin peer education about ASD so that his peers would understand why Connor was tattling when rules were broken to reduce peer teasing.
2. Institute peer buddy program for unstructured parts of the day to minimize Connor's anxiety and to reduce opportunities for peers to physically attack him.
3. Provide resource room services to both pre-teach and review math concepts with Connor.
4. Develop a hierarchy of school rules for Connor so that he would not think he needed to tattle when any school rule was broken. We recommended that Connor learn that he could only tattle when someone was hurting or threatening to hurt him or another student.
5. Limit Connor's discussions about his obsessive interests (e.g., Pokemon) by making rules that he could only discuss these interests at lunch time and while waiting for the bus after school. During speech therapy, teach Connor social scripts that he could use to include his peers in his interests (e.g., "Do you have a favorite Pokemon character?"). Practice these scripts during role plays and then in the lunch room.
6. Teach Connor to identify his irrational thoughts and replace them with more rational thoughts. For example: "Crooked thinking is when I think that I will never pass another test in math because I lost my Pokemon ruler. I need to do some straight thinking. Straight thinking is when I think that I don't need a Pokemon ruler to pass my math test. I will pass my math tests if I study hard."
7. Teach Connor progressive muscle relaxation techniques. When Connor started to become agitated, his teachers could prompt him that he was getting upset and needed to "take a chill out." Send him to a quiet place (e.g., nurse's office) for 5 minutes to

calm down and engage in his relaxation activities. Give Connor a cue card that listed both the steps involved in progressive muscle relaxation and the coping statements he had learned to promote rational thinking.

Connor was successful in using and implementing the skill-based interventions described above. He was able to learn a hierarchy of school rules and stopped his tattling behaviors. Furthermore, he followed rules about when he was allowed to discuss his obsessive interests. It was more difficult for Connor to implement techniques that were less scripted. For example, although he learned to use progressive muscle relaxation to calm himself and he learned to identify his irrational thoughts and use thought-stopping and restructuring techniques, he needed adult prompts to identify situations in which he should use these techniques. Thus, it was most effective when his teachers, parents, and therapists worked as a team and encouraged him to implement these techniques across settings. School personnel were concerned about implementing peer education and instruction, as they were reluctant to identify a single student's disabilities. As a result, these recommendations were not implemented. Connor did not develop friendships in the school setting. However, teachers reported less peer difficulty as a result of decreasing Connor's inappropriate social behaviors. Thus, cognitive-behavioral anxiety reduction techniques were effective in treating an adolescent with ASD.

Depressive Symptoms in ASD

Approximately 17–27% of children with ASD experience various depressive symptoms (Kim et al., 2000; Leyfer et al., 2006). Symptoms of depression may include displaying increased aggression, placing increased demands on parents, and having poor relationships with parents and teachers (Kim et al., 2000). It is likely that these depressive symptoms are triggered by negative life events, low self-worth, low self-esteem in social situations, and difficulties handling the stressors that accompany the diagnosis of autism (i.e., maintaining social relationships, experiencing learning and attention difficulties, feeling that one is different, etc.; Capps, Sigman, & Yirmiya, 1995; Ghaziuddin, Alessi, & Greden, 1995; Ghaziuddin, Wieder-Mikhail, & Ghaziuddin, 1998).

Depressive symptoms in individuals with ASD may be linked to social skills difficulties and underlying cognitive impairments. In our clinical work, students with ASD who are high-functioning enough to recognize their differences and who want friendships like their peers tend to become depressed. Furthermore, theory of mind impairments lead to difficulties understanding feelings in themselves and others (see Attwood, 2005, for a discussion). For example, adolescents with ASD may have trouble understanding that the reason they are feeling sad and upset is because they feel socially isolated or have few friends, and they may instead interpret their feelings as anger or hostility toward parents for things such as making sure they complete homework assignments or chores around the house. Rigid rule-based thinking may also lead to depressive symptoms. For example, a high school student with ASD who is focused on making the honor roll may become upset each time she receives a grade lower than an A. Despite the efforts of her teacher and parents to explain that she can still get a final grade of A in classes where she receives occasional Bs, the student is so focused on wanting to earn an A that she may not understand that one poor grade will not affect her total grade.

Assessment of Depressive Symptoms

A variety of assessment instruments have been used to measure comorbid symptoms of depression in children and adolescents with ASD. However, similar to the assessment of anxiety symptoms, depression rating scales have not been tested to examine whether they are reliable and valid measures in this special population (Leyfer et al., 2006). The Autism Comorbidity Interview—Present and Lifetime Version (Leyfer et al., 2006) is a parent interview that can be used to diagnose comorbid depression in students with ASD. In the school setting, self-rating scales of depressive symptoms may be most realistic. However, because students with ASD often have difficulty understanding their own emotions, assessments may need to be made clearer by using pictorial modifications such as a bar graph or emotion thermometer (Attwood, 2003). It may also be helpful for parents, teachers, or the students themselves to keep a mood diary so that possible antecedents or cycles can be identified. Students with ASD often have difficulties understanding the varying intensities of emotions and may need education about these emotions so that they can better understand them and learn how to cope with them.

Interventions for Depressive Symptoms

Though there are no gold-standard interventions to help children and adolescents with ASD learn to cope with depressive symptoms, many cognitive-behavioral methods used with individuals with typical development can be applied with slight modifications or additions. Attwood

(2003) discussed the fact that affective education can be used to combat depression in individuals with ASD and noted that the goal of this program would be to learn why one has emotions, how they are used and misused, and how to identify varying levels and intensities of emotions. For example, in a group setting, an emotion such as happiness or sadness could be explored by having each participant write about it, draw pictures, utilize photos, and cut out magazine clippings. Students can use emotion thermometers to monitor the degree to which they and different individuals in the group are feeling that emotion. Emotion journals may also be a helpful tool. Students could create a scrapbook of pictures, activities, ideas, thoughts, and words that they think make them feel a particular emotion (i.e., happy, sad, angry). The various cues and effects of specific emotions could then be shared and discussed among group members so that they can compare and contrast different emotional experiences.

Similar to interventions for anxiety symptoms discussed above, irrational beliefs can be identified and corrected through cognitive restructuring (Attwood, 2003). Students with ASD can identify negative self-statements and develop an appropriate rebuttal or thought-stopping technique. For example, if a high school student believes that every time a classmate makes eye contact with him, the classmate is judging his physical appearance and clothing, it will be helpful to discuss the illogical nature of the thought and come up with a rebuttal such as "I can't read people's minds or know for sure that they are thinking about me. I feel good about how I look and that is what matters." In addition to affective education and cognitive restructuring, the individual with ASD may benefit from engaging in more pleasurable activities to increase positive affect. For example, one child with ASD may benefit from writing a short story or poem when he or she is feeling sad, whereas another child with ASD may benefit from spending time engaging in an activity associated with a different intense interest (e.g., taking a bus ride).

Conclusions

The issue of whether children and adolescents with ASD should receive comorbid diagnoses of anxiety or mood disorders remains controversial. However, there is growing evidence that children and adolescents with ASD experience significant symptoms of anxiety and depression. As more individuals with high-functioning autism and Asperger syndrome are diagnosed, interventions geared toward this specific group of individuals are needed. As a result, there has been a recent focus on implementing CBIs for this purpose. However, it is imperative that CBIs be adapted to fit the unique cognitive difficulties experienced by children and adolescents with ASD. Underlying cognitive impairments lead children and adolescents with ASD to attend to idiosyncratic details; engage in rigid, inflexible thinking; and have difficulty understanding other people's perspectives. These cognitive difficulties lead to the social, anxiety, and depressive symptoms experienced by children and adolescents with high-functioning ASD. Furthermore, as students with high-functioning ASD are included in regular education environments, it is clear that their social skills, anxiety, and depression will influence their academic performance. The school setting provides an excellent opportunity to implement the CBIs discussed in this chapter. Whereas mental health and special education professionals may have the expertise necessary to develop an individualized education program that includes CBIs, the interventions themselves are relatively straightforward and can easily be implemented in the regular education setting.

Although there is limited empirical support for the use of cognitive-behavioral techniques in the treatment of students with high-functioning ASD, there is a growing literature based on case studies and a few small, uncontrolled intervention studies suggesting that cognitive-behavioral techniques can be used effectively to treat social skills impairments, anxiety, and depression in this population. To date, the literature supports the use of social scripts, affective education, social problem-solving vignettes, and peer support to facilitate social skills in students with ASD. These techniques have been used successfully to teach students with ASD how to initiate appropriate social interactions, identify their own and other people's emotions, and follow social rules. Although there are several techniques designed to teach students with ASD to understand other persons' perspectives (including the use of peer buddies and emotion rating scales), research is needed to document whether these techniques are effective. There is also a growing body of literature examining the effectiveness of cognitive-behavioral techniques in reducing anxiety in individuals with high-functioning ASD. The techniques that have the most empirical support include the identification of emotions, use of fear hierarchies, use of gradual exposure, identification of irrational thoughts, and use of coping statements. More research is needed on these techniques as well as other techniques including the use of progressive muscle relaxation. Finally, similar cognitive-behavioral techniques are beginning to be used in treating depression in individuals with ASD, although to date there are no studies supporting the effectiveness of these techniques in reducing depressive symptoms. Overall, the use of cognitive-behavioral techniques in individuals with ASD is a new field that holds significant promise for the future.

References

American Psychiatric Association (1994). *Diagnostic and statistical manual of mental disorders* (4th ed.). Washington, DC: Author.

Attwood, T. (2003). Frameworks for behavioral interventions. *Child and Adolescent Psychiatric Clinic of North America, 12*, 65–86.

Attwood, T. (2005). Theory of mind and Asperger's syndrome. In L. J. Baker & L. A. Welkowitz (Eds.), *Intervening in schools, clinics, and communities* (pp. 11–41). Mahwah, NJ: Erlbaum.

Baron-Cohen, S. (2001). Theory of mind and autism: A review. *International Review of Research in Mental Retardation, 23*, 169–184.

Barry, T. D., Klinger, L. G., Lee, J. M., Palardy, N., Gilmore, T., & Bodin, S. D. (2003). Examining the effectiveness of an outpatient clinic-based social skills group for high functioning children with autism. *Journal of Autism and Developmental Disorders, 33*, 685–701.

Bauminger, N. (2002). The facilitation of social–emotional understanding and social interaction in high-functioning children with autism: Intervention outcomes. *Journal of Autism and Developmental Disorders, 32*, 283–298.

Bauminger, N., Shulman, C., & Agam, G. (2003). Peer interaction and loneliness in high-functioning children with autism. *Journal of Autism and Developmental Disorders, 33*, 489–507.

Beebe, D. W., & Risi, S. (2003). Treatment of adolescents and young adults and high-functioning autism or Asperger syndrome. In M. A. Reinecke, F. M. Dattilio, & A. Freeman (Eds.), *Cognitive therapy with children and adolescents: A casebook for clinical practice* (2nd ed., pp. 369–401). New York: Guilford Press.

Bellini, S. (2004). Social skills deficits and anxiety in high functioning adolescents with autism spectrum disorders. *Focus on Autism and Other Developmental Disorders, 19*, 78–86.

Bellini, S. (2006). The development of social anxiety in adolescents with autism spectrum disorders. *Focus on Autism and Other Developmental Disorders, 21*, 138–145.

Buron, K. D., & Curtis, M. (2003). *The incredible 5-point scale: Assisting students with autism spectrum disorders in understanding social interactions and controlling their emotional responses*. Shawnee Mission, KS: Autism Asperger.

Capps, L., Sigman, M., & Yirmiya, N. (1995). Self-competence and emotional understanding in high-functioning children with autism. *Development and Psychopathology, 1*, 137–149.

Cardaciotto, L., & Herbert, J. D. (2004). Cognitive behavioral therapy for social anxiety disorder in the context of Asperger's syndrome: A single subject report. *Cognitive and Behavioral Practice, 11*, 75–81.

Casey, B. J., Gordon, C. T., Mannheim, G. B., & Rumsey, J. M. (1993). Dysfunctional attention in autistic savants. *Journal of Clinical and Experimental Neuropsychology, 15*, 933–946.

Centers for Disease Control and Prevention. (2007). *Prevalence of autism spectrum disorders—Autism and developmental disabilities monitoring network, 14 sites, United States, 2002. Morbidity and Mortality Weekly Report, 56*(SS-1), 12–28.

Clark, L. (2002). *SOS help for emotions: Managing anxiety, anger, and depression* (2nd ed.). Bowling Green, KY: SOS Programs and Parenting Press.

Constantino, J. N., Davis, S. A., & Todd, R. D. (2003). Validation of a brief quantitative measure of autistic traits: Comparison of the Social Responsiveness Scale with the Autism Diagnostic Interview-Revised. *Journal of Autism and Developmental Disorders, 33*, 427–433.

Courchesne, E., Townsend, J. P., Akshoomoff, N. A., Yeung-Courchesne, R., Press, G. A., Murakami, J. W., et al. (1994). A new finding: Impairment in shifting attention in autistic and cerebellar patients. In H. Broman & J. Grafman (Eds.), *Atypical cognitive deficits in developmental disorders: Implications for brain function* (pp. 101–137). Hillsdale, NJ: Erlbaum.

Farrugia, S., & Hudson, J. (2006). Anxiety in adolescents with Asperger syndrome: Negative thoughts, behavioral problems, and life interference. *Focus on Autism and Other Developmental Disabilities, 21*, 25–35.

Fombonne, E. (2005). Epidemiological studies of pervasive developmental disorders. In F. R. Volkmar, R. Paul, A. Klin, & D. Cohen (Eds.), *Handbook of autism and pervasive developmental disorders: Vol. 1. Diagnosis, development, neurobiology, and behavior* (3rd ed., pp. 42–69). Hoboken, NJ: Wiley.

Garretson, H. B., Fein, D., & Waterhouse, L. (1990). Sustained attention in children with autism. *Journal of Autism and Developmental Disorders, 20*, 101–114.

Ghaziuddin, M., Alessi, N., & Greden, J. F. (1995). Life events and depression in children with pervasive developmental disorders. *Journal of Autism and Developmental Disorders, 25*, 495–502.

Ghaziuddin, M., Wieder-Mikhail, W., & Ghaziuddin, N. (1998). Comorbidity of Asperger syndrome: A preliminary report. *Journal of Intellectual Disability Research, 42*, 179–283.

Grandin, T., & Barron, S. (2005). *The unwritten rules of social relationships*. Arlington, TX: Future Horizons.

Gray, C. (1998). Social stories and comic strip conversations with students with Asperger syndrome and high-functioning autism. In E. Schopler, G. B. Mesibov, & L. J. Kunce (Eds.), *Asperger syndrome or high functioning autism?* (pp. 167–198). New York: Plenum Press.

Gray, C. (2000). *The new social story book*. Arlington, TX: Future Horizons.

Gray, C. (2002). *The sixth sense II*. Arlington, TX: Future Horizons.

Green, J., Gilchrist, A., Burton, D., & Cox, A. (2000). Social and psychiatric functioning in adolescents with Asperger syndrome compared with conduct disorder. *Journal of Autism and Developmental Disorders, 30*, 279–293.

Greig, A., & MacKay, T. (2005). Asperger's syndrome and cognitive behavior therapy: New applications for educational purposes. *Educational and Child Psychology, 22*, 4–15.

Gresham, F. M., & Elliott, S. N. (1990). *Social Skills Rating System (SSRS)*. Circle Pines, MN: American Guidance Service.

Happe, F. (1995). The role of age and verbal ability in the theory of mind task performance of subjects with autism. *Child Development, 66*, 843–855.

Happe, F., & Frith, U. (2006). The weak coherence account: Detail-focused cognitive style in autism spectrum disorders. *Journal of Autism and Developmental Disorders, 36*, 5–25.

Kim, J. A., Szatmari, P., Bryson, S. E., Streiner, D. L., & Wilson, F. (2000). The prevalence of anxiety and mood problems among children with autism and Asperger disorder. *Autism, 4*, 117–132.

Klin, A., Jones, W., Schultz, R., Volkmar, F., & Cohen, D. (2002). Visual fixation patterns during viewing of naturalistic social situations as predictors of social competence in individuals with autism. *Archives of General Psychiatry, 59*, 809–816.

Klinger, L. G., & Dawson, G. (2001). Prototype formation in autism. *Development and Psychopathology, 13*, 111–124.

Klinger, L. G., Klinger, M. R., & Pohlig, R. L. (2007). Implicit learning impairments in autism spectrum disorders: Implications for treatment. In J. M. Perez, P. M. Gonzalez, M. L. Comi, & C. Nieto (Eds.), *New developments in autism: The future is today* (pp. 76–103). London: Jessica Kingsley.

Krasny, L., Williams, B. J., Provencal, S., & Ozonoff, S. (2003). Social skills interventions for the autism spectrum: Essential ingredients and a model curriculum. *Child and Adolescent Psychiatry, 12,* 107–122.

Kunce, L. J., & Mesibov, G. B. (1998). Educational approaches to high-functioning autism and Asperger syndrome. In E. Schopler, G. B. Mesibov, & L. J. Kunce (Eds.), *Asperger syndrome or high functioning autism?* (pp. 227–261). New York: Plenum Press.

Leyfer, O. T., Folstein, S. E., Bacalman, S., Davis, N. O., Dinh, E., Morgan, J., et al. (2006). Comorbid psychiatric disorders in children with autism: Interview development and rates of disorders. *Journal of Autism and Developmental Disorders, 36,* 849–861.

Lopata, C., Thomeer, M. L., Volker, M. A., & Nida, R. E. (2006). Effectiveness of cognitive-behavioral treatment on the social behaviors of children with Asperger disorder. *Focus on Autism and Other Developmental Disorders, 21,* 237–244.

McGee, G. G., Morrier, M. J., & Daly, T. (2001). The Walden early education programs. In J. S. Handleman & S. L. Harris (Eds.), *Preschool education programs for children with autism* (2nd ed., pp. 157–190). Austin, TX: PRO-ED.

Mottron, L., & Burack, J. A. (2001). Enhanced perceptual functioning in the development of autism. In J. A. Burack, T. Charman, N. Yirmiya, & P. R. Zelazo (Eds.), *The development of autism: Perspectives from theory and research* (pp. 131–148). Mahwah, NJ: Erlbaum.

Mottron, L., Dawson, M., Soulieres, I., Hubert, B., & Burack, J. (2006). Enhanced perceptual functioning in autism: An update, and eight principles of autistic perceptions. *Journal of Autism and Developmental Disorders, 36,* 27–43.

Myles, B. S., Trautman, M. L., & Schelvan, R. L. (2004). *The hidden curriculum: Practical solutions for understanding unstated rules in social situations.* Shawnee Mission, KS: Autism Asperger.

Orsmond, G. I., Krauss, M. W., & Seltzer, M. M. (2004). Peer relationships and social and recreational activities among adolescents and adults with autism. *Journal of Autism and Developmental Disorders, 34,* 245–256.

Ozonoff, S., & Jensen, J. (1999). Brief report: Specific executive function profiles in three neurodevelopmental disorders. *Journal of Autism and Developmental Disorders, 29,* 171–177.

Ozonoff, S., & McEvoy, R. (1994). A longitudinal study of executive function and theory of mind development in autism. *Development and Psychopathology, 6,* 415–431.

Ozonoff, S., & Miller, J. N. (1995). Teaching theory of mind: A new approach to social skills training for individuals with autism. *Journal of Autism and Developmental Disorders, 25,* 415–433.

Pascualvaca, D. M., Fantie, B. D., Papageorgiou, M., & Mirsky, A. F. (1998). Attentional capacities in children with autism: Is there a general deficit in shifting focus? *Journal of Autism and Developmental Disorders, 28,* 467–478.

Reaven, J., Blakely-Smith, A., Nichols, S., Dasari, M., Flanigan, E., & Hepburn, S. (2007, May). *Cognitive-behavioral group treatment for anxiety symptoms in children with high-functioning autism spectrum disorders.* Paper presented at the International Meeting for Autism Research, Seattle, WA.

Reaven, J., & Hepburn, S. (2003). Cognitive-behavioral treatment of obsessive-compulsive disorder in a child with Asperger syndrome: A case report. *Autism, 7,* 145–164.

Reber, A. S. (1993). *Implicit learning and tacit knowledge: An essay on the cognitive unconscious.* New York: Oxford University Press.

Renner, P., Klinger, L. G., & Klinger, M. R. (2006). Exogenous and endogenous attention orienting in autism spectrum disorders. *Child Neuropsychology, 12,* 361–382.

Reynolds, C. R., & Kamphaus, R. W. (2004). *Behavior Assessment System for Children* (2nd ed.). Bloomington, MN: Pearson Assessments.

Robertson, K., Chamberlain, B., & Kasari, C. (2003). General education teachers' relationships with included students with autism. *Journal of Autism and Developmental Disorders, 33,* 123–130.

Rogers, S. J. (2000). Interventions that facilitate socialization in children with autism. *Journal of Autism and Developmental Disorders, 35,* 399–409.

Russell, A. J., Mataix-Cols, D., Anson, M., & Murphy, D. G. (2005). Obsessions and compulsions in Asperger syndrome and high-functioning autism. *British Journal of Psychiatry, 186,* 525–528.

Schniering, C. A., & Rapee, R. M. (2002). Development and validation of a measure of children's automatic thoughts: The Children's Automatic Thoughts Scale. *Behavior Research and Therapy, 40,* 1091–1109.

Sofronoff, K., Attwood, T., & Hinton, S. (2005). A randomized controlled trial of a CBT intervention for anxiety in children with Asperger syndrome. *Journal of Child Psychology and Psychiatry, 46,* 1152–1160.

Spence, S. H. (1998). A measure of anxiety symptoms among children. *Behavior Research and Therapy, 36,* 545–566.

Townsend, J., Courchesne, E., & Egaas, B. (1996). Slowed orienting of covert visual-spatial attention in autism: Specific deficits associated with cerebellar and parietal abnormality. *Development and Psychopathology, 8,* 563–584.

Wagner, S. (1999). *Inclusive programming for elementary students with autism.* Arlington, TX: Future Horizons.

Wagner, S. (2001). *Inclusive programming for middle school students with autism.* Arlington, TX: Future Horizons.

Williams, D. (1992). *Nobody nowhere: The extraordinary autobiography of an autistic.* New York: Times Books.

Williams, S. K., Johnson, C., & Sukhodolsky, D. G. (2005). The role of the school psychologist in the inclusive education of school-age children with autism spectrum disorders. *Journal of School Psychology, 43,* 117–136.

PART VI

THE FUTURE OF COGNITIVE-BEHAVIORAL INTERVENTIONS

CHAPTER 13

The Cognitive–
Ecological Model

Paradigm and Promise
for the Future

JALEEL ABDUL-ADIL
PATRICK H. TOLAN
NANCY GUERRA

Recent advances in research and practice on the prevention and treatment of youth mental health problems have emphasized the central role of the child's developing cognitions (Boxer & Dubow, 2002; Compton et al., 2004; Guerra, Boxer, & Kim, 2005). Children actively participate in a variety of contexts (e.g., home, neighborhood, school) that provide the settings and experiences that shape their subsequent cognitive, emotional, and behavioral development. Guerra and her colleagues summarized this cognitive–ecological view of child development:

> The developing individual is seen as an active participant in a learning process linking individual (e.g., irritability, impulsivity) and environmental (e.g., community violence, poverty) risk factors to social behavior through cognitive structures, such as beliefs, rules, and schemas, and skills, such as attention, attribution, and problem solving. This *cognitive–*

ecological view posits that problem behaviors emerge through interactions between individual predisposition and contextual socialization and are maintained over time and across situations by cognitive "styles" that are shaped by direct and observational learning experiences. Cognitive styles are learned across multiple contexts and, in turn, influence responding across these contexts. The term "ecological" refers to the nested contexts of child development, providing a stage for social interactions, opportunities for social engagement, and a normative or regulatory structure that includes costs and benefits of distinct courses of action. (p. 277)

Thus, to advance our understanding of cognitive-behavioral models of prevention and intervention, researchers and practitioners should expand notions of cognitive development to incorporate the multiple contexts and interactions.

The purpose of this chapter is to highlight the contributions of the cognitive–ecological view in advancing intervention science with children and adolescents. We first discuss the viability of the cognitive–ecological view for improving knowledge of and impact on mental health problems of contemporary youth. We then explore the application of the cognitive–ecological model to youth interventions, especially those programs that are appropriate for, and based in, school settings. Finally, we explore implications for future research and practice with the cognitive–ecological model and other multisetting approaches for prevention and intervention with youth experiencing mental health problems.

The Cognitive–Ecological Model: Enhancing Cognitive Research and Practice with Youth

As defined above, the cognitive–ecological view is one of the most promising among current cognitive-behavioral mental health models for advancing the prevention and treatment of child problems. Traditional cognitive-behavioral models emphasize the role of individual functioning apart from traditional intrapsychic models. For example, traditional cognitive-behavioral models begin by assessing the role of individual deficits and distortions in cognition. These models subsequently implement strategies to modify these dysfunctional cognitions to enhance an individual's emotional state and behavioral practices.

For example, a child who is getting into arguments with peers in a classroom may be referred to a traditional cognitive-behavioral treatment program. This traditional program would identify the child's difficulties with cognitive schemas and processes that underlie these peer conflicts. This type of program would subsequently seek to replace these problematic cognitive phenomena with more prosocial ideas that enable adaptive emotions and behaviors with peers. Although acknowledging context, the traditional treatment approach does not place equal emphasis on modifying environmental factors in conjunction with individual factors.

In contrast, the cognitive–ecological model builds on the traditional cognitive-behavioral emphasis on individual functioning by placing these individual attributes in specific social contexts. The cognitive–ecological approach guides modifications of individual cognitions *and* contextual factors to enable comprehensive assessment and treatment of child behavior problems. Thus, the cognitive–ecological viewpoint permits important distinctions in conceptualizing the fundamental problem and identifying targets for the derived intervention.

The cognitive–ecological approach also assesses and addresses the reciprocal influences on cognitive characteristics in the classroom setting, such as ideas and behaviors of peers who have conflicts with the identified child, and of the classroom teacher, whose messages and behaviors shape the classroom context. Contextual interventions might include combining individual skillbuilding with classwide interventions that reinforce these same skills among all students.

The Cognitive–Ecological Conceptualization of Child Behavior

The cognitive–ecological conceptualization of child behavior uses a multifactor framework that emphasizes the confluence of individual, environmental, and situational factors (Guerra et al., 2005). Individual factors include temperament, arousal, brain structures, and other personal characteristics. Environmental factors include family, neighborhood, and social characteristics. Situational factors include perceptions, mood, stress, and other immediate contextual characteristics. The individual, environmental, and situational factors interact over time to shape and maintain cognitive structures that subsequently influence emotions and guide behaviors. In the cognitive–ecological conceptualization of behavior, social cognition influences both behavior and treatment. Practical experiences, derived knowledge, and memory process derived from children's social contexts and experiences produce distinct cognitive styles that become characteristic of individual children over the course of development. Although these cognitive patterns can shift with temporary personal tendencies and environmental cues, children will ultimately internalize and replicate general orientations toward distinct cognitive styles across various social situations. Children will attend to pertinent social information, act according to their individual personality temperament and causal attribution, learn from environmental consequences, and reproduce those selected responses that attain or approximate their intended goals. Thus, children develop and internalize *scripts* (i.e., response patterns for given situations) that facilitate selecting and processing pertinent information and then generating appropriate behaviors in social contexts.

Yet the type of script developed, how it changes over time, and how it is reinforced depends on the context of development. For example, children who are exposed to community violence may form general orientations that are hypersensitive and prone toward peer conflict due to excitable individual temperament, external causal attributions for violent incidents, and consistent "rewards" of peer respect and personal safety for aggressive behavior. Consequently, these youth will most likely internalize aggressive scripts for dealing with perceived and actual hostility from other youth in their schools and neighborhoods. Although individual behaviors and contextual dynamics can vary over time, these child scripts and their situational sources can be valuable targets for intervention given that they represent the intersection of predisposing cognitive style and what is promoted by and reinforced by the contextual influences. Therefore, in designing interventions, the focus is on the child's tendencies but also targeting and changing environmental factors to better promote positive rather than maladaptive behaviors.

The focus on changing child tendencies as well as environmental factors is being increasingly advanced by several theorists, practitioners, and researchers (Crick & Dodge, 1994; Dodge & Pettit, 2003). For example, Dodge and Pettit presented a biopsychosocial model that is congruent with notions of social cognition and scripts. This model argues that (1) biological dispositions, social context, and early and ongoing life experience of developing youth lead to distinct social knowledge comprising related cognitive-emotional phenomena (e.g., relational schema guiding declarative and procedural information processing, and social scripts reflecting beliefs about how social events occur in daily life); (2) this social knowledge about their surrounding world is memorized by children and used as a guide for subsequent behavior; (3) children use this social knowledge to guide information processing and generate related specific cognitive, emotional, and behavioral responses to social stimuli (e.g., peers, parents, teachers); and (4) these social information processing patterns mediate effects of prior experiences on subsequent behaviors and, consequently, offer an important target for prevention and intervention activities. Thus, an increasing number of current cognitive-behavioral models converge in emphasizing a multicontextual intervention framework that enables targeting multiple influences for changing cognitions and behaviors, including entrenched and automatic negative patterns.

Cognitive–Ecological Prevention and Intervention for Children

The multicontextual framework of the cognitive–ecological approach provides multiple opportunities for enhancing prevention and intervention efforts with children. When multiple influences on development can be considered and therefore varied, interventions can be designed to addresses multiple risk factors, draw from multiple treatment modalities, and overlap with and relate what could be otherwise disparate intervention activities. An integrated model can increase the likelihood of effective intervention. In conceptualizing, designing, and applying interventions from this perspective, both the intervention focus and modalities can help guide the particular approach.

Intervention Focus

Although many potential environmental influences on development might be the target of an intervention, three are most salient for children and, therefore, the most apt targets: family, peer relations, and schools. In addition, across cognitive–ecological interventions, there are variations in the intervention focus. Some interventions focus on individual behavior change, some on affecting families or other influential relationships, and others emphasize changing the contextual norms, structures, and behavioral regulations (Hanish & Tolan, 2001).

Families, communities, peers, and schools all play vital roles in the cognitive–ecological approach to youth intervention. Families are obvious influences owing to their primacy in youths' lives. Although parents and caretakers wield varying influence depending on their role and family structure, they nevertheless continue to influence youth by the ideas, actions, and messages they convey (Gorman-Smith, Tolan, Henry, & Florsheim, 2000; Sheidow, Gorman-Smith, Tolan, & Henry, 2001). The communities in which families reside also provide a context for shaping ideas, emotions, and behaviors via their social, economic, and political characteristics. Moreover, youth increasingly respond to, seek acceptance in, and are influenced by their peer groups as they age (Tolan, Gorman-Smith, & Henry, 2003). These family, community, and peer-focused models primarily aim to (1) change perspectives and build skills in youth and adults; (2) improve interactions between youth and other members of their social network; and (3) remain relevant for, and congruent with, the daily living context of program participants (Kerns & Prinz, 2002; Tolan, 2001).

Although families, communities, and peers are important foci for intervention, schools may be the most important focus for contemporary youth. Schools are where youth spend much of their time and interact with a wide variety of children and adults. Schools are primary venues for promoting positive social behavior and managing antisocial behavior. In some communities, schools can be the sole stable access to children and their families, especially those whose communities have violent incidents, insufficient resources, and other environmental stressors that increase risk and impede services. Moreover, schools offer a venue for guiding interaction, coordination, and consistency of behavioral expectations and consequences across multiple child providers and contexts that compose the developmental ecology of children. This role of schools as a service delivery site coincides with an overall shift from predominantly inpatient, residential, and outpatient mental health treatment settings to alternative and accessible community-based settings (Ringeisen, Henderson, & Hoagwood, 2003).

Although schools offer important access and intervention opportunities for mental health providers, schools also involve several obstacles to successful service delivery (Gerber & Solari, 2005; Mayer & Van Acker, Chapter 1, this volume). Key obstacles include (1) continued debates and disagreements about added pressures for providing psychological as well as academic services that strain schools' limited staffing and financial resources; (2) recent legislation such as the No Child Left Behind Act (2002) that have forced schools to often become preoccupied with standardized test scores rather than nonacademic support services; (3) ongoing research and practice challenges related to training, implementation, generalization, sustainability, and cultural context for mental health interventions; and (4) chronic incongruence and fragmentation of the youth service delivery system, both within schools (e.g., between mainstream and special education services) and between institutions (e.g., between schools and mental health agencies, child protection workers, juvenile justice staff, primary care providers, crisis intervention workers). Despite these significant obstacles, schools remain a central community site for daily interactions and potential mobilizing mechanism for integrated youth services. Consequently, schools remain a valuable resource and necessary focus for mental health professionals to increase access to and implementation of cognitive-behavioral interventions for contemporary youth and their families.

Recent research has substantiated the diligent efforts of mental health providers to continue striving to overcome obstacles and tap resources related to schools as a service delivery site. Schools are one of the most (if not *the* most) viable community-based intervention settings for children and adolescents (Ringeisen et al., 2003; Rones & Hoagwood, 2000). Of children who receive mental health services, 70–80% will receive services in schools (Burns et al., 1995). In addition, many of these children who receive school-based services are often recipients of special education or other intensive services that these children would not have received through mainstream mental health institutions as schools have become the de facto mental health system for youth in the United States (Van Acker and Mayer, Chapter 4, this volume). Moreover, schools are an optimal venue for intervening with these youth and their peer groups, an important contextual influence on child cognition and behavior. For example, children are often influenced by their peers in terms of establishing and maintaining self-concepts, social relationships, close friendships, and clique formations. Consequently, these peer influences can directly precipitate or reinforce these children's associations and activities with either deviant or non-deviant peer groups. As such, schools remain a viable site for flexible and collaborative programs that are constructed in congruence with school mandates, missions, and peer dynamics.

Intervention Modalities

Many cognitive–ecological interventions are a synthesis of individual, family, and contextual modalities in an integrated intervention. The cognitive–ecological model, however, can also emphasize one of these modalities to suit intervention objectives.

Individual modalities are designed to address individual child behavior including such risk factors as chronic patterns of dysfunctional behavior, distinct styles of difficult temperament, and gender-based forms and meanings of maladaptive behavior. For example, individual interventions may include teaching children to properly regulate their emotions, accurately interpret cues, and select appropriate behaviors for interactions with other children and adults. In addition, reinforcement systems to increase frequency of prosocial behaviors and decrease frequency of negative behaviors are important elements of individual intervention approaches.

Family interventions are geared toward modifying family interactions, including risk factors related to parenting styles, socialization practices, and communication patterns. These may be composed of teaching the targeted children, their parents and guardians, and other family members about consistent and appropriate discipline, warm and effective communication, collaborative problem solving, and case management for family stressors (e.g., poverty) that are not child centered yet are debilitating to family functioning.

Contextual modalities are focused on changing structural, logistical, institutional, or other elements of the youth's surrounding environment in an effort to alter the youth's cognition and related behaviors. Contextual interventions can include making changes in the child's social, academic, and community environments, such as correcting the child's misattributions about hostility from peers and teachers, putting the child in prosocial peer group activities, strengthening home–school partnerships by rewarding positive academic performance and behavior in both settings, and establishing plans for monitoring in the child's neighborhood to avoid negative situations (e.g., gatherings involving drug and alcohol use). Moreover, these contextual interventions can include coordinated schoolwide programs to either reward or discourage specific shifts in self-awareness, cognition attributions, interpersonal communication, and prosocial behaviors, such as shared language among school staff and classroom competitions and rewards for intended behavior changes.

Intervention Integration

Although interventions may be focused on individuals, families, or schools and may be undertaken through different modalities, the developmental–ecological framework favors integrating the different foci and different modalities. An example of such integration is a case in which a child is referred for aggressive conflicts with peers and defiance toward teachers in the classroom. The individual modality can be geared toward teaching the child to correctly interpret cues that enable him or her to distinguish aggressive from nonaggressive peers. This modality can also include teaching the child "calm down" techniques for when angry or upset with peers. In addition, a tangible technique could be a reinforcement system for the classroom that awards points for positive and peaceful behaviors and subtracts points for negative behaviors. The family modality can involve teaching the child and his or her parents about constructive alternatives to hostility and violence in dealing with adults and peers. In addition, the family modality can design and implement a set of messages and discipline about appropriate conflict resolution in the classroom that can also be practiced in the home. As needed, the parents can also receive case management services, such as psychoeducation about dealing with aggressive children and adult treatment for any mental health issues that might be reducing parents' ability to implement the assigned interventions. Finally, the contextual modality can include enrolling the child in prosocial park district activities, coordinating parent participation in the classroom during high-conflict periods in the day, and helping children avoid associating with delinquent peers in the local neighborhood.

Contemporary Cognitive–Ecological Program Exemplars

The elaborate nature of a cognitive–ecological approach to child intervention may imply that such interventions are implausible or impractical. In fact, there are many examples of intervention efficacy. However, as with other approaches, there is less certainty about how the evident potential translates to effectiveness for large-scale implementation. A number of programs and interventions based in the cognitive–ecological approach have shown promise for reducing aggression; improving achievement and social functioning; and reducing rates of delinquency, drug use, and other associated adolescent problems (Conduct Problems Prevention Research Group, 1999; Greenberg, Kusché, & Mihalic, 1998; Hawkins et al., 1992; Henggeler, Mihalic, Rone, Thomas, & Timmons-Mitchell, 1998; Tolan, Gorman-Smith, & Henry, 2004). These programs emphasize various aspects of the developmental ecology of youth in their family, community, and school contexts. In addition, their treatment focus ranges from universal prevention with youth at risk for mental health problems to more intensive intervention strategies for youth with severe psychosocial difficulties. The remainder of this chapter highlights selected programs that illustrate these types of ecological models dealing with children and adolescents.

Individual Child Emphases

The Promoting Alternative THinking Strategies (PATHS) multiyear, universal prevention program for elementary school-age children (particularly grades K–5) combines school-based and family-based strategies (Greenberg et al., 1998). It seeks to both promote emotional and social competencies and reduce aggression and behavior problems, and its school-based implementation is designed to simultaneously enhance the educational process in the classroom. Classroom teachers receive developmentally appropriate instructions and materials to promote youth social–emotional competencies, including (1) cognitive strategies for thinking, planning, and resolving conflicts; (2) identification, management, and constructive expression of emotions; and (3) verbal and nonverbal communication strategies with adults and peers. In addition, parents receive information and join school-based activities as a means of promoting youth outcomes across home, family, and school contexts.

The PATHS program has been successful in improving protective factors and reducing risk factors among program youth compared with control group youth (Greenberg et al., 1998). In particular, the PATHS program has demonstrated improvements in using self-control, understanding and recognizing emotions, tolerating frustration, thinking and planning, and using effective conflict resolution strategies. The PATHS program has also reduced emotional and conduct problems, especially aggression, anxiety, and depressive symptoms (Conduct Problems Prevention Research Group, 2002).

The PATHS model has also played a role in FAST Track, a comprehensive child-focused intervention encompassing home, school, and community strategies for multiple settings and populations (Conduct Problems Prevention Research Group, 1999). FAST Track is a multiyear, universal prevention program that includes school-based strategies for youth, such as social skills training to strengthen social-cognitive and problem-solving skills and academic tutoring to improve reading skills. FAST Track has successfully incorporated the PATHS model as its classroom intervention component to provide an intensive home–school component to the overall model. To augment these school-based activities, the FAST Track model trains caretakers in cultivating academic skills and appropriate behaviors in youth as well as encouraging parental involvement in school. These parent-focused strategies are reinforced by regularly scheduled home visits by program staff (Conduct Problems Prevention Research Group, 1999).

FAST Track is an example of a coordinated, multicontextual, and multimodal intervention with promising preliminary outcomes. Initial evaluations indicate that program participants improve in behavior toward adults and peers. Parents also report less need for and use of corporal punishment, more warmth and involvement (mothers), and more parental involvement (Conduct Problems Prevention Research Group, 2002).

Family Emphases

The Schools and Families Educating (SAFE) Children program emphasizes family functioning via school-based strategies for young children (Tolan et al., 2004). The SAFE Children program is a single-year, universal prevention model for first-grade children that seeks to improve academic and behavioral development of youth, parenting techniques, family relationships, and parental involvement in school. The intervention consists of multiple family groups that strengthen family functioning, including through topics such as constructive discipline, family communication, and family cohesion. These family-focused group activities are enhanced by individual phonics tutoring to support educational success and re-duce school failure, which contributes to child academic and behavioral difficulties in school. It should be noted that in some cases the phonics focus may not be consistent with the school's approach to first-grade reading instruction. However, this is rare, and we have not encountered much problem integrating this work with set school curricula. This may be due, in part, to a focus on engagement of staff to support the program and to help with its implementation.

Among program participants, child aggression has declined, reading scores and academic functioning have improved, children have shown an improved ability to concentrate and demonstrate prosocial behavior, and parents have maintained involvement in school. In addition, SAFE has successfully launched an effectiveness study in collaboration with local community mental health agencies to investigate whether these effects will continue when providers are community-based staff rather than the university-based graduate students as used in previous studies (Gorman-Smith et al., 2007).

Although SAFE and similar programs target early-age and universal prevention, multisystemic therapy (MST) is an intensive community-based example of the cognitive–ecological model that focuses on ad-dressing family and community factors in seriously antisocial delinquent adolescents (Henggeler et al., 1998). MST is an intensive, short-term in-tervention for adolescents who are juvenile offenders that recognizes their complex network of interconnected systems (individual, family, and extrafamilial peers, schools) and neighborhood factors. MST treatment strategies focus on using structural, strategic, and cognitive-behavioral family therapy strategies to strengthen the caregiver and other supports for the targeted youth.

Extensive empirical evaluation indicates that MST has had signifi-cant success with juvenile offenders and other youth with severe prob-lems. MST outcomes include reductions in long-term rates of rearrests, recidivism, out-of-home placements, and mental health problems. In addition, MST has led to improved family functioning. These types of intervention effects have been obtained with varied groups, including youth of different races/ethnicities and rural and urban youth (Heng-geler et al., 1998).

School Classroom Emphasis

The Seattle Social Development Project (SSDP) is a multidimensional in-tervention that emphasizes school-based services to decrease adolescent problem behaviors (Hawkins et al., 1992). Using a social development model, SSDP integrates social learning principles at individual and peer levels to increase prosocial bonds and behavior as well as school attachment and commitment for grade school and middle school children. SSDP instructs teachers in classroom management, interactive teaching, cooperative learning, and communication and conflict resolution skills. SSDP teacher training is intended to strengthen and clarify classroom rules and rewards, improve children's academic performance, and increase prosocial peer interactions. SSDP also offers optional parent training in family management, parent–child communication, and drug use prevention.

Compared with youth in a control group, SSDP program participants had lower levels of aggression, alcohol use, self-destructive behavior, and delinquent peer association. In addition, these youth demonstrated higher levels of commitment, attachment, and success in school over a multiyear evaluation period (Hawkins, Catalano, Kosterman, Abbott, & Hill, 1999).

Schoolwide Emphasis

Whereas SSDP emphasizes classroom-based interventions, the Positive Behavioral Intervention and Supports (PBIS) program seeks schoolwide solutions to dealing with students with severe emotional and behavioral disabilities (Freeman et al., 2006). PBIS has been an important component in special education law (e.g., the 1997 and 2004 Individuals with Disabilities Education Acts), and its schoolwide format offers a promising opportunity for comprehensive cognitive-behavioral interventions with students having a range of mental health needs.

PBIS uses a multitiered, data-driven approach to identifying and addressing an intensifying level of psychosocial student needs through positive language, derived strategies, and contingent reinforcements that are implemented on a schoolwide basis. This model of synchronized slogans and activities among teachers, staff, and students throughout the school enables a consistent message toward maximizing positive outcomes. In addition, PBIS uses a three-tiered treatment continuum comprising universal prevention, early intervention, and intensive intervention that resolves youth problems in the least restrictive strategies and settings. This schoolwide approach also reduces the likelihood of using disjointed services and providers within the school setting or requiring segregated classrooms and other exclusionary approaches that unnecessarily isolate and alienate severely troubled students. Although most research to date has yet to explicitly evaluate outcomes with special education students, PBIS has an inclusive nature and systematic approach that may offer a much-needed systemwide framework for schoolwide cognitive-behavioral interventions to benefit the full range of mainstream and special education students.

Beyond Demonstrations: Future Directions

The available evidence suggests that a cognitive–ecological approach to prevention and intervention can provide a more sensitive and comprehensive understanding of child mental health and can more effectively guide intervention than a simple focus on the child or a given developmental setting. Moreover, theories of child developmental influences across levels can help integrate intervention foci and modalities. Exemplary programs have shown positive impacts on the academic, behavior, and social functioning of students with such changes in attitude, behavior, parenting and family relationships, and teacher and school behavior (Tolan & Gorman-Smith, 2003). Yet these results remain more a promise than a reality. We suggest two particular areas that might aid further development and utility of this approach, as well as some remaining challenges to realizing the full potential of this perspective.

Conceptual Development

Contextual Processes and Complexity

The relationship between context and child development (and risk) underscored by a developmental–ecological approach has broadened what we assess, how we design interventions, and how we measure effects. However, it has also brought into relief the limitations of how context is commonly conceptualized in developmental psychopathology and intervention design (Tolan & Gorman-Smith, 2003). Most often it is considered a static marker of difference in resources (e.g., socioeconomic level). However, as research unpacks such markers and identifies the critical interpersonal and social processes and sociological structures that compose them, the poverty of these conceptualizations becomes evident. Thus, there is a need to greatly improve the characterization, specification, and differentiation of various processes and how processes relate to structural characteristics, such as the economic status of a community. Similarly, it is becoming evident that although even gross differentiation of neighborhood and other key contexts is a step forward, it may carry assumptions that limit how informative such an approach can be. The impact and its antecedents may be so complex and intertwined that reducing them to a simple and homogenous influence is impossible. For example, an assumed "bad" neighborhood (e.g., a setting that is rife with poverty and violence) may be typically dismissed as a barrier to successful intervention with urban children. This same setting, however, may have important protective resources for children, opportunities for shaping cognition and behavior, or manageable obstacles to effective interventions for targeted youth. Also, the impact of key neighborhood processes and norms may be different for adolescents and younger children. Teens, by the nature of their developmental stage, for example, are more susceptible to peer influences and thus at higher risk for gang involvement. However, this same neighborhood may offer additional buffers to gang involvement for lower risk youth, from positive adult mentors within the family, prosocial adolescent activities within the community, social supports in local faith-based centers, and school-based resources for successful academic and behavioral performance. By considering this variation in access to and use of protective elements, interventions that build on these natural opportunities are likely to be more successful and sustainable.

Similar conceptual complexities can be identified for schools and neighborhood informal relations. With further development of how we characterize and approach contextual effects, we are likely to greatly enhance the effects of interventions as well as the fit to those environments.

Power and Potential of Schools

Despite their critical role as a resource for identifying and serving children, schools have yet to view interventions for behavior and social problems as a key purpose. Moreover, the power of schools to affect development through intervention that target school conditions as well as their role as an opportune venue for intervention delivery is just being realized. For example, the School Health Policies and Programs Study 2000 indicated that the three most common forms of school-based services are individual therapy, case management, and evaluation/testing (Brener, Martindale, & Weist, 2001). These three activities are primarily limited to the diagnosis, treatment, and resource identification of individual children without equitable emphases on the assessment, modification, and enhancement of contributing factors in the children's overall developmental ecology. Consequently, the growing needs and scarce resources for school-based mental health services suggest a need for a paradigm shift that can produce efficient, effective, and sustainable school-based services across developmental contexts.

The power and potential of school-based prevention and intervention may be fully realized by adopting more ecologically oriented service delivery models (Ringeisen et al., 2003). For example, the ecological model (Atkins et al., 1998) and the expanded school mental health model (Weist & Christodulu, 2000) both adopt multidimensional and multicontextual intervention approaches that integrate individual, classroom, and school dimensions. Furthermore, the cognitive–ecological model (Guerra et al., 2005) extends these ecological principles by advocating structured treatment principles for implementation across these three intervention dimensions. These types of interventions use cognitive-behavioral principles to target multiple sources of influence on child cognition, including the student, teacher, classroom, and school interactions that shape and sustain children's ideas, emotions, and behaviors. Hence, ecological interventions (especially those with specific substantiated strategies such as cognitive-behavioral treatments) can be very useful in advancing school-based research and practice with child mental health.

Boon and Bane of School-Based Service

Although schools remain a promising site for both prevention and intervention activities, school-based programs also involve a number of facilitators and inhibitors of service delivery (Gerber & Solari, 2005; Mayer & Van Acker, Chapter 1, this volume). On a positive note, schools provide direct and structured access to students, many of whom are underserved or unserved by mainstream mental health institutions. Moreover, this access is provided through a preexisting school structure that is based on identification, provision, and evaluation of student service needs. In addition, schools offer a number of professionals and paraprofessionals who can collaborate with researchers and practitioners to individually or collectively implement and support these school-based interventions.

Despite these possible benefits, schools face serious challenges to successful service delivery. First of all, schools struggle to adequately provide psychosocial supports while maintaining their primary mission of academic excellence in this era of shrinking resources and increasing demands. Moreover, schools are facing severe pressures to focus attention and resources almost exclusively on academic test scores as indicators of progress and justifications for continued operation (e.g., avoiding closures, firings). Administrators and staff at these schools also face related job performance pressures that limit or prevent time for mental health training for implementing sophisticated mental health interventions. Finally, adaptation of structured interventions to the culture of the student and family background as well as the school setting and operation remains a challenge for successful intervention implementation.

Special Education System

One of the most important factors in successful school-based service delivery is the special education system (Van Acker & Mayer, Chapter 4, this volume). Although it primarily targets youth classified as having "emotional or behavioral disorders," the special education system is a microcosm of the strengths and strains of general school-based services for children with psychosocial needs. On a positive note, with the passage of key laws including the No Child Left Behind Act (2002) and the President's New Freedom Commission on Mental Health (2003), the special education system offers a legally sanctioned emphasis on school mental health. In addition, a concurrent rise in school-based service foci for research and practice as a means of addressing service disparities among contemporary youth provides additional possible treatment options and resources for special needs children. Unfortunately, the special education system also faces significant impairments to effective and coordinated service delivery, including (1) an overflow of children with multiple complex needs that strain the availability and structure of special education services; (2) a limited amount of providers, teachers, and other personnel who have the necessary training to implement the requisite interventions; (3) multiple and often incongruous placements during the school day that impede comprehensive and consistent intervention approaches across school staff and settings; (4) punitive administrative responses to unacceptable school-based behavior that characterizes most special education students; and (5) implausibility of randomized control trials and other rigorous research methods to evaluate and enhance program outcomes. Thus, school-based programs in general and the special education system in particular must design activities to capitalize on facilitators and resolve or avoid inhibitors in service delivery to maximize cognitive-based program success.

Unique School-Based Opportunities for Parental Involvement

While possibly increasing intervention access, structured, school-based programs also offer unique opportunities for maximizing the engagement and involvement of parents. Parents of children with significant mental health needs are often extremely difficult to engage and retain in mental health interventions (McKay, Atkins, et al., 2003). Yet school-based mental health programs may offer greater opportunity for successfully recruiting and retaining parents in mental health interventions. For example, Atkins and colleagues' (2006) school-based mental health model showed significant increases in initial and ongoing parental involvement (80%) compared to a clinic-based model (0%) for 12 months. Moreover, school-based mental health programs that *do* successfully involve parents in collaborative and consultation activities can improve children's mental health outcomes (Lowie, Lever, Ambrose, Tager, & Hill, 2003; McKay, Atkins, Hawkins, Brown, & Lynn, 2003). For example, parental involvement in children's schooling is associated with improved academic performance as well as improved behavior at home and school (Atkins et al., 2006; Gorman-Smith et al., 2000; Henderson & Berla, 1994). Consequently, the natural links between school activities and parental presence in supporting children's academic and behavioral performance suggest that school-based programs remain a largely untapped resource for advancing parental roles in ecologically appropriate interventions.

Challenges for Advancing a Cognitive–Ecological Approach

To realize the full advantages of a cognitive–ecological approach, the field needs additional work and advances (Guerra et al., 2005). We identify five areas of critical importance.

1. *Developmentally informed and sensitive assessment and intervention.* Although some interventions are designed with the developmental stage and needs of the targeted group in mind, many are not, and many others do not explicitly consider the developmental specificity of the intervention formulation. Just as cognitive development follows developmental patterns in form and substance, developmental influences and their impacts are dependent on context. Yet these aspects are not yet incorporated into many interventions, even among those applying a developmental–ecological approach.

2. *More tests of context modification effects.* Most interventions still focus on changing individual child cognitions and behavior, or changing parent or teacher cognitions and behavior. Far fewer consider how these might be constrained by, promoted by, and dependent on contextual characteristics. It may be that positive impacts could arise from changing contextual influences such as reinforcement of parent and teacher behaviors; organizational communication methods; physical characteristics of the contexts; and opportunities for positive behavior by children, parents, and teachers. Similarly, changing group norms may also lead to important effects. An important step forward in this effort is current approaches such as the PBIS model. However, there are methodological and practical challenges to such work, even though these approaches are sorely needed (Multisite Violence Prevention Project, 2004).

3. *The need to consider implementation strategies and challenges.* Current trends toward evidence-based practice and other applied research efforts require careful consideration of "real-world" practicalities (e.g., who can deliver the intervention, what the logistical and fiscal factors in sustaining these programs are, how to ensure rigorous fidelity while maintaining manageable implementation). Yet there are relatively

few studies of the role these practicalities play in the results (i.e., how variations in approaches or lower fidelity might enhance impact, sustainability, or engagement of providers and recipients). The field would be greatly enhanced by advances in our understanding of effective implementation, what makes a difference in program use and impact in real-world use, and what modifications are critical to attaining success within practical realms.

4. *More attention to integrative and multidimensional programs.* Applying multiple components simultaneously should, in theory, have a greater impact than applying them individually—they are more than the sum of their parts. At the least, when applied simultaneously they are complementary and additive. Yet few studies have tested this assumption. Moreover, many multicomponent programs arise from conceptually different predecessors and therefore may not be well-integrated for providers or recipients. Studies that examine the simultaneous application of multiple components can lead to a better understanding of how multicomponent and multidimensional interventions can avoid conflicting with one another and be translated across foci and modalities.

5. *The need to expand tests of service delivery systems.* In most cases, the available evidence for effects is drawn from relatively small-scale, well-controlled demonstration tests. There are few examples, and even fewer studies, of intervention delivery systems. As with other larger scale research, these tests require considerable resources and collaboration that can be quite challenging to manage. However, the lack of understanding of these promising interventions within service systems renders the knowledge most tentative. It maintains a gap between what could be done to aid children and what is likely to be done, such that the promise is not turned into practice. This is important to change, and appropriate research is needed to do so (Multisite Violence Prevention Project, 2004).

References

Atkins, M., Frazier, S., Birman, D., Abdul Adil, J., Jackson, M., Graczyk, P., et al. (2006). School-based mental health services for children living in high poverty urban communities. *Administration and Policy in Mental Health and Mental Health Services Research, 33*(2), 146–159.

Atkins, M. S., McKay, M. M., Arvantis, P., London, L., Madison, S., Costigan, C., Haney, P., et al. (1998). An ecological model for school based mental health services for urban low-income aggressive children. *Journal of Behavioral Health Services and Research, 25*(1), 64–75.

Boxer, P., & Dubow, E. E. (2002). A social–cognitive information-processing model for school-based aggression reduction and prevention programs. *Applied and Preventive Psychology, 10,* 177–192.

Brener, N. D., Martindale, J., & Weist, M. D. (2001). Mental health and social services: Results from the School Health Policies and Programs Study 2000. *Journal of School Health, 71*(7), 305–313.

Burns, B. J., Costello, E. J., Angold, A., Tweed, D., Stangl, D., Farmer, E. M., et al. (1995). Children's mental health service use across service sectors. *Health Affairs, 14*(3), 147–159.

Compton, S. N., March, J. S., Brent, D., Albano, A. M., Weersing, V. R., & Curry, J. (2004). Cognitive-behavioral psychotherapy for anxiety and depressive disorders in children and adolescents. An evidence-based medicine review. *Journal of the American Academy of Child and Adolescent Psychiatry, 43*, 930–959.

Conduct Problems Prevention Research Group. (1999). Initial impact of the Fast Track prevention trial for conduct problems: I. The high-risk sample. *Journal of Consulting and Clinical Psychology, 67*, 631–347.

Conduct Problems Prevention Research Group. (2002). Predictor variables associated with positive fast track outcomes at the end of third grade. *Journal of Abnormal Child Psychology, 30*, 37–52.

Crick, N. R., & Dodge, K. A. (1994). A review and reformulation of social information processing mechanisms in children's social adjustment. *Psychological Bulletin, 115*, 74–101.

Dodge, K. A., & Pettit, G. S. (2003). A biopsychosocial model of the development of chronic conduct problems in adolescence. *Developmental Psychology, 39*(2), 349–371.

Freeman, R., Eber, L., Anderson, C., Irvin, L., Horner, R., Bounds, M., et al. (2006). Building inclusive cultures using schoolwide PBS: Designing effective individual support systems for students with significant disabilities. *Research and Practice for Persons with Severe Disabilities, 31*(1), 1–32.

Gerber, M. M., & Solari, E. (2005). Teaching effort and the future of cognitive-behavior interventions. *Behavioral Disorders, 30*, 289–299.

Gorman-Smith, D., Tolan, P. H., Henry, D. B., & Florsheim, P. (2000). Patterns of family functioning and adolescent outcomes among urban African American and Mexican American families. *Journal of Family Psychology, 14*(3), 436–457.

Gorman-Smith, D., Tolan, P. H., Henry, D., Quintana, E., Lutovsky, K., & Leventhal, A. (2007). The SAFE Children prevention program. In P. Tolan, J. Szapocznik, & S. Sombrano (Eds.), *Developmental approaches to prevention of substance abuse and related problems* (pp. 113–136). Washington, DC: American Psychological Association.

Greenberg, M. T., Kusché, C., & Mihalic, S. F. (1998). *Promoting Alternative Thinking Strategies (PATHS): Blueprints for violence prevention* (Book 10). Boulder: University of Colorado, Center for the Study and Prevention of Violence, Institute of Behavioral Science.

Guerra, N. G., Boxer, P., & Kim, T. E. (2005). A cognitive–ecological approach to serving students with emotional and behavioral disorders: Application to aggressive behavior. *Behavioral Disorders, 30*, 277–288.

Hanish, L. D., & Tolan, P. H. (2001). Antisocial behaviors in children and adolescents: Expanding the cognitive model. In W. J. Lyddon & J. V. Jones, Jr. (Eds.), *Empirically supported cognitive therapies: Current and future applications* (pp. 182–199). New York: Springer.

Hawkins, J. D., Catalano, R. F., Kosterman, R., Abbott, R., & Hill, K. G. (1999). Preventing adolescent health-risk behaviors by strengthening protection during childhood. *Archives of Pediatrics and Adolescent Medicine, 153*, 226–324.

Hawkins, J. D., Catalano, R. F., Morrison, D., O'Donnell, J., Abbott, R., & Day, E. (1992). The Seattle Social Development Project: Effects of the first four years on protective factors and problem behaviors. In J. McCord & R. E. Tremblay (Eds.), *Preventing antisocial behavior: Interventions from birth through adolescence* (pp. 139–161). New York: Guilford Press.

Henderson, A., & Berla, N. (1994). *A new generation of evidence: The family is critical to student achievement.* Washington, DC: National Committee for Citizens in Education.

Henggeler, S. W., Mihalic, S. F., Rone, L., Thomas, C., & Timmons-Mitchell, J. (1998). *Multisystemic therapy: Blueprints for violence prevention* (Book 6). Boulder: University of Colorado, Center for the Study and Prevention of Violence, Institute of Behavioral Science.

Kerns, S. E., & Prinz, R. J. (2002). Critical issues in the prevention of violence-related behavior in youth. *Clinical Child and Family Psychology Review, 5*(2), 133–160.

Lowie, J. A., Lever, N. A., Ambrose, M. G., Tager, S. B., & Hill, S. (2003). Partnering with families in expanded school mental health programs. In M. D. Weist (Ed.), *Handbook of school mental health: Advancing practice and research issues in clinical child psychology* (pp. 135–148). New York: Kluwer Academic/Plenum.

McKay, M. M., Atkins, M. S., Hawkins, T., Brown, C., & Lynn, C. J. (2003). Inner-city African-American parental involvement in children's schooling: Racial socialization and social support from the parent community. *American Journal of Community Psychology, 32,* 107–114.

Multisite Violence Prevention Project. (2004). Lessons learned in the Multisite Violence Prevention Project: Collaboration: Big questions require large efforts. *American Journal of Preventive Medicine, 26,* 62–71.

No Child Left Behind Act of 2001, Public Law No. 107-110, 115 Stat. 1425 (2002).

President's New Freedom Commission on Mental Health. (2003). *Achieving the promise: Transforming mental health care in America. Final report* (DHHS Publication No. SMA-03-3832). Rockville, MD: U.S. Department of Health and Human Services.

Ringeisen, H., Henderson, K., & Hoagwood, K. (2003). Context matters: Schools and the "research to practice gap" in children's mental health. *School Psychology Review, 32*(2), 153–168.

Rones, M., & Hoagwood, K. (2000). School-based mental health services: A research review. *Clinical Child and Family Psychology Review, 3*(4), 223–241.

Sheidow, A. J., Gorman-Smith, D., Tolan, P. H., & Henry, D. B. (2001). Family and community characteristics: Risk factors for violence exposure in inner-city youth. *Journal of Community Psychology, 29,* 345–360.

Tolan, P. H. (2001). Youth violence and its prevention in the United States. *Injury Control and Safety Promotion, 8*(1), 1–12.

Tolan, P. H., & Gorman-Smith, D. (2003). What violence prevention can tell us about developmental psychopathology. *Developmental and Psychopathology, 14,* 713–729.

Tolan, P. H., Gorman-Smith, D., & Henry, D. B. (2003). The developmental ecology of urban males' youth violence. *Developmental Psychology, 39,* 274–291.

Tolan, P. H., Gorman-Smith, D., & Henry, D. (2004). Supporting families in a high-risk setting: Proximal effects of the SAFE Children prevention program. *Journal of Consulting and Clinical Psychology, 72,* 855–869.

Weist, M. D., & Christodulu, K. V. (2000). Expanded school mental health programs: Advancing reform and closing the gap between research and practice. *Journal of School Health, 70*(5), 195–200.

CHAPTER 14

Future Challenges
to Cognitive-Behavioral
Interventions
in Practice and Policy

MICHAEL M. GERBER
EMILY SOLARI

In this chapter, we discuss the future of school-based, cognitive-behavioral interventions (CBIs) for students with emotional and behavioral disorders (EBD). Our discussion is limited to the potential of CBIs in everyday school practice and not to their clinical applications as part of noneducational therapies (e.g., see Gerber & Solari, 2005; Maag, 2006; Polsgrove & Smith, 2004). For most of their childhood and adolescence, children and youth with EBD will be in public schools, and it is in these places, through individually tailored special education, that the opportunity is available to address their individual needs. Moreover, we believe that the problem of applying CBIs in schools is never about the ability to prepare a single teacher under relatively supported and controlled circumstances. The real problem, we contend, is how to bring valid knowledge about this or any scientifically valid or high-potential practice to bear generally and at some significant scale.

An Implicit Curriculum for Self-Management

Although schools, through their teachers, often have academic and social self-management as an explicit goal for students with EBD, it is also an implicit goal for all other students. Students with EBD tend to receive special notice because self-management often is seen as a skill in deficit and, therefore, as a necessary component of intervention. However, although students *without* EBD may already engage in "normal" academic learning and related social behavior, teachers have expectations that students can and should become *increasingly* self-regulating over time. These expectations may derive from knowledge of child development but also may reflect increasing need for efficiency in classroom instruction and management as children get older and the curriculum becomes more demanding.

Either way, teachers express their expectations for increasing self-regulation chiefly by gradually transferring greater responsibility for managing assigned tasks to students. In so doing, teachers act to motivate and instruct their students to control task-oriented behaviors, such as attention, perseverance, timeliness in beginning and ending tasks, following directions, and other social behaviors that directly facilitate learning and also help maintain a classroom environment conducive to learning. In an important sense, then, teachers engage in an implicit, but pervasive, cognitive-behavioral instruction all of the time and for all students. That is, learning to manage oneself constitutes a universal, although sometimes tacit, curriculum in all classroom-based education. What seems critically different, however, is how *explicit* teachers need to be in implementing a particular CBI for students with EBD compared with the largely *implicit* nature of the self-management curriculum for all students that emerges from normal classroom instruction.

Cognitive-Behavioral Aspects of Teaching

As a relatively hidden part of daily instruction, a given student's ability to learn self-regulation and self-management depends primarily on how well teachers coordinate and manage multiple goals during classroom teaching (Perry, 1998; Perry, Phillips, & Dowler, 2004; Perry, VandeKamp, Mercer, & Nordby, 2002). It follows that teaching is of *high quality* to the extent that teachers are able simultaneously to teach students domain-specific knowledge and skills (i.e., how to decode words, how to compute, how to write a report) and teach *general strategies* for managing one's learning in *any* domain (e.g., how to manage and maintain time on task, how to monitor and if necessary repair comprehension, how to formulate and solve problems alone and in cooperative groups; e.g., see Reid & Lienemann, 2006). High-quality teachers, then, are those who regularly create and execute "lessons" that also include substantive opportunities to practice self-regulated learning.

Teachers naturally vary in their ability to be effective instructors, especially when their students have learning characteristics that are particularly challenging. These variations in teachers' abilities to provide effective classroom instruction and behavior management are most tolerable when students are most behaviorally compliant and can, without explicit instruction, acquire useful self-management skills. However, management of classroom teaching that is effective in delivering both the overt (domain-specific) as well as the tacit (cognitive-behavioral self-regulation) curriculum requires the presence in *teachers* of a significant degree of self-awareness, self-knowledge, and self-discipline as well as domain expertise. That is, beyond merely complying and conforming with rules, students become *disciplined* learners when their teachers are highly *disciplined* instructors.

Disciplined instructors not only engage overtly in teaching self-management to their students but also must engage in a significant amount of cognitive as well as behavioral self-management *while* they are teaching. True, teachers must have knowledge of the *domain* in which they are teaching (e.g., reading). Also, they need to have knowledge of *students,* including *general* knowledge about children or adolescents who are *like* those whom they are teaching as well as *specific* knowledge about the particular students whom they are teaching *at the moment.* However, knowledge of students, even together with knowledge of a domain, is not sufficient to produce high-quality, let alone expert, teaching or teachers.

What makes expert teachers different from domain experts or child development experts is their ability to formulate effective instructional plans and, then, behaviors *in real time* that optimally elicit criterion performance from the specific students whom they wish to instruct and regardless of sometimes extreme individual differences among those students. Fact or declarative knowledge of a domain and, similarly, knowledge about students is inert, however expert it may be, unless teachers also possess an expert kind of procedural knowledge we call *knowledge of pedagogy.* The distinction we wish to make is between knowledge *of* practice—the kind of knowledge represented by lunchroom conversation, lecture, and professional writing—and knowledge *in* practice—that is, the actual use of knowledge that teachers demonstrate in the moments that they are teaching.

Skilled teachers display extensive knowledge of pedagogy. That is, they know about and can execute behaviors that translate their *intent* that students should learn something into *explicit* and *coordinated* actions that produce the desired learning. In a superficial sense, this knowledge might represent what is popularly known as *effective practices*. But having a knowledge of pedagogy is not the same as possessing a repertoire of tried and true techniques. Rather, pedagogical knowledge exists as a body of *principles* for translating what teachers know about a domain (e.g., reading words) into explicit and coordinated instructional behaviors (e.g., asking questions to promote and guide responses) that are optimal for eliciting desired performances from a *particular* group of students. These principles might be represented in formal ways for purposes of professional education, but they are a kind of procedural knowledge that is pruned and validated for actual practice by teaching experiences over time in classrooms with varieties of learners.

When teachers confront very difficult (i.e., uncontrollable) students, students who diverge significantly from the behavior and responsiveness expected from students who are the same age or grade level, their implicit pedagogical knowledge must become explicit. In teaching difficult students, teachers are forced to examine their knowledge directly. Specifically, they must determine why, in a particular circumstance, their pedagogical knowledge is not producing the expected result, and what can or should be done about it. This is precisely what happens in the case of students who have EBD. The problem facing teachers in such circumstances is not merely that they may not possess a particular teaching skill in their repertoire, but rather that their experience with students, perhaps together with their experience teaching in a particular domain, fails to provide them *spontaneously* with plans and actions that have a high probability of yielding desired results (i.e., desirable student behavior).

In the face of unresponsive or poorly responsive students, what previously might have been rather automatic now takes on the character of a problem that must be overtly, explicitly, and laboriously thought about, investigated, and solved. Moreover, these are problems that occur *during* teaching and, therefore, impose requirements for rapid formulation and execution of effective actions to reach a desirable outcome. It is during this kind of problem solving that teachers most resemble their students in their efforts to be successfully self-managing. It is the disciplined kind of thinking required of teachers who confront uncontrolled behaviors of students that most resembles the kind of disciplined thinking we hope to induce in students. At these moments, teachers are called upon to engage in the kind of cognitive-behavioral instruction that is part of the implicit curriculum for self-management, but also the formal requirements of skillfully administered, CBIs.

Why CBIs Are Difficult to Implement in Schools

CBIs, as discussed in this book, represent a class of explicit techniques and procedures that require specialized kinds of declarative, as well as procedural, knowledge applied with a high degree of precision. In short, these are not simple techniques, and their effective deployment is highly sensitive to the skill of the user. As we noted earlier, the chief problem in applying CBIs in the schools resides less in the ability to provide single teachers knowledge and skills in the use of a repertoire of techniques than in promoting a generalized increase in the ability of many teachers to acquire and apply this repertoire. That is, there are very significant theoretical and qualitative differences in what may be required to build particular teachers' skills versus requirements for embedding those same skills at a very large scale. For the latter goal to be achieved, empirically validated behavioral techniques have to become scalable behavioral technologies. From a century of experience with behavior management in public schools, it seems generally true that *any* management technique that teachers may usefully employ, including explicit application of CBIs, can become generally applied *technologies* of instruction only to the extent that they can be *reliably* applied by *most* teachers in *most* extant school settings *despite* variations both in teachers and in the environments in which they teach.

A 2000 survey (Gottfredson et al., 2000) suggested that schools are severely limited in their capacity to implement research-derived behavioral management programs. Moreover, analyses of treatment effects for all behavioral programs in secondary schools were overestimated and could not be generalized to typical school settings. The researchers argued that schools in which these programs were implemented for research reasons have a higher level of implementation than that of which a typical school is capable. Schools involved in research have support from the program creators. In general, these schools have consented to the program, and in many cases teachers who are willing to try the program are targeted.

It appears, therefore, that effective implementation of relatively sophisticated (i.e., knowledge- and skill-demanding) techniques such as CBIs makes demands on school leadership and administration, on teachers' professional education and development, and on the families that prepare and support students for schooling. That is, programs of professional education and development that intend to build teachers' knowledge of domain, students, and/or pedagogy must also incorporate the goal of training them to effectively address the implicit curriculum for academic and behavioral self-management. School administrators and leaders must be committed—and *act*—to organize and sustain personnel training, administrative, organizational, and financial and other material support for the effort required of teachers to deploy such higher level instructional knowledge and skills. Finally, it is logical to expect that successful implementation of relatively sophisticated techniques would be better facilitated where students are *more* behaviorally compliant and *more* predisposed to acquiring useful self-management skills *without* explicit instruction. In part, students' preparedness to learn in the implicit curriculum of self-management derives from the same sources as their preparedness to learn in the formal academic curriculum. Variations in prior socialization and learning are a fixture of a universal, public education system. Where students are less well prepared, for whatever reason, teachers must be more than ordinarily prepared to make the implicit curriculum explicit. The need for increased preparedness of teachers translates to a call for an increased level of commitment to provide substantive supports to schools and teachers necessary to meet increasing challenges in behavioral management and related classroom instruction.

The inevitable interplay between differences among teachers and the school organizations in which they work presents additional significant and continuing challenges to successful implementation at *any* significant scale of CBIs or *any* other behavior-focused instructional practices derived from rigorous research. To the extent that teachers cannot reliably manage a range of behaviors displayed by students and instruct toward better self-management, and to the extent that schools do not promote and support such skills among teachers, schools may fail to produce the self-regulating learners they desire and certainly will fail to provide appropriate responses to students with EBD in inclusive settings.

Teaching Improvement and the Problem of Agency

Let us consider more deeply the complexity of promoting scientifically validated or other high-potential practices like CBIs in actual schools at some significant scale. Attempts by policymakers or administrators to apply treatment knowledge that has been empirically developed and validated by researchers under controlled circumstances confronts what is called the *principal-agent problem* (Ferris, 1992) or more simply the *agency problem*. School personnel act as "agents" for researchers, developers, administrators, or policymakers who believe they possess and wish to frame knowledge of practice in ways intended to improve student outcomes. But those who wish to implement knowledge *of* practice are not the ones who must implement that knowledge *in* practice.

Teachers ultimately, at the end of this chain of intentions, act as agents for other actors in the educational system and are expected to integrate the intended practices into their everyday pedagogy. It may not matter that the strategy, method, or technique at stake was carefully developed or validated by research if development and validation did not include the costs and efforts required to implement in natural settings with randomly selected teachers. Teachers cannot simply be ordered to behave more effectively any more than children can be ordered to be better achieving. This is why policy mandates—weak and remote behavior management plans for organizations—cannot, by themselves, produce more effective teachers or practice. Teachers must *learn* to teach more effectively and be motivated to do so. Because the organizational ecologies in which they work are complex, teachers also may be protected from inadequate incentives or powerful counter-incentives arising naturally in the work environment, just as students with EBD must be protected from inadequate incentives and counter-incentives in their environments (i.e., risk and protective factors, as discussed within a public health framework). Nor is there a short or easy path for teachers to acquire the necessary expertise, just as there are no short or easy paths for students with EBD to become reliably and successfully self-managing. Rather, these are learning processes that require motivated effort, time, and ample opportunity for practice with feedback.

What makes this learning process—what we can call *professional development*—so difficult is that school systems act as a kind of refracting lens that alters proposed innovations of practice—such as those contained in policy mandates—as they move to and through the organization. One explanation for weak effects in top-down innovations could be the push back from those whose behavior must change the most (Honig, 2006; Weatherly & Lipsky, 1977). Teachers and administrators may work to implement mandates in a manner that is at once legally compliant but also consonant with local capacity, conditions, and values. For example, a survey of more than 13,000 secondary teachers by Gottfredson and his associates found that 76% of schools reported using a "prevention curriculum, instruction, or training" including use of "cognitive-behavioral modeling methods of instruction," and 64% of these schools reported using behavioral or behavior modification interventions. However, 47% of all prevention activities claimed by schools were evaluated as inadequate, even when "research-based" programs were being implemented (Gottfredson et al., 2000).

Moreover, only slightly more than 57% of elementary and high schools with students who are classified as having EBD had conflict resolution or anger management programs (Wagner et al., 2006). Barely a third of students with EBD in these schools received training in learning strategies or study skills. Although about 70% of students with EBD in elementary and middle schools had behavior support or management plans, only about half of such students in high school received these services. In fact, across all schools, only about a third of students with EBD actually received behavioral interventions, and only about 40% received mental health services (Wagner et al., 2006).

Recent comparative research on comprehensive school reform, for example, has shown that different models of schoolwide improvement generate differently patterned ways of organizing change within schools and that these patterns, in turn, produce differences in implementation and success (Correnti & Rowan, 2007; Rowan & Miller, 2007). For example, comprehensive school reform models that promote "procedural" rather than "cultural" or "professional" means for addressing the agency problem tend to produce more desirable changes in the classroom behavior of teachers. In behavioral terms, if the agency problem is to get teachers to adopt better teaching practices, then policy (i.e., any other kind of externally encouraged improvement plan) ought to provide not only positive encouragement and incentives, but also sufficiently direct guidance, monitoring, and feedback, as well as substantive resource supports. Just as students' improved outcomes require deliberate, active, and effective actions on the part of teachers, school administrations must deliberately, actively, and effectively promote learning (i.e., professional development) by their teachers.

Applied researchers might recognize the problem of teacher behavior change as a problem of achieving and maintaining *fidelity of implementation*. However, changes in the intended fidelity of implementation occur not only because of the personal characteristics, preferences, and discretion exhibited by administrators, teachers, or students. Schools also refract intended improvement efforts because of each school's particular distribution of relevant knowledge, talents and motivations, the prevailing dynamics of social and professional relationships, the structure of work and the work day, the habits of administrative and instructional decision making, the adequacy and patterns of resource allocation, the manner and flow of information, and even the configuration or adequacy of physical space.

All of these organizational factors contribute to shaping the behavior of individuals in schools as they respond to any externally presented (e.g., professional development) plans for improvements and reforms. Consequently, the actual construction of educational practices may result in significant divergence from that intended by outsiders (e.g., researchers, developers, administrators, policymakers). Schools' difficulties in implementing new practices arise, therefore, not only from individual differences in human actors, but also from individuals' hierarchical and transactional organization within schools. As a consequence, no matter how well developed the scientific understanding of treatment effectiveness or potential, successful application of new practices at nontrivial scale ultimately requires additional and different knowledge about the organizational propensities and variations of schools and the degree to which these characteristics of schools contribute to teachers' successful problem solving under various challenges to their teaching.

The point to be made is that although an evidentiary basis exists for the effectiveness of cognitive-behavioral training in self-control and self-regulation for students with EBD under some circumstances, it is challenging to implement this knowledge reliably, and at a desirable scale, in everyday classroom-level practice. The school personnel who ultimately must be implementers of CBIs must be supported by their schools in the learning effort—both pre service and in service—that will be required to acquire and apply CBIs effectively as part of normal practice. The research record thus far suggests that larger scale implementation and broad uptake of CBIs by teachers in schools requires significant changes in how teachers are supported in becoming effective overt managers of student behavior in classrooms (Corno, 2006).

The First Hurdle: Effective Classroom Management

One might suppose that a solution to the apparent problem of implementing difficult interventions like CBIs is to enhance teachers' professional education. Indeed, the professional preparation of teachers with regard to managing behavior in the implicit curriculum appears to have lagged significantly far behind scientific knowledge of behavior. However, the implicit curriculum for teaching self-management begins with effective classroom management. Teacher education programs tend to give priority to disciplinary and domain-specific knowledge and teaching strategies without recognizing that behavioral instruction towards self-managed learning is a necessary component of academic instruction. That balance needs to change to help ensure adequate attention to knowledge, strategies, and skills that facilitate integrated application of student self-management in teacher preparation programs.

Furthermore, teacher education programs need to devote more time and energy to addressing basic principles of behavior management to the extent that teachers actually require it (Evans & Tribble, 1986; Gottfredson et al., 2000; Veenman, 1984). Under No Child Left Behind, federal education policy seeks to ensure a "high-quality teacher" in every classroom, and both state departments of education and schools of education have taken steps to respond to that mandate. However, No Child Left Behind's treatment of teacher quality has emphasized content rather than pedagogical knowledge under the assumption that content expertise relates strongly to ability to teach content to higher achievement levels. In fact, in criticizing state licensing systems, the U.S. Department of Education stated in its first annual report on teacher quality that some teaching skills ought to be acquired while in practice:

> Such a streamlined system will shift much authority away from state certification officials and to local school principals. But that is only fair, as these principals are the ones who will be accountable for student academic achievement, as required by the *No Child Left Behind Act*. They have strong incentives to make good hiring decisions. . . . If they find certain pedagogical skills essential—training in research-based reading instruction or classroom management, for example—they will be free to seek out individuals with these skills. Local teacher training programs, unleashed from their monopoly on the teacher preparation business, will likely respond to this demand by producing teachers with those skills that are in high demand. (Darling-Hammond, Holtzman, Gatlin, & Heilig, 2005, p. 40)

In addition to providing improved teacher education in behavior management, schools must provide appropriate professional development opportunities once new teachers begin to work as a natural extension along a time continuum of career-long professional improvement. In schools in which students with EBD are educated, only 17% of elementary teachers received professional development pertinent to the needs of their students with EBD (Wagner et al., 2006). A little more than 20% of middle school teachers received such support, and only 6% of high school teachers did. Fewer than *half* of elementary school teachers who taught students with EBD had received at least 8 hours of professional development in behavior management in the previous 3 years. Far fewer teachers in middle (39%) or high schools (32%) had received this kind of basic instruction.

Similarly, support of teachers' behavior management in typical schools requires improvement nationally. Although almost every one of more than 800 schools surveyed in 2000 reported being engaged in multiple prevention efforts, only 20% of these schools reported attempting to implement packaged "systems" for preventing or reducing serious behavior problems (Gottfredson et al., 2000). Of these, principals reported that less than 5% of the prevention "packages" used directly promote behavior management skills for teachers (Gottfredson et al., 2000, p. 3–28).

In a more recent, larger survey, more than 77% of more than 3,000 schools from a new, nationally stratified sample reported the occurrence of violent incidents, for an overall rate of 31 per 1,000 students (Nolle, Guerino, & Dinkes, 2007). Yet 90% of surveyed schools cited multiple efforts to reduce or prevent crime in the schools, including behavioral interventions, varieties of psychological and therapeutic interventions, and "individual attention, mentoring, tutoring, or coaching of students by students or adults."

The unavoidable conclusion is that schools often have difficulty implementing sound and effective behavior management programs, especially for high-risk students. Educators attempting to meet the needs of these high-risk youth, especially in high-risk schools in clear need of significant professional development and support in program implementation, are in clear need of greater support. Nolle et al.'s (2007) 2006 survey, for example, showed a *third* of sampled schools cited "lack of or inadequate teacher training in classroom management" as a factor in limiting efforts to reduce or prevent crime, and a third of schools also cited "inconsistent application of school policies by faculty or staff" as a limiting factor. Moreover, the public schools suspend about 3 million students a year (e.g., see U.S. Department of Education, 2002). However, as many as 90% of out-of-school suspensions and expulsions are *not* in response to violent or dangerous behavior (Committee on School Health, 2003). Instead, the most common reasons for suspension are *disruptiveness* and *defiance of authority*.

Nearly half of elementary (48%) and middle school (52%) students and more than a third (39%) of high school students with EBD in one study were involved in fighting during a school year (Wagner et al., 2006). However, behaviors disruptive to classroom order and instruction were more frequently reported for these students. About two thirds (66%) of elementary students with EBD were observed "very often" to be distracting, 54% were reported to be impulsive, and 40% seen as frequently arguing with others.

Teachers clearly understand the association between students' behavior and the perceived difficulty of teaching. The Gallup organization has polled teachers nationally for Phi Delta Kappa over several decades. A substantial proportion of teachers *continually* view lack of discipline as a "fairly" or "very" serious problem—49% in 1984, 50% in 1989, 49% in 1998 (Langdon & Vesper, 2000). These data are consistent with findings from other sources. Gottfredson and his associates (2000) found that 27% of teachers in surveyed schools felt that students' behavior kept them from teaching. In urban schools considered "safer," 38% of teachers responded that students' behaviors kept them from teaching. For urban schools considered "less safe," this percentage rose to 74%. Even in suburban, safer schools, almost 1 teacher in 10 reported that students' behaviors kept them from teaching (Gottfredson et al., 2000, pp. 2–29).

Despite the common experience of behavior management difficulties in teaching across many generations, it remains difficult to institutionalize, either in the practices of professional development programs or in schools, the fact that there are actually *three* facets to what we usually characterize as *discipline,* and each has implications for the future of CBIs in everyday school practice.

The Three Disciplines

There are really three *disciplines* to be achieved in effective classrooms and schools. The first discipline, what we normally think of as *classroom* discipline, relates to a required sense of orderliness and civility in which individual impulses are subordinated to teachers' needs to create and maintain an environment conducive to group teaching and learning. Teachers tend to believe that good order arises from presenting highly motivating lessons while maintaining a classroom environment that is appealing to the students in it. When these principles seem to fail, teachers are prone to using mass incentives or sanctions as a means for manipulating motivation to comply with general rules of deportment. It is this "discipline" that is most observable to an outsider visiting a classroom— soft voices, task-related movement, politeness, and general attentiveness and responsiveness to the teacher.

The second discipline concerns self-management of behavior by individual students. We imply this discipline when we refer to a child positively as "disciplined." Some cognitive and behavioral self-management constitutes a tacit product of school curriculum—what we have termed the *implicit curriculum* for teaching self-management. In specialized form and content, disciplined self-management is the explicit target of CBIs. From an information-processing perspective, disciplined self-management of social and academic behavior has much in common. That is, comprehension of social threats and challenges and the subsequent formation or selection of strategic actions require the same cognitive-behavioral self-management as comprehension of text and the formation and selection of skills employed in subsequent performance. The social as well as academic learning success of students, particularly those with EBD, requires not only suppression of behaviors that are noxious or generally maladaptive or that otherwise interfere with learning, but also the *positive* employment of skills that *facilitate* learning; reliable performance of academic skills; formation and maintenance of friendships; achievement of important goals within a community while respecting others; and feelings of self-worth, competence, and happiness.

The third discipline in classrooms—perhaps the least visible or discussed—is the discipline exhibited—or not exhibited—by *teachers* who must continuously and deliberately select actions calculated to attain the other two disciplines (i.e., classroom orderliness and individually self-regulated learning). Moreover, teachers' must engage in such ongoing and consequential choices while controlling their own emotional responses, thoughts, and behaviors. This critical third kind of discipline might emerge naturally as a function of sufficient and reflective teaching experience, but teachers' self-discipline does not develop spontaneously and without effort (Payne & Manning, 1988), or else the other two disciplines would be easier to attain.

In cinematic portrayals of teaching, consonant with the lay public's view of schools, apparent orderliness in classrooms signifies that meaningful learning is occurring. But in real life, without attention to the other two disciplines, there can be no classroom education that matters, only compliance with behavior standards that, by themselves, afford, but do not produce, learning. The future of CBIs in schools is very much tied to the fact that all school teaching, regardless of grade level or subject matter, aims to teach cognitive and behavioral self-regulation and that, to accomplish this end, all school teachers themselves must be highly self-disciplined if they also are to be highly effective.

For CBIs to become part of teachers' repertoires of research-based, effective practices, there must first be a new behavioral ecology of classrooms and schools. Teachers, just like their students, exhibit patterns of behavior that are produced by their learning histories and conditioned by their circumstances. One would suppose that successfully teaching students to become better at regulating their maladaptive behaviors would be highly reinforcing to teachers. Yet there is substantial evidence that school and classroom experiences tend to shape teachers away from being effective with even very simple behavior management practices (e.g., contingent reward) and make effective implementation of more complex and effortful practices such as CBIs much less likely.

Continuing Use of Punishment

It is a well-established scientific fact that administration of punishment, even when deemed appropriate and adequate, cannot produce the kinds of student or teacher self-discipline that productive learning environments require. Yet punishment has been difficult to eradicate from public schools as a primary behavior management strategy. As an extreme example, although corporal punishment in schools has decreased by two thirds over the past 30 years, approximately 300,000 students still received corporal punishment in 2002–2003. In all, 28 states now ban such punishment, but 21 states still permit it in some form (U.S. Department of Education, 2002). Also, although teachers generally do not impose corporal punishment on students, they tend, nonetheless, to be punishing (e.g., through reprimands, shouting, restriction, assignment of tasks meant to punish) in their habitual response to students' misbehaviors. Even when teachers are induced to use various systems of management, they are quicker to learn and apply the punishment than the reinforcement components.

The reasons may relate in part to the prevailing models that surround teachers and their own social histories (Cohen & Amidon, 2004). That is, disposition to assert control over students' behaviors by means of punishment reflects exposure to social modeling (e.g., other teachers and administrators) or an embrace of conventional wisdom rather than the needed reeducation we might expect from professional education programs. Its use also produces models of social problem solving that negatively instruct students about the apparent effectiveness of the use of punishment, or threat of punishment, to solve their own problems. This effect is precisely antithetical to the positive kinds of social problem solving we profess we should teach to students with EBD. As we know, however, behaviors that eliminate or deter the noxious behaviors of others are reinforced by that effect. So teachers are rewarded even when a mild reprimand has the desired effect of stopping unwanted student behavior.

However, positive approaches to teaching adaptive student behaviors require time and effort, often without dramatic or immediate effects. The behaviors that teachers have to learn and reliably execute to be good behavior managers are initially unrewarding. Therefore, teachers, too, require motivational as well as technical support. In recent years, behavior management research and implementation has turned to an approach that might provide both the motivational and technical environment that teachers need. *Schoolwide* positive behavioral support (PBS) programs can be a means of increasing teachers' likelihood of learning and using positive management approaches with their students. PBS programs can accomplish this result by changing the predisposition that schools have toward positive strategies.

Schoolwide PBS

Originally, PBS emerged as a nonaversive behavioral management approach to support individuals who exhibit significant problem behaviors (Horner et al., 1990). Specifically, PBS attempts to alleviate students' disruptive behavior by defining and teaching expected student behaviors, rewarding these behaviors, and continually evaluating the implementation effort itself (Carr, Horner, Turnbull, Marquis, & Magito-McLaughlin, 1999; Gresham, Watson, & Skinner, 2001). Schoolwide PBS has been seen as a "community-based" approach, actively involving teachers, administrators, parents, and students in its implementation and evaluation. An understated assumption, however, is that teachers as much as their students work within the specialized social ecology of a school and that ultimately it is this ecology that influences how well both teachers and students become self-disciplined.

Schoolwide PBS programs now have been implemented in hundreds of schools nationwide. These programs have been seen as an alternative to "get-tough" approaches of discipline characterized by increasingly strict consequences for problem behavior with the hope that as the consequences get more and more severe, students will "get it" and problem behaviors will decrease (Sugai & Horner, 2006). In contrast to reactive get-tough behavioral management programs, schoolwide PBS is a proactive preventive behavior management program that is based on an applied behavioral analysis framework, but more important it addresses directly the organizational issues—school or district—that can create supports for teachers' efforts to improve their classroom management (Lane, Wehby, Robertson, & Rogers, 2007).

Limitations of PBS and other Schoolwide Behavioral Programs

To date, evaluations of the effectiveness of schoolwide PBS have mainly concentrated on the schoolwide outcome variables, leaving individual-level treatment effects understudied. In a review of the PBS literature, Carr and colleagues (1999) found that the most commonly used behavioral strategies in PBS research were skills training, antecedent-based approaches, and consequence-based approaches. By comparing "problem behaviors" of students at the end of baseline data collection and the end of the intervention period, Carr and colleagues found that proactive behavioral management programs and those that were less proactive showed similar results as PBS approaches. The review also found that most of the current research investigating the effects of PBS failed to provide long-term maintenance and generalization data (Carr et al., 1999). With long-term results rare, it is difficult to conclude whether more proactive approaches such as PBS have better long-term results than more consequence-based behavioral management programs. In general, overall effectiveness of PBS programs with individual cases has not been comprehensively evaluated. The use of functional behavioral assessment as a fidelity component of PBS implementation has been investigated. But evaluation of assessments cannot substitute for a comprehensive evaluation of students' near and longer term outcomes.

Mental Health Services in Public Schools for Children with EBD

One approach to providing more sophisticated behavioral treatments to students with EBD in schools is to bypass teachers and to rely on wrap-around mental health services. Some current literature suggests that children receive the majority of mental health services in school settings (Burns et al., 1995). Two presidential commissions (President's New Freedom Commission on Mental Health, 2003; U.S. Department of Health and Human Services, 1999) called for changes in the way in which the mental health system provides early identification and interventions for students at risk for EBD. The commissions called for the mental health system to work in conjunction with the public school system to identify and intervene with at-risk students. In a review of the literature on mental health services for children, it was found that schools are the primary sources of mental health services for children (Burns et al., 1995).

The use of three different mental health programs has been well documented in school settings: CBIs, tailor-made interventions for individual students such as crisis interventions, and programs based on the Systems of Care reform movement (Hoagwood & Erwin, 1997). For the most part, these interventions have been led by therapists, clinicians, and researchers, not teachers. The Systems of Care reform movement is a co-ordinated network of resources for children with severe emotional and behavioral problems. The Systems of Care reform suggests that one system alone cannot fully address the needs of at-risk children; instead, it is suggested that communities a whole (schools, parents, teachers, students, community programs) address the behavioral needs of the most challenging students.

However, in a review of the literature that evaluated the effectiveness of mental health services within school settings, Hoagwood and Erwin (1997) found that overall, very few studies have employed experimental or quasi-experimental methods, and few studies have implemented specific, well-articulated interventions. One finding of particular importance was that the majority of implemented CBIs occurred in university-based labs, not in school settings. Although intervention effects have been good, these effects cannot be generalized to interventions conducted in school settings.

The Expanding View of the Teacher's Role

In today's classroom, teachers have very limited resources; one very limited resource is time. CBIs when implemented correctly are, in nature, complicated and time consuming. Both general and special education teachers may be prepared or motivated to learn and/or implement behavioral programs such as CBIs that require specialized training. In order for CBIs to be successful at the classroom level, teachers must be trained in the development and implementation of CBIs. Yet CBIs are not widely taught in teacher preparation programs, and there is limited availability for inservice time devoted to CBI training, given competing priorities within schools. This disconnect suggests at least two distinct remedies that can be facilitated through federally funded incentives to university preparation programs and school systems: (1) grants to teacher preparation programs to include CBI training, and (2) grants to school districts to provide supplemental training to school staff outside of normal work hours with financial remuneration to participants.

Research has also suggested that teachers are generally not well prepared to deal with basic behavioral problems that occur within classrooms. In a study by Myers and Holland (2000), teachers were asked to read fictional stories that included common behavioral problems that occur within classroom settings and to determine the function of the student behavior. Teachers had a difficult time differentiating between behaviors that sought to seek attention and those that were avoidance behaviors. Perhaps more important, only 17% of the general education teachers and 42% of the special education teachers reported receiving instruction on functional behavioral analysis in their teacher education programs. If teachers are not able to identify the function of student behaviors, behavior interventions, from very basic to complex systems such as CBIs, will have an increased likelihood of failure, leaving teachers less motivated to use such interventions. Research has demonstrated that when inservice teachers are provided with training to identify the function of behaviors, they are able to not only successfully identify the function of behaviors, but develop behavioral interventions to reduce the problem behavior (Sasso, Reimers, Cooper, Wacker, & Berg, 1992).

Daunic, Smith, Brank, and Penfield (2006) researched the effectiveness of teacher-directed cognitive self-regulation curriculum. Although overall the study reported positive effects on teacher ratings of student behavior after the curriculum was implemented, there were strong teacher effects across all treatments. This suggests that teacher characteristics, such as classroom discipline style and level of motivation for implementation, must be taken into account.

It is important to remember that teachers are not therapists and they are not researchers; they are teachers who teach in classrooms that are complex, dynamic, and at times unpredictable. Classrooms are not controlled settings, which makes the implementation of complex behavioral management programs such as CBIs even more challenging. In this highly charged environment, teachers are responsible for fulfilling each student's individual academic and behavioral needs. For these reasons, it is not surprising that schools are turning toward schoolwide behavioral programs that assume that same function of schoolwide academic curricula, acting as a blanket approach to behavior with individual behavioral needs being addressed in extreme cases of noncompliance. However, for the individual interventions to be successful, especially interventions as complex as CBIs, teachers must be highly trained in their use so that they are successfully implemented and teachers are motivated to use them.

Administrator and Staff Roles

If teachers are to be expected to implement CBIs in classrooms, support from other staff, the administration, and the school system as a whole is required. Schools must provide training opportunities for both general and special education teachers, and the administration must support teachers in the implementation processes. Schools must also provide general education teachers with greater knowledge and resources about challenging students and their challenging behaviors. With movement toward schoolwide inclusion for all students, remaining reliant on a special education teacher to deal with all challenging student behaviors is unreasonable and increasingly unfeasible.

Gottfredson and colleagues (2000) referred to "organizational capacity" as an obstacle to successful implementation of behavioral programs on a schoolwide level. Specifically, *organizational capacity* refers to the ability of the organization (school) to implement strong behavioral programs. Obstacles that must be overcome for programs to be implemented successfully are low school morale or a feeling that "nothing works" with the most challenging students; budget and resources for implementation; support and training for the program; and perhaps the most important, the level at which the proposed program can be implemented within the school's existing organization.

Student Role

Given the nature of CBIs as based on self-management/self-regulation of thoughts and ultimately behavior, students play a large role in successful implementation. It is logical to assume that students who require such complex individual behavioral intervention lack self-management strategies inherent to the majority of students. These students must be explicitly taught self-management strategies and therefore must be highly monitored at the onset of CBIs. Studies have demonstrated that self-management interventions are most effective when students are provided with high levels of modeling and practice, receive feedback about acceptable behaviors, and are provided with opportunities to use new techniques in different settings (Gottfredson et al., 2000). A guiding assumption of CBIs is that, with practice, students will employ self-management techniques in order to regulate their own behavior.

A fundamental question at the student level is the following: How hard are CBIs for students to learn and implement? Research addressing this question at the student level is limited. Daunic and colleagues' (2006) 2005 study investigating the effectiveness of CBIs in preventing aggression in fourth- and fifth-grade students through classroomwide, teacher-led interventions found that after students received the CBI-based curriculum, they reported having a better understanding of problem solving and teacher ratings of students' behavior increased. This seems to suggest that students as young as fourth grade can successfully be taught cognitive techniques in order to regulate their own behavior. However, direct observation of problem behavior was not included in the study design, therefore actual problem behavior reduction could not be assessed.

Future Possibilities

In this chapter we have argued that the formal theories and methods of CBIs intersect with a naturally occurring implicit curriculum. This curriculum has the same teaching goal for all students, namely self-regulated academic as well as social behavior. Students with EBD are characterized by having needs in this respect because their behavioral deficiencies are often both acute and conspicuous. Whereas CBIs are implicit for most students, they must be explicit for students with EBD. However, most teachers face a triple threat in their ability to deliver such intervention. First, the everyday effort of managing classroom instruction, particularly in schools experiencing high rates of disruptive student behavior, often causes teachers to expend so much energy on the overt aspects of academic performance and classroom order that they rarely pay conscious attention to the implicit cognitive-behavioral curriculum on self-regulated behavior. Second, teachers are chronically disadvantaged by inadequate preparation in their professional education programs. Third, lack of consistent and effective response to teachers' behavior management challenges by school administrators and colleagues further undermines teachers' ability to consistently address self-management as part of their normal instructional routine.

Conclusions and Recommendations

In this chapter, we have argued that self-management—both in academic as well as social contexts—is an implicit goal in all classroom teaching. If true, our position implies that CBIs for students with EBD represent only a highly specialized, and somewhat technical, form of instruction aimed at precisely the same goal. A teacher's ability to manage a classroom, including providing instruction, is foundational not only to his or her ability to learn to effectively use CBIs but also to his or her ability to deliver the implicit curriculum to support student self-management objectives. Teachers need not only skills but understanding of why and how academic achievement and discipline, in all of its meanings, are necessarily fused. The more effectively achievement and classroom, individual, and teaching discipline are addressed, the better we might expect outcomes for all students, including those with EBD, to become. That is, high-quality instruction should be understood to include high-quality instruction in self-management along with high-quality instruction in academic knowledge and skills. Therefore, the appropriate national concern for teacher quality ought to imply a concern that teachers possess sophisticated behavior management and instructional skills, not only knowledge of the academic domains in which they teach.

Unfortunately, in national policy discussions there has been greater emphasis on teachers' knowledge of curriculum than teachers' ability to manage instruction and its supportive contexts. However, it will not matter if classroom teaching is well aligned with a high-quality curriculum if teachers cannot deliver instruction that fosters learning that steadily increases students' ability to adaptively manage their cognitive and behavioral responses to the environment. Lane and her colleagues nicely illustrated this point in a recent study (Lane, Little, Redding-Rhodes, Phillips, & Welsh, 2007).

Although it is clear that students with EBD often display academic deficiencies, Lane, Little, and colleagues (2007) indicated that there are very few empirical studies in which improved behavior for students with EBD was approached through instruction to improve academic instruction. Even the few extant studies noted produced only weak effects. Lane, Little, and colleagues stated that the purpose of such interventions should be to produce effects that are both "immediate and collateral" (p. 48). However, what we think makes the Lane, Little, et al. study so interesting is not only that it attempts to apply a more effective treatment than previous research, but also that it argues persuasively that normal teachers, not specially prepared research or auxiliary staff, must be able to deliver the instruction and attain the desired joint effects of academic and behavioral improvements.

The results showed improvements in reading skills of students with EBD but, disappointingly, uneven or no improvement in "engagement." The authors noted that there was no monitoring and apparently no specific training related to managing "disruption." In recommending future research, Lane, Little, et al. (2007) suggested that decreases in disruption must occur as a precondition for improvements in engagement (p. 66). This means that not only must natural teachers be trained and induced to implement more effective academic interventions, they must also be trained and induced to combine those interventions with instruction that is designed both to decrease disruption; capture, hold, and direct attention; and simultaneously teach and encourage self-management of learning.

In order to support the academic and social, emotional, and behavioral success of students with greatest need—those with EBDs—as well as those who are more normally achieving and behaving but who would benefit nonetheless, the educational system must develop training, implementation, and organizational supports that enable schools and teachers to do these things as a part of normal instruction. With this type of commitment and support, effective use of CBIs, along with other beneficial practices, has a greater chance of becoming a more widespread reality in schools.

How can we help teachers achieve these complex skills? How can we create and promote such high-quality teachers on a national scale? Clearly, if schools, through their teachers, are held accountable for using evidence-based practices, professional education programs must teach them and, moreover, be accountable for teaching them. It is difficult to find evidence that this goal has been widely attained in teacher preparation programs, or even at a large enough scale to ensure that most teachers learn explicit instructional behaviors and how to be disciplined in their application during instructional episodes.

We propose that the change required have a national platform and visibility. It must have several coordinated elements if it is to change the overall quality of classroom teaching for students with serious emotional and behavioral problems as well as for their nondisabled peers. First, the policy definition of teacher *quality* must be expanded to include the requirements of expertise in instructing students, not merely expertise in the domain knowledge that is to be taught. Moreover, teacher quality must require explicit knowledge and skill in managing the social behaviors of children in classrooms so that effective instruction is supported. Furthermore, teacher quality must be defined in terms of ability to instruct children to be self-managing—including use of CBIs—both within academic tasks and in those specific social behaviors that afford and support learning in schools and classrooms. Specifically, professional preparation programs need to develop more explicit training to promote teachers' abilities to manage and control their own teaching behaviors while teaching, in essence, to apply CBIs in professional education (Bodrova & Leong, 2006; Jack, Shores, Denny, & Gunter, 1996; Manning & Payne, 1989, 1993; Payne & Manning, 1988; Perry, Hutchinson, & Thauberger, 2007; Randi, 2004).

Finally, a fertile ground must be created for teaching quality to be sustained. This may be accomplished by a combination of two strategies. First, new policy incentives should be created for states to approve and professional preparation programs to adopt requirements for training skills in the three characterizations we have presented about discipline—classroom management, teaching self-management, and teachers' self-management in their teaching practices. States and preparation programs must not view behavior management skills as naturally developing or somehow auxiliary to good teaching. State certification boards and teacher training institutions must be persuaded instead that the true, multifaceted nature of *discipline* in classrooms is fundamental to the quality of education and that curricular reforms alone will not be successful in closing achievement or behavior gaps, nor will they reliably improve the outcomes for any students who are at high risk for academic and social failures.

Second, there needs to be a new, significantly larger investment in research and dissemination centers to create a more complex and integrated knowledge base about the professional practice of teaching. Such centers must be charged to conduct applied research at classroom, building, and district levels to determine (1) the instructional conditions that must be created and sustained to address the cognitive-behavioral training needs of students with EBD, (2) the requirements for establishing schoolwide systems of PBS in schools that do not self-select for this effort, (3) how instructional designs can embed cognitive-behavioral approaches within normal academic instruction, and (4) how cognitive-behavioral approaches can be applied productively to the professional preparation of teachers themselves. If these actions are taken, it is possible that the future of CBIs will brighten and hold greater promise, not only for students with EBD. If we as a society and professional community make these proposed changes, not only will there be greater educational opportunity for students with EBD in the public schools, it is also quite possible that they will produce a radically different public education environment for all students.

References

Bodrova, E., & Leong, D. J. (2006). Self-regulation as a key to school readiness: How early childhood teachers can promote this critical competency. In M. Zaslow & I. Martinez-Beck (Eds.), *Critical issues in early childhood professional development* (pp. 203–224). Baltimore: Brookes.

Burns, B. J., Costello, E. J., Angold, A., Tweed, D., Stangl, D., Farner, E. M. Z., et al. (1995). Children's mental health service use across services sectors. *Health Affairs, 14*(3), 147–159.

Carr, E. G., Horner, R. R., Turnbull, A. P., Marquis, J. G., & Magito-McLaughlin, D. (1999). *Positive behavior support for people with developmental disabilities: A research synthesis.* Washington, DC: American Association on Mental Retardation.

Cohen, J. H., & Amidon, E. J. (2004). Reward and punishment histories: A way of predicting teaching style. *Journal of Educational Research, 97*, 269–280.

Committee on School Health. (2003). Out-of-school suspension and expulsion. *Pediatrics, 112*, 1206–1209.

Corno, L. (2006). Commentary on Vollmeyer and Rheinberg: Putting the teacher in research on self-regulated learning. *Educational Psychology Review, 18*, 261–266.

Correnti, R., & Rowan, B. (2007). Opening up the black box: Literacy instruction in schools participating in three comprehensive school reform programs. *American Educational Research Journal, 44*, 298–339.

Darling-Hammond, L., Holtzman, D. J., Gatlin, S. J., & Heilig, J. V. (2005). *Does teacher preparation matter?: Teacher certification, Teach for America, and teacher effectiveness.* Palo Alto, CA: Stanford University, School Redesign Network. Available online at *srnleads.org/research/research.html.*

Daunic, A. P., Smith, S. W., Brank, E. M., & Penfield, R. D. (2006). Classroom-based cognitive-behavioral intervention to prevent aggression: Efficacy and social validity. *Journal of School Psychology, 44,* 123–139.

Evans, E. D., & Tribble, M. (1986). Perceived teaching problems, self-efficacy, and commitment to teaching among preservice teachers. *Journal of Educational Research, 80,* 81–85.

Ferris, J. M. (1992). School-based decision making: A principal-agent perspective. *Educational Evaluation and Policy Analysis, 14,* 333–346.

Gerber, M. M., & Solari, E. J. (2005). Teaching effort and the future of cognitive-behavioral interventions. *Behavioral Disorders, 30,* 289–299.

Gottfredson, G. D., Gottfredson, D. C., Czeh, E. R., Cantor, D., Crosse, S. B., & Hantman, I. (2000). *National Study of Delinquency Prevention in Schools. Final report.* Rockville, MD: Gottfredson Associates.

Gresham, F. M., Watson, T. S., & Skinner, C. H. (2001). Functional behavioral assessment: Principles, procedures, and future directions. *School Psychology Review, 30,* 156–172.

Hoagwood, K., & Erwin, H. (1997). Effectiveness of school-based mental health services for children: A 10-year review. *Journal of Child and Family Studies, 6,* 435–451.

Honig, M. I. (2006). Street-level bureaucracy revisited: Frontline district central-office administrators as boundary spanners in education policy implementation. *Educational Evaluation and Policy Analysis, 28,* 357–383.

Horner, R. R., Dunlap, G., Koegel, R. L., Carr, E. G., Sailor, W., & Anderson, J. (1990). Toward a technology of "nonaversive" beahvioral support. *Journal of the Association for Persons with Severe Handicaps, 15,* 125–132.

Jack, S. L., Shores, R. E., Denny, R. K., & Gunter, P. L. (1996). An analysis of the relationship of teachers' reported use of classroom management strategies on types of classroom interactions. *Journal of Behavioral Education, 6,* 67–87.

Lane, K. L., Little, M. A., Redding-Rhodes, J., Phillips, A., & Welsh, M. T. (2007). Outcomes of a teacher-led reading intervention for elementary students at risk for behavioral disorders. *Exceptional Children, 74,* 47–70.

Lane, K. L., Wehby, J. H., Robertson, E. J., & Rogers, L. A. (2007). How do different types of high school students respond to school-wide positive behavior support programs? Characteristics and responsiveness of teacher-identified students. *Journal of Emotional and Behavioral Disorders, 15,* 3–20.

Langdon, C. A., & Vesper, N. (2000). The sixth Phi Delta Kappa poll of teacher's attitudes toward the public schools. *Phi Delta Kappan, 81,* 607–611.

Maag, J. W. (2006). Social skills training for students with emotional and behavioral disorders: A review of reviews. *Behavioral Disorders, 32,* 5–17.

Manning, B. H., & Payne, B. D. (1989). A cognitive self-direction model for teacher education. *Journal of Teacher Education, 40,* 27–32.

Manning, B., & Payne, B. (1993). A Vygotskian-based theory of teacher cognition: Toward the acquisition of mental reflection and self-regulation. *Teaching and Teacher Education, 9,* 361–371.

Myers, C. L., & Holland, K. L. (2000). Classroom behavioral interventions: Do teachers consider the function of behavior? *Psychology in the Schools, 37,* 271–280.

Nolle, K. L., Guerino, P., & Dinkes, R. (2007). *Crime, violence, discipline, and safety in U.S. public schools: Findings from the School Survey on Crime and Safety: 2005-06* (NCES 2007-361). Washington, DC: National Center for Education Statistics.

Payne, B. D., & Manning, B. H. (1988). The effect of cognitive self-instructional strategies on preservice teachers' locus of control. *Contemporary Educational Psychology, 13,* 140–145.

Perry, N. E. (1998). Young children's self-regulated learning and contexts that support it. *Journal of Educational Psychology, 90,* 715–729.

Perry, N. E., Hutchinson, L., & Thauberger, C. (2007). Mentoring student teachers to design and implement literacy tasks that support self-regulated reading and writing. *Reading and Writing Quarterly, 23,* 27—50.

Perry, N., Phillips, L., & Dowler, J. (2004). Examining features of tasks and their potential to promote self-regulated learning. *Teachers College Record, 106,* 1854–1878.

Perry, N. E., VandeKamp, K. O., Mercer, L. K., & Nordby, C. J. (2002). Investigating teacher-student interactions that foster self-regulated learning. *Educational Psychologist, 37,* 5–15.

Polsgrove, L., & Smith, S. W. (2004). Informed practice in teaching self-control to children with emotional and behavioral disorders. In R. B. Rutherford, Jr., M. M. Quinn, & S. R. Mathur (Eds.), *Handbook of research on emotional and behavioral disorders* (pp. 399–425). New York: Guilford Press.

President's New Freedom Commission on Mental Health. (2003). *Achieving the promise: Transforming mental health care in America. Final report* (DHHS Publication No. SMA-03-3832). Rockville, MD: U.S. Department of Health and Human Services.

Randi, J. (2004). Teachers as self-regulated learners. *Teachers College Record, 106,* 1825–1853.

Reid, R., & Lienemann, T. O. (2006). *Strategy instruction for students with learning disabilities.* New York: Guilford Press.

Rowan, B., & Miller, R. J. (2007). Organizational strategies for promoting instructional change: Implementation dynamics in schools working with comprehensive school reform providers. *American Educational Research Journal, 44, 252–297.*

Sasso, G. M., Reimers, T. M., Cooper, L. J., Wacker, D., & Berg, W. (1992). Use of descriptive and experimental analyses to identify the functional properties of aberrant behavior in school settings. *Journal of Applied Behavior Analysis, 25,* 809–821.

Sugai, G., & Horner, R. R. (2006). A promising approach for expanding and sustaining school-wide positive behavior support. *School Psychology Review, 35,* 245–260.

U.S. Department of Education, Office of Postsecondary Education, Office of Policy Planning and Innovation. (2002). *Meeting the highly qualified teachers challenge: The secretary's annual report on teacher quality.* Washington, DC: U.S. Government Printing Office.

U.S. Department of Health and Human Services. (1999). *Mental health: A report of the Surgeon General.* Rockville, MD: Author.

Veenman, S. (1984). Perceived problems of beginning teachers. *Review of Educational Research, 54,* 143–178.

Wagner, M., Friend, M., Bursuck, W. D., Kutash, K., Duchnowski, A. J., Sumi, W. C., et al. (2006). Educating students with emotional disturbances: A national perspective on school programs and services. *Journal of Emotional and Behavioral Disorders, 14,* 12–30.

Weatherly, R., & Lipsky, M. (1977). Street-level bureaucrats and institutional innovation: Implementing special education reform. *Harvard Educational Review, 47,* 171–197.

Index